Dark Star

Also by Leatrice Gilbert Fountain

Love to the Irish

and by John R. Maxim

Platforms
Abel/Baker/Charley

Dark Star

◆ ◆ ◆

Leatrice Gilbert Fountain

with John R. Maxim

SIDGWICK & JACKSON
LONDON

For my father

First published in Great Britain in 1985
by Sidgwick and Jackson Limited

Originally published in the United States
of America by St. Martin's Press, Inc.

Copyright © 1985 by Leatrice Gilbert Fountain and John R. Maxim

ISBN 0-283-99260-3

Printed in Great Britain by
The Garden City Press Limited, Letchworth, Hertfordshire
for Sidgwick and Jackson Limited
1 Tavistock Chambers, Bloomsbury Way
London WC1A 2SG

ACKNOWLEDGMENTS

THE facts and the impressions collected in this book are the accumulations of a lifetime. I am indebted to many, many people. Listed below are some of those whom I have spoken to, or who wrote letters and shared with me their memories of my father. To each of them I am profoundly grateful.

Cleveland Amory
Marjorie Bennett
Eleanor Boardman
Clarence Brown
Virginia Bruce
Ben Carré
Alice Charles
Lenore Coffee
Marc Connelly
Joan Crawford
Bosley Crowther
Viola Dana
Marlene Dietrich
Douglas Fairbanks, Jr.
Robert Florey
Lillian Gish
Harold Grieve
Howard Hawks
Arthur Hornblow, Jr.
Leila Hyams
Leatrice Joy
Howard H. Strickling
Blanche Sweet
King Vidor
Robert Wallsten
Richard Watts, Jr.
Rowland V. Lee

Mervyn LeRoy
Beatrice Lillie
Bessie Love
Bert Lytell
Jack McEdward
John Lee Mahin
Rear Admiral Gene Markey,
    USNR (Ret.)
Sarah Y. Mason & Victor
    Heerman
Lewis and Kendall Milestone
Colleen Moore
Conrad Nagel
Barbara O'Neil
George Oppenheimer
Anita Page
Aileen Pringle
Hazel Gibbons Ross
Adela Rogers St. Johns
Irene Mayer Selznick
Donald Ogden Stewart
Marie Stoddard
Irvin Willat
Carey Wilson
Lois Wilson
Margery Wilson

A NOTE OF THANKS

There are people who opened doors for me, Suzanne Vidor, King Vidor's daughter, for one. In the earliest days of the book, she opened her home and all her resources and made it possible for me to begin. Charles Higham, who once thought of writing a book on John Gilbert himself, turned over material to me. Herbert Nusbaum helped me gain access to the MGM archives. Sam Marx gave generously of his time and advice. (We didn't always agree!) Herman G. Weinberg, Charles Turner, and Spencer Berger shared their stills and their film collections. Andrew C. McKay sent movie reviews. I am indebted to the Film Department of the Musuem of Modern Art, to Eileen Bowser, Mary Corliss, Charles Silver, Steve Harvey, Jon Gartenberg. At the Library of the Performing Arts at Lincoln Center, Paul Myers was an invaluable source of help. At George Eastman House, James Card treated me like visiting royalty. George Pratt and Marshall Deutelbaum helped continuously and Herbert Reynolds even drove me from Rochester to Greenwich, Connecticut, one snowy day when I was stranded by an airplane strike.

Ted Ashley, then president of Warner Brothers, who owned my father's house on Tower Road, invited me to see the place late one night after work because I was leaving the next day for home.

I will always remember Celia McGerr, who researched *me* in the course of writing a monograph about my father when she was a student at Sarah Lawrence College. She stayed, and did scrupulous research and helped me in every way. She should be a major film writer before long.

My thanks to James Powers (American Film Institute), Jack McLaughlin (United Artist TV), Chris Steinbrenner (WOR-TV), Herbert Yuen, and the John Gilbert Fan Club. Special appreciation to Kevin Lewis, Henry Wuckert, the Danish Film Museum, the Library of Congress (Motion Picture Section), and Digby Diehl (*Los Angeles Times*).

To my mother, Leatrice Joy, my warmest love and thanks for opening her heart and her memories so generously.

To Kevin Brownlow, who has been my mentor and friend through it all and who made corrections and read through at least three different versions, offering help and advice, my affection and gratitude.

To my husband, who endured eleven years of off-again-on-again chaos without complaint, my undying love and the belief that every woman who writes should have such a husband.

I am, at last, profoundly grateful to my co-author, John Maxim, an extraordinarily intelligent writer, who was able to absorb huge amounts of material in a stunningly short time and help me sort it out with sensitivity, skill, and unfailing good humor.

Still-Picture Acknowledgments

Cinemabilia
Marlene Dietrich
International Museum of Photography at George Eastman House
Douglas Fairbanks, Jr.
Robert Florey
Leatrice Gilbert Fountain
Harold Grieve

Peter Hanson Collection
Leatrice Joy
John Kobal
Library of the Performing Arts at Lincoln Center
Museum of Modern Art
Eugene Poddany
Edward Steichen

INTRODUCTION
by Garson Kanin

JOHN GILBERT!

A niagara of images comes flooding through memory at the sight or sound of his name.

He was the epitome of dashing, daring, glamorous action—the quintessential Movie Star, the role model for a generation of would-be lovers.

Those who saw his unforgettable silent films still carry indelible impressions in their minds' eyes: the blazing love scenes with Greta Garbo in *Flesh and the Devil*; the shattering climax of *The Big Parade*, as he stumbles, one-legged, down the hill, returning to the French girl he had loved and left; the glittering waltz with Mae Murray in *The Merry Widow*; the poignant death scene in *La Bohème*; the unbearable tension of the gambling in *Cameo Kirby*.

Those piercing dark eyes that not only looked, but saw. That dazzling smile which disarmed and conquered. The incomparable physical grace and aesthetic elegance.

His real work and, therefore, his real life virtually ended with the coming of sound.

Three generations have not known his magical presence, and the story of his life has been blurred by gossip and untruth and invention. Up to now we have had no more than flashes, snapshots, quick cuts, teasing intimations of the complex private life of this luminous, mercurial, mysterious, and maddening shooting star.

However, in the pages that follow, there is at last a full-length portrait. More, a completely dimensioned monument; a memorial in which the moral judgment we too often pass upon one another is tempered by compassion and understanding and, above all, love.

In this heartbreaking yet heartwarming account, we see how corrupt power tortured and annihilated a fine and sensitive human being. What is even worse, it destroyed a great artist and his talent. There is but small difference between killing a man and not permitting him to live.

In the gross fashion of the day, we have seen too many gratuitous vilifications of famous parents—usually deceased—who are castigated, criticized, blamed, and belabored.

Dark Star, the story of John Gilbert by his daughter, comes as a fresh and refreshing change.

Leatrice Joy Gilbert was born a few months after her illustrious parents ended their four-year marriage, and her relationship with her father was fitful until the final years of his life.

John Gilbert was not destined to be a husband or a father; he was far too handsome, gifted, humorous, sexually magnetic, high-flying, and joy-loving for any role so prosaic. He was possessed not only of a roving eye, but of a roving heart as well.

His wife, Leatrice Joy—an exquisitely radiant star in her own right— understood all this. Thus the separation was without bitterness or re-crimination. Instead, friendship supplanted marriage and in time proved to be more necessary.

His eloquent daughter recounts the legend of his downfall with rea-soned clarity and brilliant perception, at the same time clearing the record of the myths and apocrypha that have long plagued it.

According to the long-circulated version (which she demolishes): John Gilbert's descent from glory began when the most celebrated, vir-ile, lusty, masculine screen lover of his time spoke from the sound screen in his first talking picture, ironically titled *His Glorious Night*. The voice that emanated from the image did not match it. It was "squeaky" or "high" or "effeminate," depending upon who is reporting or repeating. As a result, he was laughed off the screen by the premiere audience and was never able to achieve a successful return. (Has every-one forgotten that virtually all early talkies got all sorts of laughs, often because of audience surprise or nervousness? Someone eating celery brought down the house again and again.)

As a professional filmmaker, let me add one more element that gives the lie to this fabrication.

In the making of any film, one part of the process has to do with the "dailies" or "rushes." These are the prints, usually screened each morn-ing, of the previous day's shooting. At major studios in the thirties the results of all pictures in work were seen by all of the executives.

Here then are the questions: During the thirteen shooting days of *His Glorious Night*, did no one viewing the rushes notice anything odd or unseemly about John Gilbert's voice? If it was as wrong as it was said to be at the premiere, why was nothing done or repaired or changed? Why was the filming permitted to continue? Did something happen to the soundtrack prior to the premiere?

*   *   *

It has been said that a single anecdote can often reveal a person as well as a book. Here is a characteristic one about the audacious John Gilbert:

He and his great love, Greta Garbo, had in common a mutual loathing of manufactured publicity and routine interviews. In her early days at MGM she had been forced to do what was called "cheesecake"—leg shots and bathing suit poses, also group photos with college track teams and squaring off with champion boxers. These degrading adventures understandably soured her on the whole principle. She and John Gilbert thought it all a rude intrusion and failed to see the benefits other than a justification of the studio's vast exploitation department and a service to the proliferating movie magazines—sixty-six of them being published at the time.

At length John Gilbert found a way of being relieved from the nuisance of interviews.

The studio had pressured him into an on-the-set session with Ruth Waterbury of *Photoplay* magazine. She was a prim and proper young lady, new to Hollywood.

She asked the usual pro forma questions and received the accustomed answers until she inquired, "And how did you happen to become an actor, Mr. Gilbert?"

"It was ordained," he replied. "My mother and my father, you see, were both on the stage. For a time they ran the stock company in Salt Lake City, and I went on whenever they needed a child in the play."

"How fascinating!" exclaimed Miss Waterbury.

"Yes, isn't it? I remember once taking a curtain call with my parents after the first act of a play—we took calls after each act in those days. My mother was wearing a long dress with a bustle and a train—it was a period piece." Miss Waterbury was scribbling away as he continued. "Well, she stepped forward to take her solo call—we had one of those roll-up curtains that rolled up and down like an enormous window shade—and somehow the train of my mother's gown got caught in the roll curtain, and up, up, up it went. And do you know," he added, his eyes misty with loving memory, "that was the last time I ever saw my mother's ass."

"Thank you," whispered the stunned Miss Waterbury as she fled.

And do you know, he did not see an interviewer's pad for quite some time.

As the penultimate chapters of this haunting biography unfold the metaphor of a bullfight is unavoidable. We see the brave-hearted, stalwart beast desperately attempting to stay alive, to return to his field, to do what nature intended him to do—but he is doomed. The odds are dead against him as they were against the hapless John Gilbert, whose most grievous sin was that of offending the wrong people.

The analogy fails, however, on one small but significant point— toreadors and matadors and picadors do not hate the bull; their motive is fortune and fame. In the case of John Gilbert's ruiners, money was involved, of course, but the major spurs were hatred and vindictiveness, jealousy and revenge. Moreover, a bullfight is not a tragedy—the lamentable life story of John Gilbert is.

He managed somehow to cram a hundred years of living into his meagre thirty-six, adding to the fatal strain.

Leatrice Joy Gilbert is unsparing in her telling. She does not see John Gilbert through a haze of rosy, doctored remembrance. Neither does she offer an apologia for his weaknesses, errors, and follies. She has searched long and painstakingly to find the truth about her errant father—the whole truth, not merely *her* truth—and having found it, she recounts it with candor and courage, providing a rare, seemingly new-discovered document. It is an important contribution to film lore, a daughter-to-father mash note, an antidote to falsehood and slander.

Fate, not always kind to John Gilbert, gave him a gifted offspring to tell the story he cannot tell himself.

A loving daughter has recreated a memorable father and shares him with us.

We are in her debt.

In the time of Hollywood's most glittering days, he glittered the most. He received ten thousand dollars a week and could keep most of it. He lived in a castle on a hill. Thousands of letters poured in daily telling him how wonderful he was. The caliphs for whom he worked bowed before him like a reigning prince. They built him a dressing room such as no actor ever had. It was a small Italian palace. There were no enemies in his life. He was as unsnobbish as a happy child. He went everywhere he was invited. He needed no greatness around him to make him feel distinguished. He drank with carpenters, danced with waitresses and made love to whores and movie queens alike. He swaggered and posed but it was never to impress anyone. He was being John Gilbert, prince, butterfly, Japanese lantern, and the spirit of romance.

—Ben Hecht

"My God, Jack! Are you still in the acting game? Get out, lad. Get out before they lick you."

—Bob Stewart,
Los Angeles policeman and former actor

"You're finished, Gilbert. I'll destroy you if it costs me a million dollars."

—Louis B. Mayer

·one·

SOMETIMES it's hard to believe that he was real.

John Gilbert. My father.

It's harder still to imagine that all the stories told, all the passions fired, could have been centered on just one man. And on one very brief lifetime.

But what stories! And what a lifetime!

He began as an unloved and unwanted boy, set on his own when barely in his teens, who went on to become the most fiercely blazing star of an age when motion pictures touched more lives more deeply than ever before or since.

People remember him as a lover. *The* lover. To tens of millions of filmgoers he was "The Great Lover of the Silver Screen," a title created by Irving Thalberg—to John Gilbert's eternal embarrassment. But the great-lover image was hardly an invention. Thalberg, head of production for Metro-Goldwyn-Mayer, simply recognized a quality, a magnetism that the camera witnessed, and gave it a name. Thalberg knew that Gilbert exuded this magnetism, along with a certain elegance of style, in his private life, and was one of the rare few who could translate it to the screen with the same intensity.

He did so even to the extent of bringing the genuine passions of his private life onto the screen. He was, on screen and off, the single greatest love in the lifetime of Greta Garbo. This fascinating, complex woman shared his life and his home, though they never married, for more than three years.

Marlene Dietrich loved him, with supreme unselfishness, during the last year of his tragically short life. She was near collapse at his funeral.

Mother was there, of course. Tiny Leatrice Joy, Jack Gilbert's second wife and a major De Mille star in her own right. Although Mother had divorced him, she'd never quite stopped loving Jack Gilbert. She never has. Even today. Nor for that matter had the two exquisite women he'd married after her; brilliant Ina Claire and the innocent, star-crossed Virginia Bruce.

And I was there. Leatrice Joy Gilbert. Age eleven.

I remember King Vidor and John Barrymore looking over to see how Mother and I were holding up. Mother sat stiffly, gripping her hands to keep from trembling, her head down and her shoulders forward. She looked smaller than ever, even to me. And every so often her body would shake.

But I didn't cry. I didn't cry for a very long time.

During the service, I sat there in numb disbelief. Someone would say or do something that would remind me that my father was dead and I would push the thought away. It was not possible for John Gilbert to be less than exuberantly alive. I'd only just found him, discovered him, begun to revel in being able to talk to him and touch him. He was happy and so was I. He was filled with new hopes and dreams. No one else seemed to know that but me. They all thought he was sad, lost, and miserable, even his closest friends. They said it so often, and magazines wrote it so often that after a while I began to believe it myself. What could I know? I was a sad little eleven-year-old girl who got acquainted with her own father by writing him a fan letter. A fan letter, for God's sake! All I knew were bits and pieces of him, private lunches and quiet walks along the beach. How could I know what John Gilbert was like? Was the real John Gilbert the faded star, laughed out of Hollywood when his thin and piping voice was heard in talking pictures? The manic-depressive who drank himself to death at the age of thirty-six, a dark and brooding shadow of what he'd once been? A bitter relic, a shell of a man unable to live with failure? A reclusive paranoiac who slept with a gun nearby, convinced that the enemies who'd brought him down were not yet finished with him?

But I did know my father. I knew that he listened carefully when I talked with him and that he answered my questions thoughtfully. He wasn't like most grown-ups, who would sort of half listen just long enough to catch the gist of what you were saying and then bore you to death with advice. My father asked questions. And he touched. He would brush at my hair with his fingertips while he was thinking aloud or while I was telling him what I thought. He'd put down what he was doing when I spoke to him, and he'd turn those fantastic brown eyes and that smile toward me and the whole room would light up. I'd feel that I was the only person in the world who mattered to him. Later, when I learned that he made almost everyone he liked even a little feel that way, I didn't really mind. I didn't mind that he made other people feel special too.

[2]

Life goes on. I grew up about as normally as one would expect for the daughter of two screen idols. We were surrounded by a certain amount of glamour but we didn't really know it. I did have my turn at a movie career, and might even have been a star. After appearing in one minor film for MGM, I was astonished to be offered the lead in *National Velvet*, to be made in 1937. A publicity buildup of thirteen-year-old Leatrice Joy Gilbert was well under way when the project was delayed for one reason or another and then shelved. *National Velvet* wasn't revived until late in the war. By that time, I was a gawky adolescent, so they gave the part to some kid named Elizabeth Taylor. (She wasn't too bad, for a second choice.)

During all those years of growing up, eventually finding a dear, reasonable husband, and raising a family, I grew closer by degrees to the man who was my father. I had Mother's memories, which she shared with me, most of them tender and moving. She never played the star when she talked about Father, just a woman who loved a man and who cried at what might have been. I would see the light in Douglas Fairbanks, Jr.'s eyes when he talked about his friend. Sometimes Doug would be quiet for a moment and then chuckle and shake his head over some secret thought or reminiscence that he'd decided was not suitable for my young ears. There were boxes full of my father's memorabilia— letters, photos, clippings, favorite poems, stories he'd written, random thoughts, copies of interviews. Taken together, they painted a portrait of a man very much like the father I came to know during that one golden year. A lovely man who was superbly talented, a thoughtful and witty conversationalist, an engaging speaker, a man who read good books, a man with a riotous sense of fun, and a man who had his share of inner devils.

During those same years, quite another portrait of John Gilbert was emerging in Hollywood folklore. John Gilbert? Wasn't he the silent-screen ham with the fruity voice who drank himself to death because people laughed at his first talking picture? A shallow twit who would fold if asked to do anything more demanding than stand in front of a camera looking pretty?

In *A Star Is Born*, Fredric March and later James Mason played a role supposedly based upon John Gilbert's crash from the heights. The character was a boozing actor who drowned himself one morning because he couldn't face the fact that his career was in decline while his wife's star was rising. In truth, that picture never had the slightest connection with John Gilbert. It was patterned after an actor named John Bowers, a handsome leading man who could find no work after the coming of sound, became an alcoholic, and actually did drown himself the same year John Gilbert died.

The legend that audiences broke into giggling fits upon hearing Gilbert's voice was played for laughs in *Singin' in the Rain*. The scene showed Gene Kelly squirming in the back of a theater as the audience roared at his "I love you, I love you, I love you," in a setting copied from John Gilbert's heroically misnamed first talkie, *His Glorious Night*. Meanwhile, book after book about early Hollywood appeared, each apparently using all the others as source material. Most described the scene in which audiences laughed at Jack's voice. No two ever agreed on the basic facts. No author had seen the movie. None quoted a witness. Yet the story grew. Even people who knew better heard it so often that they began to believe it. John Gilbert was laughed out of the movies because of his voice; it was fey and high-pitched. The guy chirped.

Did he?

To begin with, I heard him talk. I don't remember anything at all wrong with my father's voice. Secondly, John Gilbert's first talkie, which was supposed to have driven him from the screen, was by no means his last. He made nine more movies after that, a whole career for most actors. Who makes nine movies with a drunken actor who talks like a bird? Thirdly, he was only thirty when his first talkie hit the screen. An attractive human being who reads and thinks, washed up at thirty? Acting was all he knew? Hardly. This was a man who was making a thousand dollars a week as a director when he was only twenty-one.

Nor, for the record, did he drink himself to death. It's true that he drank, sometimes a lot. But Marlene Dietrich says he didn't drink at all during her last year with him. His death was brought on by a heart attack, his third. And he was not a bitter man when it came.

I thought I knew the truth about my father. A lot of other people thought they knew a different truth. And I was old enough to know that whatever the real truth was, it probably rested somewhere in between.

I suppose it was inevitable that I would feel his shadow all these years. I knew him so briefly and he'd left such an indelible mark. From time to time, I'd ask questions about him—everyone seemed to know him—and I picked up hundreds of stories. I met his old directors: King Vidor, John Ford, Clarence Brown, Howard Hawks. I met the women he acted with, some he had loved: Marlene Dietrich, Lillian Gish, Joan Crawford, Colleen Moore, Eleanor Boardman, and, of course, my mother. Jack even left a four-part autobiography in *Photoplay* magazine that I was able to authenticate.

It was a voyage of discovery for me. I located his father's family and found out what his name really was (which he didn't know himself). In time I was able to tell which stories about him were true and which were the creation of others, some from the MGM publicity department.

I'll never forget the words Rowland V. Lee, perhaps his oldest friend, said to me. "There will always be those who count Jack as a failure or a tragic figure. But by God, there's not one man in ten thousand who touched as many hearts as he did. I'm not talking about fans. I'm talking about the people who knew him. That's how you measure a man's life, Lea. If there's anything tragic about Jack, it's the number of people now living who have no idea what they've missed."

I didn't miss it.

I was just in time.

·two·

H E was born John Cecil Pringle on the morning of July 10, 1899. Not 1895 or 1897, the two dates most often appearing in film biographies. He lied about his age until he was about thirty, for reasons that will become obvious.

The place was Logan, Utah, about seventy miles due north of Salt Lake City. He'd mentioned at one time or another that no doctor or midwife was in attendance because he was born during the worst flood of the decade. A massive summer storm had caused the Logan River to burst from its canyon and fan out over the Wasatch Valley. The storm was easy to verify from meteorological records. It was 1899, July 9 through 11.

The house belonged to Jack's maternal grandfather, William Henry Apperly. Apperly was a retired schoolteacher and himself the child of Mormon pioneers who came from the village of Week in Gloucestershire, England. Apperly's father, also named William, had served in the Royal Marines and was sent to India, leaving his wife behind in Britain. While he was gone, she converted to the Mormon religion and apparently had no trouble converting William almost as soon as he stepped off his troop ship.

Their only son, schoolteacher William Henry Apperly, married a bad-tempered but eminently fertile woman named Lydia Mangreen. Lydia had been orphaned in infancy and grew up as a servant girl in Washington, Utah. It took her ten years and eight children to realize that schoolteachers lived basically on the charity of the community and that the situation wasn't likely to improve. Nor was she crazy about kids, particularly in large groups. By all accounts, she paid them scant attention once they were born, asserting that no one gave her any mothering when she was growing up and she turned out just fine.

Lydia ran off to San Francisco one year, was followed and retrieved by her husband, and then ran away for good. This time, William sued

[6]

for divorce and seven of the eight children ended up scattered all over Utah. All except Ida Adair Apperly, his favorite daughter.

Ida Adair, as she called herself, was born with a burning desire to be an actress. She certainly had the looks for it. Ida was tall, with dark eyes, a voluptuous figure, and a strong sensuous face. She cultivated a certain dramatic flair in the way she moved and dressed and used her voice, and she practiced elocution and singing every chance she got. When a traveling stock company came to town in 1898, someone told the leading lady to break a leg and she did. Ida was hired on the spot to replace her. She lost no time in marrying her deliverer, the show's producer, John Pringle, and began her life on the road.

The little stock company toured from Oklahoma to Ottawa, performing the popular sudsy melodramas of the day and a sprinkling of classics. Ida was a perfect leading lady, tall and regal with a firm commanding voice and attitude, but most of the better and more sympathetic parts went to ingénues. Ingénues got better lines too, like: "Rags are royal raiment when worn for virtue's sake"—sure to bring a tearful, cheering audience to its feet.

Accordingly, Ida hated ingénues. It was said that none remained long with the company or returned to work with her again. And plays were soon being chosen with the role of the leading lady in mind.

Nothing ever went well for Ida for very long. Within the first year of her marriage, she carelessly became pregnant and returned home to her father's house, where she bore the child who was to become Jack Gilbert. Ida was back on the road within two weeks, determined never to get careless again.

As one might expect, Ida's maternal instinct was recessive to say the least. The baby was an accident, an inconvenience, and an intrusion. She swore like a sailor during a difficult labor, and when it was over she refused even to look at the result for twenty-four hours. Jack heard the story many years later in a bar in Fresno, California, when he was approached by a woman who turned out to be his aunt. He remarked afterward that he could have lived without knowing that.

Ida's first act after Jack's birth, when the rain stopped and the roads were passable again, was to hitch up her father's wagon and go calling on relatives in the Wasatch Valley, hoping to find someone who would take the child off her hands. But times were hard and no one could take him in. Ida wrapped him in a borrowed blanket and took off to join the company in Montreal, where at Pringle's request Jack was baptized in the Church of England. She didn't hang around Utah long enough to register his birth.

John Pringle was the son of German emigrants. His grandfather was a circuit-riding Methodist preacher in Missouri, who claimed to have ministered to Jesse James and his brothers. Pringle's name was actually Priegel, but English-sounding names were more acceptable on the stage. It hardly mattered. Ida and John were divorced before Jack had any clear memory of his father, and he never used his name. Jack would not see or hear from him for twenty-six years. John Pringle went one way with his stock company, playing in tents before rural audiences, while Ida went another, an itinerant actress touring the dingy provincial theaters of America around the turn of the century.

It was a life with little glamour and few rewards, driven by a need to perform and a dream of playing the Palace. The actors of Ida's day, however, were despised as a group. They were considered little better than vagabonds by the very people who flocked to the theaters to see these miscreant curiosities perform. Almost every town had its Opera House where touring companies performed the current plays. Most offered variety acts imported from New York or all the way from London.

In Cincinnati, where Ida performed each year with the Forpaugh Stock Company, she developed something of a following. But still the pay was low, the boardinghouses were drab, the hours were as eccentric as the people, and life for little Jack was at times witheringly lonely. He grew up in unheated rooms with chocolate-striped wallpaper peeling off the walls, boardinghouses that he would always remember for their smell of boiled cabbage and for the rough hands of the chambermaids who frequently minded him. Nearly all his afternoons and evenings were spent backstage, in quiet corners, keeping out of the way of adults, or wearily trying to keep his balance on the high stools of grim all-night restaurants.

On rare occasions, one of his mother's fans would invite "the actress's little boy" home to spend the night. There he would see another world. He'd see fires burning in a hearth and bowls of fruit that he could sample any time he wished and shelves holding nothing but books. The children went to bed at the same time every night, and even earlier if they were tired, and they played with real toys. Jack never owned a real toy. Certainly not a bicycle or a football. These were luxuries few traveling actors could afford for their children. And those actors who could afford them didn't have them because of the need to travel light. Jack never even had a Christmas tree, except those set up by the community they happened to be playing during that season. And most Christmas presents he remembered were from community charities, handed out to indigent, homeless, and otherwise unfortunate children.

Jack went to school whenever he could. He bought himself a big red alarm clock and kept it under his pillow. The loud ticking made sleep difficult but it did get him up in the morning. He learned as a toddler to dress himself, fumbling with buttons front and rear. One morning at Cincinnati's Olympia Theater, a character actress named Marie Stoddard went backstage to collect some clothes from the dressing rooms. She noticed a light burning in the star's cubicle and went to investigate. She found Jack, then about six years old, trying to iron a shirt for school. He was too short to reach the ironing board and was having trouble lifting the heavy old-fashioned iron:

I finished it for him, poor creature, and did it many times after that. We called him Cecil then. He was a natty dresser even in those days. His little shirts had to be just so. He liked them made of white piqué with a raised pattern, tiny horseshoes or shamrocks. He didn't often get what he liked. He didn't really exist for Ida Adair. She was a good trouper. I always enjoyed working with her because I could hold my own, but she had a blind spot about that boy. She hardly knew he was there. And he was such a nice little fellow, always polite, but his face was pinched-looking, too old for his years. You wanted to hug him and make him laugh.

There wasn't a whole lot to laugh about, least of all when they dressed him up for the occasional girl's part in one of his mother's plays. According to Marie, Jack had been appearing on stage since birth (the great Eddie Foy carried him out at two weeks!) whenever the script called for a child. He was handy and the price was right. He played the little lost prince in *A Winter's Tale* and one of Nora's children in *A Doll's House*. She said he suffered dreadfully from stage fright and was particularly self-conscious when boys his own age were in the audience.

Jack seldom stayed in one town long enough to make friends or to know his way around a neighborhood, nor did he spend enough time in school to be considered educated. He taught himself to read largely through scripts left lying around backstage. He would sit in dim light behind the proscenium and follow the action on stage, picking out words as they were spoken. Eventually, he could read almost an entire script and began picking up any book, newspaper, magazine, or playbill he could find. He'd discovered a marvelous new universe, books that would talk to him, keep him company, and teach him with infinite patience anything he could possibly wish to know. Secretly, he began to collect books, hiding them among the stage props or burying them in his mother's huge wardrobe trunks when they traveled. If she found them, they were confiscated; actors could not afford excess baggage and it often seemed to Jack that he, as well as his belongings, fell into that category, particularly when Ida's various lovers arrived on the scene.

Many times, with a great show of apparent affection, she would wake her little Cecil in the middle of the night to meet his new "daddy." He would climb out of his bed in his nightshirt and solemnly shake hands with the new addition to the family. But often before Jack could become familiar with the man's name, he was replaced by another. Jack's earliest memory was of a handsome Irishman named O'Hara, whom he'd believed for years to be his real father. His mother never told him differently.

Ida's temperament was volatile, to say the least, and Jack often felt whipsawed between the extremes of her emotions toward him. One moment she would smother him with kisses, the next she would throw him across the room or lock him for hours in a closet. Early in life he learned to guard himself against his mother's moods, neither taken in by floods of affection nor dismayed by her cruelty. He later wrote in his journal, "Sometimes I think she hated me. Children have a curious sense of honesty of emotions. I would strain my small self distrustfully back into her arms when she could catch me up with dramatic tears and love words. I knew it wouldn't last, that in a moment she would push me impatiently aside or throw a chair at my head."

When Jack was six years old, Ida left him in New York with a seamstress, a woman she barely knew. He remembered her as grossly fat with dark bristles on her chin. She appeared at Ida's hotel to collect him, calling him "lovey" and promising to look after him as if he were her own child. She did just that. Her own daughter was a prostitute who worked out of the furnished room they shared on Amsterdam Avenue. Jack walked up five flights of steps to the dark, unheated flat and was given a mat in the corner to sleep on. For ten months, Jack was exposed to the ugly scenes that went on in that room. The daughter's patrons were told to pretend that he wasn't there. When a patron objected strenuously enough, the boy was sent away on errands. He was often sent to the corner saloon for a pail of beer. "I was so short," he said, "that I couldn't see over the bar. I was hungry enough to eat out of garbage pails, though I don't remember that I did. . . . My feet came through my shoes. . . . Abused by that dressmaker . . . I was only seven but I knew more about the world than many people ever discover . . . the bitter lessons of life from chambermaids, drunkards, livery stable hostlers, street women."

One winter day, while lugging a pail of beer back to the Amsterdam Avenue flat, he caught sight of a familiar face. Incredibly, it was Marie Stoddard, the woman who'd been kind to him in Cincinnati, standing on the curb waiting for a trolley. Jack dropped his pail and ran to her, clutching her skirts and crying. She didn't recognize him at first; he was covered with grime and dressed in ragged clothes. But finally she realized who it was and swept him up into her arms.

Years later, when she was teaching acting classes in Hollywood, she told me the story of Jack's rescue, how she climbed five flights of stairs and confronted the wretched woman. The fat seamstress denied any mistreatment of the boy and swore he was a lying little devil, ungrateful for the loving care she and her daughter lavished on him.

"You had only to look at him," Marie said, still furious at the memory. "I marched him out of there and bought him a coat and shoes and a ticket to Rochester where his mother was performing with Bert Lytell. I had little enough money to spare, but what could I do?"

Ida, enjoying her career and a private life unencumbered by a child, was not entirely pleased to see him. A few weeks later, she sent him to his grandfather's farm in Utah, where he remained for almost a year.

He rejoined his mother at about the time of her marriage to a comedian named Walter Gilbert. Marie Stoddard remembered Gilbert as a cheerful type but a man who was careful with his money. Gilbert flatly refused to call his stepson, now eight years old, Cecil. He thought it was a silly effeminate name—as opposed to "Jack," for example. Cecil became Jack. Later, when Walter adopted the boy, he became Jack Gilbert. His mother persisted in calling him Cecil.

Marriage seemed to stabilize Ida's life for a while. She returned to Cincinnati as leading lady and played many demanding roles, of which one critic said, "Miss Adair won distinction for good and effective comedy acting." Since Ida was less than a barrel of laughs offstage, she must indeed have been a pretty fair actress. The marriage soon deteriorated into one more or less of convenience. Ida resumed taking lovers, began drinking heavily, and Jack was in the way again. Back he went to his grandfather's house in Logan.

He was never happy there. Jack was a city child, used to noise and people. The stillness of the Utah nights kept him awake. During the day, the wide empty horizon to the west and the looming mountains to the east made him feel small and vulnerable. The farmyard smells made him sick. Eating was one thing, murdering screaming animals and dismembering them was quite another.

He had cousins to play with, but nearly all the games in which they excelled were new to him. They rode horses as if born in the saddle. Jack counted it a good ride if the horse didn't throw him or try to bite off his toe. One cousin, Clifford Apperly, did go out of his way to be kind to Jack. He taught him the basics of baseball and finally got Jack to where he could manage a horse, if not master it. Jack never forgot the kindness, and remembered Cousin Clifford in his will. All things considered, however, the relatives had little use for him. He was a book-worm, which meant that he read whatever he could find, and they read not at all except for the Book of Mormon and the Sears, Roebuck cata-logue. He was a snob, which meant that he did not share their convic-tion that the simple godly country life was infinitely preferable to life upon the wicked stage. Jack missed his mother desperately. For better or worse, they understood each other.

During a period of relative prosperity while Ida and Walter were play-ing San Francisco, Jack was sent away to a boarding school, the Hitch-cock Military Academy in San Rafael, California. It was, again, a difficult adjustment for him because he'd had no coherent formal edu-cation up to that time. The youngest child at Hitchcock knew more about spelling and arithmetic than he did. The teachers, apparently unaware that Jack was largely self-taught, decided he was lazy and stu-pid and said so out loud. It did not help his standing with the other boys or his self-esteem. On balance, though, Jack seems to have enjoyed the experience of being among city children of the same age and he cer-tainly liked wearing the bright-blue, carefully tailored uniform.

Ida's health began to fail during the summer of 1910. She spent sev-eral months in a tuberculosis sanitorium while Jack toured with Walter Gilbert. It was rarely dull. While they were playing one small town in Arkansas, the manager disappeared with the receipts. The same night, a cyclone came through and the town almost disappeared too. Jack and his stepfather were stranded. They had to go to work washing dishes in a little railroad lunchroom to earn enough money to get out.

Come fall, Jack went back to school and Ida recovered enough to join Marjorie Rambeau's company in San Francisco. She was now reduced to playing second leads and heavies. Jack wrote from school for permis-sion to visit her during the next holiday break. Ida agreed and arrange-ments were made. Jack had not seen his mother in many months. She'd be surprised, he thought, at how tall he'd grown. He carefully brushed his uniform, shined his brass buttons, and put an extra spit polish on his shoes. His most successful English paper, a critique of *Macbeth*, was folded in his pocket.

The train reached San Francisco at noon. Feeling his normal mix of apprehension and excitement at the prospect of seeing his mother, he made his way to the theater, went backstage, and knocked on the door of her dressing room. There was no answer. He quietly pushed the door open and saw her. She was slumped at the dressing table, her head resting on her arms, smeared and running makeup from the night be-fore still on her face. She raised her head and squinted at his image in the mirror as if trying to focus.

"What the hell are you doing here?" she croaked at last. She had forgotten he was coming.

Jack stayed for a few minutes talking to her, then went out, leaving his prize paper on her dressing table. He spent the day walking around San Francisco. Lunch was a sandwich in Golden Gate Park. In late afternoon, he walked once more through the theater district and caught the five-o'clock train back to school. That evening, he told his classmates about lunching with his mother in a fine French restaurant and taking a pleasant drive in her carriage. Then, pleading understandable exhaustion after such a magnificent day in the company of his mother the stage goddess, Jack went to bed early and cried himself to sleep.

Ida Adair's career was moving quickly to its end. The next year, 1911, she played one last engagement at the Garrick Theater in Salt Lake City. After that, her health deteriorated and she died of tuberculosis on September 29, 1913. She was not yet forty years old.

Jack was in school when his mother died. He was summoned home to Logan, Utah, for the funeral. As he left Hitchcock Military Academy, he had a feeling that he would not be returning, that his formal education was now over. It was. Jack never finished the ninth grade.

Ida's body was laid out in the small crowded parlor of his aunt's house in Logan. Jack looked down at the wasted face of his mother and could feel no great sense of loss. The face was almost that of a stranger. His various aunts sat around the room weeping and occasionally saying how young and lovely she looked. Jack wondered why they bothered to pretend. She did not look young. She looked old and sick and dead. And anyway they had never liked her, nor she them.

The family left for the funeral in hired carriages through a steady pouring rain. Jack found himself alone with a young girl, his cousin Clara, who smiled comfortingly and took his hand. Her concern and sympathy warmed him and, on impulse, he leaned toward her and kissed her cheek. He never saw Clara again, but he remembered the purity of the moment for the rest of his life. She had cared.

Ida was buried beside her father and other members of the family in a sandy graveyard at the foot of the Wasatch Mountains. Jack looked across the open grave at his aunts and uncles standing in the chill autumn rain. Stern, hard-faced Mormon farmers. He wondered how he and his gypsy mother could ever have grown from roots such as these. He could see in their eyes a certain satisfaction. Jack was sure they saw the hand of God in her defeat and death.

"Poor mother," he wrote later, "all she ever wanted was to gloriously play New York. Nothing, no one else in her life, was ever quite as important as that one fundamentally trivial goal. That fact was the real tragedy of her life. But trivial or not, it was a goal, and she made a grand try. That ought to count for something. She'd auditioned in New York for David Belasco and Charles Frohman, bringing with her great piles of good reviews, but nothing ever came of it. Mother should have been a Rachel or a Duse. But life condemned her to wander from one filthy dressing room to another, harried by debt and with something tearing at her . . . the desire to do great things and the bitter knowledge that she would not do them."

After the funeral, Jack received another shock. Walter Gilbert could no longer take care of him or pay for his education. It was time for Jack to earn his living. He handed Jack ten dollars and took him to Salt Lake City's Union Station, where he put him on a train for San Francisco. A fine place to start, Walter said.

Jack was fourteen years old and on his own. There was no question of staying in Logan. He had ten dollars, his mother's makeup case, and a sheaf of her clippings and posters. Her other valuables, Walter told him, were sold to pay for her long illness and burial expenses.

The apparent utter lovelessness of his childhood came as a shock to me. I'd read most of his own account when I was much younger, but I really thought that business about living with an Amsterdam Avenue hooker was a particularly tacky example of press-agentry until Marie Stoddard confirmed it. Marie also made the point that Ida's ever-growing coldness toward her son wasn't all that uncommon in show-business families. A child getting bigger reminded an actress-mother that she was getting older. Worse, it reminded the producers. Better to keep the kid out of sight.

It should have been a spirit-crushing childhood by almost any standard, but Jack never appeared to have been beaten down by it or turned into a loner. On the contrary, he showed more than the normal resiliency of children and became quite resourceful. It's hard to doubt that he resented—even hated—his mother or that some of those feelings would eventually turn inward. But by and large he felt sorry for her. Jack knew a personal demon when he saw one.

·three·

I N 1913, San Francisco was where the jobs were. Money had been pouring into the Bay Area in anticipation of the 1914 opening of the Panama Canal and the commerce that would subsequently be funneled through the best deep-water port on the West Coast. The construction trades had, of course, been booming since 1906, when the earthquake and fire destroyed most of the city. Half the town seemed to be looking for ways to spend money while the other half was looking for ways to take it.

Jack wouldn't starve, Walter figured, even if he had no idea what he wanted to do. Something would turn up for a healthy young man who'd learned to be self-reliant since infancy. Why not the theater? Any time there was money to be spent, it would find its way to a ticket booth.

But Jack had had enough of the stage in general and the San Francisco theater district in particular. Too many unhappy memories. Too many lonely boardinghouses in strange towns. Too much of his life already spent owning nothing that couldn't fit in a trunk. Besides, what could he do in the theater? He'd played a few children's parts in his mother's troupe but he was hardly a credentialed actor. Anyway, they'd laugh at him. Jack was tall, much too thin, had a long stringy neck and a face that he thought was funny-looking.

From his last visit, he remembered walking past whole blocks full of saloons; every one of them seemed to employ a boy or two not much older than himself. It was a place to start. He began by canvassing the waterfront area where saloons were in greatest profusion and where living quarters were cheapest. All of them seemed to have back rooms fitted for extra-legal pursuits, ranging from tiny roped-off areas for bare-knuckle boxing to larger pits where patrons bet on the number of rats a terrier could kill in sixty seconds. The implied availability of rats and the general gracelessness of the clientele caused Jack to focus his search upon a better part of town. He found work on the third day in a saloon that was marginally more genteel although radical enough to have a ladies' entrance. For several weeks he scrubbed floors and washed dishes for two dollars a week and meals, while keeping an eye open for more promising employment.

One day a patron chanced to remark that the B. F. Goodrich Company was looking for a tire salesman. Jack questioned him and was told that he was probably much too young. Jack claimed to be eighteen, but the knickers he wore caused the listener to doubt it. Seeing his point, Jack decided to invest in a secondhand suit, his first pair of long pants ever except for the Hitchcock uniform, and applied for the job. To his astonished delight, he was hired. The salary was seven dollars a week, more than he'd ever had before, and he saw before him a clear future as a business tycoon if starting out was this easy.

But if it was easy it was also boring. There's only so much that the well-rounded young man wants to know or discuss about a tire. The newspapers he read between customers evoked dreams of being a journalist. A want ad for reporters, placed by the Portland *Oregonian*, inspired him to take a few days off and a train to Oregon, where he talked his way into the job. Unhappily, although he could gather and write a story, the paper felt that it needed someone with more traditional ideas of spelling and punctuation. It was suggested that he cast about for something more suitable. The only other job that was both suitable and available, if not entirely desirable, was the position of stage manager for the Baker Stock Company in Spokane, Washington. He took the job and enjoyed it in spite of himself. Like it or not, theater was where he felt most confident and most at home. He stayed with the company until it went broke.

Nearly two years had passed since Jack first arrived in San Francisco and he was going nowhere. He never made more than a dollar a day and that was only when he worked. His dreams and his confidence were beginning to fade and he was poor. Then, like a lot of other poor people, Jack discovered the movies. They were terrific, marvelous, truly better than ever. Movies had improved vastly since the early nickelodeon days of sappy twenty-minute stage plays or vignettes put on film. Now there were real stories. They were like books for people who couldn't read and a godsend to immigrants who spoke no English. They were like a magic time machine that could carry a whole audience to any spot in the world or to any place in history. Even the educated were beginning to take them seriously, or had, at least, when Griffith's *Birth of a Nation* played to three-dollar-a-ticket crowds in the East. And the actors! They were much more natural than before, more like real people. Unlike the studied poses and sweeping gestures of the stage, this was a kind of acting that was done mostly with the face, with the eyes. Eyes that could look out upon thousands and thousands of people in a single day and make them laugh or cry. And they didn't even have to learn lines. Jack was crazy about the whole idea of movies. Like almost everyone in the audience, he began to dream of being a part of them.

One afternoon, Jack went to see *On the Night Stage*, starring William S. Hart. The movie had barely begun when a title flashed across the screen introducing "Black Jack Malone, the ugly villain of the piece." And there was the evil Black Jack, leaning against a bar, one foot on the rail, a glass of whiskey at his lips. A shock of recognition hit Jack and he leaned closer for a better look at the actor's face. My God, he thought, that's Herschel Mayall up there. Mayall had been a member of his mother's stock company in Cincinnati. In fact, the last time Jack had seen him he was standing in exactly the same position. It was in a saloon near the old Olympia Theater. Jack had gone there with Walter Gilbert on the day the company closed and all the actors were having a last drink together. That was in 1910 and Herschel looked as if he hadn't moved since. "Either he held his liquor extremely well," Jack recalled later, "or it was a very long time between drinks."

He left the theater believing that if Herschel Mayall could break into the movies, so could he. But he had no idea where to start. Learning to be an actor was as good a place as any, he decided, and promptly made plans to see Walter Gilbert, who was then working as a director in Portland. Surely his stepfather would train him in some parts. With the few dollars he'd managed to save, Jack boarded a train for Portland.

Walter Gilbert couldn't help him, certainly not with an acting job. He tried to make Jack understand that this was his first crack at directing and he simply could not afford to risk it by casting a stepson who was little better than an amateur. Times were too hard, he told him, and his own status as a stage comedian was beginning to show signs of wear. He needed this directing job. It was the beginning of his future.

As for this movie business, however, Walter did have a thought. He had a friend, Walter Edwards, who was directing movies for Thomas Ince, of the New York Motion Picture Corporation. Their studio, he told Jack, was called Inceville and was located in Santa Monica, California. He'd write to his friend if Jack was interested. Jack almost leaped at him with his reply.

Walter Gilbert's letter contained a warm recommendation and two recent photographs. Jack watched the mail for a week, barely able to eat. Finally, a letter arrived from Santa Monica. "Mr. Ince," it read, "says he will pay the boy fifteen dollars a week if he cares to come down."

[17]

"I became a bit hysterical," Jack admitted later. His moods vaulted from a dancing, leaping euphoria to a black pool of disbelief and despair. I'm going to be a movie actor, he told himself. I'm going to be a star. He would imagine himself on the screen and see crowds crying and cheering. And then he'd know it was impossible. He was ugly, much too ugly to photograph. He'd never taken a decent picture since he was a child. How could he? He was a one-hundred-and-fifteen-pound beanpole with a "stringy neck and a long beak of a nose." Clothes almost flapped when he hung them on his body. Impossible, he thought. But it's going to happen. I'm going to be a movie actor. He walked around Portland telling it to anyone who'd listen. He'd stop often to study his face in store windows. Then he'd feel the need to say it out loud again. By the time he arrived in Los Angeles, thanks to a ten-dollar loan from Walter, he'd almost convinced himself.

"This is Jack Gilbert," he announced into the public telephone. Arriving at Union Station, he'd asked the central operator to connect him with the Inceville studio. He told the man who answered that he'd arrived in Los Angeles.

"What of it?" the voice asked.

It had crossed Jack's mind that they might send a car for him, but he was slowly coming down to earth. "Well, how do I get there?" he asked.

"Walk!" the voice said curtly, and clicked off.

Confused, Jack fished out another thirty cents, and tried once more. The same voice came on again, asked Jack who the hell he thought he was, told him that he could go to hell, and hung up a second time.

Jack got a few swear words out of his system and then set out on his own. After first taking the wrong trolley, he took two more, plus the interurban railway, then a bus, and then finally arrived on foot at the gate of the famous Inceville studio.

Inceville, in 1915, was a sort of Disneyland of moviemaking. Thomas Ince had acquired some eighteen thousand acres along the shore above Santa Monica and built a fantasy world. Five years of making movies had left the property scattered with sets of every imaginable description. Beyond the cluster of buildings where Sunset Boulevard now meets the ocean, there were western towns, desert forts, Babylonian temples, an English manor house, Civil War battlefields complete with cannon—even a real operating Japanese fishing village. Nearby was a pier where Ince's "navy" was moored. It contained the shells of warships, Chinese junks, sampans, gondolas, and various sailboats. A ratty old schooner could become a square-rigged pirate ship or an Arab dhow in a matter of days. Ince, who produced a great many westerns, had put an entire

Wild West show on the payroll, including real Indians, cowboys, horses, even a small herd of buffalo. Sets, once built, stayed built, collecting dust until they were used again.

Tom Ince had been called the first prophet of modern cinema. What Henry Ford was then doing for the mass production of automobiles, Ince had already done for the making of movies. Once a story was selected for filming, many of which Ince wrote himself, he would plot out each scene in sequence, describing every action and emotion in detail, leaving no room for interpretation by individual directors but also no room for wasted footage or the possibility of an incoherent story. Every finished script was stamped with the words PRODUCE THIS EX-ACTLY AS WRITTEN, and anyone who didn't was fired.

Ince's purpose was not to stifle creativity but rather to focus it upon the planning stage, where it belonged. Far from discouraging innovation, scenes often involved some technique that had not been tried before, such as dream sequences shot through a lens smeared with petroleum jelly or covered with a layer of gauze, or new lighting techniques, or camera setups in airplanes or under the hooves of stampeding horses. Much of it was trial and error. But Ince was breaking new ground almost daily. His tight production methods resulted in a steady stream of fast-paced stories that could capture and hold an audience's attention. He made everything from tender love stories to historical epics.

With understandable awe, Jack approached the main gate of the Inceville studio and an aging guard who dozed near a sign that said NO ADMITTANCE. Again he introduced himself and stated his purpose, and again the announcement was met with absolute indifference. Jack moved toward the swinging gate but thought better of it when the guard's hand dropped across the butt of the six-gun he wore. Jack had neglected to bring the letter that had promised him a job and was not at all sure the old man could have read it if he had. As far as the guard was concerned, Jack was just one more kid trying to break into the movies. Dozens like him were already arriving each week, grimy and broke, horrified to discover that the studios they had to canvass were not only scattered over fifty-five square miles, but were literally armed camps. Tough cowboys also doubled as guards and carried loaded six-guns and Winchesters. The patents war, in which Edison's Motion Picture Patents Company tried to collect tribute from everyone who made or showed movies, was still a fresh memory. Hired thugs had sabotaged films, started fires, even shot at producers and directors. Cecil B. De Mille routinely carried a sidearm.

This final barrier left Jack in despair. There was no way to telephone, no way to get a message through. He was tired and weak from hunger. It had been three days since he'd eaten a regular meal or slept in a bed. He sat down, near collapse, upon his suitcase.

At that moment, a Ford bus came chugging up the road from Santa Monica to collect homegoing actors and crew from Inceville. The gate swung open, and through it came a group of men in western costume heading for the bus. One face in the crowd almost caused him to faint from relief. It was Herschel Mayall.

"Herschel!" Jack sprang after him and grabbed his arm. The startled actor turned, no recognition on his face.

"Don't you remember me? It's Cecil Gilbert." He was a foot taller than when Mayall had last laid eyes on him in Cincinnati. But finally Mayall gave a shout and threw his arms around Jack. He then escorted him safely through the gate to the office of Walter Edwards, who was expecting him after all. Edwards, to Jack's even greater relief, seemed pleased with the way he looked and introduced him to the stocky blond man sitting at the next desk. It was the legendary Tom Ince himself. Both men spoke to him cordially and welcomed him to the studio. If there were a heaven, Jack felt, it couldn't be more thrilling than this. In his exhaustion, coupled with the intoxication of being in Tom Ince's company, he began to babble. He talked about his trip, his phone calls, his burning desire to succeed as a movie actor, movies he'd seen, leaping from subject to unrelated subject, often in midsentence. He knew that he was babbling. He could see the glazed expression on the faces of the two men but couldn't stop. Eventually, Ince excused himself and Edwards silenced him with an understanding slap on the back. He invited Jack to dinner, and pretended not to notice as Jack stuffed food into his mouth almost faster than he could swallow it. Later, he helped Jack find a room at the Waldorf Hotel in Santa Monica and told him his first call would be at five o'clock the following morning. Jack didn't care how early it was. He was going to be a movie actor.

But two weeks went by before he was asked to do anything. He would come to the studio, he'd collect his pay, he'd be treated respectfully, even deferentially, but no one asked him to do any work. At the end of that period, he realized what had happened. Jack had been seen being personally greeted by Thomas Ince and one of his top directors. It was hardly the type of reception one would expect for a fifteen-dollar-a-week extra. The presumption, therefore, was that some special relationship existed between Jack and Tom Ince, and no one was willing to risk ordering him about.

The confusion was finally straightened out and Jack learned his proper place in studio society. There were three basic social strata among the actors and they rarely intermingled. At the top were the "hams," or featured players, and at the bottom were the extras. The extras, Jack's group, called themselves the "bushwa," a probable corruption of "bourgeois" (and perhaps a euphemism for "bullshit"). In between, or in a world of their own, were the cowboys. They were the real thing: wild and rough men, the last of a breed being pushed off the plains by progress and civilization. Many elected to drift farther west to Hollywood, still basically a frontier town, where the makers of movies had no interest whatsoever in taming them. They were expected to be what they were and, given that encouragement, they were even more so. They would gallop like the Wild Bunch onto the set, guns blasting, scattering actors and crew alike. They were coarse men, proud of their roughness, and with an intimidating contempt for anyone farther along on the Darwinian scale. The result was that everyone was afraid of them—except Tom Ince, who simply fired them if they got too far out of line. And except Jack, who seemed to have developed a knack for getting along with almost everyone.

During those first idle weeks, he became friendly with the owner of the Café de Yellow, a hash house for actors that operated on the beach. The proprietor was a giant-size, dangerous-looking Italian who was known to have a long prison record. Even the cowboys treated him with care. Jack once saw him break up a fight between two cowboys just by lazily drawing a knife from his belt and moving, with a sigh, in their direction. Otherwise, Jack enjoyed the big man. He liked hearing him sing operatic selections as he served plates of franks and beans to the extras. More privately, the Italian would gave him free Coca-Colas and regale him with chilling stories of prison life. So, from the outset, the owner of the Café de Yellow was presumed to be a friend of Jack's and protective of him. No cowboy ever dared intimidate Jack. Several became good friends.

Also during those first weeks of wandering and observing, Jack noticed how young almost everybody seemed to be. Tom Ince, the man who'd built all this, was himself only thirty-three. And many of the featured players, including several stars, were hardly older than Jack himself. Lillian and Dorothy Gish, over at Biograph, were eighteen and twenty, respectively, and had already made over seventy-five pictures between them. Mae Marsh and Mary Pickford had both made their first films at sixteen and Norma Talmadge at fourteen. Many male leading men were also in their teens. This emphasis on youthful actors had to do with the film quality and lighting technology available at the time. Klieg lights hadn't been invented yet, reflective lighting was still experimental, and the film stock could not distinguish between soft shading and dark shadow. The result was that any facial line was enhanced and then enlarged upon the screen. Most actors in their early twenties seemed to be at least ten years older. Youth was king. Jack reflected happily upon this fact of Hollywood life. Stardom might be only a matter of months away.

His first day of actual work began in the wardrobe room, where he was issued a blue cavalry uniform, a rifle, an Indian breechcloth, and a can of dark body makeup called Bole-Armenia. He followed the other extras up a hill to the boys' dressing room, where he was assigned a makeup shelf and a cabinet for his clothes. He made himself into an Indian and then walked, nearly naked, to the set.

He had no idea of the name of the movie. All he knew was that he was supposed to climb on a pinto pony and ride, whooping and shouting, in wide circles around the camera. His only previous riding experience was out in Logan with his cousins. There at least he had had a saddle and stirrups. Jack crashed to the ground several times during the filming and feared that he'd ruined the scene, but no one else seemed to mind. As far as the director was concerned, Jack falling was just another shot Indian.

After taking a pounding all morning, Jack was lame and sore. He hobbled back to the dressing room, where he became a cavalryman and spent the afternoon standing behind a stockade shooting the same rifle at the now imaginary Indian he had been that morning. The cavalrymen were dismissed at sundown.

Jack dragged himself back down to the dressing room, dreaming aloud of a hot bath and a bed.

"No such luck," said fellow bushwa Roy Coulson, grinning. "We're working tonight."

"Tonight?" Jack was aghast.

"Yup," Coulson answered. "With Richard Stanford down in Sulphur Canyon."

A trickle of blood was running down Jack's leg from one of his falls. Coulson noticed it and laughed. "You'll harden up in a few days," he promised.

Jack almost didn't live that long. Stanford had set up a mine-disaster scene at the bottom of an old shaft. The script called for five boys to be found dead among the burning rubble, and Jack was one of them. Jack was laid out in a suitably grotesque and uncomfortable position and warned not to move no matter what happened. Next, kerosene was poured over everything, the flares were lit, a torch applied to the soaked timbers, and the camera started rolling.

Jack lay still, the flames licking all around him. He felt his feet grow warm and then hot. Opening one eye, he noticed that his left shoe was burning briskly. As he watched, the cuff of his trousers began smoldering then burst into flame. Moving as little as possible, he tried to kick out the flames.

"Lie still, you dirty coward!" the director shouted.

"Nuts to you!" Jack yelled, and leaped out of the fire. The action stopped and someone ran to him with a blanket to smother the flames.

"You killed the scene, you yellow rat!" the furious director screamed, starting after Jack. Jack reached for a timber and held it like a club, but one of the other boys grabbed his arm.

"Don't say a word," he whispered. Jack dropped the timber, the director blew off a bit more steam, and the incident passed without escalating into a confrontation that would probably have ended in Jack being barred from that or any other studio. They finished shooting at midnight and Jack was back at work at dawn the next day.

The moviemaking world that Jack chose for himself in 1915 was a tough one. There were no union hours, no lunch breaks, no workmen's compensation. The sets were dangerous and the casualty rate among actors was high. Each year, several were killed. But as Roy Coulson promised, Jack did toughen up. And there was no place else in the world where Jack Gilbert wanted more to be.

He wrote: "I rode cow ponies for Ince and made no impression on the directors . . . but I collected my extra's wages at the end of each day and carried them home. . . . Even though I was not succeeding quite as I'd hoped, I was happy. For the first time, I belonged."

And he was taking the first steps to success. He was learning about the making of films and he was following a route toward manhood that no powder puff would have survived, let alone chosen. He also turned out to be wrong about making no impression on directors. A few, among them Reginald Barker and Clifford Smith, had their eyes on the gawky youngster. They began to move him closer to the camera lens.

·four·

THE year was 1915. There was lanky young Jack Gilbert, boy actor, cannon fodder in a series of shoot-'em-ups, and occasional unintended stuntman, watching and learning and waiting for his big break. It came, after a fashion, when Jack was given a small role in William S. Hart's western classic, *Hell's Hinges*.

Jack actually didn't have much to do in the picture but he made the most of what he had. If you see the film today and look for Jack, you'll see that he manages to stay subtly visible all through it. He dogs the camera, swaggering in front of a saloon, listening conspicuously to what the other actors are saying, and otherwise hovering in the background, using any excuse whatever to be seen. He was seen, most of all, by William S. Hart himself, who practically walked into Jack every time he turned around.

But Jack did make a positive impression. The horse-faced actor mentioned Jack's performance in his autobiography, *My Life—East and West*: "He was one of the fifteen-dollar-a-week extras, 'actor boys' we called them. I noticed his eagerness to please and I could see he had training. I asked who he was and recognized the name of a well-known stock actress." (If Ida Adair couldn't teach scene-stealing, nobody could.)

Hart evidently decided that Jack might as well have a scene worth the effort, and offered him a substantially stronger part in his next picture, *The Apostle of Vengeance*. The plot was vintage William S. Hart, with the forty-five-year-old cowboy manqué from Newburgh, New York, playing a firm-jawed, country minister whose heaviest cross was his firebrand kid brother. The brother, the second lead, was a dangerous young punk who was ripe for a redeeming death in the last reel. Hart told Jack that the part was his if he thought he could handle it.

Jack grabbed at the chance, naturally, but Tom Ince balked. Jack was too inexperienced for a role that Ince felt was the meatiest part in the picture. But Hart, who had made over twenty successful westerns and had a star's clout, was adamant.

"All right," Ince told him, "but if the kid ruins the picture, we won't release it and you'll lose your salary."

Hart shrugged off Ince's concerns and began working. The picture was being shot along a creek bed in a narrow canyon up behind the studio. The canyon walls blocked out all direct sunlight, which was fine because the script called for a rainstorm. But rainstorms need rain and the answer was a steady stream of spring water that played on the actors all day through a battery of fire hoses. With the wind coming off the ocean, funneling up the canyon, the result was a raw, bitter cold that drove right through Jack's clothing. After two days of watching Jack under these conditions, Hart began to wonder whether his confidence was justified. The kid who was supposed to be a firebrand was shaking like a wet dog and looked as if he were scared half out of his mind.

"Jack was thin to the point of emaciation," Hart wrote, "shaking to pieces and frightened to death that he would lose the part. He was actually shedding tears from the cold. It was really brutal. I put an arm around the boy and said to him, 'Look here, laddie, we've got to go through this and we're going to do it. So just lock your teeth and let's go. And just remember you're making good, that no one is going to hurt you or take the part away from you.'"

By Hart's account, his display of kindness and support was all Jack needed. He stiffened his quaking legs, clenched his jaw, doubtless hitched his belt, and then sailed right through the scene. Hart wrote: "It was bitter work. I still shiver when I think about it, but the picture was a success and the young actor made a hit."

Tom Ince, as well, had to admit a somewhat grudging respect for Jack. He was still too inexperienced and too skinny for anything resembling a romantic or action lead, but he had gumption and a good camera sense, and, above all, he was willing to do anything that was required of him. Ince gave him three more featured roles in quick succession. Now Jack's name was being listed in the credits. Ince decided, when pressed, that he was probably worth a three-dollar-a-week raise. Jack Gilbert, a featured contract player with six roles behind him, was making eighteen dollars a week.

During this same period, according to Jack's own account, he had his first taste of sex, Scotch whisky, sudden tragedy, and guilt. He'd met an actress named Effie Stewart when he wandered out to the Venice Pier on an idle, lonely weekend. An actor he knew, Langdon Gillett, noticed him outside the Ship Café and invited Jack in to round out a foursome. He shyly agreed and was paired off with a small blonde actress who was several years his senior. After a few drinks, the first hard liquor of his life, Effie asked if he wouldn't rather go home with her than face the long trip back to Santa Monica. By morning he was in love.

Effie, for whatever reason, seemed genuinely to care for this rail-thin sixteen-year-old who still had pimples on his face. She was almost certainly lonely herself, and, like most of the actors and actresses of the time, lived a life of near starvation and crushing disappointments relieved by only occasional rays of hope in the form of minor roles.

At first, Jack was supremely happy. His relationship with Effie was probably the most sustained, intimate, human contact of his young life. After a long, sometimes bruising day at the studio, they would shop together, cook dinner together, read poetry, and make love. Her little beach cottage, with its blue wicker furniture, Japanese prints, and potted geraniums, was infinitely more inviting than his tiny hotel room. But Effie's caring soon turned into needing and Jack began to chafe under her demands upon his time and his thoughts. Needing turned to clinging.

That, at least, was Jack's perception. He was totally inexperienced in anything resembling a give-and-take relationship and doubtless didn't handle this one well. As he had done with his mother, he began putting up walls. Effie tried to hold on to him by promising to change whatever it was that made him uncomfortable. But those efforts became even more suffocating. Finally, after three months, he broke off the affair. He told her of his decision on the bus to the studio where they were both extras in Ince's first big spectacle, later called *Civilization*. Effie was hurt, but chose not to regard his decision as final. She would win him back. There would be plenty of opportunity. After all, working on the same picture, he wouldn't be able to avoid seeing her at least several times a day.

For *Civilization*, an anti-war allegory, Ince had built a replica of the Potsdam Palace, representing a mythical Teutonic kingdom where the evil hun was about to loose the dogs of war upon the rest of Europe. Jack was one of a troop of mounted lancers shouting oaths to the war gods while Effie and the other ladies of the court watched from the balcony. Suddenly, there was a grinding sound and a snap. The balcony crumbled and fell away, pitching Effie and the other ladies into the courtyard. People screamed and horses bolted as masonry fell, but miraculously there was only one casualty. Effie Stewart was dead on arrival at Santa Monica Hospital.

Jack was overcome with guilt. He had broken her heart and now she was dead. More than that, he despised himself for the feeling of relief that crept in through his remorse. Whatever his other feelings were, Jack kept them to himself. No one knew about his relationship with Effie. Jack told the story ten years later, after two marriages and God knows how many love affairs.

Jack responded to Effie's death by plunging fully into his work at Inceville. Inceville absorbed him just as completely. Jack was among the first to arrive at the studio each morning and often had to be told to leave at night. He noticed that several of the newer actors were just as reluctant to return to the real world of hotel rooms and cheap restaurants. Why should they? Their work, if it could be called work, was enormous fun, for all the risks, long hours, and uncertainty. They were living such an incredible dream that it almost seemed it would all disappear in the night if they didn't stay and hold on to it.

Jack had at least one advantage over most of the other young hopefuls he knew. He had a contract. His salary was eighteen dollars a week by 1916 and, best of all, it was steady income. It was true that on a daily basis he earned no more than a free-lance extra's three dollars, a fact that galled him from time to time, since he'd appeared in several featured roles, but extras, on the other hand, rarely worked steadily. Moreover, in the days before central casting, they had to appear every morning for a longshoreman's sort of shape-up. But a contract didn't mean that Jack would automatically be assigned to key roles or even that such parts would permanently lift him out of the ranks of extras. Today's featured player could be tomorrow's extra. Jack knew that. He also knew that featured parts were where you found them. It would be up to him to get himself noticed and known. There was a lot of luck involved, of course. A lot of being in the right place at the right time. Or having a friend in the right place at the right time.

Such a friend was Lee Garmes. Lee, who was about Jack's age, came to Hollywood to be an actor but soon developed a greater interest in the technical side of filmmaking. (He went on to become an Oscar-winning cinematographer and a pioneer in lighting techniques that are still being used today. One of the many high points of his career was the filming of the first third of Gone With the Wind.)

He happened to be within earshot one day when Reginald Barker suggested to another director that Jack might be just right for an upcoming picture if only the kid had a decent wardrobe. In those days, actors were expected to supply their own clothes except for costume parts.

Lee interrupted Barker's conversation, saying, "Why don't you give the kid a break? You know Jack's a good actor and he'd love to get this part. Why can't the studio advance him some money for clothes and take it out of his salary over the next few months?"

Barker, instead of wondering who this nosy kid was, wondered why no one had ever thought of advancing clothing money before. They talked it over for a few minutes and Barker agreed on an advance of fifty dollars. Lee Garmes ran off to tell Jack, who stared for a while in disbelief before letting out a sudden whoop of joy and bear-hugging his startled friend. They took off on a shopping spree the next day.

In 1916, fifty dollars could provide an adequate actor's wardrobe. A good shirt could be had for a dollar. A wool suit at Forman & Clark's went for fifteen dollars and evening clothes went for twenty. Jack decided to spend twenty dollars on just a dinner jacket—as long as it was perfect. Everything had to be absolutely perfect, even if the fitters had to work all afternoon. Lee Garmes watched in amusement as Jack went through the racks of clothing like a child in a candy store. He would pose in front of the dressing-room mirrors, his expression moving from a rapturous smile to a critical frown and then back again as minuscule tucks were taken in every seam and cuff.

"Your dad was a born dandy," Lee Garmes told me. "There was always a kind of elegance to him even before he had the right kind of trappings. As a matter of fact, when he showed up on the set—I think the picture was *Hater of Men*—nobody recognized him at first. The director even stood up to be introduced to him. To Jack, all this was like magic. One or two good-looking outfits and he was suddenly transformed into a gentleman. I don't think he ever forgot the difference those clothes made. He took very good care of them."

Rowland V. Lee, the director who later became famous for atmospheric chillers like *Tower of London* and the Fu Manchu series, was a lifelong friend of my father's who started with him at Inceville. In the beginning, he was probably more of a big brother. For more than two years they both lived in the Waldorf Hotel, really a rooming house, in Santa Monica. Jack had his two-dollar-a-week room with an ocean view—if he leaned far enough out of his window. Rowland lived in the Waldorf's penthouse—actually on the roof, which he shared with his brother Bob and his sister Zarah. The Lees paid sixteen dollars a week. On the whole, the Waldorf was a gloomy, peeling place, but it did cater to show people at a time when some hotels hung out signs forbidding actors, Chinese, and dogs.

Jack's room was small, but it was his own for as long as he could pay rent. He built in the bookshelves he'd always wanted and bought a silk shade for the naked light bulb in the ceiling. Jack stretched his salary by eating only what was necessary to stay alive and had little to do with girls, particularly after Effie Stewart.

The Lees were all actors at first, but the older, Columbia-educated Rowland soon maneuvered himself into a director's job while Bob began writing scenarios. Zarah, an actress getting reasonably regular work, noticed how underfed Jack looked and began inviting him up for dinner with the family. By dumping extra helpings onto his plate she got him to the point where he looked as if he might survive, although at a hundred and fifteen pounds and almost six feet he was something less than robust. According to Rowland Lee:

Jack was so thin you could see through him on a bright day. He hadn't much confidence then, he was struggling to overcome his background. . . . Later he became a very literate guy. He sort of grew into his star personality but in those days he was a very lonely kid. My sister was keeping house for my brother and me and one night she invited Jack to have dinner with us. I don't think he had ever tasted home cooking before and he tried not to show how hungry he was. After that, we more or less adopted him.

Dreaming about stardom, even dreaming about climbing the first couple of rungs, is an indulgence every actor permits himself. But few actors are ever quite able to believe it's happening when it comes, even a fairly modest success like a first leading role for an eighteen-dollar-a-week actor. Rowland Lee remembered how it happened to Jack:

It was a picture called *Princess of the Dark* and Jack was given the lead. He was absolutely floating on air. He couldn't believe his luck. Not that it was much of a part. I mean, it was awful. He played a hunchback crippled boy in love with a beautiful blind girl who, of course, couldn't see that he was crippled, and everything would be perfect as long as she didn't try to give him a backrub. Really corny stuff. The picture was actually a pretty good showcase for the star, Enid Bennett, but we were sure it wouldn't do much for Jack. He was basically romantic lead material, given a few more plates of pork chops and noodles. Thrashing around like Quasimodo with pimples wasn't going to move him very far in that direction. But he really didn't care about the romantic lead business. Not even later. The more offbeat a part was, the better he liked it.

William S. Hart, Jack's first champion and mentor, was famous for proposing marriage to his leading ladies, and it seems to have been catching. Jack promptly fell in love with Enid Bennett. She was a fragile-looking girl, an Australian with china-blue eyes and golden hair, who had come to Inceville by way of the New York stage. She'd been touring with Otis Skinner when Tom Ince spotted her and lured her into the movies. Enid's part required a tenderness and caring toward her crippled leading man, which almost guaranteed that Jack would succumb to her.

Enid was older than Jack (almost everybody was), but she grew quite fond of him, as almost everybody did. Enid and her two sisters lived downtown at the old Engstrom Apartments, near the Philharmonic. They enjoyed and encouraged Jack's frequent visits.

Each visit was easily a three-hour round-trip by trolley and on foot. Given Jack's long hours, his visits were limited to living-room conversations, as much by time as by his lack of cash. Enid, upon learning that Jack more or less knew how to drive, had a terrific idea. Jack would buy a car; she'd lend him the necessary four hundred dollars, and he'd pay her back as soon as he could. Jack was dumbfounded. A car! That was like giving him his own magic carpet! When he recovered from his disbelief, he decided that it was the most intelligent, practical suggestion he'd ever heard. It would add hours to his day. No more waiting for trolleys that poked along at fifteen miles an hour. No more living his life by the studio bus schedule. And it meant time he could spend with Enid. He calculated that he could pay her back fully in six months, and swore that he would. It must have been a very quick calculation, because four hundred dollars amounted to almost exactly five months' pay. But who cared! Jack Gilbert and Enid were going to have a car. He must have looked at fifty before he settled on a little yellow Saxon with an open top.

Jack and Enid saw each other frequently but not exclusively, at least as far as Enid was concerned. She'd been going out with Fred Niblo, the director, well before she began seeing Jack, but Jack didn't seem to have considered Niblo a serious rival. After all, Niblo, forty-two-years old, was twice the age of Enid Bennett, who therefore could not possibly have felt anything for him beyond a certain respectful fondness. Jack liked Fred Niblo well enough. He was bright and personable, in fact one of the most likable men at Inceville. Old, though.

Enid told Jack one evening that Fred Niblo had proposed marriage and she'd accepted. They would not be able to see each other anymore. Jack was appalled. When he pointed out Niblo's age, Enid pointed out that Jack was at least four years younger than she, a fact that Jack considered irrelevant. What was relevant was that the woman he loved was making the worst mistake of her life. The man was obviously too old to offer her any kind of happy life and just as obviously a phony. Even his friendliness, Jack decided, was artificial. "No one is ever as glad to see *anybody* as Fred Niblo is to see *everybody*."

Enid went on to become a major star, later playing Maid Marian to Douglas Fairbank's Robin Hood, then semi-retired from the screen to assist her husband in directing *Ben-Hur*. It was a good marriage and it lasted until Niblo's death, in 1948.

Enid was lost to him, but Jack still had his car and no shortage of other friends of both sexes who liked him a lot. Rowland V. Lee remembers one day when Jack literally drove his car into the ground. He was driving to the studio at his usual clip when, as he reached the top of the last hill on Motor Avenue, the whole damned engine fell out on the street. Poor Jack managed to coast down to the studio, where he told people what had happened. Word somehow got back to the studio's motor department and the mechanics stopped what they were doing and went out looking for Jack's engine. They found it still lying in the middle of the street and brought it back and put the car together again. It was ready in time for him to drive home that night. There was a crowd waiting at the gates when Jack drove through, and they all cheered. Jack was happy as a baby. And those guys wouldn't take a dime for it either.

The Triangle Film Corporation came into existence at the end of 1915. The movie business had begun to attract Wall Street investors and an army of hustlers and promoters who saw there was money to be made. Harry Aitken was one of them. With his brother Roy, plus two ex-bookies named Adam Kessek and Charles Baumann, and the backing of Kuhn, Loeb & Company, Aitken came West with a scheme that put film producers and businessman, distributors and exhibitors, all into one centrally managed profit-sharing organization.

Harry Aitken's idea made a lot of sense. He'd bring together the three most creative men in pictures, Ince, Mack Sennett, and D.W. Griffith—hence the name Triangle—and provide each with his own studio, a liberal budget, and almost total freedom to do what he was good at. Triangle would then distribute and exhibit the films and divide the profits fairly.

"Fairly" was the key word. The matter of profits ending up in the hands of those who earned them had been a sore point for years. Distributors leased out the film and were supposed to pay a certain percentage of their revenue back to the film's producers, but did so almost on an honor system. The problem was that there were hardly any honest distributors and no way at all to monitor their sales. A year earlier, Aitken had taken a financial bath when Griffith's *Birth of a Nation*, which he backed, yielded surprisingly modest returns for a picture that was playing to packed houses in almost every theater in the country. One of the grossest examples of inequitable reporting came from a young Boston wheeler-dealer who sewed up franchising rights to the New England states. Aitken got fifty thousand dollars and the Boston entrepreneur later boasted that he made almost a million dollars on the deal, so much in fact, that he came West himself to get in on the money machine. His name was Louis B. Mayer.

To house the new operation, Ince acquired twelve acres in the growing suburb of Culver City. Triangle later bought another thirty acres so that there would be enough room to film outdoor pictures without trekking all the way up the coast to Inceville. The new facility was vastly larger than anything ever before seen. There were eight covered stages; complete shops for carpenters, plumbers, and electricians; a wardrobe department, a restaurant and commissary; three hundred dressing rooms; and a scenario department with a full-time staff of writers.

The writers as a group were Jack's best friends at the studio. Early film writers were mostly ex-newspapermen, clever, hard-bitten types, and to Jack they represented a kind of worldly glamour and skill that was more impressive than mere acting. When Jack was not on the set, he could usually be found hanging around the scenario department making himself useful and asking questions. The writers, in turn, enjoyed Jack and were flattered by his interest. Several assumed responsibility for his education and lent him books to read. They encouraged him to try his hand at writing, and they allowed him to sit in on story conferences to see how it was done.

Among Jack's special friends were Monte Katterjohn, J. G. Hawks, C. Gardner Sullivan, and John Lynch. Lynch was a Cornell Law School graduate turned writer, and part owner of an honest-to-God Mexican gold mine. Lynch was particularly generous with his time and talent, and also with his money when Jack later found himself one stale doughnut away from starvation. But at this point he was helping to nurture a writing talent in Jack, sometimes using Jack's ideas in his own scenarios, and otherwise advising him. One piece of advice involved the right way to demand raises and how to negotiate contracts. Armed with it, Jack went to Tom Ince and got himself a new contract calling for thirty dollars a week the first year and with an optional forty dollars the second.

This was in March 1917, and Triangle was already in trouble. D. W. Griffith was pulling out because of one too many broken promises of non-interference in the creative product. Tom Ince left in June of that year, squeezed out by the Aitken brothers. Harry Aitken was pressing for more sophisticated movie fare to appeal to a middle-class audience. Ince

argued that such an audience simply wasn't there and that the unedu-
cated, blue-collar masses who made up the moviegoing public would
stay away if they didn't get what they thought they were paying to see.
The Aitkens didn't believe him until it was too late, and in the mean-
time voted him out. Tom Ince took this development calmly, largely
because he personally owned the original twelve acres of Culver City on
which the management was then sitting. "All right, boys," he said, undoubtedly with great relish. "Now that I'm fired, will you kindly get
your studio the hell off my land?" The Aitkens were forced to pay him
an exorbitant rent for the next year until he finally gave up his title.
Ince used the money to start a new studio.

Jack was deeply upset by this turn of events. Making movies wasn't
fun anymore with these supervisors and executives crawling all over the
place. With Tom Ince gone, so were his standards. The production
department was being managed by a man, H. O. Davis, who had a
background in carnivals and midway shows. Critical decisions were
being made by people with no knowledge whatsoever of making movies.
Budgets were being slashed and poor pictures were being made that
might never be released because the distribution system was falling apart
as well. Jack had his new contract and he was getting one part after
another, but what good was that if he might not even be seen? Actors
had to be seen if their careers were going to grow. Every week, two or
three big names would leave for another studio. Jack couldn't leave; his
contract had another eight months to run, but he felt that his career was
going nowhere.

A conversation he heard outside the scenario department didn't help
matters. Jack's name was mentioned, and he realized that his friend
Monte Katterjohn was recommending him for a part in an upcoming
picture that was to be directed by Irvin Willat.

"Oh, no!" he heard Willat answer. "Not Jack Gilbert. For one thing,
he's terrible, and for another, his nose is too big. He looks Jewish."

Jack didn't wait to hear Katterjohn's answer. He was devastated. He
crept back to his dressing room and sat in anguish until dark. Jack despised Willat, a notorious anti-Semite, but didn't blame him for what
he had said. Willat was right. His nose was a monstrosity. How could
he ever have dreamed of being an actor with a nose like Pinocchio's? He
was a washout!

Margery Wilson, a colleague of Ida Adair's, said such overreactions
were typical of him. Once she was playing a feature role opposite Jack
in a murder melodrama called *The Eye of the Night*. When he came on
the set that morning, his mood was uncharacteristically bitter. He was
getting nowhere, he told Margery. He was a hopeless failure. She tried

to cheer him up but it was impossible. In their next scene together, Margery had been accused of murder and now the mob of angry villagers were coming to arrest her. Jack, playing her brother, stood at the door defying and berating the crowd. The camera moved in to get a close-up of Jack. Margery watched him closely.

"There was a genuine fire," she said, "a righteous anger in his face and body. He acted with his whole being and everyone was moved by it." Afterward she said to him, "Could you feel what you were doing? How good you were? Much too good to talk about quitting. Give yourself time, Jack. You have everything it takes to be an actor."

At Triangle, in the latter part of 1917, the collapse of the company was accelerating. Personal rivalries led to further defections. Too much money was being spent against anticipated income that either did not arrive or vanished once it entered the system. Distributors were reporting revenues that bore no resemblance to studio box-office estimates, and several were compiling private fortunes. It seemed as if almost everyone with access to money was skimming off his share while he could. Triangle had begun feeding on itself.

At any other studio, Jack might have already become a star. One of his last Triangle pictures was a western called *Golden Rule Kate*, starring Louise Glaum. He played a wild young drifter in whom a saloon owner, Louise, saw something worth saving. It was a good three-dimensional part in which Jack could demonstrate the force of his personality, the grace with which he moved, and his now highly developed skills with horse and lasso. Paul Killiam, the film archivist, said of Jack's performance: "It was all there. John Gilbert's good looks and confident manner were so striking in this and other early roles that it's something of a mystery why top-flight stardom eluded him until the mid-twenties."

A possible answer might have been Jack's growing interest in writing, coupled with an increasing disenchantment with the sort of films he'd been making for Triangle. Virtually the entire scenario department, the writers he admired so much, had already left Triangle to join a new studio, Paralta Pictures, which had opened on Melrose Avenue in Hollywood. Many of the original Inceville crowd followed. Louise Glaum made the move shortly after the completion of *Golden Rule Kate*, hoping to escape the vamp stereotype—which, incidentally, was not necessarily a heavily made-up Theda Bara type, with exotic costumes and an occasional snake twining around her neck. A vamp was basically the strong femme fatale who seldom got the man and even more seldom got sympathetic parts. Louise's interesting face was her curse as well as her blessing. She was more handsome than she was beautiful. You could be attracted to her if you were a man, and you could like her, but you knew she wasn't the sort of woman who needed your arms around her. Louise never did escape her image, and perhaps it was a mistake to try. In any case, her departure was the last straw. Jack requested a release from his Triangle contract. Triangle refused.

Soon after, Jack was approached by Monte Katterjohn, the writer, a good friend who'd spent a great deal of time helping Jack to develop his own writing skills. Monte, who would later write *The Sheik* for Rudolph Valentino, asked Jack why he didn't stop making those lousy pictures and join him over at Paralta.

"I'd love to," Jack answered. "But they won't release me from my contract."

"To hell with your contract. It's not legal anyway. You're underage. Remember?"

Jack knew that it was true. He was still a minor according to the law and could not legally be held to a contract. But that technicality was roundly ignored in Hollywood, where a large percentage of movie people were underage. Legal or not, breaking the contract would have been a breach of faith. How could he then sign an acting contract with Paralta and expect to be taken seriously?

"You're swimming in the middle of a pool of sharks," Katterjohn said with a snort, "and you're worried about biting *them*. Anyway, they're too busy eating each other to notice. And who said anything about an acting contract? I want you to come to Paralta and write. The job pays sixty bucks a week."

Jack jumped at it.

Jack happily wrote screenplays the rest of 1917. Some were produced, but never as he wrote them. A few were unrecognizable. He was learning what writers like Scott Fitzgerald, Ben Hecht, and Anita Loos discovered later. It was neither necessary nor likely that a finished film product bear any resemblance to the written work that inspired it. After all, what are directors for? To say nothing of stars, executives, cameramen, their wives, and even casual visitors to the set.

By then America was at war. During Jack's last glum days at Triangle, he'd gone with Rowland Lee to enlist but was turned down because he was not yet eighteen. Now that he had reached that birthday, the glumness had passed and he was well launched into his new career as a writer. Besides, Rowland was already in France and without him it wouldn't have been the same. Jack decided to sit tight. His draft number would be coming up soon enough.

[3 5]

Paralta Studio, the safe haven for so many Triangle escapees, collapsed with appalling suddenness the week before Christmas of 1917. Bankruptcy was declared without warning. One day Jack felt secure in his job, the next he was out of work with no money saved.

With Paralta dead and Triangle dying, and several other studios with their backs to the wall, a panic swept over the entire industry. Payrolls were being cut and hiring was almost nonexistent. Jack had to forfeit a deposit on a new car he was buying and had barely enough money for food. By March, he was borrowing money to pay his rent. Once again, he tried to enlist in the service, the Navy this time, but was turned down because he was too thin. Jack was now desperate, but once again salvation came at the last possible moment. "Just once," he grumbled to Lee Garmes, "I'd like to see fate deal an ace in my direction without waiting for the last card in the deck."

The last card in this case was the reopening of Paralta under a new general manager. He was Robert Brunton, formerly Tom Ince's production manager, and a man who remembered Jack Gilbert as an actor, not a writer. In April 1918, Jack went to work on a picture called *One Dollar Bid*, opposite Louise Glaum. Jack was to play a young gambler passionately ensnared with Louise, and getting soundly vamped. The good influence, or countervamp, in this case, was the gambler's sweet little sister, who was played by a recent import from the studios of Fort Lee, New Jersey. She was a Southern girl, from New Orleans. Her name was Leatrice Joy.

"I came to the set while Jack was doing a scene with Louise Glaum," she recalled. "She was a big star and I was thrilled to be in a picture with her. I had never seen Jack before. He was sitting at a gambling table dressed in a dinner jacket. He had just lost all his money and was laughing about it. There was a wild look in his eyes. I thought he was the most attractive man I ever saw. What impressed me was his air of confidence. He seemed to know exactly what to do and I wondered if I'd ever feel that sure of myself in front of a camera."

Leatrice was extremely nervous. She hadn't made many pictures. She'd been out of work for several weeks, with a mother to support, and was suffering from the same panic that affected Jack. Before her first scene with him, she rubbed her arms with a white body paste called Wheatcroft enamel. Its purpose was to give the skin a flattering alabaster glow. It also rubbed off on anything it touched:

> I was supposed to come into the gambling hall looking for my
> brother and then beseech him to come home to our dying mother.
> My knees were shaking so I could hardly think. Jack could see that

I was scared. He put his arm around me and we talked about the scene. He told me what I should be feeling and how he was going to react to me. He made the whole thing real for me and he made me feel that I could do it.

When the camera started rolling, the newly confident Leatrice Joy went wild. She burst in upon Jack, begging him, enticing him, pulling at his sleeves and twisting his collar and throwing her arms over his shoulders and back. In seconds, Jack's cherished twenty-dollar dinner jacket looked as if it had been attacked by a demented Tom Sawyer. White greasepaint was everywhere in streaks and slashes. Jack, seeing the violence being done to his wardrobe, roared in outrage and tried to pull away. Leatrice presumed he was still acting. It wasn't the reaction he'd described a few minutes earlier, but what did she know? She kept right on tugging, begging, and smearing until the words "You're destroying my goddamned dinner jacket" alerted her that the make-believe part was over. Jack wiped furiously at the stains but only made them worse. Stripping off the jacket, he ran for the wardrobe department in search of a cleaning solvent. Leatrice followed after him in tears.

The stains never came out. The jacket could be photographed but otherwise it never looked the same again. Leatrice completed the scene, her only one in the picture, and said good-bye to Jack, apologizing one more time. Jack forgave her, of course, but only after extracting a promise that she would never, ever, under any circumstances use Wheatcroft enamel again.

"I did, though," Leatrice told me later with a giggle. "The same thing happened in a movie with Richard Dix and again with Thomas Meighan."

"But why did you keep on using that stuff if it caused so much trouble?" I asked.

She replied with the look of a person patiently explaining the obvious: "Because it made my arms look so pretty."

·five·

DESPITE his ruined jacket, Jack Gilbert thought Leatrice was the prettiest girl he had even seen. He tried to reach her after the shooting was completed. But she and her mother had already moved from the address Leatrice had given him, and no one seemed to know where they had gone. He had a hard time forgetting her dancing green eyes and, of course, her unusual name popped into his head every time he had to use his ravaged dinner jacket.

Jack made two more films for Paralta in early 1918, both with Louise Glaum, before the studio went under for the last time. By this time, the panic had grown into a full-scale depression in the movie industry and elsewhere. The war had substantially reduced the living standards of the dependents servicemen had left behind, and inflation increased everyone's cost of living. Except for Britain, the lucrative European market for American films no longer existed. This meant fewer people in the theaters, less revenue for the production of subsequent films, and therefore fewer new movies. Hollywood tried to liven up the market with a stream of war movies—good atrocity stuff, with evil huns raping blond nurses and throwing babies out of windows. However, Hollywood and moderation being strangers, this sort of picture soon glutted the market.

To actors, unemployment then was more of a disaster than it is now. There was no unemployment insurance or any other kind of social benefit, not even a soup kitchen for those who were starving, and many were. Other employment was hard to come by, even if an employer could be found who would take a chance on hiring an actor. Going elsewhere in search of work was impossible for free-lance players who didn't have the price of a meal in their pockets, let alone train fare. Quite a few handsome actors became hoboes and many pretty young actresses moved in with any man who could feed them, or became prostitutes.

Jack, without a contract since the first Paralta collapse, was as bad off as anyone, except for an occasional free-lance role at whatever salary a studio was willing to pay. That money had to stretch over the long, dry periods when there was no work at all. Jack had gone hungry many times in the past, but not once during that year did he ever have enough to eat. He said later that the experience stayed with him in unpleasant ways. Money became increasingly important to him, almost an obsession in subsequent years. He cared for money but not in terms of what it could buy, or even as a barometer of success. Money, to Jack, meant never being hungry again.

In desperation he tried once more to join the service, this time the Army Flying Corps. Again he was rejected, this time because the air service was taking only men with a high-school education. Two more months went by without any work at all. Then there was one job at Pathé, playing Frank Keenan's son in *More Trouble*, followed by another hungry spell. He borrowed some money from his gold-mine-owning friend, John Lynch, to buy food, but when he could not pay it back he refused to borrow more.

He was leafing through a newsstand copy of *Theater* magazine in the fall of 1918 when he found his name mentioned for the first time. "John Gilbert," the item read, "has completed his picture *Sons of Men*, with J. Warren Kerrigan, and has been engaged by the Vitagraph Company to play opposite Bessie Love in her first production for the company. Young Gilbert has been coming along rapidly during the past year and has done some excellent work. He should make a very good opposite for the popular Bessie." Jack didn't have enough money in his pocket to buy the magazine.

That same month, Jack applied for a part in another J. Warren Kerrigan picture called *Three X Gordon*, an independent Jesse D. Hampton production also starring Lois Wilson. The movie was a western, with the handsome Kerrigan, already famous as "The Gibson Man," playing the classic virile and virtuous hero. Jack was trying for the role of his sidekick.

When he entered the outer office, he saw a girl on her knees in a dark corner, obviously negotiating a deal with the Almighty if he would help her get the part of the ingénue. It was Leatrice Joy. Jack was more than pleased to see her again, and she him. As she stood up, Jack noticed that she was wearing a large black straw hat trimmed with real garden geraniums that were already limp and faded. Coming from New Orleans, she had never seen such blossoms before and was sure they added a touch of exotic elegance. Jack knew that geraniums were as common as tumbleweed in Southern California and about as exotic, even when they weren't wilted. He told her so as tactfully as he could, with some flattering words about roses needing no adornment. With lingering doubts, Leatrice dropped the moribund geraniums into the nearest wastebasket and sailed into the casting office.

Leatrice's prayers apparently worked for both of them. They were hired, and celebrated the occasion by going to the nearest drugstore for a Coca-Cola. Jack asked her if she'd go to a movie with him that night, but Leatrice could not. It was Wednesday and she'd promised to take her mother to church. They were devout Christian Scientists. Inwardly, Jack made a face. This revelation, on top of her earlier prayer scene, suggested that a continued relationship might offer limited satisfaction. Anyway, he was seeing another Southern lady at the moment.

One of the casualties of Jack's financial condition had been his room at the Waldorf Hotel. He moved into an old-fashioned boardinghouse in the Palisades where for less money he could have a room, plus one meal a day. The other guests, none of them movie actors, were infinitely less interesting than the Waldorf crowd. There was a schoolteacher, a widow who lived on a pension, a retired Shakespearean actor who felt that movies were loathesomely inimical to everything that was cultural and fine, and an insurance salesman who could work the certain eventuality of death and fire into the most casual conversation. Jack avoided each of them with varying degrees of vigor. Apart from the other guests, there was a Southern family, the Burwells, newly arrived from Mississippi and looking out of place in their surroundings. The family consisted of Mrs. Burwell, two daughters, and a consumptive son-in-law, whom they'd brought to California in the hope of improving his health.

Jack admired the women. Despite the summer heat, they always appeared in freshly starched white cotton dresses and they had soft and gentle Southern voices and manners, which he'd always liked. They were characteristically reserved and they very nicely but firmly rebuffed Jack's attempt at friendliness. Each night after dinner, they would withdraw to one end of the veranda and Jack would sit at the other end, listening to the quiet charm of their speech.

One afternoon as Jack came home from work, Olivia, the younger Burwell, stood on the veranda and called to her sister, who was sitting on the lawn in the full sun. "Come out o' that sun, sugah," she drawled. "Yo' gonna bake yo' brains!" Jack laughed, and the girls, to his delight, laughed with him. The ice was broken, and a few days later Jack took Olivia and her mother to the movies in his car. That earned him Mrs. Burwell's limited approval, and he was then allowed to take Olivia out alone. They went dancing at the Ship Café.

In August, Jack received his notice from the draft board. He was to leave for Kelly Field in Texas in ten days. He'd known it was coming eventually—but it was still a shock, expecially when he'd just landed an acting job. He was going to France, to fight a war that was already one of the greatest slaughters in history. The way his luck was running, he would certainly be killed. All that he had worked for would be nothing. And worse, there was no one in the world who would miss or mourn him. His name would appear one last time on a casualty list and then it would be gone as if he never existed.

That night he took Olivia for a drive in the Hollywood Hills. They parked overlooking the lights of the small, growing city, lights that meant homes and families and security and safety. The sight depressed him even more than he had been. He chain-smoked for an hour before Olivia asked him to stop. It was bad for his health, she said.

"Who cares?" Jack said, shrugging. "I don't think it matters to anyone whether I live or die."

"I care," the girl said quietly.

Only someone who had known Jack's life up to that point could imagine the effect those words had on him. Someone cared. Even if he never came back from France, even if he was killed, something would remain of him at home. He asked Olivia to marry him. Olivia smiled and said that she would. Three days later, on August 26, they were secretly married in a small Methodist church in Hollywood. Olivia did not tell her sister or her mother, who would surely have interfered. The only witnesses were the minister and his wife. On the marriage license, Jack added three years to his age. Olivia was at least that much older than he was.

They were married a week, still not long enough for the other Burwells to get used to the idea, when another message came from the draft board. All troop movements had been canceled because of the Spanish influenza. The plague was sweeping across the world, eventually killing twenty million people. It would kill more American servicemen than the Germans. The only effective weapon was isolation. All inductions and troop movements came to a halt.

The indefinite delay of Jack's military service changed everything. Instead of going off a hero, Jack was now a husband with a wife to support. And roles were not being offered to an actor who might be called up at any time. He finished his picture with Leatrice Joy, to whom he was ashamed to mention his impetuous marriage, and had nothing else waiting. For weeks no money came in. He moved with Olivia from the boardinghouse to a grim, hall bedroom in downtown Los Angeles, where at least the presence of her family would not keep reminding them of their foolishness.

Jack approached Tom Ince and begged him for a part in an upcoming picture. Ince, in fact, had a part for which he thought Jack was perfectly suited if it weren't for this draft thing hanging over his head. Jack had seen the scenario, a baseball story called *The Busher,* with Charles Ray and Colleen Moore already cast in the leads. The unfilled part was that of a spoiled rich kid riding around in a souped-up sports car and throwing his money around. The shooting script had not yet been drawn up. Jack realized that Ince could easily shoot Jack's scenes first, so that the picture could be finished even if he was called up again. Ince agreed and Jack got the part. He was superb in the role. His performance is all the more impressive when one realizes, watching the expensively dressed, self-indulgent rich kid arrogantly trying to buy his way into Colleen Moore's attentions, that Jack was in real life desperately in need of money and only a jump away from starvation.

Jack's draft call, when it finally came, required him to report for duty on November 11, 1918, the day the Armistice was signed. The Great War was over. Jack reported for duty as ordered, was bureaucratically given a uniform and sent home wearing it the next day, an honorable discharge in his pocket. Half-embarrassed to go home, he walked the streets of Los Angeles and watched the celebration. Shops and factories had closed early and thousands of people were in the streets parading and blowing horns. Girls were kissing any man in uniform. Flags were everywhere. Newsboys walked through the crowds shouting headlines and were sold out before they'd covered fifty feet. This was the real thing, not like the false armistice that had been announced four days earlier. Saloons were jammed with soldiers and sailors, and in most bars drinks were on the house for anyone in uniform. Guiltily, Jack began taking the drinks that were offered him.

He went home reluctantly, having realized in recent weeks that he barely knew Olivia. They had absolutely nothing in common. She knew nothing about the movies, nor did she read, nor was she particularly bright. Conversations of the sort he'd had with the Bennett sisters or the Lees were impossible. Jack had to explain almost everything he said. In the beginning he'd affectionately called Olivia his "Mississippi bubble," and now he realized that the phrase had a deeper meaning. Worse, he had to find a way to support her. He had to make the best of it.

The influenza epidemic had hit the studios as well, closing them down, eliminating any chance of finding an acting job. Jack tried other sources; he didn't care how menial, he was just one more returning serviceman scratching for any kind of job at all. His beloved car had to be sold; his equally treasured books went next.

When the studios reopened in 1919, Jack began making the daily rounds on foot, sometimes covering thirty-five miles in a day, but he found nothing. He was either too this or too that for any of the roles that were being cast. Coming home to Olivia was no comfort. He knew that when he walked through the door she would be sitting there silently, her big eyes watching him. She was never reproachful, she never questioned him about his efforts that day; she would just watch like a dog waiting to be fed. The eyes haunted him and her stoic silence hung like a weight around his neck.

In desperation, he wrote to his stepfather, Walter Gilbert, asking for a loan. Walter was then operating his own stock company in San Francisco. Never before had he asked Walter for help except for the loan to get to Inceville, which he'd quickly repaid. Jack knew that Walter was tightfisted and it crushed him to have to admit his own failure by asking, but he could not bear to see Olivia go hungry.

Gilbert's answer came by return mail. He chided Jack for not putting money away for hard times and advised him to be more frugal in the future. As for the loan, he suggested that instead of being a borrower or a lender, Jack "should pray for guidance and believe in the mercy of God." Jack was furious. He realized that Walter had his own problems and he was prepared for him to regretfully decline his request, but Jack could have done without the accompanying folk wisdom, which he knew was gleaned from one of Walter's melodramas.

Jack was at the lowest point of his life when out of the blue came a call from the famous French director Maurice Tourneur, who had recently arrived in Hollywood after several years in the East. Tourneur's work was already legendary. There probably wasn't an actor anywhere who didn't know and admire him. Tourneur had originally trained to be a painter, but he gravitated toward the movies, making pictures for the Eclair Studio in Paris, and soon gained an international reputation. Tourneur's painter's eye led to unheard-of uses of light and shade while filming and to a uniquely close collaboration with his set designer and cameraman. "We three make the picture," he said, "the art director, the cameraman, and the director. The actors are incidental."

Jack didn't care whether he was incidental or not. This was Maurice Tourneur and he was actually calling Jack Gilbert. Maurice Tourneur, incomprehensibly, was familiar with Jack Gilbert's work and was offering him a featured role in his next production. Jack accepted the offer in a state of near shock, not bothering to inquire about money. It was enough that he'd be working . . . and working for Maurice Tourneur.

The picture was *The White Heather*, and Jack played opposite Mabel Ballin. Before the filming was finished, Tourneur was impressed

[43]

enough to offer Jack a permanent contract. Needless to say, Jack accepted. All this and a contract too after more than a year of free-lancing and extremely hard times. "But," he asked cautiously, "will you pay me between pictures?" Tourneur assured him that he would receive half wages when he wasn't actually working. That same night, Jack and Olivia moved to a better hotel, and the next morning he used most of his pay envelope for a down payment on a Buick roadster. Over the next three weeks, Jack and Olivia lived in the happy certainty that their troubles were over. But by the time the picture was completed, Tourneur had taken a new look at his expenses and income. A contract with Jack Gilbert became an unnecessary luxury. "I have nothing for you in my next picture, Mr. Gilbert," he said, dismissing his earlier promise with a Gallic shrug. Jack was destroyed. Perhaps the unkindest blow was the knowledge that he had been slapped down by a man he'd almost come to idolize.

It would be another four months before he worked again. There was now no use pretending that he could support or even feed Olivia. For the last time, Jack borrowed money from his friend John Lynch, and used it to send Olivia back home to Mississippi. He kissed her good-bye at the station and promised he would send for her when whatever curse he was under finally lifted. Then Jack turned away from those big dark empty eyes. They never saw each other again.

In the summer of 1919, his luck turned at last, although it would be years before he could quite believe it. He found work in a picture called *The Man Beneath*, with Sessue Hayakawa and Helen Jerome Eddy. After that, Jack was never again without work.

He felt alive and free once more. He sent money regularly to Olivia with bright cheerful letters, but did not ask her to return. Many reasons for not wanting her back simmered inside of him, but perhaps most of all was the conviction that she would no sooner arrive than his world would collapse again. And his world, compared to what it had been, was glorious. He could buy clothes and eat in decent restaurants. He could pay back loans. He could put a down payment on a car and get to keep it this time—as long as Olivia stayed where she was.

More parts were being offered than he could accept. Even Maurice Tourneur called to cast him in an upcoming film, and Jack had the enormous satisfaction of telling him to go to hell. Instead, he went over to First National and made *Heart o' the Hills*, with Mary Pickford.

The picture was vintage Pickford, well and warmly acted, beautifully photographed, expertly directed by Sidney Franklin. It still can be seen today. The blockbuster scene in the movie is one in which Mary Pickford tries to outdo Jack Gilbert at a church social in a marvelously ad-libbed dance that looks like a hoedown ancestor of the jitterbug. It brought down the house everywhere it played. Sidney Franklin said the dance was Jack's idea—and a good one.

Later that year, Jack was put up for membership in the Los Angeles Athletic Club. He was quickly accepted, and the club was a dream in itself. It offered comfortable rooms, a pool and tennis courts, but most of all, it offered the club dining room, which had become a gathering place for the most notable men in Hollywood. Jack would often find himself seated at the same table with Charlie Chaplin, then earning a quarter of a million dollars a picture. Or he'd share a meal with Richard Barthelmess, Latin lover Antonio Moreno, James Kirkwood, Marshall Neilan (who was Hollywood's highest-paid director while still in his twenties), or Raymond Griffith, whose most memorable film role was that of the dying French soldier in the trench with Lew Ayres in *All Quiet on the Western Front*. The men around Jack were all assured, rich, and thoroughly successful. They welcomed him among them as if he belonged without question. Jack, however, could not quite believe it. The feeling never left him that their acceptance of him was a charade, a practical joke of some kind. Surely the day would come when someone would tap him on the shoulder and tell him to leave, the joke was over.

Well into 1919, soldiers were still returning from the war. Jack heard that Rowland V. Lee was back from France and rushed off to see him. Happily he told Rowland of the success that seemed to be coming to him from every direction and that he was now making two hundred and fifty dollars a week. That was more in a month than he'd ever earned in his best year.

"I guess it paid to stay home," Lee replied coldly.

Jack was deeply hurt. He reminded Lee that he tried to enlist first in 1917 and twice in 1918, that it wasn't his fault that the war ended on the same day he was finally drafted. "I know two days don't count for much, but I tried and I *was* in," Jack protested.

They shook hands after that but Lee didn't apologize. Rowland, like many soldiers, had seen too many splendid young men blown apart to be free of some level of bitterness toward those who stayed where it was safe and grew rich. "I still should have apologized," Lee said later. "I never imagined what a tough time Jack had had up until a few months before he came to see me. He could have told me and made me feel ashamed but he didn't. He was too nice a guy for that. He'd rather have me think poorly of him than make me feel like an ass for saying what I did. Next thing I knew, he put me up for membership in the Athletic

Club so that I could get quickly back into the movie scene. We ended up sharing rooms together for several years after."

Maurice Tourneur kept calling. He was a stubborn man and Jack's refusal to work for him was an irritation he could not ignore. Perversely, it made him value Jack's services above those of most other actors. After several curt refusals, Maurice Tourneur called at the Athletic Club in person and cornered Jack. He listened patiently, even docilely, as Jack purged himself of his anger and told Tourneur what his callousness and his broken promise had caused. The months of hunger and despair. The loss of his wife. The humiliation of trying to borrow money and the loss of almost everything he had except his self-respect, which, god-damn it, was sufficiently intact to keep him from working for such a duplicitous son of a bitch no matter how much he admired him. When Jack was finished, Tourneur began apologizing, mostly in French, and cataloguing his own shortcomings both as a human being and as a director. Soon Jack was contradicting him and reminding him of his greatness. He would hear no more self-deprecation. Only a fool could fail to recognize the director's genius or to overlook certain minor behavioral eccentricities. In the end, Jack agreed to do another picture. Jack allowed him a smile of satisfaction before he told him that it would cost him exactly twice what he had paid the last time.

The picture was called *The Glory of Love*, starring Lon Chaney as an old sculptor who falls in love with his model. Jack played an American tourist who eventually got her. Tourneur made this picture shortly before he broke off from his sponsors, Jules Brulatour, who was the distributor for George Eastman Film, and Paramount Pictures. Possibly for that reason, release was held up, and it wasn't shown until 1923, under the title *While Paris Sleeps*.

Jack Gilbert and Lon Chaney worked together harmoniously enough, but they were far from friends. "I never have anything to say to that man," Jack told a friend. "He looks right through me." Given the polar differences in their personalities, it would have been more remarkable if their relationship was otherwise. Chaney was a stolid, humorless man who lived only for his work. He would often arrive at the studio at four in the morning to begin applying his elaborate makeup, and he was just as ponderously dedicated throughout the day's filming. Physically, Chaney looked like the classic Marine drill sergeant: powerfully built, close-cropped hair, strong square jaw. He cared little about money or about anything else, including himself, except his art. Jack's recently acquired interest in money seemed superficial to Chaney, as did Jack's flashy and wisecracking playboy demeanor. Jack, for his part, had trouble understanding why anyone would choose such a monkish existence if he had the means to enjoy pleasure and comfort, which Jack felt was the point of having money.

Tourneur, on the other hand, grew increasingly fond of Jack. He treated him with a certain gruff affection and Jack responded in kind. A writer from *Motion Picture Classic* magazine interviewed Jack the day he signed his new two-year contract with Tourneur. Whenever the interviewer probed Jack for details about himself, Jack quickly turned the subject back to Tourneur as if he couldn't help it. "His feeling of hero-worship is real," the interviewer wrote. "Tourneur must be conscious of it. Jack said he was happier than he had ever been in his life before." He quoted Jack: "A director can make or break his people. It means everything, absolutely everything, to be with the right one and Tourneur could bring out the best there was in you. He would praise you to the sky when you did anything well and perhaps break a chair over your head when you did badly. He won't let people overact and he doesn't kill your enthusiasm. He makes you want to do your very best every minute because you know that work you are doing with him will live. That means something."

Clarence Brown, who started out as Tourneur's assistant in 1915 at Fort Lee, went on to become one of Hollywood's finest directors. He later explained the unusual relationship between the two men:

When Jack Gilbert joined the company in 1920, I was getting ready to direct my first picture, although still under Tourneur's close supervision. I'd been his assistant for six years and he taught me everything I knew. Tourneur was not only a gifted director, he was a great teacher. He shouted at you, he'd blow up and scare everybody off the set, but that was his temperament. He wasn't malicious but he did use sarcasm. When he felt I was ready, he pushed me into directing. That meant he needed someone to take my place as his assistant. Jack asked for the job. He'd been hired as an actor but Tourneur took a liking to him. He could see he was smart and eager to learn. There was no reason why Jack couldn't be his assistant and act too. Jack adored Tourneur but he wouldn't toady up to him as some did. Jack had a lot of pride and Tourneur respected him for it. He would have been a great director. He was always asking questions, he had to know the reason for everything and Tourneur was usually patient with him. I guess he'd mellowed since my own early days. He was gentle with Jack, almost like a father to him.

Tourneur kept Jack close to his side in the cutting room and in the laboratory, where his films were hand-tinted in blue or rose or amber, depending on the desired mood. Ben Carré, Tourneur's art director, taught Jack how to create special effects:

> In *The White Circle* we had a scene of moonlight shining through the clouds. I had to make a moon, a globe hanging in a tree with lots of gauze. It was a gorgeous shot and Jack loved it. He wanted to know how it was done, so I took the whole thing apart and showed him. He put it back together exactly right. There wasn't anything about the movies Jack wasn't interested in. He had a mind like a sponge. He told me he wanted to make his own movies someday. He said, "I want to be prepared when the time comes. I want to know everything Mr. Tourneur knows."

Jack was spending eighteen hours a day at the studio. He was established by then, and probably making less and working harder than he would have as a free-lancer. But being any place else would have been unthinkable. He told Clarence Brown, "I still can't believe they're paying me real money for doing what I enjoy so much."

Clarence and Jack collaborated on the first picture Brown directed. As Brown remembered:

> It was pretty much a hokum piece about a cowboy artist who is sent to jail, where he meets a convicted murderer who's due to be strung up in the morning. The cowboy spends the night drawing pictures on the walls of his cell, including one of Jesus smiling with outstretched arms. In the dead of the night, the murderer wakes up and sees a shaft of moonlight shining on the face of Christ and thinks he's been saved. He falls to his knees and goes to his death happy and sanctified. Hokum or not, it was surefire stuff for the audiences of the times. My problem was to get a picture out of it that we'd feel good about.

He tried to write the scenario for several days and couldn't get it right. Clarence called Jack in to ask him what he thought, and they ended up spending three days in Clarence's room at the Garden Court Apartments putting a script together. "We worked around the clock arguing and yelling at each other, living mostly on coffee and doughnuts, but we got it done. We went to Tourneur and showed it to him. He seemed surprised. He said to Jack, 'Mr. Gilbert, already you are my leading man *and* my assistant director. Now you tell me you are a writer?' Jack admitted modestly that he'd done a little writing. Tourneur said, 'Splendid! By tomorrow you will please write for me "The Pavilion on the Links."' Luckily, Jack was familiar with the Robert Louis Stevenson story and he turned in a passable rough draft by the next morning. I don't know when we slept in those days. People just worked and took catnaps when we could. The pay wasn't that much but nobody minded. We were making movies."

Clarence finished his cowboy picture and invited Jack to the first studio showing. Once again, the finished product was substantially different from the scenario Jack helped to write. He was furious. He stormed out of the projection room and roared at Clarence, "You've ruined my script! That's the worst thing I ever saw. How could you do that to me?"

Clarence said, "I was crushed. Certainly we changed a few things in the course of filming but most of Jack's stuff was there. I thought his reaction was out of line and I felt rotten. I walked away damned near in tears. Mr. Tourneur came after me and put an arm around my shoulders. He said, 'That was a wonderful picture and I have great confidence in your future.' Later, even Jack admitted he liked it. But you know, it took a lot of energy to be Jack's friend."

"The Pavilion on the Links" was retitled *The White Circle*. Jack cowrote the script, was Tourneur's assistant director handling all the location shots, and played the lead opposite Janice Wilson, who was Lois Wilson's younger sister. Burns Mantle wrote in *Photoplay*: "Here are foggy nights on the moor . . . shiveringly realistic. . . . Here is a nicely toned and sanely screened adventure . . . with enough Stevensonian atmosphere to hold an audience through to the last scene . . . a good straight performance by Jack Gilbert as the hero."

Jack plunged immediately into another picture, an undersea adventure called *Deep Waters*. Again, Jack did three jobs. The movie was being filmed at Balboa Beach, eighty miles south of Los Angeles. Jack would drive down each morning and return to the studio each evening to see the rushes and consult with Tourneur. Late one afternoon, he was walking past the studio dressing rooms when a pretty girl swung around the corner, stopped, and called "Hi!" Jack stopped in his tracks. It was Leatrice Joy. "He looked taller, and he'd put on weight, but it was the expression on his face that was so different. He seemed a lot older, more relaxed. He looked happier. Jack was always handsome, but now he was breathtaking. At least he was to me."

When I was ten, like any little girl, I asked my father about how he and Mother got together. This is how I remember his answer. "Well, you know we had worked together, we knew each other before, but it was when we bumped into each other at Tourneur's studio that I knew I wasn't ever going to let her get away again. I looked at her that day and I thought she was the most beautiful girl in the world. I still see it. The late-afternoon sun caught the curls in her hair and made them shiny and put a gold light on her face. Oh, those green eyes and that smile. She was so pretty it would break your heart just to look at her."

Jack took the dainty hand Leatrice extended and did not let go. "Where have you been?" he asked her. "I've looked all over the place. I've asked people but no one has seen you. Are you all right? You look just beautiful."

Leatrice was out of work. She'd been away for ten months acting with a stock company in San Diego, both for the experience and because she couldn't find any movie jobs. She was in town visiting a friend and also hoping that someone would offer her a part. Jack explained what he was doing and invited her to come down to Balboa with him the next day. Leatrice said she'd be delighted. She was very glad to see Jack and would have gone with him in any case. The chance to renew an old acquaintance with Maurice Tourneur wouldn't be bad either. They walked together to the parking lot and said good-bye until morning.

That night at the Athletic Club, Jack shared a table with Charlie Chaplin. Jack told him of his meeting with Leatrice, and then there was a long silence. Chaplin could see that Jack had something darker on his mind.

"It's Olivia, isn't it?" Chaplin said. The two men had become close friends and confidants. Jack had spoken to him several times about his impetuous marriage to Olivia and his guilt over not sending for her now that he could afford it.

Jack nodded.

"Do you or do you not love Olivia?" Chaplin asked.

"I don't even know her," he answered sadly.

"Do you or do you not want her back? It's time to be honest."

"No!" Jack straightened. "No, I do not want her back."

"Then end it."

Jack wrote to Olivia and her mother that night.

He picked up Leatrice before dawn and they drove south along the coast. Although Leatrice didn't understand why at the time, Jack was behaving as if a great weight had been lifted from him. The world was more beautiful than it had ever been before. Time after time he would stop the car and, pointing to a distant snowy peak or a thundering beach or a browsing deer, shout, "Look at that!" Leatrice would glance at him and smile at the joyous way he was driving, his head back, his hair blowing in the wind. She thought then that the two of them made rather a handsome couple. Others thought so too when they arrived at Balboa. They were followed and stared at most of the day.

Leatrice watched him direct a beach scene for a while, but everyone was busy and paid little attention to her. She soon wandered off through the village. In no time, people were asking her for her autograph. They had no idea who she was, only that she had come to town with the movie company and anyone that pretty had to be somebody. Leatrice obliged them, walking slowly down the street, aware of being watched and followed, pausing now and then to primp in a store window. She adored it and always had. Then, as now, her personality was geared toward pleasing an audience, any audience. But when Jack came looking for her at the luncheon break, he'd put on dark glasses, and tried to take her to some place where they could be alone and unnoticed. That made no sense at all to Leatrice. The whole point of being an actor or an actress was having people look at you, having them know you were special. Being special and deliberately choosing not to be recognized was too silly for words.

At the end of the day, a Wednesday, Jack hesitantly asked Leatrice to stay for dinner and seemed surprised that she accepted.

"No church tonight?" he asked.

"Oh, pshaw!" Leatrice answered. "I don't go all the time. Just that once. I promised Mother."

Jack was relieved. He admitted, in fact, that he'd been relieved the other time when he asked her out and she'd declined. If he'd taken her to the movies then, he didn't know what he would have used for food the next day.

They dined and danced at the old Bay Club, a weathered frame building with a wide veranda overlooking the water. Later, they sat outside watching the full moon shining on the water, and talked about their lives and their careers. Leatrice says they fell in love that night.

They made a date for the following evening. Jack suggested the familiar Ship Café in Venice, which was now a speakeasy that catered to the movie crowd. On the afternoon of their second date, Leatrice decided she'd wear her best evening gown, of soft black "wedding ring" velvet. She piled her black hair on top of her head to make herself look taller. But something was missing. The black velvet made her skin look washed out and pale without the right kind of makeup, a subject that the convent-educated Leatrice knew comparatively little about.

But one of her neighbors would know. Only two houses away in the bungalow court where Leatrice lived with her mother lived the notorious vamp, Theda Bara. Leatrice had only a nodding acquaintance with her, but that didn't stop her from walking up to Theda Bara's door and ringing the bell. That action produced a sound of distant gongs like exotic temple bells, and moments later Theda Bara appeared.

Theda had just turned thirty and her sensational career was effectively at an end. She'd made over forty movies since 1914 and had been the prototypical vamp from the beginning. Her first major film, based on Rudyard Kipling's poem *The Vampire*, had set the mold. The name Theda Bara was an anagram for "Arab Death," and she was supposed to be the illegitimate child of a French artist and his Egyptian mistress. In fact, she was born Theodosia Goodman, in Cincinnati. Theda had eight films released in 1919 and none after that until one in 1925, and another in 1926. After that she vanished and was not heard from again until her death twenty-nine years later. Theda's vamp roles were simply a phenomenon that had run its course. The exotic, high-powered emoting that had so fascinated early audiences was laughed at by the more sophisticated moviegoers of the flapper era. Since Theda had been purely a manufactured star, right up to the white limousine driven by a "Nubian slave" and her "fascination" with symbols of death such as snakes and human skulls, the studio publicity machine that created her left her no place else to go. She valiantly tried sympathetic roles such as *Kathleen Mavourneen*, but audiences could not accept her in them. Theda Bara was one of the first big idols to fall. Although little has been written about her, she apparently did so with grace.

Leatrice explained her dilemma breathlessly. Tonight's date with Jack Gilbert was very important to her. She wanted to be a knockout, but she just didn't know what to do with her face.

Theda Bara was delighted to help. Leatrice followed her through the sitting room, stepping over velvet ottomans and fur rugs, through a beaded curtain into her boudoir. The walls were hung with cretonne prints and the air reeked of a heavy musk. There was a caged snake on a shelf, which Theda would stroke in the presence of the press but which slept and ate bugs at all other times. Theda lived that way because she was expected to, but now she was just plain Theo Goodman enjoying a schoolgirl conspiracy. She seated Leatrice on a carved teakwood stool and went to work. When she was finished, Leatrice was something more than a knockout. She had rings of kohl darkening her eyes and a dusting of indigo. Her mouth was arched in a deep-red cupid's bow and white powder accentuated her already pallid skin. As a final touch, Miss Bara took a rabbit's foot dipped in rouge and applied it to her earlobes.

"What's that for?" Leatrice asked.

The arch-vamp slid laughingly into a parody of herself. "Zis is for earlobes pulsing vit ze blood of love. Zis means passion. Seething passion."

Leatrice wasn't entirely sure that seething passion was what she had in mind, but who'd know better than Theda Bara? She thanked her and went home to wait for Jack.

Her mother, Mary Zeilder, took one look at her and gasped. "You're an actress, not a fancy woman. Go wash your face this instant." Leatrice, who had a doubt or two of her own, obeyed. All of Theda Bara's artistry was scrubbed away, but Leatrice and her mother both overlooked the pink ears.

Jack arrived on time, and as far as he was concerned her well-scrubbed face was perfect. "You look like a madonna," he told her. She winked to indicate she might offer just a little more excitement than that and introduced Jack to her mother. Mary Zeidler was not impressed. So this was the kind of man for whom her daughter felt the need to look like a harlot. Good-looking, but one of those flashy types. Besides, she thought she smelled liquor on his breath. In Mary Zeidler's eyes, poor Jack was licked before he started.

They left for the Ship Café, where Jack was known, and shown to a good table. The small orchestra played "Whispering" as they danced, and the tune became their love song. Jack paid the orchestra to play it several more times, until the other dancers complained.

At one point, Leatrice looked up at Jack and saw concern on his face. "What's wrong?" she asked.

"I think one of your earrings might be on too tight. You look as if you're getting an infection."

"My earring? I don't think so."

"Well, your earlobe had gone awfully red."

Leatrice suddenly remembered and burst into giggles. "That's my seething passion," she told the blank-faced Jack. "Couldn't you tell?" When she explained, describing her visit to Theda Bara's seraglio bedroom and Mary Zeidler's reaction, they both laughed so hard they had to leave the dance floor.

"Oh, Miss Joy," he said, wiping away tears, "you're a rare bird in this cockeyed aviary. I hope you never leave it again."

"Oh, Mr. Gilbert," she answered, "you can bet your life on that. I've worked too hard to get here."

❖SIX❖

L EATRICE had come a long way.

She was born in New Orleans, to Joseph and Mary Zeidler. Her father was the first practicing orthodontist in the state of Louisiana, but he became ill with tuberculosis and was unable to practice. Her older brother, John, also graduated from dental college, practiced briefly, but hated it and quit to go into the service at the outbreak of World War I.

It was clear to Leatrice, even before she left New Orleans Convent of the Sacred Heart, that she would have to work to help support the family. Her brother showed no signs of accepting such a responsibility. He considered himself an aristocrat, and aristocrats did not scratch for a living, nor did they spend their days sticking their fingers into other people's mouths. Leatrice, on the other hand, was perfectly willing to work as long as the work suited her natural gifts, foremost among which was her appearance. She was wildly beautiful. Her features were flawless and her body was slender and graceful. She was lighthearted, effervescent, something of a coquette from the very beginning, and yet always a lady. Leatrice had played the lead in her school play and then, naturally, began dreaming of being an actress. In those days, however, a convent-school student was wise to keep such ambitions to herself. Certainly from Mary Zeidler.

In 1915, the NOLA Film Company opened on St. Charles Street in New Orleans and advertised in the newspaper for an ingénue. Leatrice, citing her convent-school stardom, applied for the job after first looking up the word *ingénue* to make sure it was something respectable. She sent her graduation photograph with her application and was hired the next day.

My grandmother, Mary Zeidler, was a Victorian and then some. She didn't like the idea of Leatrice becoming an actress, but a dollar was a dollar. Perhaps with the proper kind of chaperoning, she thought, Leatrice could retain both her virtue and a decent standard of living. It hurt, however, to see Leatrice's former classmates crossing the street rather than speak to their fallen friend turned actress.

Leatrice made six pictures for NOLA before the company closed. It seemed that no matter how hard they tried, they couldn't manage to get a clear image on film. It was a phenomenon called "miasma," caused by an excess of moisture in the warm delta air. No technology of the time could cure it. The company broke up, but John Boyle, the NOLA cameraman who went to Hollywood, encouraged Leatrice to stick with the movies. He told Mary Zeidler, "She is absolutely photogenic. She has no bad angles and she can act. She ought to be a great star some-day."

Armed with that encouragement, twenty-five dollars in cash, and the help of a distant cousin who worked for a steamship company, the two women stowed away on a passenger liner going north to New York. The cousin hid them in a first-class cabin until they were safely at sea. After that, they mingled with the passengers and no one questioned their right to be there. They arrived in New York in January 1917, during one of the coldest winters ever recorded. Leatrice didn't even own a topcoat. They shivered through that winter, living on one meal a day in a rooming house on the Upper West Side. Life was hard for two Southern ladies unused to being poor, but they remained cheerful and optimistic. It never occurred to either of them that Leatrice would not become a star. Mary Zeidler was willing to wait as long as six months for it to happen.

Chutzpah often has a way of paying off. Leatrice found work opposite Fatty Arbuckle, who was just starting his own production company after years with Mack Sennett. Next she made a short series called *Suzy Speed—Girl Detective* for the Blue Diamond Film Company of Pennsylvania. Between acting jobs, she modeled for Howard Chandler Christy and other illustrators, and was thrilled to see her lovely face on the covers of popular magazines. Leatrice then went to work for Maurice Tourneur in Fort Lee, New Jersey. She accompanied him to Marblehead, Massachusetts, where she appeared in *The Pride of the Clan* as an extra and doubled as Mary Pickford's stand-in. Leatrice made six other pictures in the East, her roles growing in size and importance.

In 1918, a friend, Bernard Bernstein, wrote from California offering Leatrice a job in a series of Billy West comedies. (West was one of Charlie Chaplin's imitators.) Leatrice and her mother were more than happy to escape the severe Eastern climate, particularly if there was work at the other end of the country. She did one movie with Billy

West, *The Slave*, plus several shorts, and found a few more small jobs with different studios, including the one that destroyed Jack Gilbert's dinner jacket. But soon afterward, the same economic depression that affected Jack closed doors to her as well. There were no more offers. Leatrice heard about an opening in Virginia Brissac's stock company in San Diego and reluctantly went after it. It wasn't the movies but it was a job. And she'd be learning another thing or two about acting.

At the outset of the flu epidemic of 1918, Leatrice was playing the lead in *Rebecca of Sunnybrook Farm*. She walked onto the stage for the opening performance and was startled to see that the entire audience seemed a sea of blank white faces. Almost every person was wearing a surgical mask to filter out the deadly sickness. People had taken to wearing them in any sort of public gathering, and often on the street. Leatrice, being an earnest Christian Scientist, did not believe in contagion and thought the masks were silly. She did, however, believe in Christian charity, and promptly volunteered to work with the Red Cross. She would help tend to the sick and dying all day and then return to the theater in time for her curtain.

Between plays, or when there were no ingénue parts, she found an occasional movie bit. One was in *The Right of Way*, with Bert Lytell.

She was sitting on the set with Lytell one day when a messenger handed him a wire. Lytell opened it and read aloud: "AM INTERESTED IN USING YOU FOR MY NEXT PICTURE. CONTACT ME AT ONCE. LOUIS B. MAYER." Lytell was unimpressed. He was an important star and many people were bidding for his services. Also, he'd never heard of Mayer. Bert Lytell sent a return message: I DO NOT KNOW WHO YOU ARE. ANY OFFERS GO THROUGH MY AGENT.

The same day he received another telegram: YOU WILL REGRET YOUR ARROGANCE. MAYER.

The actor laughed it off. But years later, when Mayer had reached the height of his power, he effectively kept Lytell from being hired by any studio in Hollywood and bragged about it. Louis B. Mayer had a long memory. And he never forgave a personal slight.

It was several months later, while between jobs, that Leatrice ran into Jack at Tourneur's studio. From that point on, they were inseparable. Jack, although he'd barely turned twenty-one, was someone of substance in Hollywood. Everyone knew him as an up-and-coming actor, scenarist, and associate of Maurice Tourneur. Being seen with Jack called attention to Leatrice, and of course he bragged about her to anyone who would listen.

Mary Zeidler, however, remained implacably hostile to any relationship between Jack and her daughter. For openers, he was already married. Worse, he was on his way toward becoming a divorced man. Still worse, he was an actor, her daughter's occupation notwithstanding. He was also sassy, irreverent, not a Christian Scientist, and he drank hard liquor in violation both of the laws of his country and of ordinary Christian propriety. Leatrice could not have chosen a less suitable man if she had embraced the Devil himself.

Jack was bewildered by her antagonism. He liked older ladies as a rule, and usually got along splendidly with them. But Mary Zeidler was immovable. He kept trying. He would bring her flowers and expensive chocolates. He took her riding on Sundays in his big open touring car and she would sit glumly in the back seat complaining about the wind, the gas fumes, or the sun in her eyes until they would have to cut the day short and drive her home again. Jack never swore in her presence. He chewed mints to cover any trace of alcohol on his breath, which, of course, she saw as prima facie evidence that he'd been drinking. Mary Zeidler never relented. As Leatrice fell more deeply in love with Jack, her divided loyalties became increasingly unbearable. Eventually, rather than endure the daily insults by which Mother Zeidler hoped to discourage him, Jack stopped calling for Leatrice at her home. They would meet only at the studio and go out from there, but this dark fortress of a woman would always be glowering at the door when he drove Leatrice home.

It's doubtful whether any suitor would have met with Mary's approval unless he was wealthy, Southern, and a Christian Science practitioner with good teeth. Even then, an outsider might have been unwelcome. Mary Zeidler saw her daughter's career as her own only chance to escape being a poor relation in the homes of Louisiana relatives. Leatrice not only represented her mother's only security, but she might also be called upon to help her brother, who was beginning to get into trouble. John had received a Presidential citation, serving as a captain in the Army Medical Corps at Walter Reed Hospital. He helped develop prostheses for men whose faces had been mutilated in the war; Leatrice had pictures of his work, and they were harrowing. After he left the service, he seemed to fall apart. They suspected he was using drugs. Mary had enough to worry about without Jack Gilbert intruding and doing violence to Leatrice's sense of dedication and to their close-knit family life as well.

But the affair was already out of anyone's control. Jack and Leatrice quickly became Hollywood's darlings. They were a beautiful couple and they were appealingly, foolishly, and publicly in love. Most of the movie community had watched Jack growing up. They knew of his early infatuations, such as with Enid Bennett, and of his unfortunate marriage, but now at last he had met the first real love of his life. People were introduced to Leatrice as if they were parents of a boy bringing home the girl he hoped to marry. Leatrice was another Southern girl, and again she was at least three years older than Jack, but no one seemed to worry much about history repeating itself. They were clearly devoted to each other. The past was past.

For Leatrice, it was as if a heavy curtain had been torn from the windows and spring sunshine let in for the first time. All the sacrifices she'd made for the sake of her mother and her career, all the longings that had been put aside, erupted into a happiness she'd never known before. She tried to keep a sense of balance and to respect her mother's wishes where she could, but it was no use. Even seeing Jack across the room made her tremble. Nothing like this had ever happened to her before. She had not even imagined it possible. And Jack, in turn, was so captivated by her beauty that he sometimes forgot to speak. They would simply stare at each other in a sort of happy helplessness. Their whole world was an Eden and their future would be like a fairy tale. There was no prize they could not win, no obstacle they could not sweep aside as long as they were together.

Leatrice's career began to pick up speed. In August of 1920, Leatrice was offered the lead in a Lewis J. Selznick picture, *The Winged Victory*. It was about a bohemian artist and the innocent girl who loves him. For authenticity, the company went on location at Laguna Beach, about fifty miles south of Los Angeles, where a real artists' colony existed whose members would work as extras. Jack drove down every weekend and the lovers enjoyed their first free time together, away from the studio and away from Mary Zeidler.

Soon afterward, Leatrice signed a four-year contract with Samuel Goldwyn. Her salary was an incredible seven hundred dollars a week, almost triple what Jack was earning, but the difference seemed to present no problems at first. Mary Zeidler handled the money, and used part of it to support Leatrice's brother, who was having increasing difficulty adjusting to civilian life. Leatrice saw very little of her paycheck.

Jack, meanwhile, had his heart set on directing. Tourneur was more than satisfied with his work, and had gradually prepared him to do a picture on his own. At that time, Tourneur was in the process of breaking away from his financial backers, Jules Brulatour and Paramount Pictures. There were the normal disagreements about money, but more important were questions of artistic integrity. An artist, Tourneur felt, could not function with a banker looking over his shoulder. He decided to leave and form his own unit, Associated Producers Company, combining the talents of Thomas Ince, Marshall Neilan, Mack Sennett, Allan Dwan, and George Loane Tucker, all of whom were already legendary Hollywood directors. Jack was invited into this august company with an agreement that he would direct four pictures a year. Clarence Brown, Tourneur's other assistant, would have the same number.

Back in Fort Lee, Jules Brulatour was distressed at the thought of losing his prize director. It was he who had brought Tourneur from France in 1913 and had set him up first in Fort Lee and then in Hollywood. He valued Tourneur immensely for his ability to produce the happy combination of quality and profit, and had no intention of meekly letting him go.

Brulatour arrived in Hollywood in the late fall of 1920 ready to do battle. He brought with him his protégée and future wife, Hope Hampton, an attractive blonde who hoped to become a star. Brulatour knew that Tourneur could accomplish that if anyone could. He was anxious to have him direct Hope Hampton, and Tourneur was equally anxious to avoid it. He had seen her film début in A *Modern Salome* and decided that the task of making an actress of her was beyond his skills.

The two men met and argued for days. Brulatour alternately scolded and threatened, warning that a group of directors without the combined business sense of a newsboy would soon drive themselves bankrupt. Tourneur was not intimidated, but finally they worked out a parting agreement. Tourneur would take on Miss Hampton and make one picture with her. It was called *The Bait*, based on a play, *The Tiger*, by Sidney Toler. Jack wrote the scenario.

Before the filming began, Tourneur managed to find an emergency that occupied him elsewhere. Jack actually directed the picture with only occasional supervision. Tourneur or no, Jules Brulatour was quite pleased. He was either unaware that Hope Hampton had certain limitations as an actress or indifferent to them. She was extremely nervous, had little sense of timing, and, though a beautiful woman, was suprisingly awkward. She was the type who could stumble over dust. Jack got around these problems, mostly through careful editing, using other actors to advance the story while Miss Hampton stood around looking pretty. *Photoplay*, in December 1920, said: "Hope Hampton redeems herself in this picture, which might be called, *The Proof of Good Direction*."

During the shooting, Brulatour had begun making overtures about Jack coming to work for him. Jack could be his director, the head of

Brulatour's production unit, and the manager of his company. Jack was flattered, but he did not feel he was ready to leave Maurice Tourneur.

Tourneur, a possessive man with his employees, erupted when word reached him that Brulatour was trying to lure Jack away. He was furious at Jack and as much as accused him of treason. Jack tried to calm him, insisting that he was not even considering the offer and had turned Brulatour down. But some tension remained and Brulatour moved to take advantage of it.

He began by offering Jack five hundred dollars a week. It was more money than Jack had ever earned, but still he refused. The offer was raised to seven hundred and fifty and then to a thousand. Brulatour's final offer was a five-year contract. Jack would be paid a thousand dollars a week plus ten percent of the profits in his first year. For the remaining four years, he would receive fifteen hundred a week plus fifty percent of the profits. His first two pictures would have to star Hope Hampton, but after that he would have his own production company, with a free choice of actors and stories. Jack was flabbergasted. No director up to that time had ever signed such a contract, not even Tourneur. Whatever Brulatour's motives were, winning a round from Maurice Tourneur was certainly among them. The money meant nothing to him. Brulatour made a profit on every foot of film exposed in Hollywood. The money meant a lot to Jack. He was keenly aware that he wasn't worth it, but there it was.

Jack brooded over the offer for a week. He discussed it with Leatrice and his friends at the Athletic Club. Leatrice wished the offer had never been made, because it would mean at least a temporary separation. But it was made, it was real, and she couldn't imagine anyone turning it down. Jack's friends felt the same way. To Jack, the contract meant an end to all those lingering fears of one day being hungry again. And he would be making more than Leatrice. He had tried to tell himself that her greater financial success didn't bother him, that money paid for acting and money paid while learning directing were not the same, but now, with his own financial success within reach, he had to admit that it did bother him. Leatrice! How terribly would he miss her? How often would they see each other? Might he lose her if he moved a continent away? Charlie Chaplin counseled him that with every gain there's a loss and that every success has a price.

"What will you think of yourself if you don't try?" Chaplin asked.

"I don't know. I suppose I'd always wonder. But there's Leatrice."

"How will you feel toward Leatrice later if you turn your back on this opportunity for her sake?"

"I don't know that either," Jack told him. "I don't even know if I can do the job."

Still unsure, he accepted Brulatour's offer. Jack completed a final script for Tourneur, *The Last of the Mohicans*, and delivered it to him. Tourneur accepted it without a word and did not give Jack screen credit for the job. Nor did he offer his hand or say good-bye. To Jack, it was like losing a father.

Once he realized how alone he was, Jack implored Leatrice to go East with him. She wanted to, but she was not free to go. Leatrice was just beginning her third picture for Sam Goldwyn, *Bunty Pulls the Strings*, by James Barrie. It was her first really big role for a major studio. *Bunty* was a charming story no actress could refuse. Moreover, all the signs of her own impending stardom were beginning to appear. Important directors began dropping by on the lot to watch her work. Her face appeared on the cover of three movie magazines in a single month, and her fan mail was being delivered to her house in large canvas bags instead of handfuls wrapped in string. For all that she loved Jack and had confidence in him, she could not bring herself to break her contract. Not when she was this close after coming so far.

Brulatour, seeing Jack's anguish and fearing that he might change his mind, came up with a brainstorm that would get Leatrice to Fort Lee for at least the month it would take Jack to settle in. One morning, he and Hope Hampton showed up at Leatrice's apartment with a quack doctor in tow. The doctor, Brulatour explained triumphantly, would tape Leatrice's back from her shoulders to her hips, then report to the studio that she'd injured herself and would need a month's rest. Hope Hampton steered the disbelieving Leatrice to her bedroom, where, lisping sweet encouragement, she undressed her and called in the doctor to start taping her up.

"This isn't going to work," Leatrice protested. "You people are crazy."

"Don't worry, Leatrice dear," Hope Hampton assured her. "Brooly will take care of everything."

When they were finished, and Leatrice saw her half-mummified body in the mirror, she began to cry. "I can't do it," she said. "I just can't deceive Mr. Goldwyn." Nor was she going to wear all that adhesive tape for the next thirty days, to say nothing of blowing a part like *Bunty*.

Jack denied having any knowledge of the scheme. Leatrice tended to believe him, since she'd never known him to tell a lie, and because he fell into a giggling fit when she described the scene over the phone. Still, he had to admit the idea had its good points.

"I'll come as soon as I can," Leatrice promised.

[61]

"When?"

"The day the picture is finished."

Sadly, Jack climbed aboard the eastbound train. From every stop across the United States, he sent a telegram telling Leatrice how much he loved her.

At the end of 1920, Victor Heerman, who later won an Oscar for the screenplay of *Little Women*, was directing films for the Owen Moore Company of Fort Lee. He and Lewis J. Selznick were both renting space from Jules Brulatour. One morning, Victor was told to vacate his office; the new manager of the Brulatour Company was coming in. Grumbling, he set to work putting his things in boxes, wondering where he'd go next, when the new manager walked in:

> There was this *kid*, Jack Gilbert. I sized him up in a hurry and told him he could share *my* office. He was perfectly happy to do it. There was plenty of room and two desks. The only trouble was we had one phone between us, and Jack seemed to spend every waking hour on the long-distance phone to Leatrice. I had to go outside and use a pay phone if I had any calls to make. I don't know if it was possible to make a half-decent picture with Hopeless Hampton, but he might have if he didn't spend so much time on the phone. I don't know when he had time to direct.

Almost everyone at the studio was older than Jack, and most had more experience. These older hands were as mystified as Jack concerning what it was Brulatour saw in him, and several resented being told what to do by a twenty-one-year-old kid. The situation was difficult enough without Jack being so distractedly in love at the same time. Worse still, Jules Brulatour was in love, blind to any shortcomings Hope Hampton might have had and absolutely impervious to any suggestion that she might hold lesser rank than Mary Pickford or Lillian Gish. All she needed was the right director, and this Gilbert fellow, by God, was the one she wanted.

The movie was called *Love's Penalty*, and it was. Jack began by trying to charm the nervous Hope Hampton into a more relaxed state. These attentions, and Hope's grateful response, were noticed by Jules Brulatour, who decided he'd better stick around lest they get out of hand. He was on the set everyday, hovering at Jack's shoulder, often repeating Jack's instructions to Hope and adding a few helpful ideas of his own in mid-scene. Hope Hampton became utterly confused. Under the best of circumstances, she found it difficult to register any emotion other than bewilderment, the intensity of which could be measured by the number of times she batted her eyes. She was playing a kidnap victim, so bewilderment wasn't all bad. The trouble was that whenever she had a decent take showing an acceptable level of that emotion, Brulatour would cheer and she'd ruin the take by breaking into a broad and relieved smile. Or she'd knock over a lamp. Or she'd trip over the hem of her dress.

Each night, Jack would salvage what he could of Hope Hampton's footage and, as he'd done with her last picture, try to build the action around the other players. The difference was that this time there was no Maurice Tourneur to look at his work and assure him that he was doing the best that could be done under the circumstances. He was entirely alone. Members of the crew would look at him and laugh, probably sympathetically, but his lack of confidence was such that he felt they were laughing at him.

"It was unbelievably horrible," Jack later wrote of the experience. "The story was awful. I wrote it. I was responsible for the direction. It was ghastly. The cutting was bewildering. I did it. It was inconceivable that it could have been so bad."

It wasn't as bad as Jack thought. Burns Mantle, in *Photoplay*, called it "a dramatic story not lacking in entertainment value. . . . There are flashes of originality and suspense." *Variety* said: "*Love's Penalty* is first-rate 'hokum' melodrama magnificently produced, ably directed and well cast. Written and directed by Jack Gilbert. It makes a vehicle for Hope Hampton that will satisfy the average exhibitor and picture patron."

These were hardly raves, but they were hardly as devastating as Jack's perception either. But Jack wanted the picture to be great. He had to show Tourneur that he knew what he was doing. He wanted the picture to be a timeless epic, another *Birth of a Nation*, and what he delivered was a good little melodrama under difficult conditions.

Leatrice Joy said:

Jack was his own severest critic. The picture wasn't bad. Percy Marmont gave a wonderful performance and so did Virginia Valli. Brulatour was so anxious for Hope Hampton to succeed that he sat at Jack's elbow all through the shooting. He made Jack nervous, he made Hope nervous, and he really interfered. But still it wasn't bad. Several years later, when I made *The Marriage Cheat* with Percy Marmont, we talked about the Hampton thing. Percy said he was surprised the movie had acquired such a bad reputation. "It was all Jack's doing," he said. "Jack wouldn't stop talking about how awful it was, and really it was a nice little picture. I'm not ashamed of it." And Percy was right.

During the making of *Love's Penalty*, Jack could see nothing but failure. Alone in the cutting room or watching the rushes night after night, Jack was constantly convinced that he was in over his head. Nothing he could do seemed to make the picture better. Nothing made it good enough.

Leatrice was asleep one night when the telephone rang. It was Jack calling from his hotel room in a state of deep gloom. He told her how badly the picture was going, that the crew was laughing at him. He'd been absolutely stupid to leave Tourneur and now there was no turning back. Hope Hampton's performance was going from bad to numb and, to climax it all, Brulatour had become wildly jealous and suspected him of flirting with his protégée.

"Can you imagine that? Me flirting with anybody?" he asked indignantly. Leatrice did not think it entirely impossible, but she sympathized. Jack told her everything would be fine if only she were there with him. That way Brulatour wouldn't worry, Jack wouldn't feel so utterly alone, and Leatrice might even be able to coach Hope Hampton into a wider range of eye-batting while Jack made the rest of the picture. "If you really loved me," he told her, "you'd be here and to hell with Sam Goldwyn."

Leatrice tried to calm him. Her picture was almost over. She could not leave now because too many people and too much money was involved. She would come the minute it was over. Just two more weeks. Surely he could wait that long.

"She never loved who dared not venture all!" Jack shouted into the phone, and hung up on her.

Leatrice went back to bed, but before she could fall asleep the phone rang again. This time it was Rose, the night operator at the Algonquin Hotel in New York. She said, "I'm sorry, Miss Joy, but there's another call for you. It's from the lady in the room next door to Mr. Gilbert. She wants to talk to you."

Leatrice was too surprised to refuse. The hotel guest, who did not give her name, came on the phone and apologized, saying she could not help hearing Jack's side of the argument. "But, Miss Joy," she said fervently, "if any man pleaded with me like that I'd come to him on my hands and knees. If you have any heart at all, you'll be on the next train in the morning. Please, Miss Joy, that boy needs you." Leatrice sat up the rest of the night feeling like a traitor. But she simply could not go.

In two weeks, as promised, *Bunty Pulls the Strings* was over. She raced from the studio, her bags already packed, and boarded the evening train for New York. In Topeka, Kansas, a porter delivered an urgent telegram: RETURN AT ONCE FOR IMPORTANT RETAKES. GOLDWYN.

[64]

For a twenty-dollar bill, the porter agreed that there was no one on that train named Leatrice Joy. Goldwyn would have to manage without her.

Hope Hampton met the train when it arrived in New York early in the morning. She explained that Jack was busy at the studio, which was fine because it would give them a chance to go to the hairdresser and then do some Fifth Avenue shopping. It was midafternoon before they arrived at Fort Lee and found Jack half out of his mind with worry. By this time, he had kidnapping on the brain.

"Where the hell have you been?" was his welcome. "I know you arrived at eight o'clock this morning. What on earth have you been doing since then? Doesn't it matter to you that I've been counting every second in every minute? How could you be so cruel?"

Leatrice, who thought she was being considerate, was hurt. Since he was working, she said, she thought she'd use the time to make herself more beautiful for him. "But you're beautiful enough already," he argued. "It's ridiculous to think that you could be more beautiful. No one could be more beautiful. You should have flown to my side rather than waste time attempting the impossible."

The logic of his position was unassailable. The quarrel quickly passed and they spent a glorious week together. A relieved Jules Brulatour entertained them like visiting royalty. Newspaper reporters followed them everywhere, to Jack's annoyance and to Leatrice's unconcealed delight. The week went by too quickly.

Sam Goldwyn appeared in New York on business unrelated to Leatrice's truancy. They went to his office to plead with him for a few extra days. Leatrice was due to return to the Coast to begin her next picture, a Chinese story called A Tale of Two Worlds. They stood holding hands in front of Goldwyn's enormous desk. Leatrice's knees were shaking. She was sure Goldwyn would be angry about her telegram dodge, or at least unconvinced that Leatrice Joy could have escaped notice during four days on a railroad train. But Goldwyn was a sentimental man, touched by their romance.

"You really love that girl, don't you, Jack?"

"I'd give her the moon if she asked me," he answered.

Goldwyn smiled and wagged a finger at Leatrice. "Take my word sweetheart, don't ask." He sat back. "Well? How much time do you need? Another weekend, will that do?"

They were delighted. It was only Thursday. That would give them three more days. As it turned out, they had five. Leatrice's train ticket was to be sent to her by Red Arrow messenger, but the messenger pocketed the money for the ticket and disappeared. When the theft was discovered, it was too late to catch the Monday train and she had to wait for the Twentieth Century Limited, which left on Wednesday.

Parting then wasn't any easier. Jack went back to work finishing his hated picture. Upon its completion, he asked Brulatour for some time off to go to California and spend a week or two with Leatrice. Brulatour answered that it was out of the question. They were ready to begin a new Hope Hampton picture, perhaps the one that would solidly establish her as a star. To Jack, the very thought of going through all that again so soon was paralyzing. It would inevitably be another failure, and Jack had had all the failure he could stand for a while. The whole thing had been a ghastly mistake. The contract was a mistake. Brulatour must certainly know that by now and regret the day he offered it. Jack would let him off the hook. They would agree to tear up the contract and all would be square.

Brulatour wouldn't hear of it. He had no regrets whatsoever, he said, and he and Hope Hampton were eminently satisfied with Jack's work. Jack thought they both had to be out of their minds. All right, he decided, he would sell Brulatour's fabulous contract back to him for twenty-five thousand dollars. That was nine thousand more than Jack had already been paid. Now it was Brulatour's turn to think Jack was crazy. He wouldn't hear of it.

Finally, in self-destructive desperation, Jack marched into Brulatour's office, tore up the contract, and announced that he was boarding the next train to Hollywood. "Let him sue," he told Leatrice. "There's nothing more he can take."

Jack convinced himself that Brulatour had all this time been looking for a way to break Jack's contract, that he was going to buy him off that very day. But Clarence Brown denies the story. It was he who directed Hope Hampton's next film (which was also a disaster):

> Jack gave up too soon. Anyone can make a bad movie. I certainly did and I had six years' experience on Jack. The difference is I was able to write it off and go on to my next assignment, while he couldn't accept what he thought was a failure. The other difference is that I didn't walk out on a contract. Jack never should have done that. It wasn't necessary. All the while I was there, Brulatour and Hope Hampton were saying how much they missed him. Something could have been worked out if he hadn't been so damned impulsive.

Jules Brulatour never sued Jack or tried to get him back. But Jack was never offered another directing job when he returned to Hollywood. I asked Clarence Brown whether Brulatour put him on some sort of a blacklist after he broke the contract. His answer:

I don't think so. At least not directly. Jules Brulatour wasn't a vindictive man. It's possible, though, that people avoided hiring Jack purely on the chance that doing so might offend Brulatour. As distributor for Eastman Film, Jules was a pretty important guy. He could give a movie producer a lot of service or a little. He could sell film on credit or demand cash. Jack was a good up-and-coming director, but maybe he simply wasn't important enough to be worth the chance of getting on Brulatour's bad side. Telling everyone what a lousy Hope Hampton movie he made didn't help either.

The directing chapter of Jack's life was effectively closed. He arrived in Hollywood almost broke, with no real job prospects. He had collected sixteen thousand dollars in salary, but his long-distance phone bills were nearly a third of that. He was floundering, while Leatrice's star was rising fast.

· seven ·

IF JACK'S future was unclear to him upon his return to Hollywood
and to Leatrice, it was perfectly clear to Olivia Burwell's lawyers. He
was an established actor and director. If one film producer thought
he was worth a thousand dollars a week, why wouldn't another? In any
case, there was certainly no wisdom in rushing into a divorce settlement
with Jack while he had no money coming in. The lawyers chose to drag
their feet until Jack was back on his. And the ante, of course, would be
raised each time Jack's situation improved. Besides, everyone knew that
he wanted to marry this actress he was seeing. No settlement, no marriage. Their Hollywood sources told them that Leatrice was definitely
not the type to live in sin with him. If Olivia remained patient, and
refused to sign any papers, Jack Gilbert would eventually throw in the
sponge and settle handsomely.

Leatrice, however, had her own ideas of what was sinful and what
was not. Love was a gift from the Almighty. Rejecting the gift would be
the greater sin. She and Jack had long since consummated their relationship, and were therefore married in the eyes of God and in their
own hearts as well. She suggested to Jack that being married in the eyes
of a Mexican justice of the peace wouldn't be bad either. Since God was
everywhere, He presumably even visited Tijuana occasionally. Doing
likewise was the least they could do, and a marriage in Mexico was a lot
better than no marriage at all. Leatrice's views sounded suspiciously like
bigamy to Jack, but he was too astonished and delighted to start getting
picky at that point.

But first things first, Leatrice said. They would need a house and
some furnishings. Jack and Leatrice promptly went looking together and
settled in a single day upon a pretty little place in Laurel Canyon that
was for rent. It was a stucco cottage with a sloping red roof and leaded
glass windows. The owner had built it in the middle of an orange grove
whose blossoms made everything in the cottage smell like breakfast. To

this day, Leatrice says, she sees the house every time she squeezes an orange.

Furniture was the next order of business. Leatrice had taken only a few pieces from her apartment, leaving the rest for Mary Zeidler. Jack owned nothing at all that didn't have a handle on it or that couldn't fit in a hotel closet. Lee Garmes, who had taken Jack on his shopping spree for clothing four years earlier, now volunteered to drive them to the Barker Brothers furniture store. Jack and Leatrice selected some tables and bookcases made of mission oak and stained to look like mahogany, an overstuffed sofa and some carpets, and a particularly ugly clock. What the furniture lacked in the way of graceful lines, it made up for, unfortunately, in durability. The clock, among other items, still stands in Leatrice's Connecticut home defiantly ticking away.

Next, they hired a servant named Wong, who muttered in Chinese a lot. Then Jack decided that a dog would round out everything nicely. Leatrice never cared for dogs. They ate the most revolting things and disposed of their food in an equally repulsive and indiscriminate way. But Jack loved animals, and was so enthusiastic about owning the very first dog of his life that she couldn't bear to argue. Leatrice went with him on a tour of kennels and dog pounds in search of exactly the right dog. She assumed that he was looking for something exotic, this being a time when other actors were buying matching Russian wolfhounds or bull mastiffs. But he chose a big homely yellow hound dog that no one else wanted, and for precisely that reason Jack brought the dog home. They named him Me Too, after a comic-strip character. The dog slept under their bed. Jack and Leatrice didn't sleep too well on top of the bed because the dog had a thing about moons and howled at any that passed the bedroom window. Jack loved the hound anyway and took him walking every night in the canyon. Me Too loved Jack just as much. He learned the sound of Jack's car and would begin yelping enthusiastically long before Jack's car turned into the driveway. Sadly, the dog was hit by another car a few months later. Jack buried him in the garden, and was inconsolable for days.

The Mexican marriage took place soon after the furniture arrived. Jack and Leatrice drove south with actress Helene Chadwick, Helene's sister, and a French actor named Gaston Glass, and found a seedy old Mexican justice of the peace who was considerably less romantic than the one Leatrice had imagined. But Jack, who had fewer illusions about Mexican border towns, did what he could to make the ceremony memorable. He'd chosen a platinum-and-diamond ring with great care, and even arranged, though no one knew how, to have a hurdy-gurdy play their song, "Whispering," outside the justice's window.

On the way back home, Jack could see that Leatrice was sulking. He knew that the wedding wasn't everything it might have been, but at least they were legally married someplace. But to Leatrice none of it seemed quite right. Not even the ring. She'd told Jack that all she wanted was a simple gold band like the one her mother wore. Jack had assumed that she was being frugal. Whatever the reason, he thought she deserved much more, and now he was hurt that his surprise choice of a suitable wedding ring had done just the opposite of pleasing her. Jack listened to a few more complaints about the ring from an overtired and melancholy Leatrice and then, as the car turned into Laurel Canyon, he stopped, slid the ring off her finger, and threw it deep into the bushes lining the road. Tomorrow, he said, he'd buy her the "respectable" ring she wanted. Leatrice burst into exhausted tears.

She told the houseboy, Wong, what had happened and offered a reward if he could find the ring Jack threw away. Wong, who'd already decided that Jack and Leatrice were both more than a little crazy, wasn't surprised. For months afterward, he spent his days off crawling through the canyon on his hands and knees, but the ring was never found. It's probably still there.

Wong got some small satisfaction out of the whole business when, with Christmas coming, Leatrice bought Jack a bronze lamp for his study and made a red silk lampshade for it. She then asked Wong to decorate it with Chinese letters. He did a lovely job, and the effect was striking—black brushwork ideographs on crimson raw silk. One evening, Jack and Leatrice invited the Chinese actress Anna May Wong to dinner. She was properly impressed when Jack showed off his magnificent lamp but became evasive when asked if the inscription meant anything in particular. A bottle of wine later, and with Wong out of earshot, she translated. Up and down each panel, Wong had inscribed, "Crazy boss lady goddamned fool!" In a stroke, the lamp became Jack's most treasured possession.

Mary Zeidler didn't help matters any. If a scandal concerning bigamy appeared in the papers, Jack could be sure that Mary would deliver an underscored copy to the house and drop it on their bed. Leatrice didn't like it, but she felt loyal to her mother and would defend her actions as unpleasant but understandable. Understandable like hell, Jack would fume, reminding Leatrice that she'd married a man who was trying to be a good husband and not Jack the Ripper. Nor did he care much for Leatrice's brother, who'd recently followed the family to Hollywood and, at Mary's urging, was beginning to make sounds of outraged Southern manhood. Jack was concerned about her family. He had sympathy for her brother and knew about his work with wounded soldiers. But when John, knowing nothing about the movie business, had the effrontery to change his name to Billy Joy and set himself up as an actors' agent, Jack's sympathy ran out, especially when Leatrice would listen to her brother and not to him.

Leatrice told me a long time ago that her brother had once actually gone to their house with a gun while she was working and threatened to blow Jack's head off if he didn't get out of his sister's life. Jack, according to Leatrice, invited him in, calmed him with a drink, gave him some money, and sent him home feeling that he'd accomplished his knight-errant mission. That was all Leatrice knew or could recall.

Then, years later, at the tail end of a long conversation with Rowland V. Lee, I happened to mention Billy Joy and his gun. Rowland began chuckling at an episode that I didn't think was especially funny. He said:

Hell, I was there. Not in the house actually, but I was sure a witness. I was talking to Jack on the phone about a possible directing job when he said, "Oh, damn, what does that dimwit want?" He said it was Billy Joy, and asked me to hold on until he got rid of him. Billy was stammering about what he'd do if Jack didn't move out of the house, using lines like "In New Orleans we know what to do with men who taint our women." But I had no idea he really had a gun in his hand. Jack didn't sound as if he were taking it seriously. After a minute or two I heard Jack say, "As long as Rowland Lee is listening to all this, why don't we ask him what he thinks?" Poor Billy must have stood there not knowing what the hell to do next. Then Jack got on the phone and said Billy was there to shoot him if he didn't quit tainting Leatrice, and did I have any suggestions? Well, my first suggestion was that Billy try not to shoot himself in the foot. Jack passed on the suggestion and Billy must have realized he was standing there like a dummy with the gun in his hand because Jack told me he quickly put it away. Then I could hear Jack mixing drinks. Billy allowed as how he might take just a splash of sippin' whiskey. Billy tried to get back into his Southern-avenger role but Jack would pretend not to hear. My God, he'd get Billy talking about everything, from the "War Between the States" to his experiences in the Army hospital to the proper way to fill a tooth. The guy could charm a corpse. He asked me why I didn't come over and hear some of Billy's interesting stories, but I really didn't want to get off the phone as long as Billy had that gun. The man was just possibly dangerous. But then Billy said he had to be going. Jack gave him some money, but it was to buy roses for Billy's mother. Jack promised him he'd start untainting Leatrice that very night, and Billy left.

When Jack got back on the phone, I expected we'd have a good laugh over what happened, but he asked me to forget about it and not tell anyone. I'm not surprised that he never told it. The story, good as it is, would have ridiculed Billy, and Jack wouldn't have done that. But what happened upset him more than he let on, no matter how cool a customer he was. It was something he had to live with. He put the matter aside and we went back to discussing jobs.

Besides these problems, Jack had another. There weren't any jobs. Not directing jobs. His estrangement from Brulatour or Tourneur, or both, had, at least indirectly, closed all doors to him except those that led to acting jobs. Jack wanted no part of them. Leatrice acted because she wanted to act and because acting was what she could do. Jack wanted more substance to his life than acting promised.

Gouverneur Morris, the novelist, was a good friend of Jack's. He'd written *The Ace of Hearts*, which was the last picture Leatrice made for Sam Goldwyn, and came to know the Gilberts well. Morris was something of a black sheep from a distinguished New Jersey family. He was then making his living writing stories for the movies, but he was enormously erudite. He was also a bright, funny man, ruggedly handsome, who dressed in patched and threadbare tweed suits and a battered felt hat pulled sideways over his head. Morris lived apart from a wife in Santa Barbara and claimed to be secretly married to his collaborator, Ruth Wightman. Wightman, who had once lived with Jack London, was as indifferent to formalities as Gouverneur Morris was. "Guvvie" and Ruth particularly enjoyed Jack's company. They were impressed by his inquiring mind and the scope of his knowledge, and would spend many nights talking until dawn or playing elaborate word games. Morris understood Jack's reluctance to return to acting. "It's a mug's game," he said. "Why don't you write? You have the words and the imagination. Anyone who can talk like you and me can write."

But Morris, unlike Jack, had a small inherited income, enough to cushion the rough spots, and the security of a good education behind him. Jack had nothing or nobody but himself to rely on. He wanted to write. He wrote almost every day when he wasn't reading. But he had to make a living and he didn't think writing jobs would come his way any faster than directing jobs.

During the winter of 1920–21, Jack finally gave in to his manager, Harry Edington, who was pressuring him to accept one of several good roles he'd been offered. He signed with William Fox for the lead in a picture called *Shame*. It was a dumb story. *Photoplay* summed it up: "When the hero of *Shame* hears that his mother was Chinese, he immediately dashes to the mirror and sees himself reflected with almond eyes, long nails and a Chinese laundry. The thought drives him almost insane so he goes to Alaska and fights a wolf."

On the other hand, a review in the Toledo *Blade* said: "Intimate views of Chinatown, John Gilbert's bare-handed fight with a wolf, and some of the best screen acting we've ever seen are a few of the high spots in William Fox's production of *Shame*. . . . With a poor cast it would have been the rawest kind of melodrama . . . John Gilbert, in the role of the young millionaire, easily carries off honors in his very heavy part."

The Toledo *Blade* notwithstanding, Jack didn't think much of his performance. He'd seen with a director's eye all that the picture might have been if it hadn't been made on the cheap like most Fox pictures. Fox operated on a shoestring, making hurried imitations of other studio's successes. Fox also distributed his own pictures, but had no distribution outlets on the West Coast. The result was that even if Jack did happen to make a picture he was proud of, no one he knew would be able to see it. William Fox, however, offered Jack a three-year contract when he saw that *Shame* was so well received. His salary would be a thousand dollars a week. Jack had little use for William Fox and stalled until his money ran out, hoping that something else would turn up. Finally he signed.

The Fox contract, he told Leatrice, was better than not working at all, but not by much. "These are vile men," he said. "They're awful to work for. Fox doesn't have a friend in the world, because he's mean, cheap, vulgar, and he's notorious for breaking his word. He's a fifth-grade dropout with an absolute contempt for education. Do you know what he said to me? He said, 'Why should I read a book when I can buy the bum who wrote it?' Imagine! To him, a man like Gouverneur Morris is a bum who can be bought and then discarded. I don't know how I am going to stand it."

It was Fox who destroyed Theda Bara's career by putting her in over forty movies in five years, until people were sick of looking at her. When, in 1916, he produced a spectacular failure called A *Daughter of the Gods*, the only thing the critics found to praise was the director, Herbert Brenon. Fox recalled the picture, removed Brenon's name from the credits (substituting Al Blum's), and ordered Brenon off the lot. Brenon was lucky. Fox fired other men over petty jealousies while they were on location, even in Europe, and left them stranded with the company's debts.

But Jack did some good work in some reasonably good pictures during his time with Fox. Of *Gleam o' Dawn*, Jack's first picture under the new contract, *Photoplay* said: "John Gilbert, a new star, does splendid work in a unique and well-directed drama of the Hudson Bay country." Jack thought it was rubbish.

He made nineteen pictures for Fox, of which only two remain: *Monte Cristo*, made in 1922, and *Cameo Kirby*, made in 1923; both are competent movies, well directed, with moments of surprising beauty, and both received more than their share of favorable reviews. Jack, however, wasn't crazy about either one of them. His own high standards were out of touch with the financial realities of moviemaking. Even the best of studios had to crank out fifty or more fast and dirty pictures a year to satisfy the demands of the exhibitors. In most cases, there was literally no time for the careful preparation that would result in quality films; these were "program pictures." Of the fifty, perhaps six would be considered exceptional by the critics, and the studio didn't know which six they were until the reviews appeared. These were facts of life well known to the studio executives. For that reason, those executives had little patience with the unending parade of actors, writers, and directors who waltzed into their offices demanding to do something "substantial."

From the beginning, Jack and Leatrice had been an unlikely combination, an attraction of opposites. Leatrice was a clever woman and an excellent actress, but she was not in the least intellectual. She seldom read a book not related to Christian Science; she had no interest in music, politics, or art; she felt uncomfortable with Jack's friends and he was easily bored by hers. Leatrice never drank, did not approve of it, while Jack, by her standards, drank heavily. Jack was a listener, a toucher, a feeler, and a thinker. Leatrice didn't converse so much as she waited for her turn to talk and switch the subject to one that suited her. Not to say that Leatrice wasn't loving and kind and generous; she was all these things and more. She was also sentimental, particularly on the subject of mother love. Jack did not share that sentiment. One day, Jack came home from work and was startled to find large posters of his mother hung up all over the house. Leatrice, while rummaging through the old trunk Walter Gilbert had given him, found them and thought it would be a lovely surprise. She'd heard stories from Jack of Ida Adair's cruel indifference to him, but Leatrice, convinced that mother love was next to the divine, did not believe a word of it. No mother could be cruel to her child. And no son could fail to be proud of a mother like

Ida Adair. She tried to explain this to Jack as he walked around the house tearing posters off the walls and burying them deep within the trunk. His only reply was to laugh bitterly and ask her to never open that trunk again.

Another problem between them was Leatrice's success. When her contract with Goldwyn ran out, she decided to look around before committing herself to a new one. Her brother, acting as her agent now, thought she needed a new, more sophisticated image. Times were changing, he said. Sweetness had gone out with the Great War. The new American woman was exciting, alluring, adventurous, sensual. Billy Joy suggested that she start with some publicity stills. There was a new photographer in town, Edwin Bower Hesser, whom everyone was talking about. She must be careful, though, because Hesser's pictures were inclined to be "suggestive."

Leatrice obediently made the appointment. The session developed into a small tug-of-war, with Leatrice pulling a velvet drape closer to her throat every time Hesser tried to move it in the other direction. In the end, however, Hesser got what he wanted. He produced a set of photographs so lovely, so tender, so romantically erotic that Leatrice wept over them. She knew she was pretty. But Hesser had made her into an extraordinarily beautiful woman.

Billy Joy knew what he had. Without consulting Leatrice, he delivered the new photographs to Cecil B. De Mille, then a top director for Famous Players–Lasky. De Mille had just lost his greatest leading lady, Miss Gloria Swanson, and was looking for someone special to take her place. At the end of a week the call came: "Mr. De Mille would like to meet Miss Leatrice Joy."

De Mille, like many directors, had begun as an actor. His first pictures survive today as masterpieces, but some were box-office flops. His psychological tragedies were often over the heads of the public and many of the critics. What De Mille fully expected to be recognized as the work of genius was brushed off as "piffling" and "morbid." Thereafter, as Adolph Zukor said, "De Mille didn't make pictures for himself, or for the critics. He made them for the public." He lowered his sights and embarked upon the pompous, epic phase of his career. His formula seldom varied. He would deliver some pious message against a background of orgy scenes, near-nakedness, wild animals, slaughter, and lots of sunken bathtubs. He would patronize the audience with garrish naïveté, providing sexual indulgence, extravaganza, hokum, and title lines such as no human being ever spoke: "Be thankful for your tears, without them life would have no rainbows," or (spoken by Lois Wilson in prison),

"Doesn't this doughnut remind you of a life preserver? That's what prison has meant to most of us—a life preserver."

Meanwhile, the actor in him developed a new kind of director personality. First came the costume. De Mille decided upon riding breeches, bound to his calves with puttees, and an ever-present revolver at his hip. On the set, he had as many as eight people trained to stay close behind him and anticipate his every need. When he no longer needed the megaphone in his hand, he would simply drop it. Someone was expected to catch it. When he wanted to sit down, he sat, regardless of whether a chair was there or not. An assistant whose job it was to follow him with a chair was expected to get it under him in time. If, during a shoot, he decided to wade into water for a better look at a shot, eight people would wade in with him. De Mille's office was like a small church, complete with vaulted ceilings and stained-glass windows, designed specifically to awe and intimidate people like Leatrice Joy.

Billy Joy convinced her that he had discovered the opportunity of a lifetime now that Gloria Swanson was out of the way. Never mind that De Mille paid his actors very little. She had a chance to star in some of the most important and successful movies being made in Hollywood. Never mind that she was making seven hundred dollars a week with Goldwyn. The hundred and fifty that De Mille would pay would lead to greatness.

Jack exploded when he heard of the offer. "How can you work for that silly son of a bitch?" he asked. "He treats people like cattle and acts like he's doing them a favor by paying them anything at all for the privilege of working with him. That's what he wants you to think so he can spend that money building his ridiculous sets. You think he'll make you a star, but the fact is no one is going to notice you in those epics of his unless he has you riding around naked on the back of a Bengal tiger or wallowing in one of his sunken bathtubs." Jack urged her at least to talk it over first with his manager, Harry Edington.

But Leatrice didn't listen. Her brother had arranged the contract, and was so pleased with himself that Leatrice couldn't bring herself to question the deal he'd made. Besides, Jack was exaggerating. It wasn't all bathtubs and tigers. She saw in her mind's eye all the great roles that Gloria Swanson had played, roles that made her a star among stars. That was going to happen to Leatrice. She was going to be somebody.

Without telling Jack, Leatrice went to the studio and signed with De Mille. Jack did not learn of it until the following night. Her rejection of his advice hurt him, and he was bitterly angry that loyalty to her brother, whom he detested, meant more to her than loyalty to him.

Most irritating of all, Leatrice had been suckered by De Mille, a man he considered to be a posing, self-important ass.

Through Jack's tirade, Leatrice answered sweetly that she had no idea he would be so upset. She could not understand all the fuss. After all, he was earning more than enough money for both of them. He was really being very silly. Jack stormed out of the house and did not come back until morning.

As usual, he apologized, taking full blame for the disagreement. Leatrice took him in her arms and clung to him. She still didn't understand what could have caused such a rupture, but it frightened her because she loved him so much. Jack told her that he loved her just as much and repeated his apology. As for the hurt he felt . . . there seemed to be no use in saying more.

Under the new contract, Leatrice made two pictures for Famous Players–Lasky before making *Manslaughter*, her first film that was actually directed by De Mille. The story was about a society girl who loves speed and thrills and parties, and whose wild driving causes the death of a motorcycle policeman. The prosecuting district attorney falls in love with her. When duty requires that he must send her to jail, and when the annoyed girl rebuffs his affections, he turns to drink and dissipation. But when the heroine sees the error of her ways and does charitable work in a soup kitchen, the fallen district attorney shows up in line and she starts him on the road to recovery. With the support of her love, he runs for governor. De Mille even squeezed in his trademark, a Roman-orgy scene. During the trial, the D.A. describes the wild parties of the 1920s and the camera switches to a huge Roman-revel scene, complete with nudity and bodies intertwined in an alcoholic stupor; then Attila the Hun bursts in and chops everyone to pieces to show them the errors of their ways.

This last touch was for the benefit of the newly created Hays Office. By the dawn of the twenties, movies had begun to get a bit out of hand. Ads were appearing touting attractions like "Brilliant jazz babies, champagne baths, midnight revels, petting parties in the purple dawn, all ending in one terrific, smashing climax that makes you gasp." The actors were getting pretty wild themselves. Wallace Reid, the All-American Boy, was shown to be a morphine addict. He died in a sanitorium in 1923 at the age of thirty-two. That was a real tragedy, because Wallace was hardly a thrill-seeking drug user. He was given morphine so he could keep on working after suffering a painful injury. The more he needed, the more morphine he received; soon he was hooked and it killed him.

[77]

The most famous scandal of the day, however, was the Fatty Arbuckle case, in which the obese actor was accused of raping a poor young actress and causing her fatal injuries because of his great weight on her helpless body. Arbuckle was crucified in the press, hounded by an ambitious and unscrupulous prosecutor, and ultimately driven out of the movies. Yet Arbuckle was innocent. He was acquitted after his third trial by a jury whose foreman said that, more than an acquittal, Roscoe Arbuckle was owed an abject apology for the wrong done him.

Yet another scandal was revealed in the press close on the heels of Arbuckle's arrest. William Desmond Taylor, the suave and handsome director who also worked for Famous Players–Lasky, was murdered. Mabel Normand, of Mack Sennett fame, and Mary Miles Minter, a former child star and then an ingénue lead in the Mary Pickford tradition, both saw him on the night he died. Both were reputed to be having affairs with him and both were said to have been introduced to drugs by him. Their careers were ruined by the resulting publicity.

Aside from these scandals, which helped pave the way for the Hays Office Production Code, many of the producers and directors, De Mille included, enforced codes of their own. De Mille demanded discipline and sacrifice, as well as high moral standards, from everyone working on his set. He demanded absolute dedication to himself, with no interference from the outside. That included private lives—even husbands.

The fan magazines and newspapers had begun to report quarrels between Jack and Leatrice. Many fights were prompted by Leatrice's devotion to Cecil B. De Mille. Jack was tired of forever taking second place to a man whose posturing he considered ludicrous and whose attempts to run other people's lives he considered outrageous. At parties, Jack did scathing imitations of De Mille that Leatrice did not find amusing at all. She was spellbound by De Mille, and accepted his authority without question. To this day, she believes he was the greatest of all directors.

Jack's jealousy began to feed on itself. At one point, when Leatrice came home from a De Mille party with a gold purse she'd won in a charades game, Jack presumed it to be a personal gift from De Mille and even wondered whether the two were having an affaire. Leatrice was simply respectfully loyal to De Mille in a way that was entirely characteristic of her. She was also insensitive to Jack's feelings in the matter, and that was also characteristic. Jack complained that Leatrice had no capacity whatsoever to tell someone to go to hell.

As the Gilberts' marital tiffs began appearing in print, De Mille would carefully clip the articles and drop them in Leatrice's lap when he came on the set. The clippings were accompanied by a warning that she was coming dangerously close to violating one or more of De Mille's unwritten laws. The matter came to a head one morning, after a particularly stormy session at home, when she appeared at work with her eyes swollen from crying. Leatrice was summoned by megaphone to the main office, where De Mille and her brother were waiting:

De Mille threatened to cut me entirely out of the picture [*Saturday Night*, with Conrad Nagel and Julia Faye]. He said, "We can reshoot tomorrow with a new girl," and I believed him. He had done it before. He replaced another girl once, and never counted the cost. He said to me, "Your acting is terrible, you can't take direction, your mind is so distracted that I can't reach you." He pointed to a pile of stills on his desk and told me to look at them. I was afraid to, but I did. They were the rushes taken from the day before. I had shadows under my eyes. I really looked a little haggard. I started to cry again and reached into De Mille's pocket for his handkerchief. He waited until I calmed down and he said, "Miss Joy, your work must come first. If it doesn't, then you and I will have no reason to continue together. Is that perfectly clear?" I knew I had to be away from Jack or I'd lose everything. De Mille was right. I owed him my best. As long as he was paying me my work had to come first. That night I packed some things and moved into the Hudson Apartments in Hollywood. Jack tried to understand it but he just couldn't.

The bright side was that the separation taught Jack, and Leatrice as well, how much they meant to each other. Hard as it was, perhaps they needed some time apart. Jack sent her flowers daily and delivered a new portable phonograph with a stack of Irving Berlin's tender love songs, including "Always," "All Alone," and "Remember." She was deeply touched by these sentimental reminders of his love, but not so much that she'd defy De Mille by seeing him evenings. Jack decided he was damned if he was going to sit home alone in meek obedience to some skinhead director. He chose as his companion an exquisitely beautiful actress, already married four times, whose private life was one of the most scandalous in Hollywood. Her name was Barbara La Marr.

Several times during their separation, Leatrice drove up to the house in Laurel Canyon, but her pride would not let her go in. She also knew that she might walk in on something that would be hard to put behind her later. Leatrice wasn't terribly concerned about Jack's flirtations with Barbara La Marr, or Lila Lee, and possibly one or two others. She knew that Jack was basically a one-woman man; he did love her, and was

[79]

probably being true to her—again in his fashion. She'd also heard that Jack's divorce from Olivia Burwell had gone through. They could really be married now if they could weather these weeks. The De Mille picture was finished. Especially now, it seemed ridiculous that they remain apart. One evening she turned away from Laurel Canyon and drove straight to Gouverneur Morris's house. She pulled into the driveway, rang the bell, and burst into tears.

Guvvie and Ruth invited her in, talked a while by the fire, and then Guvvie telephoned Jack, who was at home that night. He came at once and picked Leatrice up:

> On the way home, we said we were sorry for all the dumb and selfish things that happened. And Jack assured me that his little flings meant nothing at all, that maybe he was just trying to hit back. I asked if he'd slept with the girls he'd dated and he said no, but he did admit to giving them presents. I told him I'd forgive him for that too if he gave me duplicates of whatever he gave them. He did, too. One of them was a rare jet bottle of perfumed oil, and a white enameled elephant in which to burn the stuff he'd given to Bebe Daniels. I didn't even know he was seeing her! That night the phone rang at about two in the morning. I answered it and it was Barbara La Marr. She said, "Oh, Leatrice darling, may I speak to Jack, please?" I said, "Of course, dear," and then threw the phone under the bed and went back to sleep.

At long last, Jack and Leatrice were married, in a secret ceremony in the home of Judge A. R. Summerfield. Leatrice was blissfully happy and so was Jack. But Jack, in his rapture, neglected to ask Leatrice what she'd say to Cecil B. De Mille the next time the bastard had the nerve to insist that they separate. De Mille did insist, and she said yes. Leatrice moved out again, this time to stay with her mother, thinking that would somehow lessen the blow.

Jack was no less angry than before. This time, however, he wasn't about to be faced with a choice between lonely evenings at home and another Barbara La Marr routine. And he wasn't about to start calling at Mary Zeidler's house again. He gave up the house in Laurel Canyon, put the furniture in storage, and moved in with two friends, Carey Wilson, a writer at Metro, and Paul Bern, a German writer/director and one of the town's reigning intellectuals. The house was a rundown Spanish hacienda on King's Road, north of Sunset Boulevard. Charlie Chaplin lived only a block away and spent many evenings with them reading plays aloud, experimenting with homemade gin, and sometimes trying to commune with other kinds of spirits via Ouija boards and automatic writing. One night, they held a séance and invited Harry Houdini to chair the proceedings. To no one's surprise except Jack's, a heavy teakwood table in the center of the room began to jiggle and lurch. It lifted off the ground and slammed violently toward Jack. Wherever he moved, the table would follow him. He became so rattled that he ran from the house, only learning later that Houdini had rigged a trick used by fake mediums as a practical joke.

The house and its occupants became a legend in the film colony. Colleen Moore was a frequent visitor. "It was a miserable, run-down place," she said, "and those three *nuts* lived there. They were very witty and very bright. The parties were incredible. The ordinary days were incredible. They almost blew up the house once experimenting with aniline dyes. There always seemed to be a near-fatal accident in that place but things always turned out all right."

On the same day that *Manslaughter* was finished, a popular director named Arthur Rosson was giving a housewarming party in Beverly Hills. Leatrice had adored making that picture but now it was over and she was depressed. She didn't feel like going home to her mother and she wasn't sure she knew how to go about getting back together with Jack. There was a knock on her dressing-room door, and one of the actors suggested that the party might be just the thing to pick up her spirits. Leatrice thought so too. She slipped into a pastel, ruffled gown she had worn in the picture.

Rosson's house was already crowded when Leatrice and the others arrived. Some of the men were swimming in the new pool and there was dancing on the terrace under the glow of Japanese lanterns. Around midnight, more guests arrived, coming from another party. Jack was with them, one arm around Bebe Daniels, who was dressed in heavy black satin slit down to her navel and in full Theda Bara makeup. Leatrice tried to ignore them. There was no way she could compete with a woman like Bebe Daniels. But Jack kept trying to catch her eye even while he was dancing with Bebe. Finally he asked her to dance. A few dances later, she agreed to go home with him. They slipped quietly away from the terrace and walked around the house, sticking to the shadows so that no one would see them leaving together. As they came around the front to get into Jack's car, the entire party, Bebe Daniels included, spilled out onto the lawn cheering and pelting them with rice provided by Mrs. Rosson.

The following morning, as they sat up in bed, Paul Bern appeared with a newspaper. The headline read: THE GILBERTS DEFINITELY SEPA-RATE.

Leatrice moved in and became resident den mother on King's Road until the group broke up. Carey Wilson was married, but separated from his wife, Hopie, who lived in New York with her father. Carey told them horrifying stories about her. "She's a bloodsucking, life-destroying bitch." Once, he said, she attacked him with his own silk umbrella and fractured his skull. "She's a monster. A behemoth." His friends had never seen her, but they imagined a Marie Dressler look-alike with the disposition of Caligula.

One afternoon Leatrice went to answer the doorbell. On the doorstep, she found a tiny blonde girl with tears welling up in her violet-blue eyes.

"Is my Cawey here?" she lisped. "I'm Hopie Wilthon."

After the initial shock of the introduction, Leatrice was outraged at the way Carey had misrepresented this delicate creature. She invited Hopie inside and went looking for Carey the dirty dog.

"Your wife is downstairs," she said, waking him from a nap.

"She can't be," he gasped.

"Well, she is," Leatrice told him. "I'm making her a pot of tea right now."

"Tell her I'm coming right down."

He did. Without another word, he leaped from the second-story window, slashed through the canvas top of his car, and roared away down the hill.

Somehow, Hopie managed to catch up with him later and they agreed to a reconciliation. The Wilsons bought a house in Beverly Hills and resumed married life, for a few years anyway.

Leatrice and Jack went house-hunting too. One night as they were out walking, they noticed a cottage on the corner of Sweetzer and Fountain Avenues in Hollywood. It was small and white, with a steep roof and a garden like the place in Laurel Canyon. It looked like home. They rang the doorbell and offered a ridiculous price to the elderly couple who answered. The deal was made on the spot.

After *Manslaughter*, De Mille released Leatrice to make two pictures for George Melford, who was working at the Paramount Studio in Astoria, Queens. It meant going East for three months, another long separation. Jack particularly dreaded the prospect, for several reasons beyond missing her. First, Mary Zeidler would be going with her, and Jack was all too aware of the sort of subtle mischief Mary could do. Second, he dreaded the prospect of being lonely and frustrated at Fox while Leatrice was being lionized in New York. Jack still earned the much greater salary, but most of his pictures were trashy five-reelers and he had none of the perquisites of being a star. Leatrice had her limousine and hair-

Jack, then Cecil, Gilbert at age eleven.
(*Leatrice Gilbert Fountain*)

Ida Adair, Jack's mother, who died
when he was thirteen. (*Leatrice
Gilbert Fountain*)

Jack's first lead had him playing a hunchback who falls in love with a blind girl (Enid
Bennett) in *A Princess in the Dark* (1917). (*George Eastman House*)

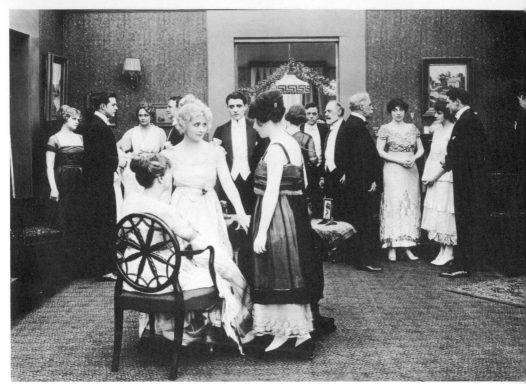

Eighteen-year-old Jack in
Hater of Men (1917). The
blonde he's pining for is
Bessie Barriscale. *(George
Eastman House)*

Leatrice Joy and Jack as
featured players in *Three X
Gordon* (1918). *(Leatrice Joy)*

Leatrice Joy (*Leatrice Gilbert Fountain*)

Jack and Leatrice Joy in Tijuana. (*Leatrice Gilbert Fountain*)

Barbara Bedford and Jack in *Gleam O'Dawn* (1922).

Left: On the set of *The Count of Monte Cristo* (1922). Standing next to camera: Robert Florey, technical director; center: Emmett Flynn, director; far right: Jack. *(Robert Florey)*

Below: Jack with Phyllis Haver in *The Snob* (1924). Jack enjoyed playing unsympathetic and offbeat roles. *(George Eastman House)*

The ballroom scene from *The Merry Widow* (1925). The servant in the lower left corner is Jack's father. Jack met him for the first time when he was hired as an extra.

Roy D'Arcy, Mae Murray, and Jack in a scene from *The Merry Widow*. *(George Eastman House)*

A rare photo from *La Bohème*; Jack as Rudolfo.

With Eleanor Boardman in *Bardelys the Magnificent* (1926). *(George Eastman House)*

Jack meets Greta Garbo for the first time in *Flesh and the Devil*, the film that sparked the romance between Jack and Garbo—both on- and off-screen. *(George Eastman House)*

Lars Hanson, Garbo, and Jack, from *Flesh and the Devil*. *(George Eastman House)*

Garbo and Gilbert *(George Eastman House)*

Taking a break on the set of *Flesh and the Devil. (Leatrice Gilbert Fountain)*

Garbo and Jack planned a double wedding with King Vidor and Eleanor Boardman. Jack posed with the wedding party while waiting for Garbo, who stood him up. Top row, fourth from left: Mrs. L. B. Mayer, King Vidor, Eleanor Boardman, Marion Davies, Irene Mayer. Second row: Jack is third from left, just behind Louis B. Mayer (with glasses). To the right of Mayer are Sam Goldwin and Irving Thalberg. *(Mrs. H. Behn)*

dresser and publicist, and was making much better movies. He begged her not to go, or at least to stay for only one picture. He knew that he was jealous of her success and was not very proud of it, nor was he proud of the quarrel they had the night before she left.

Leatrice was away the full three months. They wrote and phoned each other often, with Jack telling her frequently how much he missed her and how much he appreciated the little heart that she left next to his. (Leatrice had sewn a tiny red satin heart into his pajamas to wear while she was away.) For Leatrice, it was an exhausting trip with frustrations of its own. Gossip columns began linking her with almost any man with whom she was seen in public. In one of the pictures, *Java Head,* the second female lead, Jacqueline Logan, was having a flirtation with the director. The result was that every time Leatrice had a big dramatic scene, the director would cut to a close-up of Jacqueline looking out to sea or sniffing a rosebud—anything to attract the audience's attention to her instead of Leatrice.

When the picture was completed, Leatrice left for California, but instead of returning to Jack she moved into her mother's apartment "for a rest." "Jack thought it was a perfectly terrible thing for me to do," Leatrice said, "but it wasn't quite as heartless as it sounds. While I was East, De Mille assigned me to a very important film that I'd begin as soon as I returned. It was *The Ten Commandments.* De Mille would insist that Jack and I separate for it anyway. I didn't think I could stand another drag-out fight between Jack and De Mille."

Leatrice remembers this period of her life as insanely hectic but full of terrific fun. The separations from Jack made her very unhappy, and some of the fights made her miserable, but during those separations she dated every handsome man in town. She went to prizefights with Tom Mix, always sitting at ringside. One night, one of the fighters came through the ropes and landed at their feet; Tom Mix picked up two broken teeth and dropped them in her lap, and she nearly fainted. She went dancing with Richard Dix and Charlie Farrell, and also had a flirtation with Tommy Meighan. "Everyone fell in love with Tommy Meighan. He was such a big handsome teddy bear. You could do anything to him, upstage him, take his lines, he'd just stand there and smile at you."

Dorothy Herzog interviewed Jack for *Photoplay* for the first time in 1923. Later she wrote of that first meeting. Jack was reasonably well known but not famous, and with a reputation of being "a difficult man to get along with . . . a temperamental, bombastic, broadside slinger of ye President's English. Sol Wurtzel, Fox's studio manager, frustrated Jack's every effort to get better stories and pictures, and Jack was sick of starring in trite five-reelers made in two weeks with mediocre directors and released to small movie houses scattered throughout the country. He was having a great deal of trouble with Leatrice Joy then. They scrapped, loved and hated, and the wartime conditions of their household served as a barometer for Jack's disposition."

"Better watch your step with Jack Gilbert," Dorothy was cautioned. She approached the young actor gingerly but, to her surprise, found him relaxed and charming. He spoke of his troubles at the studio, and she reported, "His temperament comes from an unremitting desire to make good pictures, believable honest stories with enough money to make them properly. That may not be what the studio wants for him, but I would not call Jack Gilbert temperamental."

A few months later, Dorothy went to see him again. He was pacing up and down and chain-smoking.

"'What's the matter?' I asked.

"'Leatrice. She's left me again,' he said. Of course, it was De Mille's doing. He refused to put her in leading roles as long as she remained with Jack. Since Leatrice refused to abandon her career, they separated for the duration of the picture."

It was shortly after this 1923 interview that Jack was assigned to *Cameo Kirby*, a fine drama written by Booth Tarkington about a Southern gambler. It was John Ford's first movie using the name John Ford. Before that he was Jack Ford, and before that Sean O'Feeney. Rowland V. Lee's brother Bob wrote the scenario, and eighteen-year-old Jean Arthur made her movie debut in the picture. For a change, a Jack Gilbert movie was well written, beautifully directed, and properly financed. John Ford added a breakneck paddle-wheeler race down the Mississippi, the riverbanks lined with cheering spectators. It was an excellent movie, very popular, and Jack Gilbert began to attract the attention of other producers in Hollywood.

During the filming of *Cameo Kirby*, a misunderstanding lead to another separation. Cecilia De Mille, Cecil's daughter, had invited Leatrice to drive out with her in her father's limousine to watch the filming of the parting of the Red Sea. Jack had left work early that day to be home with Leatrice and had no idea where she'd gone. When, in late afternoon, he saw De Mille's limousine pull into the driveway and Leatrice emerge all smiles, he was sure she'd gone to see De Mille. Actually, she and Cecilia had spent the day dressed up as extras in the Exodus scene. Disappointed, jealous, and angry, Jack grabbed her by the shoulders and shook her violently. She was furious; no one, including Jack, had ever laid hands on her before and no one would again. She ordered Jack out of the house and he moved that night to the

[84]

Athletic Club. When *The Ten Commandments* was finished, she left for a long vacation in Honolulu.

Paul Bern telephoned her aboard ship just before sailing time. "Jack's waiting here by the phone," he said. "Just say the word and they'll hold the ship until he gets there. Make it a second honeymoon for you both."

But Leatrice was exhausted. She'd made five pictures in a row almost without a break. She was nearly hysterical with fatigue. Leatrice said no, and sailed off alone to the most romantic spot she'd ever seen.

Honolulu in 1923 was a paradise. And Leatrice was received like royalty. She was entertained by the Dillinghams, and Don Blanding, the "Poet Laureate of the Islands," wrote her a tender poem. Children were named after her and a public garden was dedicated to her. But she couldn't enjoy it entirely. She missed Jack. His brooding face seemed to be everywhere on *Cameo Kirby* billboards.

While she was away, Jack thought long and hard about their marriage, asking himself what he could do to be a better husband. He adored her, he wanted to live with her, and he also wanted a child by her.

Upon her return, he met her at the dock in his new red roadster. But Mary Zeidler was also there, and Leatrice had already planned to go home with her mother in her own limousine. "Am I at least as important to you as your limousine?" he asked quietly. When Leatrice hesitated, he walked away toward his car and stood near it for a while. Next he heard Mary Zeidler explain that the limousine was not there. Leatrice's brother had borrowed it to impress a client he was hoping to sign. "However," she said, pointing to Pauline and Harry Lucas, two friends from New Orleans who had driven her down in their car, "the Lucases will drive us home." Leatrice looked at the battered old car the Lucases drove, then at the reporters and movie fans who were watching, and then at Jack and his handsome roadster. Jack knew what she was thinking. He climbed deliberately into his car and slowly drove away. He did not speak to her again until she called him several weeks later.

They arranged to meet privately in a big Baptist church in Hollywood, halfway between their house and Jack's club. He was pacing up and down outside when she arrived. Together they went into the empty, shadowed church and sat for two or three hours in a pew near the back. They talked and wept. Leatrice and Jack agreed that they loved each other and were not happy apart. They also agreed to give the marriage another try. As for Leatrice having a baby, that was impossible, she said. It would mean interrupting her career at its most crucial point. Her fan mail already exceeded that of any other star on the Famous Players lot.

[85]

She was about to tell him what De Mille would say if he thought she was even considering such a thing when Jack put his fingertips to her lips.

"Don't mention his name, Leatrice," he said coldly. "Don't mention that name in any discussion about our child or about our lives together."

"Jack, I just can't have a baby now," she pleaded.

"Leatrice," he told her, "I'm going to have a child. If you won't have a child by me, I'm going to go out and find a prostitute who will." Leatrice was quite sure that he meant it. Just before Christmas of 1923, Leatrice "heard the rustle of angel wings."

Jack was mad with happiness. He showered her with presents, jewelry, and books on child-rearing. He dove into the role of prospective parent. Although Leatrice had an easy pregnancy and never suffered from morning sickness, Jack threw up every morning for three months. He bought Christmas toys and insisted on having a Christmas tree for the Gilbert-to-be, which he decorated himself. He was protective in the extreme. He took Leatrice to see John Barrymore in *Dr. Jekyll and Mr. Hyde* and brought her out halfway through the picture because it was "too morbid for a woman in her condition to see." He even tried to stop drinking. He didn't entirely, but he cut his consumption sharply.

Leatrice made one more picture before her condition became known. It was called *Triumph*, with Rod La Rocque. La Rocque was a family friend and one of the very few who was in on the secret. He almost had heart failure when he had to carry Leatrice out of a burning building five times before De Mille was satisfied. For the first four takes he'd been holding her like a crate of eggs.

At last, everything was beginning to go Jack's way. He had the woman he loved, his baby was on the way, and he was gaining new respect among some important people. His friend Ken Hawks scolded him for wasting his time at Fox. Ken's brother Howard took Jack to meet Irving Thalberg, Hollywood's boy-wonder producer who had achieved astonishing success before he was twenty-three years old.

Thalberg saw Jack act for the first time in *Cameo Kirby*. He said to Howard Hawks, "Fox doesn't know what they have in Gilbert. He could be a star."

Hawks himself had been hoping to sign Jack with Paramount now that Jack's contract with Fox was nearing its end. One day, when he was about to approach Jack with the deal he'd worked out, he had a lunch date with Irving Thalberg. Thalberg was late and apologized, saying, "Well, I've just signed Jack Gilbert for MGM. Now we'll see what he can do."

No one can say, of course, what would have happened had Jack signed with Hawks instead of Thalberg. In Howard Hawks he had a friend who appreciated what he could do on the screen, a man who began as a writer and became Jack's kind of director. Basically a storyteller who had few peers in his ability to sustain mood and atmosphere, Hawks went on to make such classics as *The Dawn Patrol*, *Scarface*, *Bringing Up Baby*, *Sergeant York*, *Red River*, and *The Thing*. He had little patience with the stylistic construction or the technical razzle-dazzle in which many of the directors of the period indulged themselves. His films called attention to themselves and not to the director. Perhaps, with better luck, Jack might have become just as big a star, a more lasting star, and eventually a fine director himself.

·eight·

THE year 1924 saw a collision that was one of the most dramatic and vicious in the history of the motion-picture industry. MGM had just been formed and Louis B. Mayer was on his way to becoming one of the most powerful and dangerous men in Hollywood. Jack emerged from leading-man status and became a star, soon to be one of the biggest box-office draws ever. And Leatrice let herself be swayed by one person too many and filed for divorce just weeks before I was born.

Metro-Goldwyn-Mayer began with the old Metro studio, which was owned largely by Marcus Loew, who was also president of the Loew's theater chain based in New York. For some time, Metro had been making indifferent pictures that were continually over budget. Marcus Loew had just about decided to sell the studio, but first he scheduled a visit to the West Coast to see for himself what the problems were. Metro's management, naturally, was ready for him and put on a persuasive show designed to prove that the officers were doing a marvelous job under difficult circumstances and that a better run of luck was just around the corner. Marcus Loew, however ignorant of the moviemaking business, was no dummy. While there, he decided to tour a studio nearby that seemed to be doing very well. He'd never been crazy about the head man, Louis B. Mayer, a crude and semi-literate man who spoke with a thick Yiddish accent. Mayer had grown up the son of a junk dealer and had learned to fight defending himself against Jew-baiting hoodlums. He was a complex man, a conniver and schemer with a strong sentimental streak and a regard for his mother that was close to idolatry. But Mayer seemed to know how to manage his resources. And what he lacked in polish was more than compensated for by his production chief, a bright and gracious young man named Irving Thalberg. However impressed Loew might have been with Mayer's Mission Road operation, the problem with Metro remained vexing and unsolved. Deciding to think about it for a while, Loew got back on the train and returned to New York, catching a cold en route. Marcus Loew then went to Palm Beach, where he recovered sufficiently to attend a party. There he was introduced to the president of another film company, Frank Godsol, who headed the Goldwyn Company. Sam Goldwyn was no longer involved, but the studio, which stood on the old Ince–Triangle grounds, retained his name.

Godsol, also an absentee owner much of the time, wasn't making any money either. He hinted strongly that he'd be pleased if Loew would take the Goldwyn Company off his hands. Marcus Loew began thinking. If instead of abandoning Metro they enlarged it, expanded the facilities, cranked out more pictures, and found a hands-on manager who knew what he was doing, they might be able to turn a decent profit. He sent for his partners—Robert Rubin, a New York lawyer, and Nicholas Schenck, his chief executive in charge of theaters—and arranged the acquistion of the Goldwyn Company through a simple exchange of stock. The management question was decided almost as easily. Robert Rubin, a cultivated, Irving Thalberg type, had served as Louis B. Mayer's counsel since 1915. He strongly recommended Mayer. Loew, fresh from the West Coast with a favorable impression of Mayer's ability, was quick to agree. Loew and Schenck bought out Mayer's entire studio, basically a shoestring operation, for about $76,000 and put Mayer under contract as vice-president and general manager at $1,500 per week. Much more important, Mayer and Rubin conspired to slip in a clause giving twenty percent of the profits to the so-called "Mayer group," consisting of Mayer, Thalberg, and, of course, Rubin, who'd brought them together with Loew. Marcus Loew was fully aware of the clause but he didn't much care. At this point he was only hoping for profits, and he was perfectly willing to share them if they came. But he did not expect the enormous sums of money that would be involved once the Metro-Goldwyn-Mayer Company began to take off on the coattails off such stars as Gilbert and Garbo. Schenck in particular grew to resent the arrangement, and a rift appeared between Schenck and Mayer that widened with the publication of each successive profit statement. The men became bitter enemies, each trying to squeeze the other out. The eventual winner of the battle would be the man that controlled—even more than the purse strings—the most valuable properties MGM possessed: its stars, and especially the actor who would become its biggest star. After Metro-Goldwyn-Mayer came into being, on April 10, 1924, Jack Gilbert was one of the first artists to sign an MGM contract.

Jack was, and for some years remained, utterly oblivious to the corporate struggles that were mentioned periodically in the press. He was busy having the time of his life. Corporate affairs, the wheelings and dealings of the money-men, interested him only in terms of their good or ill effect upon any movie he was making at the time. Jack wasn't naïve; on the contrary, he understood better than most the business of making movies, the need to show profits, and the uses of money. But partly to his credit and mostly to his peril, Jack never understood power.

Victor Heerman had left Fox to join MGM about the same time as Jack. He remembered visiting the lot one Sunday morning to pick up a manuscript. The sprawling studio was empty, the broad streets and stages, the stretches of lawn deserted. Ahead of him, however, he saw one lone man wandering aimlessly outside the dressing rooms. Drawing closer, he recognized Jack Gilbert, a dazed smile on his face.

"What are you doing here?" he asked. "Don't you take Sundays off like the rest of us?"

Jack grinned sheepishly. "I just can't stay away from this place, Victor. It's so great to be a part of anything like this. I just can't believe I'm really here."

Jack was in actor's heaven. To work in a studio where money was not always the first consideration, to be considered a serious and competent actor and not just camera fodder, to be told repeatedly that he had a brilliant future—these were what Jack had desired but had begun to fear would never come. Now, perhaps, he would catch up with Leatrice, even pass her. Perhaps the days of being Leatrice Joy's husband were at an end.

Irving Thalberg promised as much. He believed in Jack. More than that, Irving Thalberg was rapidly becoming one of Jack's closest friends. No other actor was ever so close to the young production chief. Thalberg, a shy, gentle, thoughtful, and literate man, usually chose his friends from among the management ranks and particularly from among the writers. Writers as a rule were far more interesting and less self-centered than actors. In general, they had better minds, quicker wits, were better conversationalists, and had ideas worth hearing. Jack was one of the very few actors of Thalberg's acquaintance who also possessed those qualities.

Thalberg had been brought to Hollywood four years earlier by Carl Laemmle to be an office assistant. Within a year he was virtually running Laemmle's studio and making big money for it. In 1922, Thalberg was introduced to another newcomer, Louis B. Mayer, who was then operating his small studio on Mission Road. Mayer was a man of similar ambition and dedication, but there the similarity ended. Thalberg's family were solid, middle-class German Jews with a scholarly bent, while Mayer's family were Russian-Jewish peasants. Where Thalberg was gentle and kind, Mayer was street-tough.

Mayer was forty years old when he met Irving Thalberg. He admired the younger man's easy grace, his education, and his class. Thalberg had been a sickly child who was heavily dependent on his mother and remained close to her, a fact that further endeared him to Mayer. Mayer hired Thalberg away from Carl Laemmle and thereafter conspired with Thalberg's mother, Henrietta, to keep her son alive and well. It would become a legendary partnership.

For all of Thalberg's brilliance, he was far from sophisticated. Sheltered by his mother, Thalberg had almost no experience with nightlife, partying, fast women, or even lively women. A night on the town with Jack Gilbert was a visit to a world he hardly knew existed. Thalberg learned that a certain amount of silliness and excess would not lead him down a path to ruin. Jack, for his part, delighted in Thalberg's discovery that women were neither frightening nor fragile and that many actually enjoyed sex just as much as men did.

Thalberg's mother, however, who had kept Irving in woolen underwear until long after his arrival in Hollywood, was less than enthusiastic about Jack Gilbert's tutelage. Her son's health was frail enough without Gilbert keeping him up until all hours as often as twice a week. Henrietta Thalberg complained to Louis Mayer, who promptly summoned Jack to his office for what would be the first and most benign of their confrontations. Mayer scarcely knew Jack, but he knew Leatrice and liked her. (He liked her so much, in fact, that she was one of the very few actresses with whom he permitted his own two daughters to associate.) Leatrice was a nice girl, a good actress who did what she was told, and she was devoted to her mother. That was enough for Louis B. Mayer. "You've got a beautiful wife," he told Jack. "Why don't you leave Irving alone and stay home with her and keep your nose clean? You gonna be a star, and gotta have dignity. You gotta keep your nose clean." Jack listened agreeably, thanked Mayer for his interest, and went on doing exactly what he pleased. So did Irving Thalberg. Leatrice, by her own account, fully understood how important it was for Jack to be seen around town and written about, whether she felt up to joining him or not, especially after signing a new studio contract. And especially in the company of Irving Thalberg. She'd made the same sort of rounds during her own buildup with Famous Players. But as her pregnancy developed she chose to stay home and out of sight. Leatrice was also beginning to experience periods of depression that she tried hard to hide from Jack.

One of Jack's more obligatory evenings out was a command appearance before a sixtyish, red-haired dowager who was a cultural phenomenon that could only have happened in Hollywood. Her name was Elinor Glyn—"Madame" Glyn, as she liked to be called.

Elinor Glyn was well educated, of good family, and British to the point of parody. She'd come to Hollywood a successful novelist, her books having caused a sensation on both sides of the Atlantic. They were popular trash, much like today's paperback romances, but they were considered quite daring and explicit for their time. *Three Weeks* was about a Ruritanian queen who had a three-week love affair with a young British aristocrat. They actually made love on a bed of roses, later switching to tiger skins. Another story was called *Six Days*, in which two lovers are on a French battlefield when a bomb goes off and buries them in a cave. Happily, the bomb also buries a priest, who is able to marry them before he dies of his injuries. The couple spends the next six days alternately making love and digging out.

With these credentials Elinor Glyn had no trouble establishing herself as the epitome of the liberated, sexually aware, modern woman. She had "It." Everyone knew that because she said so. She also reserved the exclusive right to decide who else had "It." You could be absolutely sure that "It" meant sex appeal, and then she'd confuse you by bestowing "It" on Will Rogers. Clara Bow, whose sexual adventures were later rumored to have included the entire University of Southern California football team, appeared in a movie called *It*, written by Elinor, and was publicly proclaimed to be the consummate "It" girl. However, when Clara Bow was overheard referring to the great lady as "that shit-head," Elinor tightened up her definition to include elegance and style.

Apart from writing for movies, elegance and style became Elinor's stock in trade. She'd no sooner arrived in Hollywood than she noticed that almost everyone was doing almost everything wrong. Not one hostess in a hundred had any idea how to pour. Most didn't even know what Elinor was talking about. Nor did they know how to manage servants, or how to select a wine, or set a table, or choose a guest list. In truth, Elinor had a point. Almost all the movie folk she encountered were basically simple people who'd suddenly found themselves swimming in cash and living in twenty-room mansions with only the foggiest idea of how to conduct themselves. Many had never read a book in their lives. What they knew about style they'd learned from watching movies. Elinor started by taking Gloria Swanson in hand, and soon most of the major studios were paying her to hold classes in deportment for their executives and stars. In no time, it seemed that half of Hollywood was affecting a British accent and calling each other "old chap" and "dahling" instead of "pal."

Hollywood, presuming Elinor to be the real stuff, took her very seriously. Charlie Chaplin, himself British, was one exception. But when he was summoned to the great lady's presence, he went—largely out of curiosity. He tried to keep a straight face when Elinor languidly offered him a gloved hand at a level that required either a deep bow or a genuflection, but he began to giggle.

"You disappoint me, Mr. Chaplin," she said, mentally withdrawing any suggestion that Chaplin might possess the faintest trace of "It." "I don't find you at all funny."

"That's too bad, Madame," Chaplin replied. "I think you're a scream."

The two never spoke again.

MGM had acquired the rights to another Elinor Glyn book, *His Hour*. Only an hour of lovemaking this time, but with a Russian prince and a female British aristocrat. Thalberg had decided to cast Jack Gilbert in the starring role of Prince Gritzko as his first vehicle for the new studio. Jack was unenthusiastic. He'd read the book because one couldn't walk into a Hollywood home without finding all of Glyn's works on prominent display. He thought it was a piece of trash. Besides, Jack felt he'd already played enough dashing-lover roles to last a lifetime. "Of course it's trash," Thalberg answered, "but it's what the public wants. Do this role and you'll get some of the best exposure of your career. Afterward, we'll see if we can find something more interesting for you."

Having persuaded Jack, Thalberg's next step would be to persuade Madame Glyn that Jack Gilbert was the only possible choice for the role of Prince Gritzko. That was essential because Glyn co-produced most of her movies and insisted on supervising the filming. Thalberg brought Jack with him to a reception being given for Elinor at the Ambassador Hotel, first warning Jack against any repetition of the Charlie Chaplin incident. Jack promised he'd behave.

It took some effort. When Jack was brought forward for his introduction, he found Glyn swathed in colored veils and wearing a turban. She turned her head slowly, peering at him through layers of chiffon before raising her hand to be kissed and saying, "Ahhh, behold the black stallion."

Jack bit his tongue and groped for polite small talk, in the course of which he announced that he was soon to be a father. Glyn looked stricken. She tore aside her veils and seized him by both hands. "This must not *be!*" she said fiercely. "Jack Gilbert a father? Don't be ridiculous. The Great Lover seen changing diapers? Pushing a pram? It is laughable. Every time that child appears in public, it will remind people that you are getting older. In five years you'll be the father of a five-year-old child. Then a ten-year-old child. You can see for yourself that it's out of the question."

Jack returned home that evening amused by his theatrical encounter with Elinor but also more than a little flattered. He'd had his first real taste of the star treatment. For Leatrice he acted out a full account of the evening, including Elinor's outraged reaction to the prospect of Jack having a child. Jack brushed it off, according to Leatrice, but she told me she couldn't help thinking that he half believed it, that, being so close to success, Elinor's words made him fear slipping back into oblivion. He needn't have worried. Jack's glamour and easy charm soon overcame any objections Madame Glyn may have had to his impending fatherhood—or anything else. At the studio's suggestion, he escorted her to parties and openings, including one memorable evening at the Venice amusement pier, when Jack maneuvered Elinor and her voluminous draperies over every air-jet in the floor. She was dazzled. She adored him, and soon proclaimed to the waiting world that Jack had "It" in abundance. Only Jack could do justice to the role of Prince Gritzko.

His Hour was produced, starring John Gilbert and Aileen Pringle, and directed by King Vidor, who would share some of Jack's greatest screen triumphs. Cedric Gibbons was art director in what was also his first picture for MGM. He and Jack became lifelong friends. Gibbons went on to become acknowledged as the most influential production designer in the history of American films. (He also designed the Oscar statuette and eventually won eleven of them.)

Audiences loved *His Hour*. Aileen Pringle played an Englishwoman named Tamara, and Jack was the Russian prince out to seduce her. Prince or not, he still had to fight a duel to win first crack at her from another Russian cad. Then he maneuvered her into passing a stormy night at his hunting lodge, where he pressed his advantage. The virtuous Tamara knew a fate worse than death when she saw one. She grabbed a pistol and leveled it not at him but at her own head, threatening to blow a hole in it if he didn't quit kissing her. It was a taxing situation and she soon swooned from exhaustion. Prince Gritzko became suddenly penitent and carried her tenderly to her room. Next morning, she awoke to notice that part of her bodice had been unbuttoned. Gritzko admitted opening it . . . but only to check for a heartbeat. Being nobody's fool, Tamara announced that now the viper would have to marry her and, being a good scout at heart, he did.

There is a scene near the beginning of the picture in which the two lovers are being driven in a troika, dashing across the snowy steppes, making passionate love under a bearskin rug, beginning with butterfly kisses, Jack's eyelashes brushing against Aileen Pringle's cheek, then kissing the tips of her fingers and moving upward. Apart from the humor, it remains an intensely erotic moment on film. It was a sensation on the neighborhood screen. Everyone was pleased but Jack.

Both Jack and Aileen got good reviews. But Jack was adamant about not playing any more such parts. He told Louella Parsons, "I refuse to play any more great-lover roles. Many a better man than I has been ruined by being a perfect lover. *His Hour* brought me more fame than anything else but it is the one picture in my life I would.rather not talk about."

Aside from his feelings about the Elinor Glyn sort of pap, Jack was keenly aware of the dangers of being typed in one kind of role. Playing the same part over and over again shortened a career. Natural aging took a particularly heavy toll among many romantic leads. Character actors like Lon Chaney and Wallace Beery, on the other hand, could go on forever and get a lot more satisfaction out of what they did. Romantic leads were such one-dimensional characters that they rarely got a chance to develop the craft of acting. He felt just as strongly about romantic female leads. "I like women. Women are interesting. And women are human beings just like the rest of us. I can't believe the public wants a heroine who is nothing more than that chaste dumbbell in *His Hour*."

Laurette Taylor was a vivacious forty-two-year-old who had been the toast of Broadway for at least ten years when she came west to make a movie of her greatest stage success, *Peg o' My Heart*. Laurette completed her second movie, *Happiness*, with King Vidor directing, and had a brief fling with him. That out of the way, she settled into Vidor's "magic circle," a glittery Sunday-afternoon tennis group made up of his brightest and most beautiful friends. They met each week at Pickfair, which King was renting from Douglas Fairbanks while his own new house was being built on Tower Road.

Laurette Taylor was a woman of inexhaustible vitality. Upon meeting Jack one Sunday at Vidor's house and getting to know him over the next two or three weekends, she declared that she had finally met someone who could play as hard as she did. She found him not only handsome and witty but, rarest of all, kind. She fell wildly, besottedly, and publicly in love with him.

With Leatrice pregnant and brooding at home, Laurette and Jack scampered all over Pickfair like children at play. They made reel after reel of silly home movies, some with Jack doing John Barrymore imitations and Laurette playing a simpering Mary Pickford. Soon Sunday afternoons were not enough for Laurette. She began showing up at Jack's dressing room, on the set, and even calling him at home. She would talk about the marvelous John Gilbert to anyone who would listen, and before long their romance, whether real or presumed, became the talk of Hollywood.

Leatrice's mood turned blacker. She'd taken a terrible risk with her career, and C. B. De Mille refused even to talk to her. Now it seemed that she was about to lose everything—her career *and* her husband. Lois Wilson observed Leatrice's anguish firsthand; she lived next door and they saw each other every day. She noticed that after Leatrice became pregnant she refused to go anywhere with Jack. Leatrice had ordered an extravagant maternity wardrobe, designed by Adrian, but she wouldn't go out. She was convinced she looked ugly, deformed, and nothing Jack, Lois, or even her mother said did any good. She hated the way she looked and she would not let anyone see her. As Lois Wilson said:

> She just couldn't bear it. She thought people would laugh at her funny shape. She encouraged Jack to go on up to King's house on Sunday afternoons, then she'd cry her eyes out when he was gone.
>
> Finally when she did go, very much the injured madonna, it was too late. Leatrice knew that Laurette was chasing after Jack, and she suspected Jack was enjoying it. She never forgave him. It was naughty of Jack. After all, she was risking her career just to please him; stars didn't have babies in those days. Still, it wasn't all Jack's fault either. He tried to bring her along. He didn't act like a man with anything to hide. It was all a shame, really. Jack was so crazy to have that baby.

The day Leatrice did go to Pickfair, she showed up late, in the company of the Barney Glazers. Whatever she suspected, all she walked in on was another of the group's home movies. But there was Laurette, playing both star and director, blocking out scenes and ordering people about. "No, *no*, Jack darling. You were over here with me. Don't you remember?" And then she would smile sweetly at Leatrice, who sat alone under a beach umbrella knitting furiously. Later, when the movie was shown, it was full of Jack and Laurette mugging and kissing and being silly, with frequent cuts back to Leatrice, very pregnant and scowling over her knitting needles. Leatrice seethed but said nothing.

Jack began work on his next picture. The film was *He Who Gets Slapped,* and Irving Thalberg had selected it for him without asking his opinion. It was a small romantic part, the starring roles going to Lon Chaney and Norma Shearer. The director was the brilliant Victor Seastrom, who had come from Sweden the year before. Jack read the script and became distressed and then alarmed. There were only twenty scenes for him in the entire picture. He'd convinced himself that he was rotten in *His Hour* before it was even released. Now he was sure the studio knew it too, and they were punishing him for that, for expressing independent ideas, and for pushing too hard for better stories. He was being taught a lesson; maybe they were even trying to force him out. Jack stormed into Thalberg's office.

"Look," he said, "if you want to get rid of me you don't have to give me rotten parts to do it. I'll leave today and it won't cost you a cent!"

Thalberg, not yet accustomed to Jack's soaring highs and lows, sat back in his chair and stared at him in amazement. "Have you gone mad?" he asked quietly. "That part, small as it is, will do you more good than anything you've done so far."

Jack was doubtful but relieved. On Thalberg's advice, he agreed to take the script home and read it more carefully. In the end he accepted the assignment.

The picture opened to rave reviews. *The New York Times* said: ". . . a picture which defies one to write about it without indulging in superlatives . . . so beautifully told, so flawlessly directed that we imagine it will be held up as a model by all producers." *Photoplay* said: "The acting is remarkably fine. Norma Shearer and John Gilbert as the lovers are delightful."

He Who Gets Slapped is still regarded as a small masterpiece. It's the story of a brilliant scientist, disappointed in love, who gives up the academic life to become a circus clown. Norma Shearer and Jack Gilbert play two young bareback riders in love. When the aristocrat who cuckolded Lon Chaney, now the clown, shows up with designs on Norma, Chaney gets his revenge, sacrificing himself in the process and leaving the lovers free to marry. Thalberg turned out to be right once more. Jack's popularity grew enormously after playing this small romantic part in such distinguished company. His fan mail increased and he was favorably mentioned by critics who'd overlooked him before.

Jack now began another picture, in a role he chose for himself. The studio owned a novel called *The Snob: The Story of a Marriage,* a bitter tale about an ambitious country schoolteacher who uses every means he can to move up the social ladder. The man is a scoundrel, a liar, a hypocrite, and an adulterer. He tries to reform in the end, but it's too late. His wife leaves him for a more decent man. The story had been lying around the lot because no leading man wanted to play such an unsympathetic role. Jack jumped at it. It was exactly what he was looking for, a part that would free him from being stereotyped as a lover. It called for uncommonly good acting rather than just a handsome face and a smile. Thalberg advised against the role, saying that such a negative part could cost him the support of his fans. But Jack was adamant, reminding Thalberg that he'd as much as given his word.

Despite the grim theme, the picture was a success. The reviewers raved: "John Gilbert is excellent . . . . a cruel difficult role and he did it well." "One of the finest entertainments the screen has reflected . . . . Jack Gilbert does the finest piece of acting of his career in the title role." "John Gilbert walks away with all the acting and Monta Bell's direction is deftly delightful."

Jack received a stack of angry letters from his fans accusing him of being cruel and heartless. He was delighted. Speaking of the role, he said, "A good many of my friends criticized my judgment in playing an unsympathetic character. To my mind it is the best judgment, because a leading man has almost no opportunity to show the slightest versatility. . . . The part in *The Snob* provided an opportunity for real characterization. He is likable in many ways for all his selfishness and conceit, and the character with its changes of emotions and poses gives a chance for a real psychological study of a complex personality."

Edith Goetz, Louis B. Mayer's daughter, remembers her father exploding at the breakfast table when he read one such quote by John Gilbert. "Goddamned intellectuals," he barked, "with their *cigarette holders!*" Using a cigarette holder, as Jack sometimes did, was one of the ways to convince Louis Mayer that you were unwholesome, decadent, and potentially troublesome.

But for now, Jack's troubles were all with Leatrice. Near the end of the summer of 1924, Laurette Taylor and her husband, her movies completed, packed up and left on the train to New York. The same evening, a telegram arrived for Jack, and Leatrice opened it. The wire was from Laurette, sent from the station. It read: DARLING, THANKS FOR THE ROSES. IT WAS EQUALLY HARD TO LEAVE YOU. ALWAYS, LAURETTE.

For Leatrice, after long months of unhappiness and jealousy, the telegram was the last straw. Leatrice chose to accept it as positive proof that Jack and Laurette had been carrying on behind her back all summer. Furious and humiliated, she left the house that evening and moved with her mother to a furnished apartment in Long Beach.

Jack returned home to find Leatrice gone. There was only the telegram. It took him all of a frantic night and well into the next day before he found someone who'd tell him where she'd gone. Uncertain of what to do next, he sent her an enormous basket of roses, together with a note that apologized for everything he could think of that might possibly have led to her leaving. The roses were an unfortunate choice. Leatrice telegraphed her reply: DARLING, THANKS FOR THE ROSES. IT WAS EQUALLY HARD TO LEAVE YOU. ALWAYS, LEATRICE.

He tried frantically to reach her, to talk to her. He sent a long letter that was hand-delivered by her chauffeur, but she refused to open it. Jack was desperate. He knew that if he drove to Long Beach he would certainly be turned away by Mary Zeidler, if she bothered to answer the door at all. He also knew that mother, daughter, and probably brother Billy would be having long conversations about him and their marriage. Mother Zeidler and Billy could hardly be counted on to improve the situation. What Jack needed, he decided, was an intermediary or two who were at least neutral. He prevailed upon Paul Bern, his former housemate, and Lois Wilson, and film writer Barney Glazer and his wife Alice. Each visited Leatrice, and between them they persuaded her to give Jack the benefit of the doubt. At least she would return home for the few weeks until the baby was born.

Leatrice drove back to the house without telling Jack she was coming. It was the middle of the afternoon. As she walked up the driveway, she could hear music blaring from the phonograph. The door was open and she entered. Her house was a shambles. Three drunken men were passed out on the floor. Ashtrays were spilled all over the rug and the place smelled like a brewery. Leatrice did not bother looking for Jack. She closed the door and returned to her mother. Leatrice engaged a lawyer the next day and filed for divorce on August 19, eight days later.

In her divorce papers she listed August 10, the Sunday just described, as the day she and Jack separated. She charged intemperance, cruelty, and ill temper. No mention was made of infidelity. She'd first pleaded with him, her complaint read, to give up the use of excessive intoxicants, but she left when "Gilbert and a number of his men friends were enjoying a wild carousal, wearing dressing gowns and pajamas. In the last year Gilbert continued to bring large quantities of liquor into their home. As a result her nerves became affected and on account of her delicate condition she is unable to work at present." She went on to claim she was without funds, and asked for alimony and hospital expenses prior to the trial.

If this whole business seems to have proceeded with indecent haste, considering that Leatrice was about to bear Jack's child, Jack had brother Billy and attorneys to thank for it. Both had persuaded Leatrice that she must file for divorce before the baby was born in order to make a child-custody suit more difficult. If Jack initiated such an action, and if he succeeded, she could be left with nothing at all. Even if he tried and failed, who knows what dreadful lies would be plastered across the nation's front pages? The argument touched her worst fears. It would mean public humiliation and Jack might just try it. After all, the baby was his idea, and everyone knew how thrilled he was at the prospect of becoming a father.

I was born three weeks later, on September 6, 1924. Mother named me Leatrice Joy II, *not* Leatrice Gilbert. (I learned that my name was Gilbert when I entered school.) And her brother Billy left word that under no circumstances was Jack to be allowed to see me. Later Billy assumed the title, which I called him until he died, of "Uncle Daddy."

Jack learned from a reporter that the baby had arrived. He raced to the hospital, where the nurses didn't have the heart to stop him. He held me in his arms until they had to take me from him. Jack sent Leatrice a thousand more roses, with a card that said simply, "I have seen our little daughter and I love her already." Eager to share the news with someone, he rushed to the Athletic Club and burst into the room of his old friend Rowland V. Lee, announcing breathlessly that he was a father. Rowland recalled:

> I had an early call in the morning, so I wasn't as thrilled to hear the news as I might have been another time. Jack didn't care. He raved for a while about this infant, then about how much he'd suffered during the past few weeks, how miserable he was at having failed Leatrice when she needed him, how he missed her, how he needed her. I pointed out that Leatrice probably hadn't had a great time either, and would he please get the hell out of there and let me get some sleep. He looked at me as if I were crazy. He said, "Rowland, I have a beautiful baby girl! Don't you understand? I'm a *father*."

Leatrice wrote a brief note from the hospital asking Jack to move out of their house as soon as possible, as she needed a home for her baby. Jack wrote and called; he hung around the hospital hoping she would change her mind and come back to him, but she refused to see or talk to him. He was further humiliated one day when he saw Leatrice's obstetrician, Dr. Coffee, and offered his hand. Coffee had been left with the impression that Jack had deliberately stayed away from Leatrice during her labor. He ignored Jack's hand and walked by without speaking.

Jack didn't give up, but he was hurt and becoming bitter. When he moved out of the Sweetzer Avenue house and into the Athletic Club, he left a quotation from Luke 6:38 on Leatrice's desk in a silver frame. It read: "For the same measure that ye mete withal it shall be measured to you again to full and overflowing."

In one interview, Jack confessed that he was hurt by the attitudes of some of Leatrice's friends. They still saw him as being selfishly insensitive to her state of mind during the pregnancy. And he admitted being caught up in his new career and less concerned than he might have been about Leatrice's. It was the first time in their marriage that he didn't feel inferior to her.

"I admit I was jealous," Jack told the interviewer. "But wouldn't any husband feel that way when a wife was earning a larger salary than he? She was a *star*. I wasn't even thought of for stardom at that time. I wanted Leatrice to believe I was just as good as she was.

"But she was a star first and foremost, and she couldn't forget that I was only a leading man. I couldn't tell her anything that she didn't know far better than I. She didn't want to be Mrs. John Gilbert, but Miss Leatrice Joy—De Mille star. . . . She would come home two hours late to dinner, too tired to talk about anything but *her* work at the studio. Now I wanted to do a little talking myself but I was only a leading man. . . . Love and warmed-over dinners don't go together, even in Hollywood. . . . I'd get angry and we'd quarrel. Then there were those separations for weeks at a time and the reconciliations. Each time . . . we were so much nearer the divorce courts."

Louis B. Mayer was outraged by the divorce, and particularly by its timing. MGM had just released *His Hour. He Who Gets Slapped* was being filmed; Jack's face was about to be spread across thousands of movie screens under the new MGM logo, and that "degenerate" had picked just this moment to show his true colors to the world! *Variety* headlined the story: LIQUOR IN BULK MADE LEATRICE JOY'S LIFE SAD. Almost every newspaper in the country carried a story entirely sympathetic to Leatrice, because nearly all of the stories were based largely on the language of her complaint, which was public record.

Irving Thalberg defended Jack, as did Howard Strickling, who was head of studio publicity, pointing out that the rhetoric cooked up by a teetotaler's divorce lawyer hardly made Jack a roaring drunk. He had never been known to drink while working, and, as for the rest of it, he had his own side to the story. But Mayer wasn't interested. All he knew was that Gilbert's "unwholesome" and "crazy" behavior had driven that nice girl back to her mother so the baby could be born in a decent home. It was a goddamned good thing, Mayer went on, that he was about to leave for Europe. Otherwise he would take care of Gilbert personally. "You either straighten this out while I'm gone," he told Thalberg and Strickland, "or I don't want to lay eyes on the son of a bitch when I get back."

Howard Strickling said, years later:

It was very strange, this thing between Mayer and Jack. Like he'd made up his mind to hate the guy from the first time he saw him. As far as I was concerned, Mayer was way off base in his feelings about Jack, but you couldn't tell him that. Anything good about Jack Gilbert, he didn't want to know. It was strange because Jack was always one of the good guys. I was just getting started out there and he was very kind to me. . . .

Not that he wasn't a little eccentric, and temperamental some-times. All the great actors were. But people now, today, say that Jack was crazy. It's the damnedest thing. He was one of the most interesting guys out here and one of the best liked. Jack liked to drink and now and then he'd tie one on, but he sure as hell wasn't unique. Now that I think of it, the real damage the divorce com-plaint did was to establish Jack's reputation as a boozer. Before that I bet no one ever gave a second thought to the amount he drank.

As for the effect of the divorce publicity, Jack did lose a little skin at first; he refused to defend himself in court or make coun-tercharges. But soon he began to get a lot of sympathy. There was something stark about the way Leatrice left just before the baby was born and then kept Jack from seeing it. And he was so solicitous about the baby, and about Leatrice, that people couldn't help feel-ing for the guy.

At the box office, the divorce had no negative effect at all that I could see. There really wasn't much of a mess to straighten out. Jack did a few interviews and told his side of the story, but he was careful not to take any jabs at Leatrice. I think he was still hoping to get back together with her.

Louis B. Mayer had gone to Europe to check on the progress of *Ben Hur*, which was shaping up to be the most expensive movie ever made. The picture was actually a Goldwyn project, a last-gasp attempt to re-store the prestige of that failing studio, and MGM ended up being stuck with it. The production was plagued with incompetence, dissension, and accidents, such as the near drowning of a hundred extras when their Roman galley caught fire and sank. Loew had already replaced most of the cast and crew with MGM people, including Fred Niblo as director. But now Niblo was also having trouble. Mayer visited the set, threatened to fire a few people (including Niblo), put the fear of God into everyone concerned, and then continued his tour of Europe. His second purpose was to survey the product of European filmmakers and perhaps do some talent scouting.

Victor Seastrom, who had directed Jack in *He Who Gets Slapped*, recommended that Mayer meet with another Swedish director and former colleague, Mauritz Stiller. The story most often told is that when Stiller showed his film *The Saga of Gösta Berling*, Mayer was taken with Greta Garbo, and hired Stiller as part of the package. Actually, no part of that story is precisely true. To start with, Mayer had seen *Gösta Berling* before he went to Europe. Lillian Gish asked him to look at it because she wanted the film's male star, Lars Hanson, to play opposite her in *The Scarlet Letter*. There's no record of Garbo having made a tremendous impression on Mayer or anyone else at that time. When Stiller showed the film to him again, in Berlin, he appears once more to have been less than thunderstruck. Mayer wired Victor Seastrom asking if Stiller was really that good. Seastrom wired back: he is—get him. Mayer then offered a contract to Stiller. It may or may not be true that Stiller insisted on his protégée Greta Garbo being part of the package. It seems doubtful, because Mayer wasn't all that eager to get Stiller in the first place, and he wasn't the type who was easily held up. Besides, it's usually forgotten that Mayer also offered contracts to Lars Hanson and to Mona Martenson, the other stars of the film. (Martenson didn't show up for another five years—and was a disaster when she did.) In any case, Garbo was on her way to Hollywood. The agreement stipulated that she was to arrive there not later than April 15, 1925, about four months hence. Mayer's parting words cautioned her to lose some weight before she showed up at MGM. "Americans don't like fat women," he said.

·nine·

J ACK, of course, had never heard of Greta Garbo. Leatrice remained
very much on his mind. As the year ended, he was still hoping that
she'd come to her senses before the divorce was final. The studio
didn't give him much time to brood. With Mayer in Europe, Irving
Thalberg had put Jack in another picture that he thought would move
him closer to becoming a major box-office attraction and therefore in-
dispensable to Mayer. It was during the shooting of that picture, *The
Wife of the Centaur*, that stories first began to emerge about Jack being
difficult to work with.

Leatrice recalled those stories:

> He had several arguments with King Vidor, who directed *The
> Wife of the Centaur*. But any talk about Jack being difficult didn't
> start with that picture. Remember, most actors at that time, includ-
> ing me, quietly did what they were told. Jack had been a director
> himself, and a writer, and he had ideas. Good ideas. To get along
> with Jack, all a director had to do was be courteous enough to
> listen and to understand that Jack was trying to make the best pic-
> ture possible. There wasn't any clash of egos. Jack hardly had any
> ego at all. He was his own toughest critic. But when an actor
> makes any kind of fuss, people always assume it's ego or tempera-
> ment.

King Vidor didn't think much of the picture. He said, "Jack and I
were both having hard times during *The Wife of the Centaur*. My marriage to Florence was on the rocks; Jack was still torn up about Leatrice.
The plot was silly. A neurotic writer leaves his sweet, young wife for
some older tootsie and then comes back to her. It might have hit close
to home. It shouldn't surprise anyone that Jack had his own ideas about
interpretation, or that he thought his insights were better than mine."

Another thing that upset Jack was Tom Ince's death under mysterious circumstances. He was devoted to Ince and always gave him credit for starting his career. About that time Jack said to a reporter, "Everyone that touches me seems to die young."

The Wife of the Centaur was released to reviews that were generally favorable. *Variety* called the picture "Another notch for John Gilbert." *The New York Review* said: "Gilbert adds to his growing laurels . . . not because he is probably the handsomest man on the screen today, but because of his undeniably genuine and versatile ability." *The Evening Graphic* enthused that "there was not a single flaw in his performance."

Thalberg was more than pleased. He decided to gamble on Jack, putting him in his first major production, *The Merry Widow*, and announced the decision with a blaze of publicity. Mae Murray would play the title role in the film version of this popular Franz Lehár operetta. The director would be a wild man named Erich von Stroheim. Von Stroheim had arrived in Hollywood in 1914 claiming to be the scion of a noble Prussian military family. He was actually the son of a Jewish hatter who'd emigrated from Prussia to Vienna, but no one asked many questions at the time. It was enough that he looked like a Prussian aristocrat. His appearance soon led to roles as the cruel, monocled hun, and he was made famous in studio advertisements as "The Man You Love to Hate."

The Armistice effectively ended the need for his services as an actor, so von Stroheim turned to directing. He made several movies whose themes usually centered around the sexual awakening of American women—lots of adultery and love triangles but also lots of attention to detail and to characterization. In those days of painted sets and grind-'em-out program fare, von Stroheim's meticulousness was a rarity. It was also expensive. The high costs he ran up were tolerated only because that same attention to detail was winning critical acclaim for his pictures, and in the case of *Blind Husbands*, financial success. Thalberg appreciated his genius despite von Stroheim's excesses. He reasoned that the combination of Erich von Stroheim as director and himself as the financially responsible manager could result in an occasional masterpiece that would even make money. But so far the path to these masterpieces had not been smooth. Thalberg had fired von Stroheim from a picture called *Merry-Go-Round*, but later inherited his *Greed* at the MGM merger. Not one to be content with a minor epic, von Stroheim had produced a staggering drama of human degradation. The first cut version of 47,000 feet had a running time of ten hours. (Irene Selznick remembers sitting numbly through it at the studio.) Once again, Thalberg fired him and turned the cutting over to others. Rex Ingram reduced it to 18,000 feet, with von Stroheim's approval, but the final butchered version was done by Joc W. Farnham under Thalberg's supervision. Still, some reviewers hailed the truncated version as a masterpiece, while others condemned it as "a vile epic of the sewer."

Mayer went wild. He already despised von Stroheim, having actually flattened the director when he remarked imprudently that "all women are whores." ("Nobody talks that way about women in my presence.") *Greed* didn't exactly extol feminine virtue either. Still, Thalberg, either confident of von Stroheim's genius or protecting his own production turf, insisted that the director be given another chance with *The Merry Widow*. When Mayer relented, von Strohcim almost got flattened again by announcing his terms, one of which was his refusal to use John Gilbert in the role. He wanted Norman Kerry, whom he'd worked with in *Merry-Go-Round*. Thalberg quickly took him out of Mayer's office and told him it was Gilbert or no one.

When Jack appeared on the set, von Stroheim welcomed him by saying, "Mr. Gilbert, I am forced to use you in my picture. I did not want you, but I will do everything in my power to make you comfortable." Although stung by the director's gracelessness, Jack knew that the insult was not gratuitous. It had long been part of von Stroheim's method to chop down any feelings of self-importance his actors might have, especially an actor with some knowledge of directing, then to build his characterizations from the blank and humbled shell that was left. For the first two weeks of shooting, Jack watched the process with an attempt at detachment, fascinated by von Stroheim and the way he was transforming a simple Viennese operetta. He took it out of Vienna and set it in an empoverished Balkan principality, called Monteblanco, that was temporarily between wars. Sally O'Hara, a Follies girl on tour, comes to visit and begins another of von Stroheim's sexually-aware-American-girl-gets-into-love-triangles themes with a couple of princes. Mae Murray was perfect as Sally O'Hara because she was in fact a former Zeigfeld girl and had been Vernon Castle's partner. Moreover, she'd done *The Merry Widow* on Broadway and her performance of the famous "Merry Widow Waltz" had never failed to bring down the house. It was a production number in which all the other dancers pull back to reveal Mae and her lover, Prince Danilo, doing a solo whirl.

Von Stroheim had pointed out to Miss Murray that a musical number had no place in his version of the story, adding for emphasis that only a stupid bitch would fail to see the point. Jack, although he agreed, decided that the education wasn't worth the hourly insults. He walked over to von Stroheim's chair, quietly told him he could take his movie and shove it up his ass, and walked off the set. He poured a drink in his dressing room and had taken a sip when, to his suprise, von Stroheim knocked on the door and asked if Jack had any more of that Scotch he was drinking.

The two men drank in silence for a while. When von Stroheim did speak, it was as a director to a man who understood directing. "It is not you, Mr. Gilbert," he told Jack. "It is that dreadful and difficult woman." Jack, who knew something about difficult women, did not immediately spring to Mae Murray's defense. He listened as von Stroheim listed the familiar difficulties a director faces in dealing with an established star. Mae Murray's Broadway successes, her movie stardom, the fact that she was married to a director, even her two Rolls-Royces, all combined against her seeing herself simply as an actress who must learn a specific role. She had demanded her own cameraman, her choice of camera angles, her own wardrobe. Von Stroheim wanted a realistic performance while she would give only a star performance. Jack was sympathetic and promised to help in any way he could. Von Stroheim stood up to leave.

"I hope that we may one day be friends, Mr. Gilbert."

"I hope so too," Jack answered.

"One day, perhaps," von Stroheim repeated. "I do not make friends while I make pictures."

The battle of the production number continued. Mae Murray took it to Louis B. Mayer himself, knowing full well that he was likely to take almost anybody's side against Erich von Stroheim. It worked, and von Stroheim grudgingly agreed to film the waltz. What he would do afterward in the cutting room was another matter entirely.

Mae Murray recalled later (in a somewhat fanciful biography) that Jack had no desire to do the waltz scene at all and seemed very nervous during the shooting. "I wish I were in South America," he whispered to her as they began to dance. "Oh, no, you don't," she answered. "You want only to be in Monteblanco with me and that is where you are." Jack tried but it wasn't easy. In Monteblanco, von Stroheim wouldn't be standing off to one side rolling his eyes and muttering obscenities.

"Cut!" shouted von Stroheim. "Lousy. Just as I knew it would be. The showgirl and the amateur."

Mae, who thought they were doing just fine, went bonkers. She flew at von Stroheim, pounding both fists against his chest and screaming, "Ya hun! Ya dirty hun!"

Her maid rushed in to separate them. She led Mae Murray back to her dressing room, where the star stripped off her black gown, all the while raging about what she was going to do to von Stroheim. The telephone rang. It was the studio gateman with a message for Miss Murray. "Mr. Gilbert says to tell you he has left for South America. He says forgive him and good-bye."

"Damn!" she shouted. "Which way did he go?"

"South, I guess" came the answer.

Mae threw down the phone and raced out of the dressing room. She ran off the set past the astonished von Stroheim, down the street, out across Washington Boulevard, and over to the parking lot where Jack was getting into his car.

"Jack!" she called out. "Come back, Jack. Please come back!"

He watched stupefied as Mae Murray, wearing a bird-of-paradise headdress, black satin shoes, and little else, rushed at him and threw her arms around his neck. A policeman was running across the street behind her.

"What the hell's going on here?" the policeman yelled. "Lady, you can't run around like that."

A crowd quickly gathered. Mae Murray's maid pushed through with a blanket, which she threw over the star's bare shoulders.

"Mr. Gilbert must come with me," she told the policeman. "It's a matter of life and death."

"Better go along, Mr. Gilbert," the policeman told Jack. "Why don't you go with Miss Murray and see what she wants."

Mae brought Jack back to her dressing room where, by whatever means, she persuaded him to remain on this continent a while longer. She then went once more to see Mayer. Mayer was delighted to have the excuse to fire von Stroheim, "that sex-maniac degenerate," and he did. He replaced him with Monta Bell, but von Stroheim's crew immediately quit in protest. Whatever anyone else thought of von Stroheim, they knew that he knew how to make a movie, and there was hardly a technical person in Hollywood who wasn't eager to be part of an Erich von Stroheim film. Finally, the diplomatic Irving Thalberg was called in to negotiate a settlement. The dance would remain, but in a shortened and more atmospheric version. Von Stroheim would grit his teeth and apologize to Mae Murray. Miss Murray's dancing partner would be Jack, and not a professional double.

As if there wasn't enough emotional upheaval on the set and in Jack's personal life, another shocking blow came while Jack was enjoying one of his Sundays off from filming. He had just come back to his room at the Athletic Club from playing tennis when an old actor knocked timidly at his door. His name, he said, was John Pringle. He was the father Jack had never seen.

Jack's first reaction was disbelief. But Pringle produced letters, old photographs, and a marriage certificate to prove his identity. Ida Adair, he explained, had left him shortly after Jack's birth. He had lost all trace of his son since then.

Jack's disbelief turned to anger. He simply could not believe that he would have been all that hard to find while he was growing up believing he was Ida's illegitimate child. Ida was well known in the theater. Any trade paper would have told John Pringle where his son's mother was playing. A single letter to the family in Utah would have traced him, at least until he was sent off to make his way on his own. Even more galling, this John Pringle had found himself a job as an extra on the set of *The Merry Widow*. (One can see John Pringle in the ballroom scene, one of the two liveried servants standing on either side of the doorway. Pringle is on the right, a tall man with a sharp, angular face and dark, piercing eyes. He stares straight ahead as Jack, the glittering Prince Danilo, enters the room.)

Jack sent money to his father for the rest of his life but otherwise would have nothing to do with him. He said later, "All those years when I needed a father so bitterly, when I had no big hand to hold or shoulder to cry on, and now a stranger shows up calling me 'my son.' After years, I find out that my name is Pringle. But I cannot learn to say 'father.' It's too late. How life wastes things! I'm sorry for the gray-haired stranger who is my father . . . but it's too late for the memories we should have shared."

When *The Merry Widow* was finally released, three months later, Thalberg was exuberant at its reception. His gamble with von Stroheim had paid off. Critic and playwright Robert E. Sherwood wrote: "The main things are von Stroheim's direction, von Stroheim's profound knowledge of composition and scenic effects, and John Gilbert's magnificent performance as Prince Danilo. Gilbert gives an eloquent, vibrant, keenly tempered interpretation of what might have been a trite romantic character. At every point he sparkles with brilliance and at times he bursts into flames."

Photoplay was enthralled: "Not since Rudolph Valentino . . . has there been such a performance of a glowingly romantic role as Gilbert's . . . in a role that ought to make him the greatest of them all." A sampling of others echo their approval: "It has been suspected for many months that Gilbert would someday carve a niche for himself . . . therefore his sudden rise does not come as a complete surprise." "John Gilbert scores repeatedly in his interpretation." "An excellent performance. One might almost say a perfect performance." "He has never appeared to better advantage. Where others might have invested the early scenes of promiscuous lovemaking with crudities, Gilbert manages to surround them with something of the fire of irresponsible romance."

A few reviews, as always, were less favorable. The Philadelphia *Inquirer*, for example, simply said that "John Gilbert struggles along rather ineffectually as Prince Danilo." Thalberg began to notice an odd pattern in what was written about Jack that seemed to go beyond the normal range of critical opinion. Reviewers, and even fans, seemed to love him or hate him. There was something about Jack, whether in his personality or in his acting, that got certain backs up. His admirers were growing by the thousands, but there remained a core of people who couldn't stand the sight of him. That was fine with Thalberg. Where there is disagreement, there is debate. Where there are personal attacks, there would be impassioned defenses. It could be the best possible kind of advertising.

Jack had other things on his mind. During the production of *The Merry Widow*, he'd begun seeing Leatrice again. Her initial refusals to talk to him had softened under pressure from mutual friends such as Cedric Gibbons, Lois Wilson, and Paul Bern. She began by allowing him regular visits to the baby, but Leatrice would shut herself in another room, fearing, she said, for her resolve if she so much as laid eyes on Jack. She was working again and she was determined to rebuild the career she feared had been damaged beyond repair. Her first film for Famous Players after the birth of the baby was, in fact, directed by Paul Bern. *The Dressmaker from Paris* was one of many American-boy-meets-French-girl-during-the-Great-War pictures that were then popular. Jack was about to do one something like it for MGM. Back working, and with Paul Bern's encouragement, Leatrice's confidence increased to the point where she could at least talk to Jack face to face. Jack, in turn, began to believe that he had a chance of winning her back.

He declared publicly, any chance he got, that Leatrice was the only woman he would ever love. At least weekly, he would send her books to read, or flowers (not roses), or small gifts, such as a string of Oriental pearls and a looking glass in a silver frame. One evening, he sent a Hawaiian band over from a party to serenade her. He didn't realize, however, that there had been several burglaries in the neighborhood and a band of musicians was suspected. Leatrice locked all the doors and windows and called the police.

Not long after the divorce became final, Leatrice invited the Mayer girls over for tea. They were sitting near a window when they saw Jack, dressed in a white sweater and tennis flannels, leap over the low garden fence and scoop up the baby, who was playing in the grass. The girls were fascinated. They'd never met the notorious Mr. Gilbert, although they'd heard their father rage about him at the dinner table. The teacup in Leatrice's hand began to rattle. She put it down and half ran outside to meet him, with the Mayer sisters following close behind. Irene told me, "I have never seen such looks pass between a man and a woman. Leatrice was trembling so much she could hardly walk and Jack's face was so intense it was alarming. They were as nuts about each other as ever. Edith and I tiptoed away and went home. I'll bet they didn't even know we were gone."

With the release of *The Merry Widow* and its rave reviews still months away, Jack plunged into his next picture in what he felt was the happiest time of his life.

The picture was *The Big Parade*, a motion-picture classic that had started off as a much smaller idea. King Vidor complained to Irving Thalberg about the rash of frivolous program pictures that had been assigned to him. He begged for a chance to do a big picture, one that might have a long run at Grauman's Egyptian Theater (the forerunner of Grauman's Chinese), which was then the zenith of a director's ambition.

Thalberg was agreeable to the idea. He was already convinced that good art and good box office were not necessarily incompatible. Vidor suggested a war story. The theme he had in mind would be about a young American caught up in the tide of war. He needn't be especially heroic. Just one of the millions whose lives were forever reshaped by the experience. Thalberg said that he'd think it over and would begin looking for the right story treatment.

Soon afterward, Thalberg returned from a New York business trip with Laurence Stallings, the author of *What Price Glory?*, which was then playing on Broadway. Although Stallings was drunk for most of the train ride to Los Angeles, he managed to produce a five-page outline of a script. Thalberg then gave it to Harry Behn, a writer at MGM, to flesh out. The result excited Thalberg. Given the right director and the right star, *The Big Parade* could turn out to be something lasting after all. The director was clearly King Vidor. The star would be Jack Gilbert.

Vidor hated the idea. He and Jack had argued over interpretation during *The Wife of the Centaur*, and Vidor wasn't about to go through that again, especially on a picture that meant so much to him. He complained to Thalberg that Jack was "too sophisticated, too hard to handle." But Thalberg brushed aside the objection, noting that no other director, not even von Stroheim, had ever made such a complaint about him. To make sure things started smoothly, however, Thalberg escorted

Jack to the set on the first day of production. King Vidor approached them and said to Jack, "Anything you have to say, say it now in Irving's presence. Otherwise, keep your mouth shut after we start the picture."

"I'll never question your judgment again," Jack promised, his hands raised in surrender. He didn't bother explaining what had happened to his emotional state between the earlier picture and this one. He simply said he'd never been more excited by a part and that he was thrilled by the whole vision of the movie they were about to make.

With that out of the way, the magic began almost at once. A feeling developed for the story that was so fully shared by all concerned that words between director and actor were often unnecessary. King Vidor told film historian Kevin Brownlow in 1963, "I actually remember moments when I didn't say a thing. I'd just have a quick thought and Gilbert would react to it."

Jack wrote of Vidor: "In directing a picture he seems to convey some of his ideas through his silence better than they could be explained by most producers. Renée Adorée, for instance, never knew she was even going to chew gum when we sat down in one of the most famous scenes from the movie. I had the gum and as we looked at each other I pulled it out and gave her some. . . . She didn't beforehand think of swallowing it, but we discovered afterward that she was expected to by Mr. Vidor." After that chewing-gum scene, in which the American boy gives the French girl her first stick of gum and she eats it, Vidor leaped to his feet shouting, "I'll be damned if I *ever* saw a scene as good as that!"

Thalberg shared very much in the growing excitement. As he looked at the dailies and saw a stark realism that had never before been shown on the screen, the haunted faces of soldiers moving into battle, the stunning improvisations such as the scene with the dying German, when Jack slapped the enemy soldier in a way suggesting burnt out hatred mingled with sympathy, then gave him his last cigarette. Thalberg knew something monumental was growing here. He increased the budget, encouraging Vidor to expand the battle scenes and, above all, to keep experimenting.

Vidor knew full well what he had. After one scene in which Jack and his two comrades, Tom O'Brien and Karl Dane, plunged into a trench half filled with water and huddled, caked with mud, Vidor shouted, "Cut!" and approached with his hand outstretched to Jack. "Grauman's Egyptian, baby," he said, grinning. "Grauman's Egyptian, Pops," Jack said, nodding.

When the picture was finished and the news came that Sid Grauman had indeed booked the picture into his fabulous Egyptian Theater, Jack and King Vidor did a war dance in his dressing room.

Lois Wilson was working in New York at the time of the premiere there. Jack traveled East for the opening in the company of her fiancé, Richard Dix. They shared a compartment on the train, carrying with them the three steel boxes containing the film. Lois met them at the station and went with them to deliver the film to the Astor Theater, where *The Big Parade* was to open.

Jack had already wired Leatrice, who was vacationing in New York, asking her to go with him to the opening. Leatrice was thrilled. She ordered a new gown of pale-pink crêpe shimmering with crystal beads. On opening night Jack sent her a corsage of five white orchids and called for her dressed in white tie and tails. He was gorgeous but terrified. "My God," he told her, "this picture has been given so much advance boosting. What if they don't like it? What if it doesn't come up to their expectations?"

Jack wrote later, "When we drove up to the theater, the crowds roared and cheered as they saw me assist Leatrice from the taxi. I was trembling from head to foot. The theater was jammed with the first-night crowd of stars and critics. The houselights dimmed and . . . I ceased to exist for this world. I grew numb and, riveting my eyes on the screen, sat as if dead for two hours. Then cheers and applause and thunderous acclamation. . . . It was over. I could not get my limbs to move or my brain to function. Not until all the people had left the theater was I capable of rising from my seat." Even then, Leatrice had to help him. She says that Jack tore his own large handkerchief and two of hers to bits during the picture, and didn't realize it until the lights went on and they saw the shreds of linen, like snowflakes, around their seats.

Marcus Loew gave a lavish reception the night of the opening. Jack was still trembling when he arrived. Loew handed him a flask of first-rate Scotch without comment. Leatrice forgave him one long swallow. In fact, she had occasion to forgive him many times throughout the night. He persuaded her to leave the party early, and they went off alone to Jack & Charley's 21 Club, where they danced and talked and kissed for hours. When he finally took her home to the Ambassador and returned to his own room, the morning papers were waiting for him. He "got drunk all over again" reading the reviews of the picture. He wrote: "No such adjectives had ever been used to describe a movie. I sat for hours crying and thrilling to the printed phrases. I staggered to bed and slept around the clock."

Superlatives over *The Big Parade* continued to roll in for months, and then again two years later when it was finally released to the neighborhood theaters. It had a record eighty-six-week run at the Astor Theater. Nothing like it was ever seen before or would be again until *Gone With the Wind*.

Robert Sherwood wrote: "*The Big Parade* is a marvelous picture that can be ranked among the few genuinely great achievements of the screen. He [Vidor] has made war scenes that actually resemble war. . . . When he advances a raw company of infantry through a forest which is raked by machine-gun fire, he makes the soldiers look scared, sick at their stomachs, with no heart for the ghastly business that is ahead. He has shown an American soldier, suddenly wild with the desire to kill, trying to jab his bayonet into the neck of a dying German sniper. He has shown the look on that sniper's face and the horrible revulsion that overcomes the American boy. I doubt there is a single irregular soldier, volunteered or conscripted, who did not experience that same awful feeling during his career in France . . . who did not recognize the impulse to withdraw the bayonet and offer the dying Heinie a cigarette.

The picture is essentially a love story and a supremely stirring one at that. Renée Adorée, who appears for a very short time, is never for an instant forgotten. Both she and John Gilbert are brilliantly effective."

Even Mordaunt Hall, of *The New York Times*, one of those who hadn't found much good to say about Jack in the past, was positively lyrical: "A superlative war picture . . . an eloquent pictorial epic of the world war. . . . It is a subject so compelling and realistic that one feels impelled to approach a review of it with all the respect it deserves. . . . The scenes are as perfect as human imagination and intelligence could produce. . . . The acting is flawless throughout. Possibly the scenes where Jim [John Gilbert] enjoys his flirtation [with Renée Adorée] are more delightful than any other part of the story because it seems so natural."

The next day, rapturously, Leatrice and Jack went looking for an apartment and begin talking over plans to be remarried. For a week they were as happy, Leatrice says, as either had ever been. But again something went wrong.

Leatrice, perhaps, had been spending too much time with lawyers. Once she and Jack began to talk seriously about marriage, Leatrice asked, then insisted, that he put in writing some clear intention to provide for their child. Jack was flabbergasted that the issue would even arise. From his point of view, it was like asking him to promise he wouldn't raise pigs in the living room. He considered the request insulting, but again she insisted. By the time Leatrice returned to the Coast and her next movie, there was no more talk of marriage.

Jack complained to Lois Wilson, "Leatrice always has to spoil things. We were so happy. It was all going to work out. And then she had to ruin it with a detail like that. Worse, I don't think she even understood why I was offended."

To Leatrice, the request was perfectly reasonable. She was a devoted and responsible mother. She was also earning a livelihood that could fade away at any time. For every actress or actor who made a sustained decent living there were hundreds of briefly twinkling stars who returned almost overnight to a struggling existence. Leatrice's instincts may have been sound enough but her timing was dreadful. Jack was unattached. And he was about to meet a wildly enthusiastic new fan. Her name was Greta Garbo.

Garbo and Mauritz Stiller arrived in New York aboard the SS *Drotningholm* on July 6, 1925. They were almost three months behind schedule because Stiller had had second thoughts about the contract he'd signed with Mayer and had dragged his feet hoping Mayer would break it. He also, characteristically, tried to throw in some new conditions after the agreement was signed. Mayer's response was to insist that he abide by the contract and then, once he'd arrived in the United States, to let him stew for a while. "Stew" was the right word. Stiller and Garbo arrived during a near-record heat wave. Garbo, accustomed to the natural air-conditioning of Stockholm, spent much of her time in the bathtub of her hotel room while Stiller tried to strike a better deal with MGM's New York office. He got nowhere. But then Stiller had a stroke of luck. A friend had introduced him to the photographer Arnold Genthe, who agreed to take a few informal portraits of Garbo. The results were spectacular.

As Stiller well knew, there was a part of Garbo that could not be seen any other way but through the lens of a camera. When he presented these haunting pictures to the Loew's office, revealing for the first time that startling face with all its mystery and sensuality, things seemed suddenly to change. MGM sent him some money and told him to head west immediately with Garbo. The studio even agreed to a revised contract paying her four hundred dollars a week. This concession, however, had little to do with the photographs. MGM's lawyers suddenly realized that Garbo was a minor, not yet twenty, and therefore had had no business signing the first contract. When she finally arrived in Hollywood, they quickly got her to sign a revised document stipulating that she was doing so with her mother's permission.

Garbo arrived in Hollywood the first week in September. She and Stiller were met by a small Scandinavian contingent that included Victor Seastrom and Karl Dane. It wasn't much of a reception but it was better than in New York, where on Mayer's orders their arrival had been almost pointedly ignored. Garbo moved into the Miramar Hotel in Santa Monica and Stiller rented a small house on the beach. They both settled in and began waiting again, this time for the studio to put them to work.

In early December, Stiller and Garbo were invited to attend a concert at the Shrine Auditorium featuring Feodor Chaliapin, the great Russian basso. Their host, producer Erich Pommer, had them for dinner at his house after the concert. Another of the guests was Jack's old friend Rowland V. Lee, who was delighted to discover that his dinner partner would be this new Swedish actress everyone was talking about. Rowland tried to make conversation with her, but she seemed remote and half asleep:

> She spoke very little English. Sometimes she pretended to know even less. But when Jack Gilbert's name came up—he was the hottest thing in pictures just then—her eyes lit up. Then when I told her I knew Jack Gilbert, that I practically brought him up, she roused herself to a pitch of excitement. Her English became better, but it was still a struggle. She asked me question after question about him. Jack Gilbert was all she wanted to talk about, how marvelous, how wonderful, how charming he was. It turned out she'd learned all the essential complimentary phrases. She stayed glued to my side for the rest of the evening and never once allowed me to change the subject.

Jack had not yet met Garbo and wouldn't for several months.

From December of 1925 well into 1926, John Gilbert might have been the best-known man in America, possibly Europe as well. John Gilbert shirts with long collars and French cuffs appeared on the market. There were John Gilbert neckties of navy-blue silk with tiny white polka dots. One evening, Jack arrived at a party having come straight from the studio wearing a light-blue shirt normally used in place of white for filming. His outfit was reported and the fashion caught on. Blue shirts had never before been acceptable for daytime wear. Jack thought it was all ridiculous. He was astonished that it made a scintilla of difference to anyone what he wore, what he ate, what kind of pets he had at home. Yet, although often embarrassed, he was secretly delighted by the attention. So was Irving Thalberg. Even Louis B. Mayer, when he was pressed, found something good to say about Jack.

With all the positive acclaim, of course, came the rumors and the inside "scoops." There were hints that this Great Lover was in fact less than manly. Inevitably, some stories had him a conceited ass. For every man who identified with Jack's easygoing charm and masculinity, there seemed to be another who was threatened by it or who simply didn't like him. Donald Ogden Stewart said, "I never went with him [Jack] to a public restaurant that some man didn't leave the woman he was with and come up to our table and try to pick a fight with him. Jack was a flaming, radiant person in those days, a bright and shining star. . . . *The Big Parade* had just shot him into the sky. Garbo had not yet risen on his horizon."

Odd stories about Jack's hammy behavior kept showing up in curious places. In King Vidor's autobiography, he says, "I decided that in Jack's new character of down-to-earth doughboy, he would use no make-up and wear an ill-fitting uniform. Dirty fingernails and a sweaty, begrimed face were to take the place of a perfectly made-up skin texture. Jack rebelled as I knew he would. He was well on his way to being established as the 'Great Lover' and it wasn't fair to change his character when his career, after all these years, was finally on the ascendancy. But to me the integrity of this picture was more important than anybody's career so I stood firm and Thalberg backed me up. When he had seen the first few days' rushes, Gilbert was so sold on the down-to-earth characterization that he never used makeup again."

Leatrice remembered differently. She later recalled:

> I enjoyed King's book very much, but that business about the makeup wasn't right at all. Jack always hated the "Great Lover" image. He fought with the studio, even with Thalberg, and he made some enemies that way. He was afraid of being typed. Jack thought it would limit his career and might even ruin him. Besides, it was silly and he knew it. The "Great Lover" business was all Thalberg's idea.
>
> If Jack objected at all to dirt and grime, his objection would have been based on characterization. For example, the boy he played was a rich man's son before the army took him. Jack could possibly have argued that a rich man's son would try to be more fastidious than most. I don't know but that would have sounded much more like Jack. He was very professional.

With his name and face everywhere, everyone seemed to want to know "what John Gilbert was really like." Ivan St. Johns, the almost forgotten husband of Adela Rogers St. Johns, told this story in *Photoplay*: "One day at a Hollywood luncheon the name of a famous man came up. One of the guests made a vicious and unfair remark. Another guest was the man's daughter, unbeknowst. A trying situation. A pause, the girl on the brink of tears. Instead of ignoring the remark, wisecracking or being upset, Jack Gilbert reached over and patted the girl's hand. He then said with a quiet dignity I will never forget, 'It's too bad you said those things because I know you're a regular guy and you want to know the truth. This is his daughter and she's going to tell you, and then you can help protect him in the future.'

"Well, it was amazing. The girl brightened. The man looked ashamed but not crushed, and in two minutes the situation resulted in better understanding for everyone. Jack never seems to be afraid of the truth. He performed many kindnesses for Dorothy Reid during Wally's last illness, just in a matter-of-fact kind of way, being around and ready to do anything he could. There was a very real side to Jack under a sort of schoolboy wildness."

Leatrice recalled showing Jack the Ivan St. Johns article one day. He blushed deeply as he read it. "I wish they'd all shut up," he told her. "Half the stuff they say is lies and the rest is none of their business."

In 1925, Jack was back hard at work finishing *La Bohème*. The star was Lillian Gish. She had seen two reels of *The Big Parade* before it was released, and was deeply impressed. She asked for and was given the same director, the same leading man, leading woman (Renée Adorée) and comedian (Karl Dane), so the "family" was together again. King Vidor was exercising his usual prerogative of making a play for his leading lady, and this time Jack decided to give him a run for his money.

One morning, the two went driving up the coast looking for a suitable location for an exterior shot. Every half hour or so, King would insist they stop at the next gas station, or Jack would dash into a country store for some trivial purchase. These stops went on all day. Finally, each man realized that the other was sneaking off to telephone Miss Gish, who was resting alone that day in her cottage at the Beverly Hills Hotel. They laughed and called it quits on the way home when they realized that neither one of them was getting anywhere.

Marion Davies remembered Jack standing each night at the foot of the stairs leading up to Miss Gish's dressing room with a bunch of violets in his hand. But Lillian never descended until after he'd given up and gone home. She'd recently been through an unpleasant experience being sued for breach of promise by an actor, and she went out of her way to avoid any publicity that hinted at romance. She remained isolated throughout the picture.

Jack decided he'd at least have the fun of doing love scenes with her while King Vidor squirmed enviously. But King had bad news for him. Miss Gish, he indicated, was not into heavy breathing. She'd exercised another of her prerogatives in setting the tone of the picture as a study in subdued emotions. As Mimi, in this film version of the Puccini opera, she lay eloquently dying of tuberculosis, fading a little each day, a long, sustained theme of dying passion. Romantic passion was something else again. Her idea was to avoid showing the lovers in a physical embrace in order to build up suppressed emotion in the audience, to say nothing of Jack and King. She would not allow Jack to kiss her or even to take her in his arms.

When Irving Thalberg saw the completed picture in the screening room, he asked King Vidor, "Where are the love scenes?" King struggled to explain Miss Gish's position on the matter, that the story was about a spiritual, otherworldly kind of love. Thalberg pointed out that the other world was exactly the right place for it. Gish and Gilbert were still with us, and he'd like them to act that way. Furthermore, he added, the reasonable John Gilbert fan would probably expect the Great Lover to do some great lovemaking. Thalberg ordered Vidor to reshoot.

Miss Gish was annoyed but she went through with it. "Oh, dear," a friend quoted her as saying. "I've got to go through another day of kissing John Gilbert." She still kept her distance after hours but later, she recalled, "After the opening, I received a most discreet proposal of marriage from my leading man."

Lois Wilson, with Richard Dix, accompanied Jack to the New York premiere near the end of February 1926. It was a tremendous affair: giant arc lights flooded Broadway and Mayor Jimmy Walker was there. King Vidor and Irving Thalberg both made the trip. Jack escorted Norma Shearer, who would marry Thalberg a year later. The crowds were huge and almost impossible to handle. In spite of extra police, they surged around the limousines and jostled the arriving stars. They grabbed at Jack's clothes and tore Miss Shearer's dress. Once inside, Jack was again consumed with anxiety as the picture was shown on the screen. One witness said, "Jack showed extreme nervousness. . . . It made one wonder, was it worth the agony he was evidently suffering to come all the way across the country? Mr. Gilbert sweated blood. He mopped his brow, his face, and his neck for the whole two hours."

For all of Jack's self-doubts, the picture was a critical triumph for him. *Cinema Art* said: "John Gilbert stands alone at the topmost pinnacle of film fame. There is no one who can approach him."

The *New York Post* said it was "a performance of sheer vitality and brilliance seldom if ever equaled in the cinema." "Another triumph for John Gilbert," one reviewer gushed, "one of the more fascinating and talented young men who has ever appeared in pictures." Even the *Times*' Mordaunt Hall now seemed convinced. He called it "a photoplay of exquisite beauty. . . . Mr. Gilbert's acting aroused applause last night. . . . He shows through his portrayal that he is thinking the part. You can detect it in his eyes."

But again there was the sharp division of opinion. Although the balance very much favored Jack, some reviewers didn't like the picture or anyone in it. Robert E. Sherwood, normally partial to Jack, said: "As Rudolph, John Gilbert is wrong most of the time, and there is a pronounced lump in my throat as I say that. He is one of the really fine, sensitive actors of the movies."

Lillian Gish didn't fare nearly as well as Jack. *Variety*, for example, said: "Mr. Gilbert walks away with the film's acting. Miss Gish is fairly smothered. Lillian Gish was never Mimi."

In her next picture, Lillian Gish played Hester Prynne, the leading character in *The Scarlet Letter*. The male lead was played by Lars Hanson, one of the Swedish actors who came over as part of the Garbo–Stiller package. Garbo spent a lot of time on the set of *The Scarlet Letter* watching Lillian Gish perform. She'd been parked there by Stiller while he went around trying to get a directing assignment. He felt she'd be less homesick in the company of her fellow Scandinavians and she might even learn something. Apparently, she learned quite a lot. The Griffith-trained Lillian Gish was meticulous in preparing for and rehearsing a role. She paid close attention to camera angles and she knew how effectively the correct lighting could enhance an emotion during a close-up. Garbo couldn't have had a better role model. Lillian Gish was a consummate professional who was firm in her dealings with the studio and would never accept anything that was second-rate. Miss Gish also held herself aloof from all the "nonsense" that went with her profession. She did not pose with college track teams or with boxers, as the MGM publicity department forced Garbo to do before she put her foot down.

Garbo had already made her first picture for MGM. In fact, it was released within two weeks of *La Bohème*. The movie was *The Torrent*, a romantic tragedy in which Garbo plays a Spanish peasant girl who, having been forcefully separated from her aristocratic lover, goes on to become a world-famous opera singer. She goes back home for a visit, and sees her now married lover again; he saves her life in a flash flood (hence the title), but they end up tearfully going their separate ways. The range from peasant girl to prima donna gave Garbo a chance to play several different types. This was not so much an intention as an experiment. The studio simply didn't know quite what to do with her. Was she a glamorous Gloria Swanson type, a wounded-innocence Lillian Gish type, or a long-suffering Norma Talmadge type? It was more than another case of a studio not knowing what it had: Garbo defied typing. The studio was sure of one thing, however: Garbo photographed hauntingly. Rather than rush her into another picture, Thalberg decided to wait and see whether the public and the critics could more precisely define her appeal. But as to her potential, neither Thalberg nor Mayer seemed to have any doubt. Mayer promptly tried to pressure her into extending the term of her contract from three years to five.

Alexander Walker said of Garbo in her second picture, *The Temptress:* "Her body and the way she used it . . . struck the American audience as excitingly unfamiliar. In motion, she relayed a liberated animal quite unfamiliar in Hollywood-made pictures." It was actually Mauritz Stiller who brought out her sensual and mystic qualities, in the portion of the film he directed before he was fired and replaced by Fred Niblo. Garbo played an adulterous Argentinian, married to one man, mistress to another, seducer of a third. All this carrying-on eventually led her from a life of comfort in Argentina to one of drunkenness and degradation in Paris. But the plot almost didn't matter. What mattered was Garbo's face and her eyes. Through them you could read her mind. Moviegoers saw thoughts that could never have appeared in a script. This time, MGM was sure of what they had: a new kind of seductress. Very human, often neurotic, strong yet vulnerable.

Meanwhile, just before Garbo was to begin filming *The Temptress*, the picture that would make her a popular sensation, Jack paid a ritual courtesy visit to his boss, Louis B. Mayer.

Jack's life, for the most part, couldn't have been going better. He was the most important male star in films anywhere. His salary was now ten thousand dollars a week. He'd already built the house he was to live in for the rest of his life, a Spanish hacienda built on top of a mountain, with sweeping views of Los Angeles. There was no particular woman in his life—save Leatrice, whom he saw regularly—but he had no time to be lonely. He was invited everywhere, often going to four or more gatherings in a single evening. It was almost perfect, except for his relationship with Mayer.

Jack arrived early for the meeting. Thalberg was there, along with Eddie Mannix, Mayer's bodyguard and aide-de-camp. After a suitable wait, Mayer summoned them into his inner office. There were greetings and polite congratulations; then the conversation turned to thoughts of Jack's next assignment. Jack's ambition for some time had been to do a film version of John Masefield's narrative poem, *The Widow in the Bye Street*. Mayer had never heard of it. Jack began to outline the story.

It was a stark drama set in a small industrial town in the English Midlands. In a bye street, an alleyway, a poor widow lives with and for a little son who is all her joy. She copes with their poverty in small ways, setting the table for a proper tea and keeping their home as neat and warm as possible. The boy grows up and goes to work. For the first time, there is enough money for the widow to buy herself a new pair of shoes. But soon the boy meets an older woman who is kept by a local drayman. She is voluptuous and evil. She amuses herself with this young innocent while her lover is serving a short term in prison. The lover returns, attacks the boy, and the boy kills him during a fight. He is tried for murder and sentenced to hang. The poem ends with the mother waiting outside the prison to claim the body of her son.

Mayer didn't think much of the story. "You can't make a movie about a whore," he grumbled. "A nice boy falling in love with a whore? What kind of movie would that make?"

Jack mentioned Camille, then Anna Christie. Someone had managed to make pretty good movies out of both, even though they were whores. The discussion quickly grew into an argument. Mayer told Jack that only someone like him would bring a whore into a story about a mother and her son. Once the subjects of whores and mothers were mentioned in the same sentence, Jack, the story goes, said, "What's wrong with that? My own mother was a whore." The story goes on, variously, to say that Mayer jumped up from his desk and punched Jack in the face, or that Mayer charged at him threatening to cut his balls off for making a remark like that. The later version has Jack taunting Mayer and daring him to go ahead; it would get him out of all those lousy Great Lover parts.

No one living knows what really happened. Jack might well have responded to one of Mayer's sanctity-of-mother speeches with the news that his own mother was something less than a madonna. Given Mayer's open dislike toward Jack, it wouldn't have taken much more than that for the man who had floored both Erich von Stroheim and Charlie Chaplin to start swinging.

In any case, Eddie Mannix restrained Mayer, and Irving Thalberg whisked Jack out of the room before any more damage could be done. But Mayer never forgot it. "That Gilbert is a bad apple," he told his wife. "No decent man would speak that way about his mother." Later, when Carey Wilson tried to patch up the quarrel, Mayer told him, "It's no use. I hate the bastard because he doesn't love his mother." Irene Selznick, Mayer's daughter, said that her father held those feelings against Jack for many years. Carey Wilson said he'd heard Mayer give at least three utterly different versions of what was said in that office, with Mayer getting angrier each time. "I never saw such hatred in my life," Carey told me. "It was frightening."

Jack gave Mayer as wide a berth as possible after that, trusting Thalberg to keep Mayer from taking any impetuous action that might damage his career. But he did not give up on the *Widow in the Bye Street* idea. It was a story that touched him deeply, and he wanted to do it. Perhaps the theme of a boy and the tender, loving mother Jack never had was what moved him. Whatever the reason, he stubbornly refused to abandon the idea.

Jack's next picture turned out to be a costume epic called *Bardelys the Magnificent*, set during the reign of Louis XIII. King Vidor directed again and Eleanor Boardman co-starred. The film, now lost, was the basic Douglas Fairbanks swashbuckler, with Jack leaping onto steeds and outriding and outfighting all manner of opponents. Again, the critics generally liked it and the public loved it. One critic wrote: "It is doubtful if anyone could have done more with the role of Bardelys than Gilbert. . . . That man continues to be a fine actor." To Jack, however, it was "applesauce, with John Gilbert contributing most of the sauce." After the stunning accomplishment of *The Big Parade*, everything the studio assigned to him seemed hopelessly superficial by comparison. Of that film he wrote: "No achievement will ever excite me so much. No reward will ever be so great as having been part of *The Big Parade*. All that followed has been balderdash."

Garbo wasn't happy about the way her career was going either. The studio wanted her to do a film called *Flesh and the Devil*. The plot, as far as she was concerned, was virtually indistinguishable from that of *The Temptress*. She'd play another adulteress; she'd again cause the death of her husband; she'd again come to a bad end, this time falling through the ice and drowning. Garbo was also upset by the way Stiller was being treated by Mayer. Mayer had quickly decided he had another hard-to-handle von Stroheim on his hands and began doing all he could lo makc Stiller pick up and go elsewhere. Garbo told Mayer she was not going to play any more "stupid seductresses," nor would she participate in any more of the equally stupid stunts dreamed up by the publicity department. Mayer replied that she'd do as she was told. She obeyed, for the present, but was left more unhappy, friendless, and homesick than ever. She was ripe to meet a kindred spirit who shared her distaste for silly romantic roles, the artifices of Hollywood, and especially Louis B. Mayer.

Jack had already accepted the male lead in *Flesh and the Devil* at Irving Thalberg's urging. He wasn't thrilled by the story, but his old friend Clarence Brown would be directing and another good friend, Cedric Gibbons, would be art director. He was also curious about this Greta Garbo who was probably going to play opposite him. There was no "probably" in Thalberg's mind. A major film opposite John Gilbert would shoot Greta Garbo into the top rank of Hollywood stardom. In fact, when the time was right, he would approach Jack about giving his lesser known co-star equal billing.

Jack first met Garbo on the streets of the MGM lot while preparations for *Flesh and the Devil* were under way. Recognizing her, he nodded and flashed a welcoming smile. "Hello, Greta," he said. She froze and stiffly answered, "It is *Miss* Garbo."

"I'll be damned," Jack told screenwriter Frances Marion. "Imagine upstaging *me!* I heard she was only a barber's latherer when Mauritz Stiller put her in one of his pictures. She isn't a bad looker. Bones are too large, but she has amazing eyes."

Clarence Brown remembers the day Garbo first appeared on the set. She seemed very nervous, and he tried to put her at ease. Garbo told him how much she admired Mr. Gilbert and looked forward to meeting him. Brown walked over to Jack's dressing room and suggested he come to the set and meet his leading lady. But Jack was still smarting from what he thought was a snub. "To hell with her," he answered. "Let her come to meet me."

So Brown brought the timid Swedish girl to meet the great star of *The Big Parade*. She was so nervous, and perhaps embarrassed by their last encounter, that Jack warmed to her immediately. She started to relax from the moment he smiled at her and he soon had her laughing. If it wasn't love at first sight, it was something very close to it. Garbo clearly had developed a crush on Jack before their meeting. Jack, for his part, was certainly flattered by it and charmed by her vulnerability. There were also those eyes. However it started, by the time their first love scene was filmed they were madly, exuberantly in love.

Clarence Brown remembers:

It was the damnedest thing you ever saw. It was the sort of thing Elinor Glyn used to write about. When they got into that first love scene . . . well, nobody else was even there. Those two were alone in a world of their own. It seemed like an intrusion to yell "cut!" I used to just motion the crew over to another part of the set and let them finish what they were doing. It was embarrassing.

The studio didn't share Brown's concern for their privacy. The publicity department began at once to cash in on their raging love affair with a barrage of gossip-column and fan-magazine items in order to build up the picture. Jack and Greta, now inseparable, were followed everywhere they went. They couldn't eat in public or go to the beach without a mob gathering around them. Jack began taking her home to his house for dinner. In a matter of weeks she moved in.

The house, near the top of Tower Road, stood there until 1983, when it was torn down. (Elton John was one of its last occupants.) Jack had chosen a lot directly above King Vidor's elegant home so he could, according to Jack, "throw dead bottles and other tributes onto his director's rooftop." He brought in all the belongings he'd been gathering in storage. The huge eight-foot bed that he'd used in *Monte Cristo*, his good Caucasian rugs, crates of books and phonograph records. He installed a speaker system so that music could be heard by the pool and tennis court, as well as in different parts of the house. It was not a large house by Hollywood standards; there were only two bedrooms. The master bedroom upstairs had French doors leading out to the garden; the other, tucked under the stairs, was a smaller room and bath for guests. There were separate servant quarters beside the garage.

There were touches of stained glass in the windows, dark-red quarry tiles on the floor, wrought-iron light fixtures, a heavy chandelier in the large sitting room, and Spanish wall sconces. Jack's big leather armchair stood by the window facing the ocean, near a circular table where he kept the books he was currently reading. Fresh flowers were everywhere and fruit was always within reach.

Jack took great pride in his home, the first of his life that was entirely his own. He was compulsively neat with his possessions. Because everything in the house was special to him, he mended things as they broke rather than throwing them away. Everything had a place and was put carefully away after use. Even his makeup box was kept in perfect order, the brushes lined up according to size. He kept the leather bindings of his books oiled, and instructed his servants to keep his silver bright and his windows shining.

In one corner of his sitting room there was a paneled alcove with a small cruciform window surrounded by bookshelves. He had this scene engraved on his bookplate. Soon after moving in, he sent the artist's drawing and the first copy to Leatrice. He pointed out a small candle burning in the engraving and told her it was a lamp burning in the window for her. "Someday you'll come to your senses and come home," he told her. But Leatrice didn't like Jack's house. She thought it was grotesque, particularly the guest room, which he'd decorated as a monk's cell, complete with giant ebony crucifix, narrow bed, prie-dieu, and missal. It was a replica of the bedroom in *The Merry Widow* in which Prince Danilo had tried to seduce Mae Murray. On the other hand, Jack thought Leatrice's chintz and antiques-stuffed house looked like "an Atlantic City auction room."

But for now all thoughts of Leatrice coming home were at least suspended. Garbo moved into the monk's-cell guest room. Jack called in his friend Harold Grieve, the designer and decorator, and commissioned him to turn it into something more suitable for a long-term guest. Grieve made it into a miniature Louis XVI boudoir, all blue and ivory and gold, with a black marble bathroom.

Jack had a profound effect on Garbo's acting style. From their first picture together, there is a marked change in her techniques with the camera and the use of her eyes, hands, and makeup. Jack would defer to her in camera angles and insist on retakes if he thought she appeared at a disadvantage. He willingly agreed to Thalberg's request that he share star billing with her. Clarence Brown said, "Jack helped her enormously. He watched everything she did and corrected it. Garbo was so grateful. She recognized his long experience in the movies and she hung on his every word."

This kind of respect was a new experience for Jack, at least in comparing Garbo to Leatrice. Leatrice had almost never listened to him or accepted his advice, while Garbo trusted Jack implicitly, and not only in artistic matters. On his suggestion, she signed with his manager, Harry Edington. Edington promptly put Louis B. Mayer on notice that he was paying Garbo a tenth of what she was worth, but not for long. Mayer saw Jack's hand in this and hated "that bastard" all the more.

The reticent Garbo blossomed in Jack's company as she never would again. Salka Viertel, Garbo's close friend, told George Oppenheimer, "Garbo was at her best with Jack. She came out in society, she laughed and went to parties. People will never forget how she was then, warm and vibrant and wildly beautiful." Anielka Elter, a young actress who worked with Jack in *The Merry Widow*, said, "I remember the days when Garbo was in love with Jack Gilbert. She looked as if she had a light shining from within." Clarence Brown added, "You couldn't blame Garbo for falling in love with Jack. He was such a lovely man. And a fine, serious actor."

Flesh and the Devil was a sensation wherever it played. It was one of the first pictures, if not the first, to show two lovers in a horizontal position. That scene, with Garbo in the dominant position, has been called one of the most erotic ever filmed. Another stunningly erotic moment, all the more effective for its unexpectedness, occurs during a scene in which the two lovers are taking Communion. Gilbert sips from the chalice and it is passed on. Garbo takes the chalice, glances at Gilbert, then turns it to sip from the place where his lips touched. Women moaned and swooned in their seats. On an artistic level, cameraman William Daniels did things with lights that had never been seen before. He used lights and lights alone to create moods on Garbo's face; he caught Jack's eyes in pinpoints of light. In one scene, as Gilbert lights a cigarette and offers it to her yearning lips, the glow of the cigarette softly lights her face. Daniels had secreted a tiny arc light in Jack's hand. The effect was magic. William Daniels would go on to light most of Garbo's pictures. The "divinity" so often ascribed to Garbo was due in no small part to the technical virtuosity of people like him.

The *New York Times* critic wrote of "admirable artistry, a compelling piece of work, hard and fast realism mingled with soft and poetic glimpses." The *Herald Tribune* said: "Never before has John Gilbert been so intense in his portrayal of a man in love. Never before has a woman so alluring, with a seductive grace that is far more potent than mere beauty, appeared on the screen. Frankly, we have never in our career seen a seduction scene so perfectly done." *Variety* reported: "FLESH AND THE DEVIL MARKS HOUSE RECORD, holding over for a third week, first time in seven years. . . . A total of $132,505 for two weeks despite very bad weather, shattering all previous records."

Fifty-six years later the picture was still a smash. In November of 1982, the London Film Festival, in conjunction with Thames Television, featured *Flesh and the Devil*. Carl Davis wrote an original score to be played live by the sixty-piece Wren Symphony orchestra. The event was held in the Dominion Theater for three nights. It was a complete sellout. I was there each night addressing the audience, and made appearances on British television talking about the film and about Jack. Many letters came in. One of the most touching came from a young woman who was an usher at the Dominion Theater. Most of the people in the audience, she said, had never seen a silent film. Every night the houselights would go back on and she'd see scores of young people wiping their eyes, deeply moved by the performances. They came, she went on, expecting to see a quaint relic. But they discovered an art form that in some ways surpasses anything offered by the modern cinema.

The picture completed, Jack and Greta retreated into their private lives. He built a small cabin for her at the back of his property, and he planted a pine grove there because Garbo missed the sight and smell of her native trees. He also built an artificial waterfall near the cabin. He hoped the sound of running water and the wind through the pines would help ease both her homesickness and her insomnia. Because she had difficulty learning to read English, he opened an account for her with a major bookstore in Stockholm from which she could order books. Jack taught her how to play tennis and she worked hard at her game. She held the racket in a peculiar fashion, clutching the middle of the handle instead of the end, but she played a fast, slashing game. It took her sixteen tries before she finally beat Carey Wilson at singles. Then she stopped and never played singles with him again. Garbo was, like Jack, self-educated. And like Jack she was an avid reader, hungry to learn about almost anything.

She and Jack hosted tennis parties every Sunday. The core group usually consisted of Carey Wilson, Paul Bern, Irving Thalberg, King Vidor and Eleanor Boardman, David Selznick, the Barney Glazers, Edmund Lowe and Lilyan Tashman, Harry Behn, producer Arthur Hornblow, Jr., and Juliet Crosby, and screenwriter Herman Mankiewicz.

Stiller, meanwhile, continued to live at Santa Monica. He was directing intermittently at Paramount now, in poor health, and fighting to salvage something of his career. If he objected to his protégée's highly publicized passion for Jack Gilbert, he kept it to himself. He would not have been threatened on a romantic level; Stiller was almost certainly homosexual. But he did comment bitterly on the choice of films, all vamp roles, given to Garbo. He felt her forte was innocence, as in his *Gösta Berling*.

Far from being a callous person, Garbo suffered deeply over what was happening to Stiller. She tried to divide her time between the two men in her life who were most important to her. She'd suddenly disappear from the house on Tower Road for hours and Jack always knew where she'd gone. He had no knowledge of Stiller's sexual preferences, nor would Garbo, with her typically Swedish sense of privacy, have told him. She would only say that her relationship with him ran deep but that it had nothing to do with her relationship to Jack. An unsatisfactory reply, from Jack's point of view. It led to jealousy and arguments. Jack couldn't help wondering how much Stiller had to do with Garbo's insistent refusals to marry him.

She was forthright enough in an interview with Rilla Page Palmborg, a prominent journalist married to a Swede. When asked a direct question about her intentions concerning Jack, Garbo said, "Many things have been written about our friendship. It is a friendship. I will never marry. But you can say that I think Jack Gilbert is one of the finest men I have ever known. He has temperament, he gets excited, sometimes he has much to say that is good. I am very happy when I am told I am to do a picture with Mr. Gilbert. He is a great artist. He lifts me up and carries me along with him. It is not scenes I am doing. I am living."

Garbo was true to her word. She never did marry. But her relationship with Jack was more than a friendship. Garbo loved him as much as Garbo was capable of loving. And she gave of herself as much as she was capable of giving.

·ten·

A MONG the constants in Jack Gilbert's life were Garbo's refusal to be possessed by him, or by anyone, and Louis B. Mayer's unrelenting hatred of everything about him. On September 8, 1926, the two came together in a devastating collision.

King Vidor, now divorced from his wife, Florence, had set the date for his marriage to Eleanor Boardman. The wedding would take place at Marion Davies's Spanish hacienda in Beverly Hills. With the ceremony still two weeks away, Vidor invited Jack and Greta to dinner at his house. King and Eleanor were, of course, thrilled and radiantly happy. It was equally unsurprising that Jack became infected with the spirit of the occasion and asked Greta Garbo if she would like to make it a double wedding. To everyone's astonishment, Garbo agreed.

Jack was delirious. After months of asking this Swedish will-o'-the-wisp to be his wife, she had finally and unequivocally said yes. Garbo seemed happier than Eleanor had ever seen her—happy and relieved, as if a difficult decision had finally been made. Eleanor, however, remained cautious. Garbo had backed out of promising to marry Jack before, once changing her mind on the very steps of City Hall. Although the idea of a double wedding was fine with her, she was not about to announce it to the world and then have the affair turned into a news circus starring Gilbert and Garbo if Garbo should have second thoughts. She suggested that the double wedding be kept a secret until it happened. That way the surprise would be all the greater. Her suggestion appealed to Jack's sense of the dramatic and to Garbo's passion for privacy as well. They obtained a marriage license under the names they were born with and waited for the great day.

The secret was well kept. At first, no one else knew except Marion Davies. Then, a few days before the wedding, King Vidor thought it prudent to let Louis B. Mayer in on the intentions of MGM's two most valuable properties. Coincidentally or otherwise, Garbo began to seem thoughtful and remote within a day or so of Mayer's learning her secret.

On the morning of the wedding, which dawned hot and clear, Jack looked out his window to see Garbo pulling out of the driveway in her car. Although it was hardly unusual for Garbo to go off by herself without a word, Jack began to feel his first flicker of apprehension. His anxiety mounted as the morning hours went by. He called Marion Davies, hoping against hope that Garbo had embraced the custom of not letting herself be seen before the ceremony. She was not there. Sadly, Jack drove down the hill by himself.

With the hour of the wedding at hand, Vidor and Eleanor Boardman did what they could to stall for time. King remembered some important phone calls that couldn't wait and Eleanor had the photographer take a second round of pictures. But finally the minister approached King and insisted that the wedding go on. Eleanor went to Jack, who was standing in the circular entrance hall because he could not bring himself to mingle with the guests outside, and told him gently that they could wait no longer. Louis B. Mayer had just stepped out of the guest bathroom. He walked over to Jack, slapped him on the back, and said almost gleefully, "What's the matter with you, Gilbert? What do you have to marry her for? Why don't you just fuck her and forget about it?"

With a low snarl, Jack spun toward Mayer and charged with both hands upraised. Mayer, eyes wide, tumbled backward through the door of the guest bathroom. Jack was fast on top of him, his hands seizing Mayer's thick neck, banging his head against the tile wall. Mayer's glasses flew into the air. Eddie Mannix, the ex-bouncer who was never far from Mayer, pushed his way into the bathroom and pulled them apart. Shoving Jack back into the entrance hall, he retrieved Mayer's glasses, tried to straighten them, and began wiping Mayer's face with a towel.

Eleanor Boardman, watching all this, saw Mayer push the towel away and take a step toward Gilbert.

"You're finished, Gilbert," he hissed through bared teeth. "I'll destroy you if it costs me a million dollars."

Jack leaned in Mayer's direction, but Eleanor took his arm and escorted him out the front door before any more harm could be done. Jack stayed for the exchange of vows and the first toast to the new couple. Then he quietly left to begin a night of serious drinking.

By morning he realized fully what he'd done. Mayer was a man who never forgot even an imagined insult. Jack had laid hands on him. Humiliated him. Mayer would make good on his threat if he could. Jack called Irving Thalberg, who'd also been at the wedding. "Mayer is

Mayer," Thalberg told him, "but a contract is also a contract. Just keep your nose clean and he can't touch you." Jack said he'd do his best.

Jack was, of course, furious at Garbo. When she eventually returned to Tower Road, he could not bring himself to speak to her. He sent her a note suggesting that it was time she started paying rent. She never did, but she stayed, and Jack did not force the issue.

The press, meanwhile, had got wind of this latest rumor of a Gilbert-Garbo marriage and then of the current coolness between them. *Photoplay* broke into verse on the subject:

> *Off again, on again, Greta and John again,*
> *How they have stirred up the news for a while.*
> *Making the critics first sigh with them, die with them,*
> *Making the cynical smile.*

Jack plunged back into work. He began his next picture, *The Show*, less than a month after the Vidor wedding. He also had a brief rebound affair with the lovely Renée Adorée, his co-star in this and several other movies, including *The Big Parade*. Renée, as I later learned from her sister, knew full well that Jack was desperately in love with Garbo. When the affair ended, they remained affectionate friends until Renée's untimely death in 1933.

As for *The Show*, Jack had little enthusiasm for the project, but not because of Garbo. Months earlier, he'd seen a Los Angeles production of Ferenc Molnár's *Liliom*, and begged the studio to buy it for him. The story of Liliom, a merry-go-round barker with a Hungarian carnival, is widely known today as the basis for the 1944 musical *Carousel*. Jack wanted to play Liliom and Thalberg agreed, but Mayer overruled him. Instead Mayer had the writers' department concoct another Hungarian carnival story, tenuously based on another property MGM owned, in which Gilbert would play a character named Cock Robin, who in turn played John the Baptist in the carnival show (Renée played Salome), all the time being menaced by a fiendish Greek (Lionel Barrymore) who comes to a bad end when he is bitten to death by a gila monster. Jack's character, Cock Robin, was "a conceited scalawag of low morals."

It was a terrible, silly, cheaply made picture, which used cheap painted sets such as those Jack remembered from his days at Fox. Few critics had anything good to say about it, although most admired Jack's performance. *Variety* wondered in print why a romantic star like John Gilbert would be cast in such a picture: "A sordid role, the type which tends to degrade. It will undoubtedly hurt his general popularity with women. Still, he does it to perfection."

Variety had a point. *The Show* was notable only for the fact that the studio put Jack in it at all. He was the top male star at MGM, with three pictures playing at the same time to sold-out houses on Broadway. *Flesh and the Devil* was setting house records around the world and inspiring millions of printed words about the art of making love. Yet MGM cast Jack in a forgettable piece of trash and in a role that closely matched Mayer's personal opinion of John Gilbert.

Jack, of course, hated the picture, which he dismissed as an "illegitimate spew." He now began to suspect that Mayer was deliberately trying to wreck his career. In fact, *The Show* did mark a turning point. From *His Hour* through *Flesh and the Devil*, his career had climbed steadily, each picture adding to his reputation. Jack's public and private comments about his treatment at MGM were almost entirely positive. Beginning with *The Show*, however, his movies fluctuated between good and poor. He was never again given a blockbuster like *The Big Parade* or *La Bohème*. All were, or were intended to be, low-budget movies.

With *The Show* completed, Jack was scheduled to go to New York to receive *Photoplay*'s medal of honor as the best actor of 1926 for his performance in *The Big Parade*. While there, in view of his suspicion about Mayer, he decided he'd better have a talk with the one man at Loew's who was at least as powerful as Mayer. He went to see Nicholas Schenck. Schenck was personally fond of Jack and valued him highly as a star. He also valued Mayer highly as an executive, but despised him as a human being. All that's known about their conversation is that Schenck told Jack not to worry and that he would see to it that Jack was protected. "Leave Mayer to me," he said.

Schenck encouraged Jack to stay in New York a while longer and enjoy being the toast of the town. It would take his mind off Louis Mayer. Jack agreed that he was overdue to have some fun. It might also take his mind off Garbo. Beatrice Lillie and George Oppenheimer took him in tow. They brought him to the Algonquin Hotel, where Jack was promptly welcomed to the famous Round Table. George Oppenheimer remembers introducing Jack to Dorothy Parker:

> They took to each other immediately. They had in common a great sense of fun. I have seldom seen anyone, let alone an actor, have as good a time as he had with Dottie, Donald Ogden Stewart, and Bob Benchley. They gave him hell, too. They never addressed him as John or Jack. It was always "Great Lover of the Silver Screen." He'd had the Hollywood celebrity treatment for so many years that he really enjoyed their unimpressed and joshing manner. They introduced him to clubs and speakeasies from Greenwich

Village to Harlem. I trailed along but I usually collapsed in the early hours of the morning just about the time the others were getting their second wind. This went on for a solid week. On the seventh day we rested, interrupting our siesta long enough to put Gilbert on the Chief for California.

A short while later, Dorothy Parker was hospitalized for an emergency appendectomy. She checked into the Harkness Pavilion without mentioning that she was basically broke and had no means of paying the bill. Her close friend Beatrice Ames Stewart, Donald Ogden Stewart's wife, came to visit and they discussed how they might dig up the necessary money. They agreed that they'd have to ask friends for help and Beatrice promised to see what she could do. "Just remember," Dorothy Parker insisted, "I don't take money from people I disapprove of. No rich people."

Those qualifications tended to limit the field severely. Beatrice, however, had heard Dorothy speak of John Gilbert and the riotous week they spent together. She sent him a telegram explaining the problem and Jack promptly wired back twenty-five hundred dollars. Beatrice cashed the wire in one-dollar bills and the two women celebrated by hurling money around the hospital room like confetti. Six years later, when Dorothy Parker was in Hollywood getting huge fees as a screenwriter, she sent the twenty-five hundred dollars back to Jack with a warm and grateful note. He acknowledged with a wire that simply said: THANK YOU, MISS FINLAND. Dorothy Parker knew what it meant. Finland was the only country in Europe that had paid its war debts to the United States.

Jack arrived in Los Angeles fully expecting that Garbo would have moved out. If she hadn't—according to Richard Barthelmess, who was on the train with him—he intended to throw her out. The stay in New York had cleared his head. Enough was enough.

But Garbo was still there. He took one look at her and his resolve turned to smoke. She'd missed him, she said. And she needed him. The love affair resumed as if nothing had happened.

At least one of the things she needed Jack for was his help in negotiating a new contract with MGM. In December of 1926, at his suggestion, Garbo demanded a raise from $750 a week to $5,000. Mayer was apoplectic. Whatever faults he might have had, Mayer always kept his word and expected other people to keep theirs. A contract was a contract. Garbo politely told him that she would go home now, and he knew where to reach her if he changed his mind. The figure, she reminded him, was $5,000 a week.

Mayer knew where "home" was: John Gilbert's house on Tower Road. And he knew that Gilbert was behind this. Irene Selznick said the family could always tell whether Mayer had seen Jack Gilbert at the studio by the way he came into the house at night. He would still be trembling with anger when he sat down at the dinner table, and would describe in detail the latest outrage Gilbert had committed. Jack was always trying to do something different, never what the studio wanted him to do; he was now stalling on the start of his next picture; "and now he's even inciting that damned Swede and it's going to cost a fortune."

Mayer and Garbo settled into a battle of wills. He threatened to have her deported for not living up to her contract. She blithely announced that if he tried she would simply marry Mr. Gilbert and become an American citizen. Mayer tried having the studio run a look-alike contest to find a replacement for Garbo, but the attempt was ridiculed in the press. There was no one on earth who could look like Garbo through a camera lens. Mayer threatened to put her in minor roles until her contract ran out. Garbo reminded him that she could stay home for these too. Mayer was becoming desperate. The studio was anxious to begin filming *Anna Karenina* with Garbo in the title role, and Mayer was sure that Garbo was equally anxious to play the part. Mayer tried to press her by announcing that the studio had decided to give the role to stage actress Jeanne Eagels, who was then a sensation for her portrayal of Sadie Thompson in *Rain*. But Jack counseled Garbo to wait Mayer out. Profits from *Flesh and the Devil* were piling up fast and Garbo's fan mail was inching up toward Jack's five thousand letters a week. He knew that many of the letters were demanding a new Gilbert–Garbo picture and that *Anna Karenina* was a natural, even though the male lead had already been assigned to Ricardo Cortez. Jack wanted the part of Vronsky but he was committed to a picture called *Twelve Miles Out*, which was to be shot at the same time. Garbo kept stalling and so did Jack. Jack's excuse was a bothersome appendix, which he was trying to cool down with ice packs rather than face surgery that might deny him to the studio for an indeterminate length of time. Presumably he thanked Dorothy Parker in his heart for the idea. Garbo didn't bother with excuses. She simply stayed home.

The Gilbert–Garbo love affair, meanwhile, was having its usual volcanic ups and downs. Colleen Moore, who lived only a few hundred feet down the hill from Jack, told the story of his bounding exuberantly into her backyard one day. Garbo had promised to marry him again. They were really going to do it this time. The wedding would be up in the little pine grove he had planted for her behind the house, and she would wear a Swedish costume. Colleen congratulated him and offered him a drink to celebrate. They had several. As she remembered:

It showed on him by the time he left the house. After a while, he called me distraught to say that Garbo didn't appreciate him getting drunk on this occasion and had taken off to visit Mauritz Stiller. I was on my way out; otherwise I would have kept him company and possibly out of trouble. He said he was going over to visit the Donald Ogden Stewarts, who were on one of their visits to Hollywood. The story is that Donald tried to distract Jack with a discussion of Flemish painters. He showed Jack a crucifixion scene by Peter Breughel, which he'd bought in Vienna, and told Jack about it in detail.

At the end of the discussion, Jack leaped to his feet, thanked him, and disappeared out the door. The Stewarts could hear his car roaring down that winding road and hoped he'd be all right. Then around two in the morning the Stewarts got a telephone call from the Beverly Hills police. Jack was in jail and he wondered if Donald would come immediately and bring the picture of the crucifixion with him. As far as Donald was concerned, that was a more or less normal Gilbertian request, so he did it. When he got there, he found Jack in a cell surrounded by an attentive audience of police and firemen, whom he was lecturing on the subject of Flemish art.

Between Jack and the desk sergeant, Donald pieced together what had happened. When Jack left the Stewarts' house in such a hurry, it was to rush to the Miramar Hotel so he could find Garbo and tell her all he'd learned about Breughel. When she refused to let him in, he went around outside and tried to climb the wall to reach her balcony window. Stiller was there waiting for him. Stiller stepped out on the balcony and told Jack to go home. Jack just kept climbing. When he reached the balcony, Stiller grabbed him by the shoulders and threw him back down to the ground.

Carey Wilson happened to be driving by right at this time. He was with Carmelita Geraghty and they were on their way home from a party. They both saw this body hurtle to the ground from an upstairs window, yelling like a banshee. They leaped out of their car and ran over and were . . . I was going to say they were surprised to see it was Jack, but I don't think anything Jack did would have surprised Carey Wilson. Anyway, Jack was stunned but he wasn't hurt. His conversation was limited to saying over and over again, "The son of a bitch tried to kill me." They got him on his feet, brushed him off, and put him in his car and followed him all the way home, where he promised he'd go to bed. But he evidently went out again and ended up at the Beverly Hills police station urging them to arrest someone for trying to kill him but then refusing to tell them who it was. They arrested him instead.

The story, of course, made the front pages. Jack was tried on a drunk and disorderly charge and, to his astonishment, heard himself sentenced to ten days in jail. *Variety's* headline read: ALL STEAMED UP OVER GILBERT'S JAIL TERM. The story protested what seemed an excessive punishment for a first offense by a substantial citizen. However, it went on: "Gilbert accepted his sentence gracefully and is now serving it. His cellmate is a negro charged with wife-beating. He refused to accede to a friend's efforts to have him assigned to a hospital on the plea that he was suffering appendix pain. He stated that he preferred jailers to surgeons."

"It's amazing, isn't it?" Jack said to a reporter. "The judge asked me if I thought I could get away with such stunts in Beverly Hills and I said, 'No, and I probably wouldn't do it again.' Then BANG! I got ten days."

Jack didn't serve ten days. The jailers were happy to see him go after a day and a half. On the first morning of his sentence, every starlet in need of publicity appeared at the jail with flowers, boxes of candy, and photographers. His rowdy friends came by the carload. Also his agent, an MGM representative, a small army of reporters, and his doctor, through whom he learned that there might be a problem with his appendix after all. Jack was paroled the next day after promising Douglas Fairbanks that he would not take another drink for the rest of 1927. He then went to Mount Sinai Hospital for tests on his appendix, which indicated that it should come out. Jack distrusted surgeons and preferred to give his appendix the benefit of the doubt. But he began using ice packs in earnest.

Garbo did not come to see Jack in jail. She would have no part in such a circus. But she did go back to Tower Road, which was enough of a circus in itself. Carey Wilson, who was hiding from Hopie again, also moved in and got to know Garbo very well.

Carey said:

The *flicka* and I had many quiet long talks. We'd stay up half the night discussing anything from bookbinding to radio transmission to Ibsen's plays. We never finished a conversation without my being utterly amazed. Few people knew the extent or the depth of her reading. Jack used to send to Europe for classic and current literature from all sources printed in Swedish. Garbo preferred to read in Swedish so she wouldn't miss any nuances that would have been less apparent to her in English.

She also tried hard to be a good hostess for Jack. Every Sunday, there would be an open house on Tower Road, with two dozen or so guests. Entertaining was second nature for Jack but agony for Garbo, at least at first. But when she realized that these attractive people wanted only to exchange sociability and friendship, she did gradually relax and lose most of her shyness. She was, at this period, the most intriguing woman I have ever seen. She entered heartily and effectively into all the games, from tennis to murder mysteries. She could clown with the best of them when clowning was in order. She was also perfectly capable of more than holding her own in some reasonable erudite discussions. Garbo made a lot of friends in this Sunday group.

Eleanor Boardman had a different view. "Garbo," she said, "was the most fascinating woman I ever met, but she was also the most selfish. She had no real love for Jack. She used to drive him mad, lead him on, and then disappear. She promised at least three times to marry him and then backed off. I always liked Jack. He had such an intensity. Everything came to a stop when he appeared. Men like him come along once in a million years. I wish I knew why Garbo treated him so badly but I don't. She took everything he had to offer and gave nothing."

Jack himself told a reporter, "Garbo is marvelous, the most alluring creature you have ever seen. Capricious as the devil, whimsical, temperamental, and fascinating. Some days she refuses to come to the studio. When she doesn't feel like working, she will not work. Garbo never acts unless she feels she can do herself justice. But what magnetism when she gets in front of a camera. What appeal. What a woman. One day she is childlike, naïve, ingenuous, a girl of ten. The next she is a mysterious woman a thousand years old, knowing everything, baffling."

In April, Louis B. Mayer capitulated and agreed to a compromise salary of $3,000 a week for Garbo. It would take effect after the filming of *Anna Karenina*. Mayer assumed that Garbo would go into immediate production. Garbo promptly fell ill. Her physician reported that she had an infection that would require at least a week's rest. Maybe even a month. Jack, meanwhile, reported that he was feeling much better, thank you, and was ready to begin making *Twelve Miles Out*, the picture he'd been delaying since December.

Twelve Miles Out was an adventure yarn about rumrunners. Jack announced that he had a proprietary interest in the subject and applied his expertise to helping write the screenplay. It was about two rival bootleggers, the other played by Ernest Torrence, who are friendly enemies until a society woman comes between them. The woman was Joan Crawford. Jack bursts into her seaside house while on the run from the Coast Guard. When she threatens to call the police, he kidnaps her and takes her aboard his boat. Ernest Torrence captures in turn Jack's boat with Joan on it. Both men are smitten with this cool, high-class lady, but Joan Crawford's affections lean toward the man who kidnapped her first. This sets the stage for a ripsnortin' fist-and-gun fight that is as bloody and realistic as anything ever put on the screen. Jack wins in the end, getting to die in Crawford's arms. In the original play, the hero sailed off into the sunset with her, having been reformed by the love of a good woman. But in the movie, MGM decided on the death penalty with the censors and the Hays office in mind.

The New York Times gave the picture a rave review: "It's gory, it's gruesome, but both men shoot with fierce abandon, with such mad joy in the thing even when they are hit, that it all fairly fascinates the spectator, jerking him into another world of savagery and blood. . . . It's not pretty, that's true, but it's not pap. That's great." Other critics said that John Gilbert is "at his best as the swearing, fighting, drinking, and dashing lawbreaker," and "John Gilbert gives one of the soundest performances of his career."

Jack, however, was more than usually disatisfied with the picture. Too many corners had been cut in the name of economy. A scene that he'd helped write and that he thought gave greater scope and excitement to the picture had been edited out. He saw Mayer's conspiratorial hand behind all of it. Joan Crawford, on the other hand, saw Garbo behind it. Crawford had done only two pictures for MGM and was excited by the chance to work with the studio's biggest star. She soon noticed, however, that Jack did not seem enthusiastic about the picture as filming progressed. "He was still madly in love with Garbo," she said, "and the romance was not going well. He was like a caged lion." Jack would come on the set in the morning and try to phone Greta, only to find that she was either out or not answering. That would set the tone of the day. He'd be impatient with Crawford and difficult with the director, Jack Conway. Conway, however, had been a close friend since the Ince–Triangle days and knew how to coax a good performance out of him despite the emotional undercurrents. Still, Crawford said, "Jack resented every moment he was not with Garbo." Even Jack admitted that "we go around glaring at each other like a lot of spoiled children."

The picture did well critically and financially. But Jack, never one to leave well enough alone, gave an interview to a Los Angeles reporter that was released to the Associated Press. In it he acknowledged that he and Mayer were no longer speaking and that he thought poorly of the kind of management he'd had lately. He said he was thinking of taking a vacation of five, ten, or fifteen years from the movies and then perhaps forming his own company. His contract, the article noted, had only eighteen months to run. Regarding *Twelve Miles Out*, Jack said, "I haven't seen the picture and did not even go to the preview. It is not a good picture. . . . One thing that makes me furious is that there is a good story in the bootlegging industry. There is an epic tale there and someday someone is coming along to do it." Then, while railing at length against pound-foolish studio economies, he seemed to be thinking ahead to *Anna Karenina*. While acknowledging that production costs had to be prudently controlled, he made the point that certain projects are better not even attempted if they can't be done properly. "We are making a Russian picture now built around the splendor and lavishness of the days of the Czar. The appropriation for the picture is $125,000. It can't be done on this sum. That's all there is to it."

Mayer, naturally, exploded when he read the interview. Thalberg prevailed upon Jack to apologize publicly and to withdraw his critical remarks about a picture that had just been released. The studio announced that Jack had been roundly misquoted by a female reporter with a grudge against MGM.

"Like hell I was," Jack told Leatrice Joy.

Despite the divorce, Jack had never been out of touch with Leatrice for very long, always remembering birthdays and often visiting me, although I was too young to remember. She knew all about his problems with Louis Mayer and more than she wanted to about his ups and downs with Garbo. Leatrice was not entirely sympathetic on the studio issue, because she felt that Jack tended to create his problems. Leatrice, remember, felt strongly on the subject of loyalty to one's employer.

Leatrice was still with De Mille (De Mille having set up his own studio after leaving Paramount) and had just finished doing another society-girl role in a movie called *Vanity*. On May 10, 1927, Leatrice went with Conrad Nagel to a lavish reception at the Biltmore Hotel. The occasion was the announcement of the formation of the Academy of Motion Picture Arts and Sciences, with Douglas Fairbanks as the Academy's first president. The five hundred guests included everyone of note in Hollywood. Leatrice knew, of course, that Jack would be there.

While she was dancing, she spotted Jack on the floor with Garbo, "who was wearing a bilious-green chiffon dress with her slip straps showing." Passing behind him, Leatrice gave his head a playful shove. He quickly maneuvered himself into position to do the same to her. They chased each other around the dance floor for the rest of the number, neither Garbo nor Leatrice's partner realizing what was going on. Finally, he winked at her and cocked his head toward the entrance. Leatrice returned to her table, excused herself, and met Jack at the door.

"Come on," he said. "My boat's moored at San Pedro. Let's get on it and never come back."

"W-what boat?" she stammered.

"It's an eighty-foot schooner. Big as a house. I just bought it."

"What about the baby?" she asked.

"We'll take her along. The sea's a fine place to bring up children. Hurry up. Go get your coat before someone finds out."

Leatrice considered Jack's invitation for about two minutes. It was completely irresponsible. On the other hand, her career didn't seem to be heading anywhere and her love life was less than terrific. Why not? Feeling like a wicked child, she dashed off to get her ermine wrap and bumped into Conrad Nagel on the way out.

"Leatrice? Where are you going?" he asked.

She told him.

"Are you out of your mind?" he said. "You can't do that. You're a mother and you also have a responsibility to your studio. You can't just dash off with Gilbert. He'll only hurt you again. Don't be a fool. Come with me, I'll take you home."

Leatrice always regretted her decision. "It might have been fun," she told me wistfully. "Life on the briny deep with Jack. Anyway, I never got the chance again."

The turmoil surrounding the *Anna Karenina* project continued. Garbo, while well enough to dance at the Biltmore, had still not recovered from her "infection," although she let it be known that the immediate institution of her $3,000 salary might have curative powers. On May 18, *Variety* announced that *Anna Karenina* was being suspended for extensive revisions and all previous work was being scrapped. When shooting resumed, Anna would definitely be played by Greta Garbo. Ricardo Cortez would be replaced by John Gilbert. And the picture would no longer be called *Anna Karenina*. It would be called *Love*.

Garbo, as usual, got her way in the end. Her new salary went into effect immediately. Garbo, Gilbert, and the fans of *Flesh and the Devil* also got their way. Irving Thalberg was delighted. The new casting and the new title, which was his idea, would allow marquees all over America to read GILBERT AND GARBO IN LOVE. Everyone was happy except, of course, Ricardo Cortez and especially Louis B. Mayer. Mayer knew

[141]

by now that he had another potential smash hit on his hands. But he also knew that he'd been had.

On Thalberg's instructions, *Love* was filmed with two different endings. One was the original tragic version as written by Tolstoy. Anna, the wife of a Russian nobleman, falls in love with Vronsky, a young officer, thereby forfeiting her right to her child. Realizing her tragic fate, she throws herself in front of a moving train just as the unknowing Vronsky is elsewhere offering a toast of "love." In the alternative ending, written by Frances Marion, three years have passed since her affair with Vronsky. Her husband has conveniently died. Anna visits her son at school, where she runs into Vronsky, who has also come for a visit. Time having cleansed their guilt, they are reunited and live happily ever after.

Distributors were given their choice of a tragic or an upbeat ending. New York and Boston stuck with Tolstoy. Middle America generally opted for Frances Marion, even though Jack had gone on record against a sentimentalized and truncated treatment, which he called "cheap imitation Tolstoy." Frances Marion never forgave him for those remarks.

There were also rumors of problems on the set, which was closed to all visitors. One story had it that the director, Edmund Goulding, had flared up several times because of Garbo's reliance upon Jack to tell her how to do a difficult scene. Goulding would instruct her, she would listen politely, and then glance at Jack to see if he approved. If he did not, she would play it his way. It's difficult, however, to believe that Goulding would have objected very strenuously to anything that made Garbo feel good about her performance, and *Photoplay* said it was agreed that Jack would direct her love scenes. Goulding, besides, had a reputation for being very good with actors and also for bending with the wind.

Another story that appeared in print was that the set was closed because "John Gilbert becomes painfully self-conscious when strangers watch his work." Anyone who knew Jack recognized this as nonsense. And William Daniels, who photographed the picture, said it was he, not Gilbert, who closed the set while Garbo was working. "No visitors," he said. "No one present except the director and the crew. She [Garbo] was so shy, so shy. I did it to protect her."

During the shooting, Jack was interviewed by Dorothy Herzog, who came to see him in his new star "dressing room," which was actually a large Spanish cottage with two floors and a fireplace. Disputes over the dressing room and who was to pay for it fill the John Gilbert file in the MGM archives. Herzog seemed particularly able to draw him out. She noticed the new maroon-and-gold decor, the books and oil paintings. It was the biggest and handsomest "dressing room" in the studio. And she knew, of course, that he was living, more or less, with Greta Garbo, perhaps the most desirable woman in the world at the time. She asked Jack if he was happy.

"He didn't say anything for a minute," she wrote. But then he answered, "Yes, I guess I'm happy enough now. I've worked myself into a more contented frame of mind at least. During this last year, I have been miserably unhappy in both mind and body. But I think that is all over now. I'm saner now."

"This movie game," he continued, "is like shoot-the-chutes. You're in breathtaking ecstasy one minute and down in the doldrums the next. If you make a success you're bound to run into a certain amount of disillusionment. You run into people who fawn over you and flatter your vanity, but not because you are what you are. Charlie Chaplin is the most famous man in this profession, and I think he's the loneliest.

"You can't live for your art in this game. You've got to keep a weather eye on the box office and that means you're going to do a lot of things and play many a part you don't want to. If an actor has any integrity at all, it will take the keen edges off his idealism about his work. He worries and frets. I know I do. I don't leave my work in the studio. It comes home with me.

"When I first started out, I wanted to be an actor more than anything else in the world. I wanted the respect for my work, not my personality. Then I wanted money. I hated poverty like a snake. It is a snake. It wasn't that I wanted automobiles and a fine home and servants for themselves alone, but I wanted the mental security and the opportunity to come into contact with the greater things in life that money brings. I thought that if I had artistic recognition and money, I would have happiness. Someone once said, 'Be careful what you wish for. It's liable to come true.' That's about the most cynical but the wisest observation in the world.

"Some of the things I wanted came true for me and many didn't. My marriage went on the rocks. I've played roles I haven't believed in. I've done things I wish to God I hadn't. I've had friendships I would have banked my life on go out like a match in the breeze. But with all that I love this game. If it has taken things away from me, it has given me plenty."

Love, once it finally got rolling, progressed rapidly and the shooting was completed in four weeks. The picture opened at the Embassy Theater in New York to generally enthusiastic reviews. *The New York Times* raved about Garbo: "Her singularly fine acting as Anna held the audience in unusual silence. She is ably supported by John Gilbert but it is the portrait of Anna that is the absorbing feature." *Photoplay* said: "*Love* is right. *Anna Karenina* would have been wrong. It isn't Tolstoy but it is John Gilbert and Greta Garbo . . . beautifully presented and magnificently acted. . . . Even in the new set of circumstances invented for them by Frances Marion, there is something of the original strength of their characters." The same *Photoplay* also gave Jack credit for assisting Edmund Goulding in the direction, suggesting, of course, that Jack's help could hardly have been unwelcome. *Variety* said: "They are in a fair way of becoming the biggest box office team this country has yet known. Both are strong away from each other and have proved it. But combine that double strength with a reasonable story and who or what can stop it?"

In August of 1927, just after the completion of *Love*, Jack was invited to the wedding of Nicholas Schenck in New York. He had to send his regrets because he was committed to be in Washington shooting the exteriors of his next scheduled picture. His regrets were especially profound, not only because Schenck was becoming his friend and protector, but because Schenck's bride considered herself Jack's number-one adoring fan. She was a bright and pretty showgirl named Pansy Wilcox. The marriage was a happy one that lasted the rest of Schenck's life. It was also to have an important effect upon Jack and his career. The Schencks would be Jack's firm allies against any harm that Louis B. Mayer might threaten. And Jack needed the strongest friends he could find at this time because his former protector and mentor, Irving Thalberg, was having problems of his own.

Thalberg had been demanding a greater percentage of MGM's profits, and was getting it. The money was coming directly from Louis Mayer's pockets. Jealousy at a personal as well as a professional level had also been simmering for some time. The personalities of the two men were so different that comparisons were inevitable. Almost any studio head would have looked boorish and heavy-handed in contrast to the gracious Thalberg. But Mayer, because he was there and also because of his famous temper, suffered more than most, and he came to resent Thalberg deeply.

Rowland V. Lee tells of the time he made an appointment with Thalberg to tell him about a story he wanted to sell. Lee met the young production chief late one day at Thalberg's office, where he normally worked twelve to eighteen hours a day. As Rowland was outlining his story, a door suddenly burst open and Mayer stormed into the room in a wild fury. Utterly ignoring Rowland, he lashed out at Thalberg, calling him stupid, a blundering fool, and spewing out a stream of the foulest obscenities. Then he wheeled around and left, slamming the door behind him. Thalberg never opened his mouth. When Mayer was gone, he turned calmly to Rowland and said, "Please continue, Mr. Lee. You were saying . . . after the train wreck?" Rowland was shaken by the ugly scene and he hurried through his tale. Thalberg listened carefully, said he did not think it was his kind of material, but encouraged him to come again whenever he had an idea.

"Under the surface, Mayer never changed," Rowland told me. "All those hours Conrad Nagel spent with him gave him a new veneer, but that's all. I've always been glad I never had to work with him."

Regarding the Conrad Nagel reference: Mayer had a thick Yiddish accent when Jack first met him; Nagel had one of the best speaking voices in Hollywood; Mayer commissioned Nagel to teach him how to talk. The effect, except when Mayer got angry and slipped, was astonishing. Mayer seemed quite polished, quite in command of the English language, with only a trace of accent remaining.

"And I'll tell you something else," Rowland went on. "I think Mayer drove Conrad Nagel out of Hollywood by way of thanks. It's like the Egyptians who killed the men who designed the secret chambers of the pyramids so the secret would be safe. There are a lot of ways to kill off an actor. Mayer leased Nagel out and put him in every crappy picture that came along for the next three years. Something like thirty movies, every one of them a dog. People think Nagel's career ended with the coming of sound. Not with that voice it didn't. Nagel died of overexposure."

The picture Jack had begun shooting excited him for several reasons. He'd be working with Monta Bell, his friend and tennis partner and also a very thoughtful director with an experimental streak. Bell had directed Garbo in *The Torrent*, and before that Jack's popular picture *The Snob*. His co-star would be Jeanne Eagels, who received a lot of attention from the press on her triumphant return to the movies. (She'd made two minor films ten years before. She would make only two more before she died, in 1929, of a deliberate overdose of heroin.)

But what excited Jack most of all was that his new picture, to be titled *Man, Woman and Sin*, was a thinly disguised and Americanized version of *The Widow in the Bye Street*. It was the John Masefield poem he'd wanted to put on film for so many years; the story that had almost led to a brawl with Mayer. Jack and Monta Bell had written the screenplay together. The story told of a poor boy and his mother and of his happy childhood. Upon growing up he gets a job in a newspaper's shipping department, then becomes a cub reporter. He falls foolishly in love with the beautiful society editor, who happens to be the boss's mistress. She leads him on. The two are confronted in her apartment by the girl's lover. The boy kills the older man in self-defense and is tried for murder. He is sentenced to hang. The girl admits at the last moment that she had set him up and he was only protecting himself. Jack, sadder but wiser, leaves her and returns to his mother.

It wasn't the tragic ending John Masefield had in mind but, on the other hand, Masefield wasn't writing in Hollywood. Even so, the movie was skillfully directed and wonderfully acted. Jack put his heart and soul into a striking performance unlike anything he had done before. He was trying to capture his own raw boyhood and then idealize it. In the film, he rejoices in being blessed with a tender mother, and when he falls in love, it's with all the ardor and sweet innocence of an eighteen-year-old.

Man, Woman and Sin drew critical acclaim all across the country. *Motion Picture Today* wrote: "When prizes for intelligence begin to be awarded to cinema circles, Monta Bell will receive a heavy and well-earned recognition . . . perfect in atmosphere, well related, coherent, convincing . . . tremendous entertainment. Mr. Gilbert shows new range in fine acting . . . a great big box-office entertainment." Robert Sherwood wrote: "John Gilbert is the guileless, bewildered youth, a distinct departure from his usual style and an effective one." A sampling from various major city newspapers included: "Here is a new Gilbert. No sophistication but he rises to greater heights." "Gilbert's best work since *The Big Parade*." "This time he is in a good picture and he endeavors to act for his audience, not excite it." "Gilbert brilliant." "One of the most intelligent, moving and dramatic films in many months. Gilbert's performance is all the more remarkable when one considers that in portraying the character of the cub reporter, scarcely out of adolescence, he has to overcome his age and his reputation for sophisticated roles. Yet he overcomes both."

Several critics singled out one great scene in which Jack, as the cub reporter, returns to the office after attending the Embassy Ball, still breathless from the glamour of the occasion and the company of a fascinating woman. Splendid in his evening clothes, he wanders all over the newspaper plant looking for someone to tell about the bewitching evening and the dazzling newness that has come to him. He goes down to the shipping department where he used to work, looking for his old friends and hoping that they'll comment on his borrowed splendor. But the men are working and barely notice him. He strolls through the pressroom, dying to talk to anyone. No one is interested. In frustration he sits at his desk and pours his feelings into his typewriter. All this is expressed without a single title. All pantomime and motion. It is the art of silent movies at its best.

·eleven·

MARCUS Loew, the president of MGM's parent company, died in September 1927, after a brief illness. The funeral for this theater tycoon, a grade-school dropout and son of Jewish Austrian immigrants who had parlayed a Coney Island peep show into a chain of four hundred theaters and a film studio, was an extravaganza. Everyone of importance in the industry attended if they could reach New York, or sent elaborate floral tributes if they could not.

Nicholas Schenck moved quickly into the power vacuum. Without calling a board meeting to choose a successor, Schenck simply named himself the new president. Schenck had the power, the position, and the support of everyone, with the notable exception of Louis B. Mayer. Mayer took the news hard. He was now working for a man who cordially disliked him.

A month after Loew's death, *Variety* issued a Marcus Loew Memorial in which all his friends rushed to buy advertising space. The first page belonged to Nicholas Schenck. Louis Mayer filled a black-bordered page with language such as "His friendship was one of the most precious treasures of my life." He went on about Loew's genius and love of family, and wound up saying, "It would demand the pen of a great poet rather than my feeble capacity of expression in words to depute the real feelings that stir my heart. In his memory I shall always find my finest inspiration."

A few pages later, Jack's tribute said simply, "To the passing of a great man and a greater friend."

Shortly after Marcus Loew's death, an infinitely momentous event took place, and was barely noticed at first. *The Jazz Singer* was released in New York and audiences literally stood up and cheered.

The Jazz Singer was, ironically, a last desperate gamble by Warner Brothers, one of the smallest studios in Hollywood and probably the least stable financially. The year before, Warners had formed the Vitaphone Company in partnership with Western Electric to develop a sound system for motion pictures. Vitaphone premiered a series of demonstration shorts in which records were synchronized with the film. The demonstration films were frequently disrupted by breakdowns. But a year later, Warners decided to risk everything on an all-out publicity-and-sales campaign in support of a hybrid talkie with only a few lines of dialogue and five songs, including Irving Berlin's "Blue Skies" and Gus Kahn's "Toot Toot Tootsie, Goodbye," sung by Al Jolson. (Myrna Loy, by the way, had a small part as a chorus girl.)

Except for the sound gimmick, *The Jazz Singer* was a very ordinary silent picture. Overall quality was fair, at best. Synchronization continued to be less than reliable. But the audience did cheer when Jolson spoke the historic words, "Wait a minute, wait a minute. You ain't heard nothing yet."

Encouraged by *The Jazz Singer's* success, Warners released its first all-talking film, *Lights of New York*, in 1928. It too was a success, and by then every major studio was frantically rushing to convert to sound. Fox developed a technique for recording sound directly on the film's edge, which quickly rendered the Vitaphone synchronized-disk system obsolete. But its purpose was served. Warners was solvent, and sound was here to stay.

There were many bright people who thought or hoped that talking pictures were just a fad, and Jack, at first, was one of them. Such a belief might seem today like insular, wishful thinking, but there was some good reasoning behind it. For one thing, very few theaters in the country were equipped for sound and very few could afford the substantial cost of conversion. For that reason alone, it seemed that talkies would be a scattered novelty for years to come. The economies of converting appeared to preclude rapid change. The cost of changing over both theaters and studios would end up being greater than the entire industry's income for the preceding year.

And for what? Because cameras and microphones would have to be stationary, it was technically impossible to make a sound picture that even approached the artistic quality of a silent picture. Action would be severely limited. Because vacuum-tube microphones were sensitive in only one direction, actors would have to speak into floral arrangements and lamps without turning their heads. Noisy cameras would have to be encased in a box along with the cameraman. Sound quality would range from poor to fair. The movies would simply not be nearly as good. And tremendous revenues would be lost from foreign distribution if the movies were produced in English. The man who asked "Who the

hell wants to hear an actor talk?" was actually echoing a popular sentiment. Stage plays were for hearing actors talk. Movies were for scope
and grandeur and action. The name of the art form, after all, was
moving pictures.

And what about the actors? Could they talk? How well? Clara Bow
had a Bronx honk. The Talmadge sisters spoke Brooklynese. Others
lisped. Some could talk just fine but not in English. In fact, a number
of actors and actresses who had British or European accents had been
presumed to be American all along. What would happen when their
fans heard them? Most actors, the studios realized to their horror, had
virtually no concept of good diction. Almost all, except those few with
long stage training, would need voice testing and diction coaches. Elocution experts, many with invented credentials, flocked to Hollywood as
hundreds of actors and actresses panicked.

If Jack was concerned, or if anyone else had the slightest misgiving
about his speaking voice, no film historian to date has been able to find
any hint of it. If anything, with the elevation of his friend Nicholas
Schenck to the presidency of Loew's, Jack felt more secure than ever as
he completed his last picture of 1927.

It was called *The Cossacks*, another Frances Marion rewrite of a
Tolstoy novel. Jack was happily reunited with Renée Adorée and Ernest
Torrence, both good friends. The director was George Hill, Frances
Marion's husband, but Clarence Brown was called in at the end to put
"finishing touches" on what he later described as a mess. "It was difficult
to edit, the story did not hang together well, and the production costs
were enormous. Whoever was to blame, it wasn't the fault of the actors."

In the story, Jack played a cossack named Lukashka who annoys his
father by being more interested in romancing the lovely Maryana than
in riding around killing Turks like a good cossack. Eventually the whole
town rejects him, including Maryana, who could never love a coward.
Lukashka rides off after escaping Turks and returns a wounded hero and
very proud. Now it's his pride that offends Maryana. She chooses to
marry a visiting prince and departs with the royal party. Lukashka chases
after her, kidnaps her, and leaves the royal party to be chopped up by
some marauding Turks.

The Cossacks turned out to be a pretty good Russian western and was
well received by audiences and most critics. Many of the critics, however, mentioned the "unintentional humor" in the titles, which turned
out to be a minor disaster. The subtitles were written by John Colton,

who was considered to be one of Hollywood's more intelligent scenario and title writers (until this picture).

In *The Cossacks*, Colton slipped. Jack (Lukashka) is introduced with a title saying, "He does not like the smell of blood. He is a chewer of sunflower seeds." Later, when Jack's own blood is up, he says, "We'll slit every unbelieving throat that gurgles in these mountains." After he slits a couple, he admits, "The smell of blood . . . is . . . not . . . so . . . bad."

Audiences also thought it was hilarious when Jack leaned over a bale of hay toward Renée and tried to seduce her with "I know a place where the turtle lives." Young American bloods were trying that one out on their girlfriends for months.

Ernest Torrence, who played Jack's father, didn't get off easily either. He got to "say," "Lu, when the dust settled I found my sword strung with heads like beads of a rosary."

Jack had the last word. When he returns a hero, he announces his new status with the words "I am no longer a cowslip."

Mordaunt Hall was a bit disappointed with Jack's performance, which he found to be too intense. Hall commented in the *Times* that Jack was "stirred to merriment by actions that would hardly provoke a smile." Among the scenes Hall was talking about was one in which Jack laughs uproariously, throwing back his head and slapping his friends on the shoulder. So far so good. But then the title appears, written after the film was completed, explaining what cracked him up. "I will write a letter that will make the Sultan hop like a fiend on cinders."

Leatrice says, "Whatever Jack was actually saying, it probably was pretty funny. Lip-readers have a ball watching Jack's old movies."

Jack was furious about the titles, as was Ernest Torrence. They both knew how easy it was for a title writer to make actors look ridiculous. An editor could do the same, snipping away a few feet or a few inches of film here and there to make an actor's movements seem jerky and un-coordinated or make his facial expressions seem totally out of proportion to anything that might have motivated them. Jack, rightly or wrongly, continued to suspect Mayer's hand behind anything that was both inexplicable and personally damaging to him. He was not, of course, so paranoid that he imagined Mayer personally supervising the title writing and editing so as deliberately to damage an expensive MGM production. He knew that Mayer would not do anything so overt even if he was so inclined. But he also knew Mayer could force the release of a picture before any but the most outstanding problems were corrected. Jack let it be known that he thought *The Cossacks* was "a botched-up job," and demanded the privilege of choosing and being responsible for his own pictures in the future.

Jack had also seen Mayer's hand behind a vicious article printed by *Vanity Fair* magazine in May 1928. The author was Jim Tully, a former hobo and prizefighter now trying to make a reputation as a Hollywood writer. Tully had published a few stories in New York, which he then tried to sell to the various studios. He'd never met John Gilbert, but Lenore Coffee, a film writer and a friend of Tully's, said that he had met with Mayer and he certainly knew about the animosity that existed between the two men. The title of Tully's article was "John Gilbert— the Screen's Most Romantic Hero Has No Glamour for Hollywood's Severest Critic." What followed was a hatchet job, devastating in its cruelty and in its lasting effect upon Jack's reputation.

"His emotion is on the surface," it began. "His nature is not deep. His enthusiasms are as transient as newspaper headlines. He has no sense of humor. He struts his little celluloid hours upon the set like a youthful Hannibal."

After this introduction, Tully proceeded with a capsule biography in which he presented Jack and his mother as conspirators bent upon the abandonment and ruin of Jack's father. Then, jumping ahead to Jack's beginnings in Hollywood and his period with Maurice Tourneur, Tully wrote: "To this young philanderer of superficial emotion, the Tourneur orbit was too large for the Gilbert cosmos. At this late day no trace of the greater man can be found in the lesser." Moving right along in the same vein, Tully wrote: "In *The Big Parade* he was second in ability to the gigantic ex-carpenter moron, Karl Dane. In *Flesh and the Devil* he was merely a romantic prop upon which Miss Greta Garbo hung an American reputation.

"Upon release of *The Big Parade*, it was fondly hoped and openly predicted that Mr. Gilbert would carry the romantic banner so suddenly dropped by Rudolph Valentino. But where Valentino has marched like a gallant Italian despoiler through the flower-bedecked portals of female hearts, Mr. Gilbert was only able to enthrall the weaker subjects in his kingdom. Perhaps women are wiser than we know in such things. Valentino was very much a man.

"Mr. Gilbert is not a gifted actor. He plays every role the same. Whether as Vronsky in *Love*, the American doughboy in *The Big Parade*, or the bootlegger in *Twelve Miles Out*, it is always the part of John Gilbert.

"Gilbert is blamed for much of the so-called temperament with which

[151]

Miss Garbo punished the sensitive MGM producers. He is the bane of the publicity department." Tully quoted Lon Chaney as saying, "'Mr. Gilbert is a young man with a romantic face, almost a high school education and a conceit that through pampering and soft handling has passed all belief. He is a good actor and thinks he is much better. He has forgotten the meaning of tact from disuse of that quality. He loves to impress folks with his greatness by being unpleasant to them.'

"But to be fair, Gilbert has certain qualities of loyalty which are highly praiseworthy when he so far forgets himself as to show them."

The story ended on a note of melodrama. "John Pringle, Gilbert's father, is now an extra player in Hollywood. His salary averages less than fifty dollars a week. He traced his son to Hollywood having seen him on the screen. They had not met in twenty years. This was said not to have pleased the young Mr. Gilbert. I saw John Pringle recently in the role of a convict. He stood head down in prison garb among other sad partakers of crumbs from producers' tables. I wonder what he was thinking. Perhaps of the vagaries of women . . . and children."

Jack was shattered by the article. Carey Wilson said that Jack literally threw up after reading it:

> You have to remember that almost everybody liked Jack and that Jack liked everybody too, with very few exceptions. People like that are never ready for this kind of thing. You'd think Jack would have developed a thick skin having been in the public eye so long, but he never did. The shame of it is that a little man like Tully could make a name for himself this way at the expense of a decent man like Jack. It just crushed Jack. For a while, Jack acted as if he believed every rotten thing Tully said about him.

The article was a sensation in Hollywood and New York. Everyone read it, many quoted it, and it's still quoted today as if it were an authoritative piece on John Gilbert. Tully, who freely admitted never having met Jack, reveled in the furor his article caused. For a while he became a minor celebrity and was invited to homes where he'd never been welcomed before. He sold a story to Paramount, a murder melodrama based on his own hobo freight-riding days, and Paramount rushed it into production. The picture was called *Beggars of Life*, with Wallace Beery and Louise Brooks. Louise, a fond friend of Jack's, asked Tully why he wrote such an article. Tully answered, "Because I felt like doing it. And if Jack is big enough he will get over it and I think he is big enough. You might imagine by reading the story that I'm Jack's deadly enemy. As a matter of fact, I admire him very much."

Many of Jack's friends were vocal in his defense. George Oppenheimer wrote that Tully had "a twisted mind with all the gutter instincts." James Quirk, the editor of *Photoplay*, encouraged Jack to set the record straight by writing his own life story, to be serialized in the magazine. Jack agreed and, with the blessing but not the help of the MGM publicity department, sat down to write the first of four installments, which ran from June through September of 1928. Quirk wrote an introduction in which he said of Tully: "'The ingrate of Hollywood,' he has been called; the hobo who was sheltered and petted by the motion picture people to whom he appealed for help. . . . He was sponsored by Chaplin, who gave him the run of the studio. He repaid Chaplin by describing him as a child of the London gutter. . . . He even dragged in Charlie's mother. . . . [Tully] made some money and moved to Beverly Hills. Utterly unlovable, he wanted to be loved by everyone. Failing, he turned bitter and has written more vicious stuff about motion picture people than any man . . . ever has. His article about John Gilbert is more vicious, more unfair, and in worse taste, if possible, than anything else he has written. Brutal, unfair, untrue. I know Jack Gilbert. I am glad he is a friend of mine."

Over the next six months, Jack's fan mail increased by half, some weeks reaching ten thousand letters. The outpouring of support from fans led him to remark that Tully's article might have been the best thing that could have happened to him. He didn't mean it, of course. Tully's slander continued to eat at him.

Jack's biography was a thoughtful and sometimes bewildered account of the road that took him from Logan, Utah, to the highest pinnacle of movie stardom. It now seems tame by the autobiographical standards of modern Hollywood. Jack does not "name names," nor does he catalogue his sex life, which included some of the most glittering movie queens, as well as starlets, secretaries, and several of the world's highest-priced hookers, whose company he occasionally preferred. But it does reveal a kind and decent human being who knows how lucky he's been but has few illusions about the luck holding out forever.

If Mayer read the article, it apparently did nothing to change his mind about Jack. Late in the same year, Mayer was quoted as saying of his studio, "We have no hate here. We have love. I love Irving, I love everybody . . . except John Gilbert, Sam Goldwyn, and Charlie Chaplin." He'd soon have reason to hate Jack even more.

During the summer of 1928, Mayer, who had long been interested in establishing himself as a power in politics, took time off to help Herbert Hoover get elected. Mayer managed to have himself appointed Republican State Committeeman from California and attended the 1928 Republican Convention in Kansas City. Mayer helped convince William Randolph Hearst, who controlled the California delegation, to support Herbert Hoover rather than Andrew Mellon. Mayer then claimed credit for the crucial support of the California delegation. Hoover, Mayer was satisfied, was in his debt.

While Mayer was off playing kingmaker, Irving Thalberg began to complain that he was being left with too much of the MGM load for too little money. The "talkie" crisis had compounded the ordinary problems of running a studio. Thalberg felt that Mayer was taking advantage of him and said so to Robert Rubin, the other member of the "Mayer group." Rubin agreed that a quiet talk with Nicholas Schenck was in order.

Schenck, meanwhile, was having quiet talks with William Fox. After Marcus Loew's death the year before, Loew's widow was left with four hundred thousand shares of Loew's stock, worth thirty million dollars. The stock also represented a controlling interest in a holding company of two hundred theaters, a successful studio, and a roster of star performers, notably Gilbert and Garbo. Warner Brothers and Paramount were also interested in buying the stock. But Fox was by far in the strongest position. His Fox Movietone system of sound recorded on film was clearly the direction in which the industry was headed. He'd also developed his famous talking newsreel, Fox Movietone News, and was working on a revolutionary wide-screen technique. Fox's feature films were improving in quality all the time, he was building an educational film industry by selling special films to schools and churches, and he owned his own chain of theaters across the nation. Fox began to think of himself as the future of the motion-picture industry and the one man in the world capable of running the whole thing. All of it.

Fox began negotiating with Schenck in June 1928. He offered fifty million dollars for the widow's stock, plus a bonus of two million for Schenck if he managed to push the deal through. Fox pointed out that by merging his company with Loew's, and his studio with MGM, there would be a savings of seventeen million a year through the elimination of competition and the disposal of redundant property and executives, Louis B. Mayer in particular. Nicholas Schenck quietly approached Mrs. Marcus Loew and other family members, asking their permission to enter into serious negotiations for the sale of their stock. Permission was granted on condition that the thing be done quietly.

An important part of any deal with Fox would include the guaranteed retention of those stars whose popularity made them major financial assets. John Gilbert was at the absolute apex of his career. His pictures were breaking attendance records all over the country and throughout the world. *Love* arrived at the Million Dollar Theater in Los Angeles, and *Variety* noted: "This picture hit like magic and led its nearest competitor by $3,000 for the week. That seems outstanding, as the Million Dollar had been given up as a lost cause with the last four pictures." *The Cossacks* was soon to set new records at Loew's State in Los Angeles, and *Variety* reported that William Fox was cleaning up by re-releasing many of his old Gilbert movies. Films Jack had made at Fox before 1924 were playing to packed houses.

None of this was lost upon the management at Loew's headquarters in New York. As the negotiations continued, it became clear that something had to be done to secure Jack for the company. All the other major MGM stars were tied up in long-term contracts. But Jack, their biggest moneymaker, was not. His contract had only a matter of months to run, and he'd been making noises for some time about not renewing it. Nicholas Schenck knew that he had to lock Jack in at almost any cost if he was to get the best possible terms from William Fox. If Jack went elsewhere, so would millions of dollars in lost revenues. And so might Garbo, contract or no contract.

Jack, oblivious to all this, was busy making pictures and finishing his autobiography. After *The Cossacks*, he switched gears to a gritty underworld melodrama entitled *Four Walls*. Oddly, Mayer at first resisted making the movie because the hero was a Jew, a gangster named Benny Horowitz, and Mayer didn't think the public was ready to accept either a Jewish hero or John Gilbert in the role. Jack, as usual, disagreed, but so did the critics. *Photoplay* called *Four Walls* "the best of the the season's crop of underworld offerings," and named it one of the Six Best Films of the Month. Another review said: "Gilbert plays with a quietness and restraint that is effective. Disregard his title of Great Lover. As a product of New York's ghetto, Benny Horowitz, he gives one of his best performances." The New York *Evening Graphic* also noted Jack's versatility and dedication to the acting craft: "No one can accuse this Metro-Goldwyn-Mayer star of sticking to the stilted form of handsome characterizations. He is more interested in the acting possibilities than in the romantic qualities of a picture."

Joan Crawford, his co-star, noted that Jack was a completely different man from the John Gilbert she had worked with in *Twelve Miles Out*. In her book *Portrait*, she says this time around he was "vivid, vital and dynamic. The curly black head tilted back when he laughed; his hearty chortle could be heard from Culver City to Santa Monica. His eyes were like radar. . . . From John Gilbert I learned to keep my vitality undiluted on the screen, never to let down for a moment."

Jack then took time to do a cameo role in a King Vidor movie called *Show People*. Also appearing as themselves were Charlie Chaplin, Mae Murray, Douglas Fairbanks, and Elinor Glyn. In the central story, Vidor had cast a John Gilbert look-alike named Paul Ralli as a strutting ham actor who posed and then ducked out of the way as stuntmen took over any action that smacked of danger. I asked King Vidor how Jack reacted to that. King grinned. "He said, 'Pops, you son of a bitch,' but I don't think he really minded." Leatrice thinks he did mind. It came a bit too closely on the heels of the Jim Tully article, which depicted him as a ham and even related a spurious story about Jack ducking behind two women once when a horse reared during the filming of *The Cossacks*. At any rate, Jack didn't see as much of Vidor after that. King's marriage to Eleanor Boardman was breaking up, and they sold their house just below Jack's to John Barrymore.

Jack next threw himself into another romantic role, but one with far greater dimension than anything he'd played before. The picture, *The Masks of the Devil*, was directed by Victor Seastrom, who was fresh from his brilliant film *The Wind*, starring Lillian Gish. Jack was excited at having his first chance in some time to work with a really first-rate artist. He wasn't disappointed. Seastrom took the time and trouble and intelligence to get exactly the effects he wanted. He would use sunlight and sudden showers to indicate the mood of his actors. An important Seastrom innovation was the technique of superimposing a character's thoughts on the background behind him. For example, when Jack, playing Baron Reiner, is introduced to the finacée of his best friend, Jack bows politely, but in the background the audience sees Jack making love to the girl in his mind.

The Masks of the Devil was praised for its technical achievement, but reviews of the picture generally were mixed. Jack's performance, however, drew some of the greatest raves of his career. The New York *Telegram* said: "It is a character which gives Gilbert a greater elasticity of portrayal than any other has offered him. Truly a role that might have been fashioned for John Barrymore, Gilbert meets its every requirement and brings a vitality and a study in contrasts of conflicting emotions in the makeup of this odd character so forcibly that it stamps Gilbert as one of the greatest dramatic actors of the screen. It is perhaps the most serious role yet allotted to Gilbert, and he leaves nothing to be desired."

Unfortunately, no prints of this picture are known to exist today.

There had been rumors all year that Gilbert and Garbo would be starring together again, perhaps even in a "talkie." The rumors had some basis as far as another Gilbert and Garbo pairing was concerned, but neither was in a hurry to talk on screen. Many of the stars were still holding back. Chaplin, for one, believed that sound and his style of comedy did not mix. He was determined not to make a sound picture until the process was considerably less experimental. Chaplin advised Jack to hold back as well. He said that Jack's romantic allure would be destroyed by talking. Chaplin felt that no spoken dialogue, no matter how well written, could replace the words that the audience imagined the lover on the screen to be speaking. Paul Bern also advised Jack to wait out what he said would be "a flash in the pan that would soon be over. All these big sound stages they're building will be torn down again. The dead sound they're creating will result in dead pictures." Even Irving Thalberg had been quoted just a year earlier as saying that he did not believe talking pictures would ever replace silent drama.

MGM held back as long as it could. The studio was as unwilling to risk the reputations of its stars as the stars were themselves. In the first talking picture released by MGM, *White Shadows in the South Seas*, starring Monte Blue, there was no talking, just music and sound effects. MGM executives watched and waited. Then they tried dialogue in *Alias Jimmy Valentine*—but only in the last two reels. One of the first things they noticed was the odd reactions of audiences to the "love stuff" in talking pictures. Audiences had laughed when Charlie Farrell said "I love you" in the Fox production, *Street Angel*. But they had not laughed when Conrad Nagel said it in Warner's *Tenderloin*. There were plenty of theories about the laughter. Some said that audiences laughed at Charles Farrell's "I love you" out of embarrassment at words they'd never heard in a movie before. That's probably quite true. Eleven years later, audiences also laughed out of embarrassment when they heard "damn" spoken for the first time in *Gone With the Wind*. But then why no laughter at Conrad Nagel? Some argued that it had to do with how it was said, and others claimed that the plot was what made the difference. In *Tenderloin*, for example, Conrad Nagel's character had been pretending to care for Dolores Costello. By the time he actually fell in love with her, the audience was wanting to hear him say it for her sake. That at least was the theory. The problem was that nobody really knew.

Jack was aware of the risks and respected Chaplin's advice. But he knew that he couldn't avoid romantic roles forever. He could, however, avoid a romantic role as his first sound vehicle, and he started looking about for a suitable action story. The story soon came to him in the hands of his old friend Howard Hawks, who found Jack in his dressing room. "Jack," Hawks told him, "I've got a great picture. Mayer is already interested in buying the story. He called me and wants to see me about it. It would be a cinch for your sound debut, a war story with good tough language, no love stuff. Take the script home overnight and if you like it we'll tackle Mayer together."

Jack was awake most of the night with the script. It was everything Hawks promised, a superbly written and realistic story about British fliers in the Great War. Its honest emotions and its authenticity reminded him very much of *The Big Parade*. All of the dialogue rang true. Jack was to play the role of Dick Courtney, a reckless ace pilot who is promoted to squadron commander and begins to suffer under the strain of his new responsibilities, which involve sending too many young pilots to their death.

By morning, Jack had a firm understanding of the part. He drove over to Hawks's house, and they planned their strategy on their way to Mayer's office. Mayer listened quietly as Hawks explained the story, and then Jack acted out one or two scenes to give Mayer a sense of the drama and rough humor of men at war.

When they were finished, Mayer asked, "Well, Mr. Hawks, are you sure you want Mr. Gilbert to be your leading man?"

"Yes, very much," Hawks answered. "I thought of him the moment I read it."

"And you, Mr. Gilbert, are you certain you want to make a talking picture with Mr. Hawks?"

"Yes, with all my heart."

Then, as suddenly as if someone had turned on a switch, Mayer leaped to his feet and, red-faced, began spewing every obscene word Hawks had ever heard directly at Jack. At first Hawks was shocked into silence by the vehemence of the attack. Then, as an equally red-faced Jack Gilbert moved toward Mayer, Hawks grabbed him and pushed him out the door before the two men could come to blows.

"Then," Hawks said, "I walked back across the room and picked up that little son of a bitch and shook his head against the wall. I told him, 'Don't you *ever* put me in that kind of spot again. What you think of Gilbert is your business, but don't get me involved in your private hatreds.'"

Hawks and Jack, who was still trembling with anger, went to see Irving Thalberg. He listened to them and said quietly, "I could have told you that would happen. But there's nothing I can do about it now." Thalberg would not even try to intervene. In the first place, he was in a game being played for much bigger stakes, where the merger was concerned. In the second place, he knew that Mayer would do absolutely nothing that John Gilbert asked if he could help it. Hawks now realized that Mayer had called him to the studio for the sole purpose of humiliating Jack. He eventually produced the movie two years later, at First National, with Jack's part going to Richard Barthelmess and with Douglas Fairbanks, Jr., as his best friend. The picture was called *The Dawn Patrol*.

When Jack's next picture was finally announced, all Hollywood knew that he intended to leave MGM on the day his contract expired. He made it clear that he would never again have anything to do with the studio while Louis B. Mayer was connected with it.

The new picture would be the long-heralded Gilbert–Garbo reunion, and the story would be a screen adaptation of *The Green Hat*, one of the best-selling novels of the decade. At first, the Hays Office blocked production of a movie based on *The Green Hat* because of its explicit references to venereal disease and its overall "immorality." The studio answered by changing the names of the characters, deleting any reference to venereal disease, and changing the title to A *Woman of Affairs*.

As a Gilbert–Garbo reunion, the picture turned out to be a disappointment to both critics and fans. It starts off well enough, with the two stars meeting and falling in love. But Gilbert's aristocratic father disapproves of Garbo and forbids him to marry. After that, it's all Garbo's picture and John Gilbert is forced to stand around looking brave while she marries Johnny Mack Brown and goes to Paris on a honeymoon. There, she learns that her new husband is a thief and the police are after him. Cornered, he leaps from a window to his death, and Garbo sets out to repay the victims of his crimes. After some years she returns to England, where her brother, Douglas Fairbanks, Jr., is dying of alcoholism. Jack is drawn to her again and attempts a reunion, although he has married while she was gone. But Garbo is stronger than he. She returns to France and some months later is reported to be dying. Jack comes to the hospital. He has sent roses—which the distraught Garbo uses in perfect pantomime to suggest the loss of their child (through abortion or miscarriage). That long pantomime is the high point of the film.

Critical reaction to the story itself was indifferent. Hollywood adaptations of popular novels are rarely treated kindly and this was no exception. Most critics ignored the picture's roots, however, and focused on it in terms of a Gilbert–Garbo starring vehicle. Among these reviews, virtually all the praise went to Garbo. Douglas Fairbanks's small intense role was also enthusiastically received. But Jack, after the opening love scenes, had little to do in the picture other than look alternately miserable and self-righteous. *The New York Times* said that "Mr. Gilbert does nicely as the man with whom Diana is madly in love," but concluded that his work "is overshadowed by the peculiar cleverness of Miss Garbo. . . . He is still more than a foil for this brilliant Swedish actress." Herbert Howe, writing for *Photoplay*, said: "He plays an awfully thankless, spineless part, all for love, I take it."

A number of other critics made the same observation, and wondered why Jack would have taken such a role in which his romanticism and natural ebullience is so severely muzzled. One New York reporter asked director Clarence Brown why he did it.

Clarence answered:

> Gilbert's a funny and a great fellow. There are people who delight in panning him and saying he's a poseur and a shallow thinker and whatnot. I'm here to tell you that Gilbert is the best screen actor in the business and far and away the most serious-minded of them all. I prefer him to Jack Barrymore as a screen actor. Gilbert wants to get at the heart of a character, and once you can convince him that the part he's playing is sincere and real, he'll work for you until the cows come home.
>
> As an example of Gilbert's attitude toward his work, I want to tell you what happened when Gilbert, Miss Garbo, and myself talked over the script of A *Woman of Affairs* for the first time. Gilbert's part in the film, as you may remember, is the part of a weak man, dominated over by his father. I quite naturally thought that Gilbert might object to the short footage which he had in the picture. Because in comparison with footage given his co-star, he had but a small percentage of the film.
>
> Before even waiting for any objection from him, I proposed that I add something to his part, making it a bigger and more manly role. Gilbert went right up in the air. He said, "I'd rather you didn't touch my part a bit, Clarence. If you do, we might weaken our story. My character *is* a weak character and he's got to be handled that way. Footage doesn't matter. I'd rather play the part of a butler in a good picture than have every foot in a film that's a flop."
>
> That's what I call idealism in an actor and God knows it's rare enough in Hollywood. Gilbert's one of the best.

·twelve·

URING the shooting of A *Woman of Affairs*, Jack and young Douglas
Fairbanks, Jr., became friends. So did Douglas and Garbo. Jack
often asked Douglas to carry messages to her on days when she
wasn't speaking to him. And Garbo would sometimes ask Douglas if Jack
said anything about the way she was playing a particular scene. The
dependency on Jack was still there. A mutual give-and-take still was not.

Douglas was carrying other messages as well. His father had been
urging Jack for some time to come to work at United Artists when his
contract expired the following March. Robert Rubin had already approached Jack and his agent, Harry Edington, about signing again with
MGM. Mayer or no Mayer, top management was not eager to see Jack
take his following elsewhere. Jack received Rubin's feelers coolly but left
the door open a crack at Edington's insistence. Rubin reported back to
New York that signing Jack would not be easy, in view of his attitude
toward Mayer and the management he'd been getting lately from
MGM. The Fox deal had not yet begun cooking in earnest and there
seemed to be no great rush. Rubin recommended letting Jack's feelings
settle for a while.

But then United Artists made an offer of its own. They would pay
Jack $125,000 a picture, plus the freedom either to choose his own
director or to direct himself. He would have story and cast approval. His
pictures would be financed by Art Cinema at a maximum of $750,000
each. To Jack, the deal was almost too good to be true. He'd be working
with Douglas Fairbanks, Mary Pickford, Charlie Chaplin, and Norma
Talmadge, all of whom were warm personal friends. His boss would be
Joseph Schenck, Nicholas's brother, who was equally tough, competent, and respected. Jack told Douglas Fairbanks that he didn't see how
he could refuse, and United Artists promptly announced his intentions
to the press.

The press, meanwhile, was filled with rumors about a secret studio merger that was whispered to be in the works. With the sound revolution coming, the industry was gearing itself for a change of monstrous proportions. A number of mergers seemed inevitable. Since the estimated cost of converting the industry to sound was going to be greater than all the studios' preceding year's combined revenues, many smaller studios would have to join forces or go under.

Finally, what was called the deepest secret in studio history broke into print on November 1928. *Variety* ran a front-page headline:

FOX WITH LOEW'S IN DEAL

Compared to the many speculative items that had been appearing for months, the *Variety* story had the ring of truth. It accurately revealed some of the complex financial details of the agreement and even named the lawyers who were involved.

Fox was furious when he heard the story had been leaked, and refused to be interviewed or to allow any comment to come from his office. Schenck could not be reached for comment. *Variety*, however, said Schenck reacted to the Fox proposal with "shock" when he first heard of it.

Schenck now had to act. He promptly entrained to California for a private meeting with his brother Joe. He sounded Joe out about joining the merger and taking charge of the three combined studios, Fox, MGM, and now United Artists. Nicholas was fully aware of the deal his brother had offered John Gilbert. While in California, he intended to bargain with all he had to retain the services of a man he thought of as a friend. On the day Nicholas Schenck was originally scheduled to return to New York, he went instead into a five-day conference with Harry Edington. Jack came and went during these sessions, listening carefully to what was being offered. He could scarcely believe the terms as they developed. Schenck clearly was intent on making him an offer he could not refuse.

Jack would be offered a contract running for three years. He would be required to make two pictures a year—not ten as he'd made in 1924, or even five as he'd made in 1928. Just two pictures a year, for which he'd be paid $250,000 each, with considerable latitude in choosing his own material.

Jack pointed out, however, that the United Artists proposal offered him absolute discretion in choosing script, director, and cast. Schenck was unwilling to go that far and Edington supported him, reminding Jack of several of his pictures that ended up being tremendously successful after Jack had predicted flops. Schenck settled the issue by devising the wording so that Jack could not lose. The contract permitted him to break it and go elsewhere at any time, but the studio could not break the contract under any circumstances other than failure to make his two pictures a year and, of course, the usual morals clause. Such a one-sided agreement was utterly unprecedented in Hollywood.

There was still, however, the matter of Louis B. Mayer. Don't worry, Jack was assured. Louis B. Mayer was as good as out. Obviously that could not be written into the contract, and the contract in fact specified that neither Mayer nor anyone else could touch him. Jack was told he could take Nicholas Schenck's word for it. Schenck was at least as eager as Jack to be rid of a man he despised. On that basis, Jack signed.

On December 18, 1928, *Variety* ran a banner headline:

WHO'S THE BOSS OF FILMS? LOUIS B. MAYER
LEAVING MGM IN MARCH, WITH JACK GILBERT
REMAINING AT THE STUDIO!

The story announced that Mayer would retire as head of the studio effective March 4, 1929. Joseph Schenck would replace him as head of operations, with Irving Thalberg as head of production. *Variety* spoke of the friction that had long been developing between Thalberg and Mayer and the legendary hatred between Mayer and Gilbert. The article also gave full details of Jack's new contract and mentioned his importance as a bargaining chip in the continuing merger talks. As for Louis B. Mayer, *Variety* said, he would probably go off and reap some political reward from the election of Herbert Hoover.

Mayer vehemently denied everything, although he acknowledged that there *had* been some talk of naming him ambassador to Turkey. As for the merger story, Mayer said "it was no more important than other ridiculous reports circulating recently about MGM." He added that since his present contract ran through 1933, he expected to be at the studio for a long time to come.

Mayer knew full well, however, that he was fighting for his life. And Mayer was not a man easily beaten.

During the filming of A *Woman of Affairs*, word reached Garbo that Mauritz Stiller had died in Sweden. He'd returned to his adopted country the year before, dispirited and in poor health from a respiratory illness. The always difficult Stiller had had one argument too many with the executives at Paramount and, after being replaced as director of an Emil Jannings movie, *The Street of Sin*, he found no other jobs offered to him. Stiller opted for Sweden and finally found some success directing a stage musical called *Broadway*. But he died on November 8, a few months after the opening. He was only forty-five.

Garbo, who felt almost a mystical bond with Stiller, took the news hard. On the set where the news reached her, Garbo paled and turned away to a wall, and stood silently leaning, eyes closed, for several minutes. She finished her work that day but stayed home for the next two, not eating and barely sleeping. Even Jack could not talk to her. She then begged the studio to let her go home to Sweden at once, but they insisted that she finish the picture. One month later she sailed on the *Kungsholm*. Garbo remained in Sweden for three months. She exchanged letters with Jack and called him once to wish him a happy New Year.

On Christmas Day, 1928, Jack came to see Leatrice as usual and delivered a small mountain of Christmas presents. She had moved from Sweetzer Avenue to her new Cotswold cottage in Beverly Hills, on the corner of Hillcrest and Elevado. The house cost $24,000 to build, and Leatrice paid an artist several thousand more to antique the outside by streaking the plaster and aging the roof beams. The place ended up looking like a movie set.

I was only four years old, but I remember Jack's visit clearly. I was on the stairs when he came in, and I peered at him through the railing as he and Mother stood very close together, talking quietly. Then I came down, dragging my Charles Lindbergh doll behind me. They never took their eyes off each other. I stood beside them for a while, and then, deciding I wasn't going to get noticed any other way, I picked up a bowl of colored sand from the hall table and turned it upside down on the rug. My plan worked perfectly. Mother disengaged with a gasp and Father roared with laughter and swept me up into his arms. I spent the rest of the visit firmly seated on his lap.

Leatrice says that much of their conversation that day had to do with the terms of his new contract. He was thrilled with the money but even more pleased that it freed him forever from Louis Mayer. The contract was between himself and Nicholas Schenck. Mayer, he told her, had not even been consulted. Jack then told her an ugly story that had happened only a few days before. He had been summoned to an MGM party for the exhibitors, the men who controlled the showing of the movies after they left the studio. These men were feared and generally loathed by the Hollywood people. They descended on the film colony several times each year, always expecting to be entertained with a tithing of liquor, drugs, and beautiful young flesh. Louis Mayer kept a house in the far reaches of Beverly Glen for these occasions. The Glen was a long winding canyon road with only a few houses spaced far apart. The area was thickly wood, and the noise of riotous parties would go unnoticed.

Jack arrived and found he was the guest of honor. The exhibitors were glad to see him and relieved to learn that he would continue to make movies for MGM. Jack stayed through a noisy dinner at which there were fulsome speeches and toasts. Then, at the stroke of midnight, waiters dressed as Santa Claus appeared pushing giant glittering snowballs. At a signal the balls burst open. Out of each one leaped a naked girl who performed a little dance and then ran to the man nearest her and climbed into his lap. There was much drunken laughing and slobbering as the men fell upon the girls and the real evening's entertainment began.

Now, Jack could never be called a prude. He was a frequent visitor to Lee Frances's elegant brothel in Beverly Hills and often entertained her girls at his home. But this scene turned his stomach. He started to leave the party when Louis Mayer stopped him.

"Where the hell do you think you're going, *Mister* Gilbert?" Mayer always managed to make Jack's name sound like an obscenity.

"I'm going home," Jack told him. "This may be your idea of a good time but it isn't mine."

Mayer's voice turned to ice. "You are *not* walking out on our honored guests."

Jack answered, "I'm walking out on a bunch of repulsive assholes, yourself included. Now get the hell out of my way."

Mayer showed his teeth and blocked the door. "And what about your new contract, *Mister* Gilbert?"

"You know exactly what you can do with it," Jack told him as he pushed past him into the night.

Needing air, Jack chose to walk all the way home. He sent the chauffeur back to pick up his car the next morning.

"I couldn't stand it," he told Leatrice. "Those poor innocent girls. It would be one thing if they were whores but they were just little starlets from the studio. I knew some of them. They were decent kids, hard up. What an awful business." His hands were shaking as he told her about it.

Leatrice was frightened. "But you shouldn't have called Mayer that, not in front of all those men."

Jack chuckled—a little nervously, Leatrice thought. "It's okay. He can't touch me now. That bastard can never hurt me again."

I remember Mother looking worried because she reached across and took Father's hand. But I was more concerned about our Christmas tea because that's when the presents would be opened. At last the maid rolled in the tea cart with plates of watercress sandwiches and the tiny chocolate cakes Jack adored. I began tearing open gifts. Father gave me a blue musical teddy bear, and a silver dressing table set, and a small crown made of rhinestones and seed pearls so that I could look like the princess he told me I was.

Leatrice continued to worry about Jack well after the visit was over. She had nothing against Mayer personally. She thought he was a very nice, moral man who loved his mother. But everyone knew that he never forgot an insult. A few nights later, she went to a party at the Conrad Nagels' and bumped into Norma Talmadge in the dressing room. Norma was married to Joe Schenck, Nicholas Schenck's brother, and although they'd been separated for the past two years, they were friends and he still managed her career. Leatrice thought Norma might know something about the scene between Mayer and Jack. Norma gave her a broad wink and put her finger to her lips.

"Honey, don't give it a thought," she said. "Your little boy is safe and sound." Norma didn't elaborate, but the implication was clear that Mayer was no longer a threat to anyone.

The rumors continued that Mayer would resign in March. Mayer continued to deny them. All through January and February of 1929, he also continued to characterize stories of a merger with Fox as nonsense.

But privately Mayer was having second thoughts. In December of 1928 Nicholas Schenck had signed an outrageous contract with John Gilbert without even consulting Mayer. By late January, he realized that his worst fears were probably true, but he was still unwilling to believe that Thalberg and Rubin were a party to the conspiracy. Next came a confrontation with Fox about the merger, during which Fox made the mistake of brushing him off. At the end of February, Mayer entrained for Washington to attend Herbert Hoover's inauguration. He told Hoover, while staying at the White House, that Fox and Schenck were conspiring to create an illegal monopoly. Hoover suggested that Mayer talk to his new Attorney General, William Mitchell. Mayer did just that.

Fox, of course, had already consulted with the Justice Department to make sure the proposed merger would not be challenged. His contact was a Justice Department lawyer, who gave an oral clearance for Fox's lawyer to proceed with the purchase of Loew's stock. Fox had also approached the man whom he fully expected to be the new Attorney General. That man was not William Mitchell.

On March 4, 1929, believing all was well, Fox summoned the press to his office. At his side were Nicholas Schenck, David Bernstein,

Arthur Loew, and Winfield Sheehan, Fox's production chief. Fox read a brief statement announcing the purchase of Loew's stock and the merger of the two great studios along with United Artists. Despite the long months of speculation, the news still came as a shock to the industry. Jack Warner had been hoping to buy the stock himself; his lawyers were still working on it. William Randolph Hearst, who had formed Cosmopolitan Productions, an MGM affiliate, for the express purpose of making Marion Davies's films, said angrily that he would have no part of William Fox. Aside from disliking him personally, Hearst had his own newsreel service, in competition with Fox Movietone News, and did not intend to give it up. At United Artists, Charlie Chaplin let it be known that he did not intend to work at Fox either. He'd work for himself.

But William Fox was jubilant. The deal was set. It was over. He was now the most powerful man in the entire entertainment industry. Louis B. Mayer was as good as dead.

Jack had meanwhile completed his last silent picture. It was a desert adventure story set around the South African diamond mines and was originally titled *Thirst*, with a screenplay by Leatrice's friend Lenore Coffee. It was also originally supposed to be a talking picture but Jack backed away, preferring to take Chaplin's advice and wait a bit. The name of the picture was changed to *Desert Nights*, and it proved to be a stunning suspense story with an erotic theme. Jack looked every inch a star.

His first talkie came later that same year and was actually an MGM all-star extravaganza called *The Hollywood Revue of 1929*. The studio, still justifiably nervous about making sound movies, decided to give the public a carefully controlled sampling of every major star on the lot. Jack Benny and Conrad Nagel were the masters of ceremonies for a series of skits, songs, and big production numbers. There was a minstrel chorus, Laurel and Hardy did a magic act, Joan Crawford sang "Got a Feelin' for You" and danced, a miniature Bessie Love climbed out of Jack Benny's pocket and danced across a table, and Conrad Nagel sang "You Were Meant for Me" to Anita Page. Garbo would have been in the picture but wasn't yet back from Sweden.

The Hollywood Revue of 1929 saved its best stuff for last. Near the finale, the black-and-white screen burst into Technicolor. On came John Gilbert and Norma Shearer doing the balcony scene from *Romeo and Juliet*, first as Shakespeare wrote it and then in flapper language, with lines like "Julie baby, you're the cream in my java, the berries in my pie." It wasn't as silly as it sounds. It was a satire on Hollywood's habit of trivializing classics such as *Anna Karenina*. The skit had Lionel Barrymore playing the director of the scene. At one point, he interrupted the slang balcony version to read a telegram from the head office: "MR. THALBERG THINKS WE MIGHT CHANGE THE TITLE TO 'THE NECKERS.'"

The grand finale had Charles King singing "Orange Blossom Time" in a colorful orchard surrounded by beautiful girls. In the larger theaters, orange-scented perfume was sprayed into the air.

Jack and Norma, like many of the stars, seemed a bit tentative in the beginning but they soon overcame it. Jack spoke Shakespeare's lines as if he'd done it all his life, and they both seemed to be relaxed and enjoying themselves during the comedy routine.

Mordaunt Hall said in the *Times*: "A bit nicely done is a color sequence of the balcony scene from *Romeo and Juliet*. It goes along quite seriously and then grows playful. The sound tones are quite good." Brooks Atkinson praised the film and said: "For a few minutes Jack Gilbert and Norma Shearer speak the glowing verses of the balcony scene . . . then slapstick, but while they are playing seriously, the music of the lines and the ardor of the visual emotion intoxicate the senses. You are startled by the potentialities [of sound]."

Those reviewers who commented on Jack's voice, along with those of the other stars, characterized it as "quite adequate" and "pleasing."

Greta Garbo returned from Sweden in March 1929. She arranged for Jack to meet her in San Bernardino to avoid the welcoming crowd that would be waiting at Union Station. Jack drove up in his little open-topped Ford, carrying his usual bouquet of roses. On the way to Los Angeles, he asked her for the last time to marry him.

Jack was almost thirty years old. He loved Greta deeply and he'd hated the last three months of living alone. He especially hated being alone at night. He was an insomniac and so was she. They'd both pad around the house together at night, she with a glass of warm milk and he with a stiff Scotch, and they'd keep each other company until sleep came. They were obviously made for each other.

But Garbo said no. Jack kept pressing and finally became frustrated and angry. She'd now been living in his house for three and a half years. At her whim, she would either stay in the house with Jack or retreat to the little cabin he'd built her in the pine grove behind the house. Jack could no longer live with the detached emotions Garbo presented him. He once complained to MGM publicist Howard Dietz, "When I said, 'I'm going out,' the only thing she said was 'I'll leave the door open, Jack.' What do you say to a girl like that? I said, 'I'm going out to sleep with Anna May Wong.' She said, 'I'll leave the door open, Jack.' What in hell do I do?"

"That's obvious," Dietz answered. "You go sleep with Anna May Wong."

But Jack wanted to sleep with Greta Garbo. More than that, he wanted a commitment. He wanted to be married. But Garbo told him on the road from San Bernardino, "You are a very foolish boy, Yacky. You quarrel with me for nothing. I must do my way, but we need not part."

"Not this time," he told her. "This time it's going to be all or nothing."

Two months later, he married Ina Claire in Las Vegas.

Ina Claire was a major Broadway star, famous enough for her face to grace the cover of *Time* magazine later that year. She'd come to California to make her first talking picture, *The Awful Truth*, for Pathé. Ina Claire had made two movies before that, the first back in 1915. She was older than Jack by seven years and very intelligent, aggressive, and sophisticated, although, as a child of theatrical parents, she'd had even less formal schooling than Jack. Ina Claire hardly seemed the type to be swept off her feet.

But, speaking of her sudden marriage to Jack Gilbert, Miss Claire said, "I'd only known him six weeks! We met at a party someplace. And it kind of amused me that he was playing craps on the floor with some people. And he said something derogatory about himself. Not exactly derogatory, but he sees himself as a kind of a joke, as a sex symbol. I mean he's kidding about it, whatever it was. But it made me laugh and I thought, I wouldn't have expected that from him. I'd thought he was a kind of ham, and I wouldn't be falling for a ham. It was because he was so nice."

Ina Claire had been married once before, to a newspaperman named James Whittaker. She'd divorced him, one acquaintance thought, when she ran out of things she could learn from him. "Ina absorbed information like a suction pump. If she learned that you knew something about Chelsea pottery, or the early Mennonites, or the flora and fauna of the Fiji Islands, she'd glue herself to you until she got it all. And then you were through."

A reporter who interviewed her soon after Ina arrived on the West Coast wrote, "Miss Claire is blonde, slim, urbane. She has a vigorous intellect and a shrewd intuition. She is utterly feminine, calm, poised, and unlike any of her film sisters."

A contemporary of Ina's agreed with all that, but added, "No one could ever accuse Ina Claire of being warm and cuddly, and that is unfortunately what Jack needed, poor darling."

The news that Jack Gilbert was about to elope with Ina Claire flashed around the studio. In the late afternoon the day before the wedding, May 9, 1929, Lenore Coffee dropped in to see Harry Edington, who was her agent as well as Jack's. Harry was expecting her and had left his office door ajar so that she could come right in. When she arrived, he was busy on the telephone, his back to her, so she quietly sat down at his desk. She immediately realized she could hear both sides of the conversation and that it was clearly a personal matter with considerable emotion involved. She was about to get up and leave just as quietly when she realized that the voice on the other end was unmistakably Garbo's. And she was sobbing. She was telling Edington that he must stop Jack's marriage, that Jack belonged to her and they never should have separated. This was getting interesting, so Lenore decided to stay.

Edington asked Garbo why on earth she'd waited until the last minute when everyone had known about it for days. She said she'd been on a yacht making a movie and she hadn't heard until now. Edington stammered, "B-but it's too late now to do anything about it. You know I'd do anything for you, dear, but how can I stop a wedding in a few hours? Hell, I'm the best man. There's only one person who can stop that wedding and that's yourself."

Lenore could see the sweat running down Edington's neck. The vision of Greta Garbo bursting in on John Gilbert's wedding and trying to drag him away from Ina Claire was the stuff of nightmares. When Edington finally hung up and turned around, he was surprised to see Lenore sitting there, but too upset to care.

"Did you hear all that? My God! Do you think she'll do anything? Can you imagine what the papers would do with it?"

Lenore reminded him that it was not Garbo's nature to make a public display of herself. Edington chose to take comfort in that thought and do nothing. He would certainly say nothing to Jack.

(I'm particularly grateful to Lenore for this story. She said that she agreed with Harry Edington that there wasn't much point in saying anything about it once Jack was married. But it always galled her when Garbo was quoted as saying that there was never an affaire between herself and Jack. Or saying that she didn't know what she ever saw in him. The fact is, Jack was probably the only man in her life who ever walked out on her.)

The wedding took place on schedule. The wedding party left Los Angeles on the evening train and arrived the next morning in what was then the quiet little desert town of Las Vegas. The town's entire population turned out to greet them. They cheered the bridal couple and followed them down the main street to the Town Hall, where they were married, then on to a local hotel for a ranch breakfast served with champagne brought by the Edingtons. After breakfast, Jack and Ina chartered a plane and flew back to finish the pictures they were making, Ina in *The Awful Truth* and Jack in *Redemption*, his first full-length talking picture.

Eleanor Boardman was the first to invite the newly married couple to dinner. Her impression at the outset was that although Ina seemed head over heels in love with Jack, she was struggling to keep her own personality and ego from being overpowered by his.

Eleanor reminded me of Ina's classic remark shortly after the wedding when a reporter asked, "How does it feel to be married to a great star?"

"I don't know," the new bride replied sweetly. "Why don't you ask Mr. Gilbert?"

It's true that Ina was to the New York stage what Jack was to the Hollywood screen, but there was more than a clash of egos to the gulf that quickly appeared between them. Ina, like many stage actors, always regarded movies as an inferior stepchild.

"Jack was having trouble with his movie," Eleanor said. "He wasn't used to sound. Ina wanted badly to help him but she seemed to go about it in the wrong way, correcting his pronunciation, giving little hints about 'pear-shaped tones' and telling him he had a 'white voice.' That only got his back up. Even if she was right about his voice, she was making him self-conscious about something he couldn't do anything about."

A "white voice" is a thin voice that comes from the throat instead of the diaphragm. It doesn't have enough timbre to be picked up properly by the primitive vacuum-tube microphones that were then in use. A white voice was much less of a problem even a year later, when recording techniques improved and actors learned the fundamentals of breath control and projection.

Ina Claire said, "I tried once to explain to him [about how to speak dialogue]. You see, I was being reasonable and this was something new to him. But his masculine pride, his professional pride . . . I was the *last* person he wanted to tell him anything about acting."

In fairness to Jack, he had made about ninety movies and understood every aspect of the business except sound, which no one else understood either. Ina had made only three movies over a period of fourteen years. She knew how to work a stage but he knew how to work a camera. She was teaching him how to act in a medium she didn't know, and she was telling him to enunciate when enunciation was only a small part of the problem. The problem was that of a skilled pantomime actor being forced to focus simultaneously on an element that had never been part of his craft. It was like telling a trapeze artist that he must now faultlessly recite Hamlet's soliloquy during his act without losing his concentration.

Although the craft of acting became a tender subject between them, Ina thoroughly admired Jack as a human being. She continued to be impressed by his "niceness" and his easy charm.

"I can tell you," she said, "that men liked Jack very much if they got to know him. They didn't like him as a sex symbol, they were prejudiced against him, but with people who worked with him and people who met him he was one of the boys. It wasn't women. He didn't go after women. They went after him and he ran away from them. He went to the bar."

The writer Gene Markey was informally engaged to marry Ina Claire when she fell in love with Jack and married him instead. Gentleman that he was, Gene Markey accepted his loss graciously and became a lifelong friend of Jack's. He lived down the hill on Tower Road and saw Jack and Ina frequently.

As Gene recalled:

> Jack loved to talk. He kept up a lively monologue on any subject that struck his fancy. Biography, films, women, government, people—anything. Often his opinions were brilliant and they were his own. Jack would put a glass of Scotch-and-soda on the mantelpiece of his long living room. His manservant would put another glass at the far end of the room, and Jack would stride between them, talking, warming up to his themes, sipping the liquor he liked best, on into the night.
>
> I had a feeling that Jack would have preferred to be a writer. He held no high opinion of acting . . . and his imagination offered a world of books, plays, essays to be written.

Through Ina, Jack also met Noel Coward, who came as a weekend guest. Ina was a bit nervous about the visit. Getting on well with Gene Markey was one thing, but Jack's response to the effeminate English author might be quite another. On a Saturday, Ina arrived home from the studio and as she came up the stairs she heard Noel's voice from the living room.

"Dearest Jack," he was saying, "I hope you won't mind if I fall just a tiny bit in love with you."

Ina froze. She had no idea how her virile Jack Gilbert would react to that. But after a startled pause, she heard Jack burst out laughing. "Look, Noel," he said, "I think you're swell but the rest of it's a lot of bullshit. Now, how about a drink?"

Jack's first talking picture, meanwhile, was turning into a living hell. *Redemption* was based on another dark, brooding Tolstoy work, *The Living Corpse*. A Russian wastrel (Jack) marries a nice girl (Eleanor Boardman) and has a child. But he soon returns to his wild ways. He runs off and takes up with his former Gypsy sweetheart (Renée Adorée). His wife has reason to think he's dead and remarries (Conrad Nagel). Later, she's charged with bigamy. Jack, realizing he is destroying her life, remorsefully shoots himself. If the subject matter wasn't depressing enough, there was also the continued presence of Louis B. Mayer on the MGM lot. It was now late May and he was supposed to have been gone in March.

The picture itself was shaping up as a disaster because almost nobody involved seemed to know what they were doing. Lionel Barrymore, incredibly, had been assigned as director. Barrymore as dialogue director would have been understandable. He had had a great deal of experience as a stage actor before coming West to work in films. He presumably knew something about speaking lines and about filming what, because of the stationary cameras and microphones, was essentially a stage play. But director? He'd directed only one other full-length film and that was a silent back in 1917.

Although Jack was a comfortable public speaker, his only experience as a "speaking actor" went back to his childhood days with the Forpaugh Stock Company of Cincinnati. He remembered the heavy drama of the theater, the precise elocution and the stage mannerisms of an earlier day. He reverted to his earlier training, bearing in mind Ina Claire's "pear-shaped tones," with terrible results. His *s*'s were too sibilant, he rolled his *r*'s, and his *d*'s and *t*'s were pronounced "trippingly" on the end of his tongue. It would have been all right on a stage, but on the screen it sounded affected.

Eleanor Boardman doesn't remember much about *Redemption*; she thinks she blocked it out. She does recall, however, that Barrymore was replaced by Fred Niblo halfway through the picture. When the picture was finished and Jack saw the result, he tried, so the story goes, to buy it so that he could dump the prints and negatives somewhere off Catalina Island. The studio refused to sell it but they did agree—Niblo heartily concurring—to shelve it for the time being. Relieved, Jack prepared to make his next talking picture—this time, he hoped, one a little better.

·thirteen·

T HE property chosen for Jack's second talkie—but his first as far as the public was concerned—was a lighthearted comedy about Viennese high society by Ferenc Molnár. Originally titled *Olympia*, Irving Thalberg innocently changed the title to *His Glorious Night*.

Jack was pleased with the story and especially happy with the change of pace from the turgid melodrama of *Redemption*. Just as important, the studio imported a leading lady who was entirely comfortable with speaking roles. Catherine Dale Owen was a graduate of the American Academy of Dramatic Arts and an established leading lady on Broadway. She'd also been acclaimed one of the world's ten most beautiful women. Jack could not have been thrilled, however, to learn that Lionel Barrymore was again being assigned as director.

Jack played the part of a dashing, slightly scandalous cavalry officer named Captain Kovacs, a master of both horses and women. Catherine Dale Owen played an icy princess who thaws out upon meeting Jack. Her mother tells her to break off the affaire because a proper marriage has been arranged for her and anyway she could not possibly be in love with a commoner. The princess capitulates and freezes up again. Jack hatches a clever plot to blackmail Catherine and her mother. He'll return the love letters if she'll spend just one glorious night with him in his quarters. The princess agrees and gets melted down forevermore.

It's actually a pretty amusing movie. There are some very funny scenes between the princess and her mother and between the princess and her dainty fiancé. Hedda Hopper does nicely as the wily American title-hunter. Much of the dialogue was lifted directly from the Molnár play, which leaned heavily upon irony and tongue-in-cheek humor.

The filming was completed in only thirteen days. While the editing was in process, Jack left with Ina on their delayed honeymoon. This time he was substantially more confident of the job he'd done.

The newlyweds arrived in New York on July 24, 1929, en route to Europe aboard the *Ile-de-France*. They were mobbed at Pennsylvania Station by reporters, photographers, and fans. One reporter told Jack he looked better than the last time he was in New York. "Why not?" Jack answered. "I'm happier."

The crowd followed them to the Ritz Hotel, growing larger as they went along. The lobby was quickly filled. The Gilberts were hustled up a back elevator to a room in the tower, where they posed for pictures and answered questions for over an hour. Finally they were allowed to withdraw to their own rooms. When they opened the door, however, they groaned to see that the suite was filled with chattering lady reporters.

Donald Ogden Stewart was in New York at the time. He invited Jack and Ina to spend the night before their sailing at a cottage he kept on Jock Whitney's Long Island estate. There they might find some peace and privacy. Jock Whitney, however, threw a party for them at the Creek Club and the Long Island social set dropped by. Jack seemed to be enjoying himself, but Ina hustled him out fairly early and took him to bed. Stewart and his wife got back to the cottage at around three in the morning and found Ina alone and furious. She and Jack had quarreled. He had left her "forever" and gone back to New York. Stewart drove into the city still in his evening clothes and found Jack at the Ritz bar. "The *Ile-de-France* was sailing at ten in the morning and Jack was not making much sense until eight or nine." The argument apparently had little to do with drinking. Ina, who was now on her own turf, had told Jack on their way back to the Whitney's that he was now meeting a better class of people and must learn to behave accordingly. Jack asked if he'd offended someone. Ina admitted that he hadn't but pointed out that he might have if she hadn't disengaged him.

They made the ten-o'clock sailing and were sent off in "a mist of flowers and photographers." Then, according to all reports, they proceeded to fight all the way across the Atlantic Ocean and Europe.

Back in the States, the Justice Department had begun a full investigation of the Fox merger. William Fox couldn't understand it. The Justice Department case officer had given him a green light, and now Fox was being told that he'd probably have to divest himself of Loew's shares and therefore the entire deal. He set about trying to find out who or what was behind this turn of events. A high Republican official told him that the one man who might be able to help was Louis B. Mayer.

Fox swallowed hard and went to see Mayer. He listened contritely to a lecture about the injustice done to Mayer and his associates, and suggested that a new generous contract might help to make amends. Mayer told him that would certainly be a step in the right direction. Fox decided that a bonus of two million dollars would also be in order *if* the merger went through without any further annoyance from the government. Mayer smiled and said he'd see what he could do.

Mayer, however, had overestimated his own influence. One John Lord O'Brien had been appointed Assistant Attorney General that June to head up the antitrust division of the Justice Department. Upon starting the job he found that the Fox–Loew deal was a top-priority issue. The file showed that Louis B. Mayer was strongly opposed to the deal on the principle of seeing justice done and "keeping the wily monopolists in check." However, Mayer came to see Mr. O'Brien and told him that, having thought about it, the Fox merger would be just fine after all. Mr. O'Brien pointed out that, for all Mayer's good offices, the law had, in his opinion, been broken. The case would go to trial.

If Mayer was upset, having blown a sweetheart contract and a two-million-dollar bonus, Fox was furious. Mayer had loosed the dogs and now he couldn't call them off. But Fox would keep fighting. He stayed close to Nicholas Schenck as they mapped out their strategy and their defense against the antitrust action.

It would have been better if he'd stayed a little less close. While Fox was being driven to a golf date with Nicholas Schenck, he was in a bad automobile accident. Fox's chauffeur was killed and Fox was seriously injured. The accident occurred in July 1929, shortly before Jack left on his honeymoon. Fox would be almost totally immobilized for the next few months. The case would not come to court until the fall, and its hearing would coincide with the collapse of the stock market. Although Fox couldn't know it at the time of his accident, he was already well on his long road to utter ruin. The studio merger was effectively dead. And an enormously satisfied Louis B. Mayer settled into a stronger-than-ever position as head of MGM studios.

Jack, of course, knew nothing of all this. It was just as well, because he was having a miserable enough time in Europe without knowing that Mayer would be waiting gleefully for him at the end of the line.

One problem was Ina Claire's determination to make an educational experience out of a romantic European honeymoon. In France she took Jack to an endless series of museums, cathedrals, and historic sites, which was fine except that she insisted upon quizzing him after each visit to make sure he'd absorbed sufficient culture. Jack told her that he'd prefer to absorb culture at his own speed and to have some fun like any other tourist. Ina insisted that he was *not* just any tourist. If he was to hold his own among sophisticated people, he was foolish not to take advantage of this opportunity for a crash course in worldliness. Ina's sophisticated people were another problem. Jack met many of her friends in Paris and Antibes, and was baffled by them. She introduced him to writers who didn't write, titleholders who didn't lead or govern, producers who didn't produce, and aristocrats who apparently did nothing at all except swap invitations and talk about wine. Jack was unimpressed and uninterested, which showed Ina how much of a bumpkin Jack really was. She managed to make him feel like one, referring to him as "my adored little boy" and advising him on one occasion "to say nothing at all, because we're going to be among intelligent people this evening."

A third problem was that Jack was recognized almost everywhere they went. He'd known, of course, that his pictures were very popular throughout Europe, but somehow it had never occurred to him that he was just as likely to be mobbed at Napoleon's Tomb as he was at the corner of Hollywood and Vine. This recognition, destructive as it was of leisurely sightseeing, came as a delightful surprise. But it was less of a delight to Ina, who was hardly known at all except among the "right people." Jack found himself ducking away from crowds of fans rather than, by staying, allow Ina Claire to be ignored on the sidelines. While Jack and Ina were having dinner at a Paris restaurant one evening, the band struck up "The Merry Widow Waltz." All eyes turned to Jack and the house began a rhythmic clapping, in the hope that he would do the famous dance for them with Ina standing in for Mae Murray. Jack declined as graciously as he could, saying that it was a double, not he, who had performed that dance in the movie. Jack, in fact, *had* done the dance and was perfectly capable of performing it again. But Ina, for all her talent, was an awkward dancer. Jack was too much of a gentleman to allow her to be embarrassed on the floor or to give her as the reason for his refusal.

One saving grace of the European honeymoon was Jack's visit to London. Jack adored England and was determined to come back again as soon as possible. Ina, conversely, found London boring. Paris, the city of lights, was more her style.

It's difficult to write about the European honeymoon trip without making Jack sound like the uncomplicated, nice-guy romantic, which he was, and making Ina Claire sound selfish and shallow, which she was not. Ina in her own way was warm and kind and bright. They were simply two very different people. Jack could not be the worldly sophisticate. And Ina could not be Greta Garbo.

By the honeymoon's end, Jack and Ina's friends were betting that the battling Gilberts would not arrive home on the same boat. But they did. And before the ship even docked in New York City, something happened that made them forget their weeks of squabbles, for a while at least.

Ina said:

> We were on the ship coming back. Before we arrived, the newspapermen came out—you know, they board the ship [from the pilot boat]. They came on with a couple of Metro people and they told Jack instantly that his picture was a failure. He came and said to me—he was sort of laughing—"Well, darling, your husband is a . . ." I've forgotten the word. It was a funny word that he was using at the time. It meant he was a failure. He'd told me about his trouble with the studio and now they'd come all the way to tell him *that*.

There was nothing unusual about reporters coming out to a ship to interview arriving celebrities. What was unusual was that two MGM executives showed up, selected reviews in hand, telling Jack that his talking-picture debut was an unmitigated disaster. Their expressed reason for coming was to prepare Jack for the questions of reporters. But all this assumes that *His Glorious Night*, and Jack's performance, was met with criticism. That's the way folklore has it today, but an examination of the reviews shows that this was not so. Folklore has Jack slinking out of a theater behind a turned-up coat collar, with peals of derisive laughter ringing in his reddened ears, even though he was in Europe when the film opened.

When I first began collecting the initial reviews of *His Glorious Night*, I fully expected them to be dreadful. I'd grown up hearing all the stories about how John Gilbert was laughed off the screen because of his piping voice. But I was unable to find a single suggestion that the laughter was directed specifically at Jack or that his career in talking pictures was in any danger at all.

Mordaunt Hall wrote: "It is evident that the producers intend to keep Mr. Gilbert before the public as the screen lover, for in this current narrative he constantly repeats 'I love you' to the princess as he kisses her. In fact, his many protestations while embracing her caused a large female contingent to giggle and laugh. But Mr. Gilbert's responsibility does not lie with his lines and therefore he is to be congratulated on the manner in which he handles this speaking role. His voice is pleasant, but not one which is rich in nuance. His performance is good. . . ."

The house on Tower Road (*H. W. Grieve*)

Publicity shot of Jack relaxing at home. (*Photoplay*)

Way for a Sailor (1930). Jack is third from the bottom of ladder, next to Wallace Beery and writer Jim Tully.

Jack and Leila Hyams in *The Phantom of Paris* (1931).

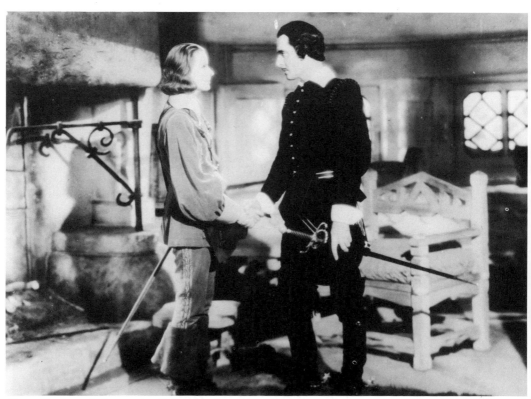

Greta Garbo tried to revive Jack's career when she insisted that he play opposite her in *Queen Christina* (1933), but it didn't work.

Jack and Virginia Bruce *(W. M. Grimes)*

Dolores del Rio,
Marlene Dietrich, Jack,
and Cedric Gibbons.

The Captain Hates the Sea (1934) was Jack's last film.

Jack's last photo session, with Marlene Dietrich in 1935. *(Kobal Collection)*

Critics by now were fully aware of the effect that "love stuff" could have upon audiences who were still unaccustomed to hearing intimate language spoken on the screen. One wrote: "The Gilbert love scenes are so intense they make the women let out nervous giggles. So you see that Johnnie is still the great lover, silent or with sound. He really gives a great performance in a role perfectly suited to him. The dialogue and situations are very sophisticated. Gilbert could not have found a better or more entertaining vehicle for his talking debut than this delightful comedy."

Another said: "Mr. Gilbert acquits himself with a certain distinction. He can speak the English language and speak it beautifully. His diction is faultless. Obvious training has been undergone, a little too much perhaps, as yet there is no warmth in the voice. His film is rather enjoyable despite a few faults. . . . It hasn't much visual movement, nor is the photography very good. But a splendid cast helps out where the film is lacking."

In the New York *American*, Regina Carew wrote: "Any doubt as to Jack Gilbert's success in the talkies is dispelled by his appearance in *His Glorious Night*. John makes the grade with ease and, if anything, speech adds to the charm. The picture leaves no doubt as to his continued popularity as a star of the talking screen."

What follows is a random selection of comments concerning Jack's speaking voice. However, there is no unique preoccupation with the voice of John Gilbert. For at least the first three years of the sound era, reviewers quite naturally focused on the voices of all the familiar silent stars.

"At the Capitol, Mr. Gilbert is disclosed as an actor of much poise and no little ability in a speaking role. He is handicapped by unaccountably poor photography and a great deal of sound recording that is not of the best."

"Gilbert reveals a remarkable command of diction, a command which might, with polish, lift him to the forefront of the talking screen. The only thing he lacks at the moment is vocal warmth."

"This is Gilbert's first sustained test in the medium and he comes off well. Without doubt he will hold his own in competition and with the public. . . . His voice is vibrant and clear if not warm. A note of self-conscious effort is excusably due to a natural anxiety about his first sound photoplay. . . . The role will lose him none of his adoring adolescent devotees."

"His first talkie reveals this idol of the screen as a star of pleasing voice, which accentuates the charms of a personality that has won him friends wherever movies are shown."

Edwin Schallert, a respected Hollywood reporter, writes in a particularly thoughtful review: "*His Glorious Night* is a diverting affair. The audience last night chose not to take the love scenes seriously, and there was therefore comedy aplenty, perhaps not wholly intended. No doubt the plot situations and their dialogue have been broadened to increase their popular appeal, but nevertheless the film version remains a work of quality. Gilbert has not yet hit quite the perfect note of intonation for the microphone but, barring a certain over-resonant delivery of lines, his enunciation is crisp and fine. . . . He will make great headway in the talking medium in light comedy. The intelligence of his work is even more marked in sound than in silents."

Schallert expressed a note of surprise that a Molnár play was adapted to the screen by Willard Mack, a writer whose past credits dealt mostly with horror, crime, or Jewish low comedy. "Add to that the circumstance that it was directed by Lionel Barrymore and one has an odd combination indeed."

The New York *Review* said: "Daringly sophisticated . . . John Gilbert's first all-talking triumph."

Where, then, were the bad reviews with which the MGM people met Jack on the ship? In truth, there were quite a few, but probably not more than for several of his previous pictures. More importantly, the negative reviews tended to focus on the picture as a whole rather than on Jack's role in it.

The New York *Review* said: "A sophisticated continental romance was robbed of its full entertainment value by bad photography and poor recording . . . with Gilbert not quite sure of himself as in his silent past. His voice is neither remarkable not displeasing but it is not that which one would associate with the Great Lover of the screen."

A critic for the New York *World* wrote: "It is not made clear as to whether *His Glorious Night* is intended as a burlesque or a bona fide Graustarkian romance, but in whichever category it is to be placed, it is not very funny, diligently as it tries to be, and not very dramatic. . . . I am surprised to know that Lionel Barrymore could have directed with so little imagination."

The *New York Post* found "the sound recording so cavernous, so unnatural and so unpleasant that what the characters have to say matters very little. . . . Mr. Gilbert repeatedly says, 'I love you, I love you, I love you.' It's all a lot of play acting and I don't believe a word of it. The audience did not always find it possible to take seriously the laughably stilted and affected dialogue."

Variety's review was crushing: "A few more talker productions like this and John Gilbert will be able to change places with Harry Langdon. His prowess at lovemaking, which has held the stenos breathless, takes on a comedy aspect in *His Glorious Night*. The gumchewers tittered at first and then laughed outright at the very false ring of the couple of dozen 'I love you' phrases designed to climax, ante and post, the thrill in the Gilbert lines. The theme is trite at best and the dialogue, while aiming most of the time for irony in the continental manner, is inane. . . . Director Barrymore apparently had a nervous reaction in the cutting room. This is borne out in the way the sequences literally grasshopper into one another. Conversation barely starts in one room when it cuts lightning-like to veranda steps and back to the bedroom or dinner table."

A week after this review appeared, *Variety's* columnist blamed the sophisticated comedy *Olympia* from which the movie was taken, noting that the less sophisticated "Capitol audiences laugh in the wrong spots." One good example was a scene in which Jack was not involved. The princess and her mother are in the royal boudoir, both in negligées, when the prefect of police is announced.

"Heavens," says the girl, "you're not going to see him in that, are you?" pointing to her mother's robe, a heavy garment trimmed with fur.

"Of course not," says the mother. She slips out of the all-concealing robe and into an all-revealing tea gown.

When *Olympia* played on the stage, this scene was always good for a nice little laugh. But the mass audience of the movies didn't know whether the humor was intended or not. Some didn't laugh at it at all. Others laughed not because they got the joke but because the queen had just done a silly and pointless thing.

The only available copy of *His Glorious Night* can be seen at the Library of Congress. It runs for nine reels, one less than the original. Even today, it's hard for anyone to view it without wincing at the awful production values, at the lines and the strained situations forced upon the actors. Jack's opening speech in the second reel has been mercifully cut from the Library of Congress copy. It was: "Oh, beauteous maiden, my arms are waiting to enfold you. I love you. I love you. I love you." But much of what remains is just as stilted.

There is one agonizingly long seven-minute scene, a medium shot showing an immobile Jack Gilbert and his co-star Catherine Dale Owen, who was wooden in any case. The camera sees them from the waist up. They are glued in place by the position of the microphones. There is no action at all except for a few spasmodic hand gestures. They stand in front of a painted backdrop, and on two occasions studio workmen are clearly visible walking around behind the scenery. Jack seems painfully constrained. One can almost see that he is aching to express himself with his body but the set-piece camera forbids any real move-ment. There are no close-ups, there are no eloquent pauses or brooding facial expressions. There is only dialogue such as this:

J.G.   Sweetheart! I thought you'd never come.

C.D.O. Careful, please. The window's open above.

J.G.   But do you know that I've been there for two hours, waiting, waiting, waiting?

C.D.O. I couldn't come before.

J.G.   But you could have sent some word. Oh, darling! Oh, darling, dearest one, what have I done but wait, wait, wait ever since I've known you.

C.D.O. I beg to remind you that if I hadn't dealt with you that way our little secret wouldn't be a secret.

J.G.   I don't wish it to be a secret. I love you. I've told you that a hundred times a week. I love you.

C.D.O. And I've told you not to tell me that again. I don't wish to hear it.

J.G.   But what is a man to do, darling, when he loves so helplessly as I?

C.D.O. You must remember what I have tried to remember. I am betrothed to another.

J.G.   Betrothed to another! You don't love him. You know you don't.

C.D.O. That's not the question. I'm going to marry him.

J.G.   Marry him! You can't! You couldn't be so cru-el, knowing how much I want you.

Catherine Dale Owen goes on to tell him that she's not being cru-el; it's just that she found out his father was a shoemaker in Riga and she couldn't possibly love anyone from such humble stock. She also tells him to knock off the "stupid poetry, your idea of social conversation." But he keeps right on being florid, reminding her of the time they danced and he held her close to his heart: "I felt the throb of your blood as it ran in tune with my pulse. Deny it!" She doesn't deny it, but he's still a peasant and she's the Princess Orsolini. But no matter. She'll make it up to him by getting him a good job as riding master for the emperor's daughter. "Arrgh!" was Jack's answering line.

After the second reel, the dialogue doesn't get much more natural but the scenes aren't nearly as stiff. Jack relaxes in both voice and manner, and the laughs begin coming where they belong. There are many gen-uinely amusing moments in the picture. Although it is not a good production by any means, and looks awkward and cheaply made, it is hardly a capital disaster. It's no better or worse, in fact, than many of the early talkies made while Hollywood was struggling with the new medium.

Critics were well aware of the difficulties of converting to sound and tended to be patient with the initial offerings of the studios. They seldom took directors to task unless their work was glaringly bad, as in the case of Lionel Barrymore. Their response to Jack's performance was mixed, but it leaned heavily toward being favorable. There were few negative comments about his voice, none at all that audiences laughed at it rather than at his lines. His voice was at worst "lacking in vocal warmth" and his speech a trifle too "mannered." Nowhere was there a suggestion that Jack's career might be finished with the coming of the sound medium. It was not until well after the picture was released that items began to appear saying that Jack's voice was unsuitable for talkies and that his acting style was out of date. Wherever those items came from, they were by no means typical of the first spontaneous reaction.

However, within weeks after the finished product was seen, rumors began to circulate in Hollywood that Louis B. Mayer had set upon a deliberate course to destroy John Gilbert. Even earlier, knowledgeable movie people were aghast at the choice of *His Glorious Night* as Jack's talkie debut. Stories with "love stuff" were highly risky. Much safer were action or mystery films, which placed less emphasis on dialogue. Even *Redemption* would have been better if it had been made halfway decently—which brought up Lionel Barrymore. How could Mayer risk the reputation of his biggest male star, first by giving him a story like *His Glorious Night*, and then assigning an inexperienced director who had just been relieved of his previous assignment because of incompetence?

Hedda Hopper wrote about the film, in which she appeared: "Talking pictures had to be approached cautiously. By the time the sound came in, 'love' was a comedy word. Use it too freely and you get a belly laugh. I watched John Gilbert being destroyed on the sound stage by one man, Lionel Barrymore. Whether by diabolical intent or accident, I'll never know, but Jack's first speech was, 'I love you, I love you, I love you.' In forming these words his mouth and nose came together almost like a parrot's beak. I used to see glee on Lionel's face as he watched Gilbert."

Hedda suggested that, competence aside, Barrymore was functioning with severely diminished capacity. He'd been suffering painfully from arthritis, and by late afternoon of a day's shooting he could barely get out of his chair.

Louise Brooks was more specific. "Barrymore was taking heavy doses of morphine in those days, and was hardly responsible for what went on. Anyone could have manipulated him and someone did. It was common talk at the studio before the picture came out. Everyone knew it but Jack."

Douglas Fairbanks, Jr., recalling the picture's extraordinarily choppy editing at Barrymore's hands, said, "If there were any intention to punish Jack in *His Glorious Night* and to bring his romantic image crashing down, one sure way to do it was in the cutting room. An awkward break or an extended pause, a jerky transition, or love words run together too quickly would have an audience howling. You've seen something like that done with a dog's ears. Shoot him with his ears down, then have a few lines of dialogue and cut back to the dog with his ears up, and there's your laugh. It could be done subtly and no one would realize it at the time. And no one could prove sabotage. I'm not saying that's what happened, but it could have been done."

Leatrice saw the picture in Milwaukee, where she was appearing in vaudeville. "I don't know whether Barrymore deliberately did Jack in, but he couldn't have done much worse if he tried. Jack's scenes with Catherine Dale Owen were dreadful. All that kissing and and saying 'I love you' looked all the more ridiculous with her because she was such a cold fish. He's hugging her and saying 'I love you' and she's just standing there like a stump. You couldn't imagine anyone feeling passion for her, which is why her career was so short. But she made Jack look silly and Barrymore allowed it. The audience laughed and so did I. I couldn't help it."

There is much conflicting testimony about what happened, if anything, to Jack's voice. Louise Brooks says that Douglas Shearer's requests for retakes were consistently denied by Lionel Barrymore. Sound technicians from Thames Television recently examined the film in a laboratory and could find no evidence of tampering.

But against the above, there is the strange story I heard from Clarence Brown in 1973, when he was in excellent health and remembered everything. We were having lunch at the Beverly Wilshire Hotel: I told him I was writing a book about Jack, and near the end I asked him if he knew what happened to *His Glorious Night*.

"I know what happened," he told me. "I was there. Douglas Shearer told me himself. He said, 'We never turned up the bass when Gilbert spoke; all you heard was treble.' Of course it was a 'mistake.'"

When I asked if Mayer had ordered it, Clarence was silent for a long time. At last he said, "Louis B. Mayer was my best friend in pictures. I was there from the early days until 1952 and we never had a cross word. I'm not going to say anything about anyone who is not here to defend himself."

Subject closed. End of interview.

Still, it was hard to believe. Notwithstanding Mayer's threat to destroy Jack, Mayer was a businessman first. Jack was too big and too valuable to throw away. It would have been more characteristic of Mayer to bide his time. Another thing that bothered me were all those bad reviews the MGM executives were said to have brought to Jack when his ship returned to New York. Where did they come from? Most of the reviews I found were, once again, not bad at all.

The first part of the question eventually answered itself. Mayer was a businessman and his motive was a business motive. The contract Jack had signed with Nicholas Schenck came at a time when Mayer was desperately paring his payroll and otherwise cutting costs to pay for the conversion to sound. Mayer couldn't break Jack's contract, but if Jack broke it Mayer would either be happily rid of him or in a position to renegotiate at more favorable terms. In *Hollywood Rajah*, Bosley Crowther's biography of Louis B. Mayer, Crowther says that Jack's contract was equally irritating to William Fox when Fox was having his abortive save-the-merger meetings with Mayer. As Mayer told it to Crowther, Fox initiated the discussion of how to dispose of Jack. "I'll tell you how to get rid of him," he said. "Give him a couple of bad parts. That'll make him mad."

Mayer supposedly drew back in horror, replying, "See here, Mr. Fox, I don't want to break contracts . . . and I don't like anybody who does."

Fox then turned and winked at Winfield Sheehan, who was present at the meeting. "We know how to break contracts, don't we, Winnie?"

Mayer stood his ground. "I won't be a party to putting my foot out in the dark and making the man stumble."

Crowther doesn't appear to believe a word of this, least of all Mayer's self-righteous response. He adds wryly: "It was on that delicate point of honor that the two men found themselves in hopeless disagreement." But there seems to be no argument anywhere that Mayer wanted Jack gone. On Mayer's terms.

Mayer may also have circulated two different versions of the same film, one deliberately made much worse than the other. A trade paper, *The Exhibitors Herald*, reported on November 19, 1929: "John Gilbert's first talkie is a very good picture. Drew fairly well but not as well as expected. It will please women especially. Ten reels. Recording good." This report came from Lampasas, Texas.

On November 30 in the same paper, Wellington, Ohio, reported:

"Not a good small-town picture. Audience laughed at the hot lovemaking. Some walked out on it. Poorest business yet on any talking picture. Eight reels. Recording fair."

Although it was common enough to film two different endings of the same picture and offer distributors a choice, there was only one official ten-reel version of *His Glorious Night*. But a nine-reel, and also an eight-reel, version was apparently made of a picture that was already badly cut. The mystery only deepened when the negatives and all but two known prints of the movie were destroyed, supposedly on Louis Mayer's direct orders.

If any doubt remains as to whether Mayer found satisfaction in the failure of his most valuable star's talking debut, it was put to rest by Mayer's daughter Irene Selznick. She said that when the first bad reviews were delivered to her father, he proudly brought them home and threw them on the dining-room table in front of the family. "That," he said, smiling, "should take care of *Mr.* Gilbert."

·fourteen·

JACK and Ina returned to New York on October 20, 1929. They stayed at the Ambassador Hotel for a few days before returning to Hollywood. Reporters who interviewed the couple thought Jack seemed uncharacteristically subdued, while Ina remained her normal vivacious self.

Was he disappointed that his first talking picture was not met with more enthusiasm?

"Certainly," Jack answered. "When I first came off the boat, the MGM publicity men were the first to reach me with clippings about my part in *His Glorious Night*. Those press notices were like a slap in the face. I really enjoyed doing the role of Kovacs . . . I looked forward to seeing it well received. And now this! Oh, well!"

Would he go back to silent movies?

"Of course not."

Was he interested in going on the stage for experience?

"No, why should I? I *will* master the talking films."

In the published interviews immediately following his return, neither Jack nor the press saw *His Glorious Night* as anything worse than a disappointment. The reporters didn't express any particular concern about his voice. They knew full well that talkies were still new for both the studios and the stars. They also knew that some stars were holding back in order to watch others test the waters, most were taking voice training, and some were joining repertory companies in order to become comfortable with speaking roles. The question of going on the stage was one commonly asked of screen actors. As to Jack's claim that he would master the new medium, there didn't seem to be much doubt among the reporters. One poor picture does not a disaster make. Jack had received badly mixed reviews before and then gone on to a new screen triumph.

Nonetheless, Jack's disappointment was profound. He knew by now that Louis B. Mayer, his hated enemy, was solidly in power at MGM. Contract or no contract, the failure of Jack's picture could only weaken his position there. The success he'd hoped for would have assured that he'd get his choice of available properties. One good picture was all he needed to wipe away the stain.

It is troubling that Jack could have told reporters how much he enjoyed playing the role of Captain Kovacs. More, that he'd gone to Europe seemingly quite confident in the success of such an indifferent picture. He'd been very critical in the past of his work in much better films. Had he somehow lost his capacity to judge the quality of *His Glorious Night?* Leatrice says that this was not so:

> You have to remember that Jack had sailed before the cutting even began. He had no idea what it looked like. You know that story about Jack slinking out of the premiere when he heard the audiences laughing? It wasn't true, of course, because there wasn't any big premiere and Jack was in Europe when the picture was released. But I think, and I don't recall whether Jack told me this, that Jack slipped off to see it while he was in New York. I don't see how he could have resisted. He would have been perfectly horrified at Lionel's butchery and at the overall quality of the picture. He probably would have heard the audiences laughing at some of his lines, but I don't think that would have crushed him in itself. He knew that love scenes were risky business, even in a so-called comedy. He would have looked at the picture through a director's eye and what he saw would have made him sick. Assuming he did see it in New York, his cheeks must have been burning all the way back to California.

On top of all this, there was Ina Claire. Jack's ego had already taken a beating during his European honeymoon with her. He had eagerly looked forward to being in his own element, in which he'd reigned supreme up until the time they left, back where Ina would be Mrs. John Gilbert and where he would no longer be her "adored little boy."

Jack and Ina were en route to California when the stock market, which had been tottering ominously for weeks, finally caved in on itself. Jack had departed a relatively wealthy man. Within days of returning he learned to his horror that almost none of his securities investments might be saved. Overnight he was sufficiently broke that he had to borrow ten thousand dollars from Ina in order to get by for a while. Then he and Harry Edington found a few forgotten bonds in his safe-deposit box. Otherwise, all Jack had for sure was his ironclad MGM contract, his cars, and his house.

The house, however, was already in a process of transformation. Ina had determined to make it her own, understandably wanting to remove as many of Garbo's ghosts as possible.

Garbo had never actually moved out. She'd gone off to make a picture about six weeks before Jack's wedding. She returned only once to collect a few belongings, including trunks she'd never unpacked after her return from Sweden. Garbo moved directly to the Santa Monica Beach Hotel because it was cheap, and then to the Beverly Hills Hotel after Harry Edington sat her down for a discussion about appropriate surroundings for a movie queen. It was bad enough that she drove a secondhand Packard. Garbo's stay at the Beverly Hills didn't last long either. Whenever she decided to take a walk, she'd send a secretary ahead to clear the way of other guests or she'd ask the management to do so. With the help of a few complaints, this behavior quickly wore thin upon the hotel's management, and it was suggested to Garbo that she either behave like any other guest or find accommodations elsewhere. Garbo then bought a house at 1027 Chevy Chase Drive, a few blocks away, and soon tried to build a wall around it. That move was blocked by neighbors who were equally unwilling to devote their lives to Garbo's privacy.

Ina, meanwhile, had hired Harold Grieve, the decorator, to help her remodel the Tower Road house. She told an interviewer, "Over there Jack is going to build a wing for me. Then each of us can have . . . a chance to get away by ourselves if we want to. I can have my maid and my piano and make all the noise I want when Jack wants to read or write. He has a great capacity for enjoyment, you know, but he has moods of seriousness." Commenting further on his moods, Ina said, "There are one or two things I should like to change [about Jack] but I wouldn't think of it. I would like to help him balance his moods. He is either plunged into the depths of gloom or he is in ecstasy. I think I could teach him how to control them. Jack is as utterly natural as a young animal. He is completely himself. He is not at all sophisticated. He said to me, 'This mustache fools you. I'm not so experienced as you think.'"

There's little doubt that Ina meant well. She did appreciate Jack as he was, but she was unable to resist trying to make him over. She'd also promised Jack that her remodeling plans would not compromise all that he loved about his house, but again she went a step too far. Ina had begun with a bedroom suite and then extended the servants' quarters to accommodate her maid. Next, however, she decided that a Venetian bridge to the swimming pool would be a nice touch. Ina called in the stonemasons, which added to the general confusion of carpenters, plumbers, and electricians.

It also added to the cost. Jack saw the bills mounting and his net worth collapsing. Under the terms of his new contract, he would get no money at all until a fifty-thousand-dollar lump-sum payment at the start of the first picture. After that he'd get fifteen thousand every Saturday morning until $250,000 added up. But the studio seemed in no hurry to schedule him in a picture, even though he and Harry Edington agreed it was now critical that he make another sound picture, a good one, and fast. But he couldn't even seem to get Irving Thalberg's attention. With these worries on his mind, he came home to his hilltop retreat and saw the foundation being built for his surprise Venetian bridge. He ordered the workmen to take it down at once. An argument with Ina followed that left her in tears. A few days later, she moved out of the house in a blaze of publicity and rented a home of her own on Linden Drive. Jack and Ina assured their friends that it was not really a separation; they simply could not manage to live together while the Tower Road house was being remodeled. They proved that assertion by going everywhere together.

It was at this time, this period of worried and frustrated idleness, that Jack began drinking especially heavily. Two factors, aside from his failure to get a film assignment, contributed to his gloom. The first was the sense of desperation that seemed to be pervading all of Hollywood. Cost-cutting alone had thrown thousands of actors out of work. Unsuitability for sound had effectively ended the careers of hundreds of featured players, and, of course, all the title writers. There were many reports and rumors of suicides among formerly free-spending actors who were now borrowing money to eat. High-priced stars who could speak perfectly well were left dangling in suspense by the studios, which saw a golden opportunity to negotiate much cheaper contracts if the stars were allowed to worry long enough. Every train from the East brought a fresh load of Broadway actors who would happily replace them at a fraction of their salaries. It didn't take a paranoid, therefore, to suspect a studio plot or fear for the worst. Jack could see lives being shattered all around him.

The second factor, related to the first, was the sudden appearance of one magazine story after another about the possibility of John Gilbert's being washed up. Even those items issued by MGM's publicity department seemed to call attention to Jack's troubles, in the guise of appearing sympathetic, when they should have been building him up. It was at this point that all the talk about his voice began to surface. One item read: "Anything that is contrary to nature seems funny to us. And that, exactly, is why Jack Gilbert's voice, which is several tones higher than most men's, sounds not heroic but humorous when we hear it."

"That's ridiculous," Leatrice told me. "Jack was a light baritone. He sounded almost exactly like Joseph Cotten."

Ina Claire agreed. "His was a high baritone. Not a tenor. He had no tenor quality at all." Ina thought he sounded exactly like Douglas Fairbanks. Still, she said, people probably did expect a deeper baritone behind "those wild-horse eyes."

In February 1930, during Jack's fourth month with nothing to do, *Photoplay* ran an article called "Is Jack Gilbert Through?" This article, by Katherine Albert, spoke of Jack's new MGM contract and the failure of *His Glorious Night.* "His enemies are glad (!), but studio officials who must pay him a million dollars in two years are turning white-haired overnight." She described the circumstances behind the contract in a way that suggested that someone had panicked and made a regrettably foolish deal for Jack's services. This "most absurd contract," she went on, even included a nice job for Harry Edington at the studio, and the right to manage Jack's affairs at studio expense. Nowhere, in fact, does anything like that appear in the contract. The article at this point sounds suspiciously like other studio plants intended to unnerve the high-priced actor and to lay a foundation of public awareness that he or she was being paid out of all proportion to reasonable worth.

Next, Miss Albert came to the subject of Jack's voice. "His friends have known for years that it was completely unsuited to the strength and fire of the man. The fans were shocked when he spoke. But while other satyrs were trotting to elocution teachers and voice specialists, Gilbert was flying to an obscure town in Nevada and getting married to Ina Claire." Mention was made of the failed picture, Jack's brooding unhappiness, his losses on the stock market, and his separation from his wife. "His career has gotten on his nerves and Gilbert must fight his battles alone. Garrulous as he is, he remains at heart a lonely soul as all creative artists are. . . . The actor, himself, takes first one side and then another. One minute he is angry and considers himself the victim of a huge plot, the next minute he is sad for what he considers a failure, but dominating it all is this spirit: Damn it! I'll show 'em. They can't ruin me with one bad talking picture.'"

Another item said: "John Gilbert has gone just a little haywire in refusing to see the press just at a time when he needs their good will as he never needed it before. He has not granted an interview, or posed for a new set of pictures, since before his trip to Europe. It is all right for Greta Garbo to hide out in seclusion . . . but!"

These articles and others all followed a suspiciously similar pattern.

Often seeming to sympathize while they undercut him, they would call attention to Jack's voice and his various other troubles, and suggest that he'd been less than fair or cooperative with the studio. They smelled strongly of studio publicity-department plants. If Jack wasn't giving interviews, who was? Who else but the studio would make it known that he hadn't posed for a new set of pictures? Several other stars, notably Gloria Swanson, were getting the same kind of treatment at the same time. They'd pick up a magazine and learn that their fans were deserting them, or that their acting styles might not be suited to the sound medium, or that their voices were in question—and always some reference to their salaries. Up until now, the high incomes of the stars were mentioned in tones of awe. They were part of their glamour. But now one began to see suggestions that incomes hundreds of times higher than the average American's annual salary were completely out of line.

Even Jack's longtime supporter, James Quirk of *Photoplay*, climbed on the bandwagon. After making the ritual mention of Jack's contract, Quirk in one of his editorials turned to the subject of Jack's voice: "I asked those scientific fellows [at AT&T] the direct question, 'Is there anything that can be done to adapt John's voice to the talking picture?' And they gave me a very direct 'No.' That is just one of the weird little tricks of fate the talking pictures have played on the Hollywood world. The camera was always very kind to Jack. The microphone played him false. Jack's voice is extremely pleasant. To the ear it is well pitched and as fascinating as a Rudy Vallee song. But it just will not reproduce in its natural quality."

Here, at least, was someone who'd heard Jack's voice both in person *and* on the sound track of *His Glorious Night*. But did those "scientific fellows at AT&T" have the same opportunity? And would they really have pronounced a pleasant and well-pitched voice to be flatly unrecordable? And, again, where did the later controversy over Jack's voice come from if it did not arise out of the immediate firsthand reaction to his talking début?

Many movie fans couldn't understand this wave of attacks on Jack. One wrote from as far away as Australia, asking, "When will the detractors of John Gilbert cease attacking one of the screen's greatest actors?" This fan said that he had admired Jack since his early Fox films and continued to do so. As for *His Glorious Night*, yes it was true that the audiences tittered when the movie was shown in East Brisbane. "But," he added, "only a fortnight before in the same theater, the audience laughed at Paul Muni's dialogue in *The Valiant*. So it seems that the manners of the audience rather than the methods of the actor are to blame."

But the attacks continued. On his voice, his life-style, his ability as an actor, his moods, and his drinking. They came from everywhere. Characterizations of his voice were given by people whom he had never met, and, in some cases, who admitted never having heard him speak on the screen. Jack was stunned. "I don't know what the hell I did to those guys," he said to Colleen Moore.

Barbara O'Neil, a contemporary actress who later played Scarlett O'Hara's mother in *Gone With the Wind*, said, "Jack had a magic about him. He was a gorgeous man. But people love to tear down idols. All the pip-squeaks in the world tear at their ankles to bring them down. With Jack it seems the first show of blood was enough to call out the vultures."

Ina Claire remembered Jack going to the studio each day in an effort to confront what was happening to him. He'd try to see Thalberg and then he'd go and sit in his dressing room:

> He would sit there all day and do nothing. He knew them well, he'd been there all his life, you see, and he knew their tricks and what they'd done to other people. They were trying to get rid of him. They practically spit on him from up above as he walked down the street. They tried to get out of paying him all that money. They tried everything to get rid of him . . . That's what it was, really. There was nothing the matter with his voice. It was not the voice they expected from those big brown eyes and those teeth . . . It was his first talking picture. Actually, if they'd wanted to, they could have at that moment done something. They could have mixed it and they could have brought it down . . . But I think maybe they did it on purpose. They wanted to get out of that contract.

Jack knew very well what they wanted and he dug in his heels. He'd go to the studio, day after day, to make it clear that he was staying. He'd serve drinks and buffet meals to friends in his dressing room, gathering what support he could from those who remained loyal to him. Some, like Cedric Gibbons, Renée Adorée, and many of the writers, stuck with Jack to the point of defiance. Others thought it prudent to keep their distance. Nicholas Schenck, chastened by the merger collapse and Mayer's apparent victory, chose to give the studio a wide berth.

Under the terms of Jack's contract, Jack was to work under the direct supervision of Irving Thalberg. The wording of that clause was actually intended to keep the production chief as a buffer between Jack and the "money-men," whoever they might be after Mayer's departure. But

Mayer did not depart and Thalberg was having his own problems of survival. After Mayer became convinced that Thalberg had dealt with Schenck behind his back, relations between the two men were never the same. Mayer remarked at the time that "Thalberg's only weakness is love of money."

One of Thalberg's survival problems involved trying to recover from the studio's comparatively late start in adapting to sound. But Thalberg went at it with characteristic energy and brilliance. He began buying up stage plays that seemed exactly right for the new medium. In short order, he purchased rights to *Anna Christie, Private Lives, The Guardsman*, and *The Last of Mrs. Cheyney*. He imported some of New York's best writers to produce scripts that had both humor and sophistication. Scott Fitzgerald, Moss Hart, Ben Hecht, Frederick Lonsdale, and Jack's old friend Dorothy Parker were among them. Thalberg gathered up some of the brightest men in Hollywood to work with him as producers and story consultants, men like the stage-trained Paul Bern, and the former English professor and drama critic Albert Lewin.

During this same period, Jack was literally hounding Thalberg's office. His career, he knew, was in deep trouble if he didn't get back on the screen in a good picture soon. Jack brought Thalberg scripts to consider, story ideas, stacks of positive fan mail, but nothing happened. More months went by. In April of 1930, Jack was stunned to learn that the studio, on orders from Louis B. Mayer, had released *Redemption*, the hated talkie he'd made twelve months earlier. Almost no one seemed able to understand the move. *His Glorious Night*, critics realized, had been a mistake. Jack should have been put into something modern and fun, preferably an adventure story, something that would make good use of Jack's personality. It still wasn't too late. John Gilbert, they knew, remained one of the most popular male stars in Hollywood. Instead came this terrible movie.

"Drab," "grim," "doleful," "dull," and "dreary" were some of the adjectives used to describe *Redemption*. Regina Carew wrote: "The director has spent a weary time telling his tale, which moves with slow and stodgy tread. . . . The Russian atmosphere is never established save by a touch of astrakhan here and there and a few bearded extras."

The *Herald Tribune* said: "*Redemption* would have been impossible for any actor. Just at a time when Gilbert needs a good film and a strong support, he is submerged in a lot of hooey."

Nowhere in the publicity accompanying the release did the studio say that this was not Jack's second talkie but his first. Nor does it mention that although Fred Niblo reluctantly took screen credit as director, much of the picture was done by the unsteady hand of Lionel Barrymore. Critics once again unanimously drubbed the editing and continuity, "flashing scenes on and off with startling rapidity and not always comprehensibly." "It jumps and stumbles from episode to episode." An example was given of a scene in which Jack, on one side of a wall, asks Eleanor Boardman in a rather diffident way to unlock the gate between them. A subtitle announces, "AND THEN . . ." and the scene cuts quickly to their wedding. "They sure cut out an awful lot," one critic quoted a moviegoer as saying.

The trade papers, without exception, blasted *Redemption*. Every publication going to the theater owners advised them against booking it. "A decided disappointment . . . a weak offering and not recommended for exhibitors." "*Redemption* would be a rotten vehicle for anyone." "Decidedly mediocre. Weak in nearly every department. Choppy, episodic, lacks movement and attention-compelling elements . . . an incompetent piece of work." All this while reviewers and exhibitors had come to expect that talkies were getting progressively better almost by the month. One trade-paper critic, clearly unaware that *Redemption* was not Jack's second picture, wrote: "This film will not aid John Gilbert's status as a talkie star. From reports, it has been finished for some time and is being released as a summer booking. It might have been better to call it in and write the loss off to overhead. Not much of a break for Gilbert."

As with *His Glorious Night*, the bulk of the criticism of *Redemption* centered upon the film's production rather than on Jack's performance or his voice. Some reviewers, in fact, were pleasantly surprised by the Gilbert voice they assumed had improved between pictures. *Liberty* magazine said: "The quality of Gilbert's voice is good. It records pleasantly, contrary to the rumors we've heard about it."

Another critic was more specific: "A good many near-libelous things have been said about John Gilbert's voice. The talkies were going to crowd Mr. Gilbert and his vocal organs right out of the cinema along with Rin-Tin-Tin. When the poor gentleman addressed the microphone, you could imagine the cat was walking up and down on the treble side of a calliope keyboard. The man simply didn't have a microphone voice. But in *Redemption*, he gives a very good account of himself. His voice certainly is not the best to be heard from the talking screen, but it is by all odds not the worst . . . Mr. Gilbert reads his lines clearly and pleasantly. . . . It is unfortunate, perhaps, that the film places him side by side with Conrad Nagel, easily one of those most accomplished on the talking screen . . . but Gilbert will get by in the talkies."

Edwin Schallert wrote of Jack's performance: "Later scenes are by far the best [after Fred Niblo relieved Barrymore]. . . . Gilbert in the mood of characterization . . . evidenced some of his inherent excellence as an actor. He achieved dramatic poignancy most effectively in the final scene."

Cheered as Jack might have been by these favorable reviews, he knew that they were only whispers compared to the volume of spurious publicity that the studio, he was sure, was leaking. The devastating verdict of the exhibitors' trade papers, with which he heartily agreed, left him now convinced that the studio had no intention whatsoever of protecting its investment in him, or of preserving his status as a star.

It was all so subtle. Jack didn't know where the next blow was coming from or how to parry it. That Mayer was behind it he had no doubt. But he could not bring himself to believe that Irving Thalberg, his friend, would be a party to anything so underhanded.

Still no new assignment came. He was worth half a million dollars a year on paper, but he was almost broke and would stay that way until he worked again. Friends drifted away. Coming home from the studio, Jack would spend more and more time by himself, with his fears, and with his bottle of Scotch nearby.

One evening, at about this time, some friends decided Jack needed company and took him with them to the Brown Derby Restaurant for dinner. One of his friends acknowledged the wave of a short redheaded man who sat at another table. Jack asked who it was. The answer was Jim Tully. Instantly, Jack, who had never seen Tully before, was up from his chair and stalking across the room toward the *Vanity Fair* author of the first and most odious of the printed attacks upon him. Here was an enemy he knew and could touch. The man who had called him a strutting ham, a minor talent, and a coward. "Get on your feet," Jack snarled as Sid Grauman rushed in too late to separate them. "Get on your feet."

Tully blinked, his eyes all innocence, and, as he rose from his table, flattened Jack with a straight right to the jaw.

·fifteen·

"ARE you out of your mind?" Donald Ogden Stewart asked Jack shortly after the one-punch fight with Jim Tully. "This is exactly the kind of thing those guys are waiting for."

Stewart was a close friend and knew his way around MGM. He was referring to the morals clause in Jack's contract. It was a standard clause, not often invoked except in cases of extreme misbehavior on the part of the star or a strong desire to break a contract on the part of the studio. It reads: "The artist agrees to conduct himself with due regard to public conventions and morals, and agrees that he will not do or commit any act or thing that will tend to degrade him in society or bring him into public hatred, contempt, scorn or ridicule or that will tend to shock, insult or offend the community or ridicule public morals or decency or prejudice the Producer or motion picture industry in general."

Don Stewart thought Jack should have counted his blessings that he hadn't landed the first punch. Jack, however, thought it would have been well worth the satisfaction, and was sure that even Louis B. Mayer, who had punched a few people in his time, wouldn't have the nerve to make an issue out of it. Anyway, he thought, Irving Thalberg would never let Mayer get away with it.

Stewart wasn't so sure. He was becoming convinced of something Jack simply didn't want to believe. If Mayer was out to destroy him, he couldn't do it without Thalberg's active complicity. Years later he told me, "Jack never said a word against him, but I believe Thalberg was just as guilty as Mayer. They ruined the poor bastard between them."

As for the Tully incident, it ended up generating considerable sympathy for Jack. Those who knew him well remembered Tully's hatchet job and wished Jack had done some damage in return. And Jim Tully himself remembered the outpouring of contempt directed at him, "the ingrate of Hollywood," after the article appeared. He now sought to redeem himself by going back to his typewriter and praising Jack for his "magnificent courage." "Jack is a warm impulsive fellow," he wrote. "His friends are loyal to him. . . . They arranged a meeting between us. With a nature completely magnanimous he has not retained the least touch of bitterness. Of course he would fight me in a minute, or Carnera for the matter. Out of it has developed a fine friendship of which I am glad."

"The heck it had," said Leatrice. "Jack couldn't stand him. Nobody could. And the people who arranged the meeting weren't his friends."

Lest it be thought that he did nothing but haunt the studio, brood, and drink during his months of idleness, it should be said that Jack did try to keep a high profile around Hollywood. Partly to this end, and partly because he had never seen Ina Claire on the stage, he and Ina arranged with the Kern Brothers, who owned a theater in downtown Los Angeles, to put on a play. It was called *Rebound*, a light comedy by Donald Stewart, with a suitably dazzling part for the leading lady. Jack bought five hundred seats on the opening night and gave an elegant party for her. He sat beside Colleen Moore, and throughout the play he kept squeezing her hand and muttering in surprise, "She's *good*. The girl can act." When the play moved to San Francisco, Jack flew up for the opening and gave his wife another gala party, then returned the following week to fly her home. It was one of their happiest periods.

Screenwriter John Lee Mahin tells of meeting Jack shortly after he arrived in Hollywood with Ben Hecht and Charlie MacArthur in 1930. Mahin says that Hecht and MacArthur went right to work on assignments but he was still free.

Jack offered to show him the town, and drove him all over the place. One afternoon, Jack took him to old Ince studio down by the ocean. Not much was left of Inceville. High up on a hill they could see the weather-beaten legs and torso of a plaster horse that once stood in the square of the Potsdam palace in Tom Ince's epic *Civilization* (where Effie Stewart fell to her death in 1915). Jack pointed out where the great Egyptian pyramid, built for De Mille's *Woman God Forgot*, in 1917, had once stood near the foot of the mountains. It had been made of wood and covered with paper, upon which sand had been glued for a rocklike appearance. The result was stone-colored sandpaper. Jack said the extras were thrown down the sides of the pyramid and a man stood at the bottom with a bucket of iodine and patched them up. He told Mahin he was making $3.50 a day back then.

John Lee Mahin, who went on to great success (Paul Muni's *Scarface* was one of his first assignments), was enthralled:

Those few days with Jack were something. I was like *Merton of the Movies*. We went to parties and Jack would introduce me to some beautiful dames. I would start to get moderately fresh and they'd respond by climbing all over me. I was never so successful in my life. It was like Utopia. They *all* wanted to go to bed with me. Later I found out that they were all professionals Jack had hired from Lee Frances, but boy, I'll never forget it. What a guy! He was a really sweet man.

In May 1930, the studio finally came through with a picture assignment, Jack's first under a contract that had been in force for almost ten months. For all the studio's insistence that they'd been waiting while searching for exactly the right vehicle for him, for all the exciting new properties they'd been importing from the stage and from best-selling books, the assignment turned out to be a minor yarn that Jack had been scheduled to make as a silent a year and a half earlier. It was called *Way for a Sailor*, a story about three seaman buddies who are left adrift when their ocean liner goes down, but are eventually rescued by a whaler. Meanwhile, back on shore, a girl whom Jack loved but who had spurned him fears that he's dead and decides she loves him after all. There's a tearful reunion and they live happily ever after.

Jack's co-star, the second of the three buddies, was to be Wallace Beery. Jack wasn't thrilled about working with Beery, who had a reputation for being difficult and mean-spirited in spite of his lovable-slob image, but he was appalled to find out who had been chosen to round out the trio. Playing the part of a seaman named Ginger, in the first and only acting appearance of his life, would be none other than Jim Tully.

Whether the studio intended to humiliate Jack through this bizarre casting decision, or whether they saw it as a way to cash in on the publicity that followed the fistfight, Jack gritted his teeth and went ahead. To do otherwise would be to break his contract. Besides, he needed the money. He would finally draw a paycheck with which he could settle his mounting bills, including the work now completed on his house and the theater parties he gave in Ina Claire's honor. *Way for a Sailor* might not have been the picture he'd hoped for but it was a picture. He would do his damnedest to give a performance that let his fans and reviewers know that he was there to stay, one that would wash away the memory of *His Glorious Night* and the critical drubbings of *Redemption* that were then appearing in the papers.

Adding insult to injury, Jim Tully was assigned the job of teaching Jack how to speak with a cockney accent for the picture. Jack's reaction to this, given that Tully was born in St. Louis and grew up in an orphanage, can only be imagined. Jack did more teeth-gritting when he was asked to pose with Tully in publicity stills, each man wearing boxing gloves and squaring off against the other.

Screenwriter Sam Marx had also just come to Hollywood, where his first assignment was as a back-lot assistant on *Way for a Sailor*. He tells of one time when they were shooting night scenes around a huge water tank. It was a raw night, with a cold wind blowing. Jack and a crowd of extras were being soaked to the skin in every shot. Marx says he felt miserable just watching them. Something always seemed to go wrong with each scene, and it would have to be repeated. So Jack was being ordered into the water tank again and again. He never refused and never complained. Sam Marx couldn't be certain whether Jack was being deliberately harassed, but several of the retakes seemed unnecessary to his eye and Jack's comfort was clearly being given less consideration than might be expected for a star of his stature.

Leatrice is inclined to doubt the harassment theory, at least as far as this particular story is concerned. The director, Sam Wood, learned his trade under De Mille and had earned a reputation for turning mediocre material into fairly decent entertainment. Leatrice says that by this time Jack would much rather have been working under a director who demanded one retake too many than under a Barrymore who demanded none at all.

A fan-magazine writer described the same water-tank story from a different perspective. "Gilbert has been much maligned," the article said, "but never by the workmen on his pictures. While certain writers and rumormongers were charging him with snobbishness and arrogance, his production crews were telling stories about his consideration and thoughtfulness." After describing the water tank and the weather conditions, this writer continued, "Between the scenes, an electrically warmed blanket and hot drinks awaited the star, but extras and the less important crew members had to stand in their places, drenched and shivering in the bitter sea breeze. Gilbert called his chauffeur, gave an order, and a few minutes later hot toddies were being prepared from Gilbert's imported stock for every extra and laborer. No matter what your sentiments are regarding the Eighteenth Amendment, you'll have to admit it was a thoughtful gesture."

After *Way for a Sailor* was completed, Jack waited anxiously for its release and for his next assignment as well. But again no assignment came. And *Way for a Sailor* was incomprehensibly delayed. It would not be released until the following November. Jack now knew in his heart that, barring a miracle, his career was as good as finished. By November, it would have been two years since the public had seen him in a halfway decent picture. After a lapse like that, he would need a picture or a part that was nothing short of sensational if he was to recapture their interest. He knew that there was nothing remotely sensational about the movie he'd just made. It was adequate at best. It would do little more for him than establish that he really could talk. Now even that small gain was seven months away. And there was nothing better on the horizon. Nothing at all.

Jack's gloom deepened, his drinking continued, and his marriage to Ina Claire began to show serious signs of crumbling. Ina was being as supportive and helpful as she knew how to be, but she warned him on several occasions that she would not tolerate his drinking forever. Nor could she be with him or available to him as much as she'd have liked, because she had her own career to think about. Jack was now beginning to be reclusive. He was less willing to attend parties, because everybody there seemed to know what was being done to him and he could not bear their pity—spoken or otherwise. He was less willing to give interviews even to those reporters he trusted, because so many of their subsequent stories turned out to be either veiled attacks or treatments that spoke of him as if he were already professionally dead.

In the summer of 1930, Paramount asked Ina Claire to star in another movie. It was to be called *The Royal Family of Broadway*, would be shot in New York, and she would have to go there for five months. Ina was anxious to do it. Her first talkie, *The Awful Truth*, was as much of a critical disaster as *His Glorious Night*, except that the picture did far more damage to the director, Marshall Neilan (another hard-drinking exuberant whom Louis B. Mayer despised and had sworn to destroy), than it did to any of the cast.

Ina Claire told Jack about the assignment, suggesting that it might be good for them to have some time apart. Jack understood. The part of a reigning stage queen wondering whether she should chuck it all and settle down in marriage to an old flame (who owned a remote plantation in South America) was perfect for her. He also knew that he was not being a proper husband and not fit company for her. It occurred to him that she might well get to New York and decide to end their marriage. Why not? Everything else seemed to be going to hell around him. In case she did make such a decision, Jack wanted some assurance that she would not claim half of all he owned under California's community-property laws. His contract, representing money still to come, was all he had. As far as he knew, it might be all he'd ever have. Ina had no moral claim on it and he wanted her to acknowledge that in writing.

Forty years later, Ina was still hurt by Jack's request:

Imagine that! I didn't marry him for his money. I said, "If this is
what you think of me, this is what's the matter with us. I don't
know anything about the laws of California, but whatever they are,
this releases you from any obligation you have to me. Go ahead
and do it if you want to." The next day, he had his lawyer around
with a contract for me to sign. A book! It was about twenty pages
long and—oh, God, even with the problems we were very, very
happy together at that time. It was written by a lawyer. I read half a
page of it and I got sick. I handed it to a lawyer, who was a nice
man. He was a judge and a Southern gentleman too. He was certainly on my side. He wasn't on Jack's side. And I said to him,
"Look, Mr. Moore, Judge Moore, this letter seems to say that everything's fine with us, but if I do *this*, I won't get *that*, and if I
don't do so-and-so and such-and-such, it sounds to me as if this is
building a defense assuming I'm going to attack in some way. I
have no intention of attacking. I know money means a great deal to
him. He thinks I'm after his money. I don't want a penny of it."

But Ina signed. She left for New York in September of 1930. She said
that she spent most of her journey East in tears.

In December, *Way for a Sailor* opened in New York to generally tepid
reviews. Mordaunt Hall wrote in the *Times:* "Mr. Gilbert endeavors to
talk like a British seaman, in which he is only partly successful. He
gives a better performance than he did in his previous audible productions. . . . Glimpses of work aboard freighters, the rescuing of men
from a sinking vessel and other such views are infinitely more arresting
than the actual doings of the characters."

A critic for the *Philadelphia Inquirer* said: "*Way for a Sailor* is the
thread by which the future of John Gilbert is reputed to hang. . . . It
must be said in fairness that whatever faults the picture may have are
not Gilbert's but the author's. . . . Gilbert's voice is pleasant and he
manages his lines intelligently and well. He gives a very creditable performance as the sailor who gives up loose ladies for the blonde Leila
Hyams. Mr. Gilbert should really have a better story next time."

Silver Screen, however, gave the picture a rave: "John Gilbert answers
his critics. And how! . . . His voice and acting are great. He plays a
tough tar constantly on the make. Beery is great in a featured role, but
Jim Tully, the writer, is terrible and should stick to his pen. Rating:
Excellent."

In a move that surprised many, most of all Jack, the studio gave Wallace Beery top billing in most of the publicity, followed by Jack's name in smaller letters. Jack's contract only specified "star billing," which means his name above the title. He'd neglected to specify that no name was to go above his, certainly not in larger type. He'd never been selfish about star billing in the past—he'd given it to Garbo when she was just becoming known—but in the past he'd always been asked.

He stormed into Irving Thalberg's office and told Thalberg that he could deal with being an actor whose appeal had peaked and receded but he was damned if he'd sit quietly and watch the studio grease the skids without giving him a decent chance. Garbo's first talkie, he pointed out, was a smash because they'd carefully chosen exactly the right property for her and even previewed it several times to gauge audience reaction. The picture was *Anna Christie*, in which Garbo played a prostitute. Her accent didn't bother anyone because she was playing the part of a woman with a Swedish accent. Garbo's first spoken line— "Gimme a viskey, ginger ale on the side, and don't be stingy, babee"— had audiences laughing with delight. Jack handed Thalberg stacks of letters from fans demanding another Gilbert–Garbo picture, pointing out that they were one of the most successful pairings in the history of the screen and yet the studio had only used them together three times. Thalberg told Jack that he was already thinking in that direction. He'd about made up his mind to star Jack in her next picture, which was to be *Susan Lenox*. He also had Jack in mind for the part of a romantic gambler in *A Free Soul*, with his wife, Norma Shearer.

Leatrice, who had made her successful talkie debut in *A Most Immoral Lady*, with Walter Pidgeon, confirms that Jack fully expected to be assigned to either or both pictures. And the papers were full of rumors of a new pairing with Garbo. But Adela Rogers St. Johns was at the studio one day when Irving Thalberg invited her to look at the test of a new actor MGM had just signed. He'd tried to crack the movies a few years before, but had no luck except for some work as an extra, notably in Jack's picture *The Merry Widow*. It seems everyone thought his ears were too big, and Darryl Zanuck thought he photographed like an ape, so he went back East to work on the stage. His name was Clark Gable. Adela liked the test and said so. Thalberg told her that he was thinking of using him to replace Jack Gilbert in *A Free Soul*. Gable did get the part. Later it was Gable, not Jack, who played opposite Garbo in *Susan Lenox*.

A number of parts were dangled before Jack and then snatched away as he reached for them. It was rumored for over a year, for example, that he would be starred in *Candlelight*, a sophisticated P. G. Wodehouse comedy that had played in New York with Gertrude Lawrence and Leslie Howard. In August 1930, Wodehouse wrote the following to his friend William Townsend:

> There was talk the other day of my making a picture out of *Candlelight* for John Gilbert but nothing has come of it yet and I don't see how the play can be twisted to make it a vehicle for a male star. . . . But ask me, I think the whole thing will blow over. Unless there's what Conan Doyle would call "villainy afoot." For a disturbing thought has occurred to me. . . . Just before Gilbert did his first talkie, they signed him up for six more at $250,000 a picture and the thought of having to pay out those million and a half smackers gashes them like a knife. The rumor goes that in order to avoid this they are straining every nerve to ensure that his next picture will be such a flop that he will consent to make a broken-hearted settlement and retire from the screen. And what is disturbing me is this; Do they feel that I am the only writer on the payroll who can be relied on to deliver a flop? When it is essential that a motion picture shall lay an egg and be a husting and a byeword, does the cry go around the front office, "Wodehouse is the man, send for Wodehouse"? It makes you think.

By the end of 1930, it was no longer possible for Jack to doubt what was being done to him. The studio had stopped all advertising of John Gilbert pictures in the fan magazines. They cited a desperate economy wave, movie box-office revenues having fallen forty percent during that year as the nation's economy worsened and more people contented themselves with listening to their radios. But at the same time Jack could see expensive publicity campaigns being launched behind new and cheaper stars, such as Gable, Robert Montgomery, and even Lawrence Tibbett. Worse, Jack found that friends he'd known for years were now avoiding him as word went out that he had been marked by Louis B. Mayer. On one occasion, a new studio guard claimed not to recognize him and denied him entry onto the lot until someone came out to identify him. Others ducked away or shut their doors when they saw him coming, lest it be reported back that they were seen being friendly toward Jack. If something malfunctioned in his dressing room, it would go unrepaired unless Jack fixed it himself. A few old friends had courage enough not to go along, particularly Cedric Gibbons, who said loud and clear that he "did not give a good goddamn what L. B. Mayer thought."

Jack became still more reclusive. If he didn't think he was fit company for Ina Claire, he didn't think he'd spread much sunshine at Leatrice's house either. He stopped coming to see us, although he would always remember birthdays and Christmas with gifts. I think now that the reason he stopped coming to see us is that he couldn't bear to listen to advice from Leatrice, whom he knew was constitutionally unable to believe that anyone, Louis B. Mayer included, would treat him so terribly.

Jack fought Mayer with the only two weapons he had left. The first, of course, was the contract. Mayer sent feelers saying that better pictures might be forthcoming if Jack was to renegotiate on "more realistic" terms. Jack answered that MGM would pay every nickel, so they might as well either make the best of it or do their worst. Jack's second weapon was his smile. Colleen Moore observed:

> After *Way for a Sailor*, Jack's contract called for five more pictures. Jack was sure he could redeem himself in one of them. Mayer was just as determined to make Jack agree to a settlement. Aware of Jack's strong pride and quick temper, he did everything he could to humiliate him, hoping that Jack would do what we were all afraid he would do, tear up the contract and throw it in Mayer's face. Instead, Jack laughed in his face. Mayer could never take that. Jack would see him on the lot and he'd give him this great big smile. It drove Mayer wild. Mayer was a great hater. Now the full force of his hatred was centered on destroying Jack. In fairness to Mr. Mayer, I must say that Jack gave him plenty of provocation. He let Mayer know what he thought of him in no uncertain terms. Then he'd remind Mayer that he had to make the remaining pictures even if they were a total loss. Either that or pay him the full amount of the contract and release him. Then he'd smile.

Among other stories Mayer spread about Jack was that Jack was a vicious anti-Semite. Almost no one seems to have taken it seriously. A great many of Jack's friends and business advisors were Jewish. And Jack was particularly adored by Mayer's own daughters, Irene Selznick and Edith Goetz.

As 1931 came in, Ina Claire's picture *The Royal Family of Broadway* had been completed and released. It was a brilliant critical success. During her five-month stay in New York, she had repeatedly denied that she and Jack were on the verge of divorce, although Hollywood gossip saw the breakup as inevitable. She denied it for the last time while being interviewed in Chicago, on the way to California, in February of 1931. She admitted to reporters that she and Jack would continue to occupy separate establishments but, she added, "Living apart has all the excitement of living in sin. I'd far rather be John Gilbert's mistress than his housekeeper."

Later she denied saying that, because when she arrived in Los Angeles, Jack was not even there to meet the train. He had a tennis date that afternoon with Ronald Colman and he sent his secretary to offer any help Ina needed. She coolly waved the secretary aside and instead accepted the assistance of a young man from the Paramount Studio, who escorted her to the Beverly Wilshire hotel. From the hotel, Ina announced their final separation. Of her previous statements she simply said, "I was misquoted about everything except that we are definitely separated."

Ina engaged a lawyer and paid him a five-thousand-dollar retainer. In her complaint she said that Jack would become angry at trifles (such as the Venetian bridge over his swimming pool) and that he often told her that they were unsuited to each other. He would tell her that she had "too much intellect for him," and that he preferred to be alone. Yet at other times he would grab her and beg her not to leave him.

She was still very much in love with Jack, according to Eleanor Boardman:

> When it was over, she came to me with tears falling down her cheeks. Jack came too, with his side of the story. It was more than the old problem of conflicting careers. Ina, with her vast stage experience, couldn't resist trying to remake him as if all his own years of experience didn't count for anything. But Ina never forgot him. For years afterward she always talked to me about him and asked me to drive her up Tower Road to pass by and look at their house.

If the divorce was a tragedy to the two people involved, the studio saw it as a rare opportunity. MGM knew that Jack had virtually no money other than that provided by his contract. If Ina could be persuaded to ask for a huge settlement, and got it, Jack might be forced to renegotiate his contract in order to raise the necessary ready cash. MGM apparently got Paramount, who in turn persuaded Ina, to hire a particular woman lawyer in addition to the attorney she'd already retained. Miss Claire remembered the events with sadness and a grim horror:

> I was talked into using this dreadful woman. She began by asking Jack for money. And I said, "No, no, no." I didn't want any money from him at all. I'd married him in good faith. I said to his lawyer and his business manager, "I'm not asking for any money, I

want you to tell Jack, and I've paid the expenses of the divorce." I didn't want anything from this man at all. I just wanted my freedom. I made a mistake marrying him. I just wanted to get out of it as fast as I could. I didn't want anything but a few expenses.

It was only fair and right. He wanted to be alone with his embarrassments and his humiliations. That I realized. The man was trying to save his life. Then that woman began asking him for money. I said, "Don't you understand? It's the only thing he's got."

Then this woman lawyer came to me and said, "You know, Miss Claire, I think you ought to know this, that I've been talking with some people. I know a lot of people at MGM and I can tell you that they would give you a very handsome present if you would just say something that would help them cancel Mr. Gilbert's contract."

Wasn't that dreadful? When you think of the millions Jack made for them, and now they were trying to get rid of him! So really, it was to have me . . . tell something. What would it have been, for God's sake?

She was very smooth, a dreadful woman. And then she went up the hill after Jack, after I'd told her I didn't want anything. She begged him to settle. "A hundred and fifty thousand dollars," she said. "Just give it to Ina as a present. She's been so nice about it, give it to her as a present."

I nearly killed her when Jack's manager called me up and said, "I want you to know about this because Jack doesn't think *you* even know about it."

Ina Claire declined to name the woman lawyer who'd hoped to milk either a public scandal or Jack's financial ruin out of their divorce.

The woman can only have been Fanny Holtzman, a well-known theatrical lawyer. Her version of the events was that she became Ina Claire's sympathetic confidante and tried to patch up their marriage. But Jack dismissed her, she claimed, confessing to her of all people that he hoped to rekindle his romance with Greta Garbo.

The divorce hearing was held behind closed doors in the chambers of Superior Court Judge Joseph P. Stone. Jack did not appear, but his good friend Paul Bern was there at his request to corroborate Miss Claire's testimony. She told of leaving Jack and returning to him twice. "Then it became impossible to live with him anymore," she testified. She said that she'd received a letter from him saying, "I have tried to make a go of it but everything is against us. I am sure that we will be giving ourselves a better chance by living apart. But I am not for company and I do not want anyone about me."

Fanny Holtzman announced to the press that a property settlement had been worked out by her, but Jack later contradicted her claim, denying that there had been a property settlement in the usual sense of the term. He said he had simply reimbursed Miss Claire, as she'd asked, for some expenditures, including her clothes and some entertainments while she was his wife. "Whatever the reasons and whatever the responsibility for the failure," he said for the record, "one thing has been established and that is the dignity of the lady who was Mrs. Gilbert. She has been more than fair in every way and has refused all offers of a financial settlement from me. In fact, I know that money has never been in her thoughts at all. She voluntarily signed away, one year after our marriage, all rights to my property."

On the evening when the divorce was granted, Jack and Ina showed up together at a party given by Fanny Holtzman at the Beverly Wilshire to honor Lady Inverclyde. The guests included Gloria Swanson, Ivor Novello, the P. G. Wodehouses, the Douglas Fairbanks, Jr.'s, and Lothar Mendes. Doug said that no one was particularly surprised to see the Gilberts together again. "Admiring each other is one thing. Living together in marriage is something else."

Fanny Holtzman told a follow-up story that seemed to prove she was unburdened by the concept of serving one master at a time. Miss Holtzman said she received a telephone call from Jack, who was staying at Malibu, where he'd leased a beach house. Would she come out and speak to him on an urgent matter? She went at once. Jack seemed to have been drinking before she arrived. His face was flushed and unshaven. She said that Jack implored her to help him, saying, "Fanny, my life is hell. I'm earning a half million dollars a year and I can't even enjoy a good meal. This stuff," he indicated a half-empty bottle, "is all I can put away."

He explained that the studio was trying to force him to break his contract and agree to a settlement, and that while they were pretending to search for new properties they were in truth doing nothing of the kind. "They're not even going through the motions of offering me junk anymore. They figure the silent treatment will wear me down.

"I can't trust agents. They're all in Mayer's pocket. How about you, Fanny? Would you take on a fight against Louis B. Mayer? Or are you committed to the studio's side too?"

Miss Holtzman gravely assured him that she was not on anybody's side. She suggested that before they go to court about it, she would first speak to Mayer and see if an amicable solution could be found.

She called on Mayer on Jack's behalf. She said to him that admittedly Jack's voice was not the best, but why make it seem worse than it was? The less likely Mayer made it that another studio would hire Jack, the more he'd cling to his contract. As for breaking the contract, a court battle could cost the studio more than to let it run its course. She suggested that Mayer stop making a martyr out of Jack by persecuting him. How would the public feel about Mayer throwing out an actor who had done so much for the studio?

"He did so much for me?" Mayer replied. "That *shikker* [drunk], if I have an ulcer, should he get the pill?"

"So leave him alone," Fanny suggested. "Maybe he'll drink himself to death, or take a swing at somebody again in public and you'll have a legal cause. But don't try to break the contract unilaterally. Let him go away and be forgotten."

Mayer, she said, nodded in admiration. "Like I always said, Fanny. A female Solomon."

When Fanny reported back to Jack, she indicated that she would expect a generous check in the mail for her services. Jack had a bit of trouble understanding exactly what those services were. Mayer had little chance of breaking the contract anyway. As for leaving Jack alone, that's what they were doing. What he wanted was to make pictures, two good movies a year and no deliberate clunkers.

After speaking to Fanny, Jack also learned that she was representing the studio's interests during his divorce while pretending to represent Ina Claire. When no check was forthcoming, Fanny complained to Jack's lawyer, Judge Samuel Moore. Judge Moore suggested that Jack send her whatever he felt her services were worth. Jack agreed, then instructed his fan club to send Fanny a large glossy of himself inscribed, "For Fanny with my very best wishes, John Gilbert." He told Judge Moore that she'd been paid in full.

·sixteen·

A T ABOUT the time Ina Claire begain her divorce action, MGM announced Jack's next picture. A look at the script and at the cast did nothing to raise his spirits.

Gentleman's Fate was a trite gangster melodrama in which Jack played a suave young man who learns that his supposedly respectable and dead father is in fact alive and a practicing Italian bootlegger. Jack goes to meet his father, only to find him dying of gunshot wounds at his hideout in New Jersey. Louis Wolheim turns up as Jack's older brother, also a gangster, and soon Jack is involved in saving the family honor. Single-handedly, he shoots up a rival gang and lives only long enough to whisper in his brother's ear, "Get out of the racket, Frank. It's a rotten racket." At best, it was a second-rate program picture.

The cast, although quite capable, comprised a sort of elephants' burial ground for actors who were being disciplined by the studio or were at the end of their careers and contracts for one reason or another. Louis Wolheim, an excellent heavy, was dying of cancer. He would not survive the year. Anita Page was being punished by Mayer for demanding a raise and refusing to work without it. Marie Prevost, star of many successful bedroom farces, made the transition to sound well enough but was now battling a weight problem that caused her to be banished to second leads. In panic and under pressure from the studio, Marie became an anorexic and literally starved herself to death a few years later. Ralph Ince, brother of Tom Ince, had directed about a hundred and fifty silent films but could not get a talkie assignment. He was reduced to playing character roles in order to eat; he soon moved to England, where he became moderately successful as a director.

Jack's co-star was once again Leila Hyams, who had been his love interest in *Way for a Sailor*. Her offense was that her real-life love interest was agent Phil Berg, who was building his clientele by approaching MGM's valued character actors and telling them they were being cheated. The director of *Gentleman's Fate* was the famous Mervyn LeRoy, except that he was not yet famous. He was a thirty-year-old who'd been directing a string of cheap program pictures for three years. He would be assigned seven in 1931 alone. One of these, however, was *Little Caesar*, which launched Edward G. Robinson's starring career and LeRoy's along with it. It was one of life's happy accidents. Following that unexpected success, he was assigned to *I Am a Prisoner from a Chain Gang*, with Paul Muni, and was on his way to a couple of Oscars.

When the assignment was announced, the studio's advance publicity again seemed designed to keep everyone away except the curious and the ghoulish. The word "comeback" was often used. Jack's past failures and his alleged voice problems were usually mentioned but then the reader was asked to forget about them. *Silver Screen* said: "There's a legion of devoted fans who would like to see this actor win out against the demon microphone. For Jack, the Great Lover, found the cards stacked against him in the talkies. His next picture is *Gentleman's Fate*. We hope it's a happy fate, Jack, for you have worked hard and you deserve it."

Louella Parsons wrote this left-handed encouragement in the Hearst papers: "*Gentleman's Fate* did much for Jack Gilbert in that it proved to his fans that he is not dead. Metro-Goldwyn-Mayer believes that Jack will come back bigger and better than ever. I don't like to use this term 'comeback,' for Jack has always been a grand actor. But dear me, so many things have been printed about his uncertain hold on his fans that I too may have been influenced."

From as far away as a London fan magazine came the following: "John Gilbert, whether willing or unwilling, is Hollywood's stormy petrel. He is rude to interviewers, petulant at the studio, quarrelsome at parties . . . has had a more precarious hold on his popularity than any other male star and has been the object of as much controversy as Clara Bow or Garbo." The writer brushes off a few of Jack's earlier pictures as "Elinor Glyn specials." "Now Gilbert is back at serious work again. This is all the more surprising since, with the arrival of the microphone, his voice was discovered to be not only high-pitched but squeaky, not only squeaky but unromantic."

Here we have a distant fan-magazine writer, who almost certainly never met Jack or heard him speak on the screen, describing his voice as "high-pitched and squeaky." Here we have Louella Parsons, who did know Jack and had heard him speak both in person and on film, admitting that she too may have been influenced by the studio slander. Even Clarence Brown, interviewed many years later, said, "As time went by,

I'd hear occasional mentions of Jack's high piping voice and the way audiences roared at the sound of it, and damned if I didn't find myself repeating them one day. Can you believe that? Me, of all people, repeating those stories. And I knew better, Leatrice, I *knew* better."

Leila Hyams remembered how professional Jack was, despite his problems:

> Jack was so charming and kind to me. He used to serve a beautiful lunch in his dressing room. A lot of the cast would go there for lunch instead of the commissary.
>
> At the end of the picture, Jack had a scene where he died and he had to cry. I always knew women could cry on demand, but Jack just lay down on the floor and cried like a baby. I asked him, "How on earth do you do it?"
>
> He said, "Leila, if the scene is true, I can cry or do anything else that's required of me. One false word and it's gone, I can't do a thing." That's why he cared so much about any picture he was in. They had to be true for him. He had to believe in the character he was playing.
>
> Jack was one of the most wonderful actors of his time or any time. He could have gone right on into the talkies except he was having contract troubles. But he never mentioned them to me. He was always anxious to keep the atmosphere happy on the set. He didn't fuss. There were some who were rebels, but most of the serious actors kept their problems to themselves while they were working. He had too much self-respect.

The New York Times recognized the picture for what it was: "In *Gentleman's Fate*, John Gilbert and a generally capable cast plough around in a morass of stale gangster melodrama without salvaging much in the way of entertainment. Ursula Parrott's story sounds as if she wrote it in a hurry. . . . All in all, Mr. Gilbert has a bad time from the start."

Other reviewers said: "The picture never achieves the slightest plausibility and you are continually awed by the persistence with which it goes on and on." And: "Gilbert still needs a picture! It seems to be Jack's fate not to find the right picture for his spectacular personality. He does some really fine work throughout. . . . The pity is that Gilbert does so well in a part that is hardly worth doing at all."

Mervyn LeRoy, on the other hand, concluded that he'd directed a good picture, going so far as to call it "the only successful talking picture Gilbert made." He went on to add, however, that, "Jack was lovely to direct, a very intuitive actor, but he was terribly unhappy and he was drinking too much for his own good."

By the time *Gentleman's Fate* was released, everyone in the industry seemed to know what was being done to Jack, and a small ground swell of indignation began to emerge. There's an unconfirmable story that Nicholas Schenck called Louis Mayer and vowed to do to Mayer what Mayer was doing to Jack. There's another that Cedric Gibbons would walk out of any room Mayer entered and let him know why. It's also possible that Fanny Holtzman's reported conversation with Mayer did some good after all. Whatever the reason, Jack was finally given a decent picture.

It was called *The Phantom of Paris,* based on the novel *Cheri-Bibi,* by Gaston Leroux, who was best known for writing *The Phantom of the Opera*. In this mystery-thriller, Jack plays a French magician-detective, Cheri-Bibi, who specializes in dramatic escapes from chains and handcuffs. A Houdini–Raffles-type character, he falls in love with a young girl, the daughter of a nobleman, who is engaged to marry the disreputable Marquis Duchais. The girl's father is murdered by her fiancé, who makes it appear that Cheri-Bibi committed the crime. Bibi is arrested and convicted but he escapes from the police and goes into hiding. Four years later, he learns that the evil marquis is near death. Cheri-Bibi goes to him and forces his confession. He then disguises himself as the marquis and goes about proving his own innocence. Cheri-Bibi clears his name and is finally reunited with his beloved.

Seen recently, the film holds up very well, with fine suspense and interesting photography. Unlike *His Glorious Night,* which was the third-least expensive MGM release of 1929, a feeling of quality pervades *Phantom*. There are some gorgeous moments in the film when Jack sparkles with his old fire. Chris Steinbrenner, of WOR-TV in New York, saw it and wrote: "Gilbert was enormously effective. He was everything you might expect in such a role. Cheri-Bibi is larger than life. He is electrifying, a dashing, flamboyant magician-detective-adventurer. The movie has all the old MGM gloss, a good European feeling to the background. Jack was elegant and graceful, quite convincing. It was the best of all his late movies."

Critics of the time were almost unanimous in their praise. The New York *Telegraph* said: "All John Gilbert's recent films have been billed as 'great comebacks' and some of them have been pretty disappointing. This one is surprisingly good. No longer the great lover, Gilbert proves himself a darn good actor. His make-up [in the disguise] is excellent. He plays a young magician convicted of the murder of his sweetheart's father. . . . It makes an exciting story."

One fan wrote to *Photoplay:* "When anyone can stir a Baltimore audience to applause, he must be great. This town as a rule has about the most unresponsive audience that is to be found. But I want to congratulate Mr. John Gilbert for doing something to wake up the audience to such a pitch that they forgot *The Phantom of Paris* was just a picture and applauded with such vigor that has not been shown here, to my knowledge, since *The Big Parade*. Mr. Gilbert, do it again."

The critics loved it, the fans loved it, but there just weren't enough fans. Movie receipts were now less than half what they'd been in 1929. The picture lost $243,000. Even without Jack's salary, it would have done little more than break even.

During the summer of 1931, while Jack was living in a leased cottage in Malibu with only his Scotch terrier, Bunty, for company, Leatrice also rented a small house down the beach. She and I settled into a long holiday between her picture assignments and vaudeville tours. It was a great place to be a child. There were low clay banks that lined the beach where quartz crystals grew. And there was a rock shelf running offshore where sea anemones bloomed and starfish lived, and soft-bodied creatures that squirted a royal-purple dye when they were frightened. The children ran in packs followed by their nannies, who supervised the crab races and treasure hunts and swimming expeditions, strictly enforcing the hour-long wait after eating before you could put so much as a toe in the water. Most of us had lessons in the morning, French or music, but the rest of the day was given over to play on the beach. Mother could tell wonderful stories about brave children captured by pirates, and tales of buried treasure that soon had us digging up half the beach.

It was one of the children—I think John Dillon, Jr.—who first told me that my father was staying there too. He pointed to the house and said, "Sometimes he sits out in front. If I see him, I'll let you know."

After that, I haunted the place every day. I was too shy to go up and ring the doorbell; I'm not sure my nurse would have allowed it anyway. But I looked for him every time I went out. Late one afternoon, I was coming in from swimming, all covered with sand and my long hair matted down and tangled, and I saw him. He was walking along right toward me with a glittery-looking blonde woman on his arm. I gathered up my courage and approached him.

"Hello, Father," I said, extending a formal hand. "They told me you were staying here for the summer and I've been looking for you." I was terribly nervous. I squinted up at his face and saw that he was smiling, but he seemed a little confused. Then he reached down and swung me, sand and all, up onto his shoulder. He nodded to the blonde lady and she smiled and walked away. Then he started carrying me home, chatting with me all the way. I told him I still had the musical blue teddy bear he had given me, and that I was going to have my hair cut short in the fall when I began a new school. He seemed very interested. I thought I'd pulled off the whole thing pretty well.

My mother was playing backgammon with a friend in front of our house. She looked up as we approached, rather startled. Then from my perch high on his shoulder I heard him whisper, "She thinks I'm her father," and I saw my mother's amused smile. I didn't know whose shoulder I was on, but it was clearly the wrong shoulder and I wished a tidal wave could have swallowed me and ended my embarrassment. Later Mother told me it was Gilbert Roland, formerly Jack's stand-in, who'd carried me home.

Another day, Jack was sitting on the beach with Adela Rogers St. Johns when a flock of children ran by. Jack noticed the small, dark-haired girl running in front and he asked who she was.

"Don't you know?" asked Adela. "That's Leatrice, Jr. Shall I introduce you?"

Adela says he looked after me for a long while, and said, "No, not now. Someday when she's sixteen or seventeen and gets her nose bumped for the first time, that's when she'll need a father. I hope she'll come to me then."

Adela says by this time all the humiliations, all the stares and whispers, all the things that had been written about him, had taken a profound toll on Jack. To see me would have meant seeing Leatrice and talking to her about the way his life was going. He preferred to keep it to himself.

But if my father was reluctant to see me, he did not reckon on my determination to find him. I hung around the Dillons' house as often as I could and kept watch on his, which was right next door. One evening, I arrived when Edith Dillon was giving a party. There were ladies in fluttering beach pajamas and men in white duck trousers and striped shirts. I found the Dillon boys, Jack and Patty, and we spent a while spying on the grown-ups. Then I heard the door open at Jack's house. I turned to see my father come down the walk, jump lightly over the fence, and then walk in and join the party. Our hiding place was in the runway between the two buildings. I started forward but Father soon was out of view and I found I was too shy to go on. We stayed pressed to the wall, watching him inside.

"He's a very handsome man," said the junior Dillon.

"I know," I said proudly. I watched as he mingled with the crowd for a time, but then he suddenly waved and left. He walked on down the beach, all by himself. It was a perfect time to catch him, but I didn't have the courage.

When I finally did talk to him, it was a surprise. I hadn't planned it at all.

I loved to swim and wasn't particularly afraid of high waves. Given a chance, I'd stay in the water until my lips were blue and my fingers looked like sponges. My nurse couldn't swim a stroke, and I would carefully avoid looking in her direction so I couldn't see her frantic signals to come in. We played this game almost every afternoon. She wasn't fooled, but she was kind enough not to report my insubordination to my mother.

One day near the end of the summer, I went swimming alone. The nurse was off for the day and our maid, Clementine, was watching me, but there were no other children in sight. Though the sky was clear and sunny, the water was rougher than usual. I plunged in regardless and dove through the breakers. Once past them, I started sculling along on my back, kicking my feet and watching wisps of cloud being blown along by the wind. I knew there was a storm somewhere out at sea and I felt myself being pulled toward it. I stopped sculling and looked toward the horizon. It wasn't there. All I saw was an enormous wave forming and rushing toward me. I knew that I'd be safe if I swam behind it, but I got frightened and turned toward shore instead. The wave caught me and it broke, slamming me down against the sharp sand and tossing me into tumbling circles. I wondered if it hurt to drown.

Then suddenly I felt an arm catch me around the stomach and I was plucked up out of the water and carried to the beach. When I could get the hair and salt water out of my eyes, I looked up and saw my father's worried eyes. He was handing me a towel.

"Are you all right now, Tinker?" he asked gently.

"Yes, thanks. That was a big one."

"Very big," he agreed solemnly. "I want you to remember something. *Never swim alone.* It's a bad idea. And keep your eye out for big waves. When there's a storm out at sea, even if the clouds don't get here, the waves do. Sometimes they're powerful, even though I can see you're a pretty good swimmer."

I don't know how any child in the world could have been more proud or pleased. I asked, "Will they give you the Carnegie Medal for that? You saved my life." I had just learned about the Carnegie Medal for bravery and was determined to get one for myself. But for my father to get one would be just as good.

"I don't think so this time," he said, smiling, "because I didn't risk my own life. I just fished you out."

By now, Clementine had arrived and I was whisked off to a hot bath and supper. I didn't see him again that year. My mother married a Los Angeles businessman and we moved to another part of town. Then I was sent off to a private school and our lives went in different ways. But I thought about him a lot. And later I found out that he was thinking just as much about me.

Adela Rogers St. Johns saw a good deal of Jack that summer. Adela had a son a year or two younger than I. Many people seemed to think that Jack was the father. More thought so when Jack left him a substantial bequest in his will. All that aside, Adela was a clever woman whose company and keen sense of humor Jack enjoyed. One evening, as she was walking home from a party, Jack almost ran her down with his Ford. He hit the brakes and skidded to a stop on the sandy road.

"Where the hell are you going this time of night?" she asked him.

Jack was obviously drunk and had no business being behind the wheel of a car. "I'm going to kill that bastard Mayer," he announced. This was about the time when he learned of the studio's pressure tactics against Ina Claire during the divorce.

"Oh, that's a fine idea," she answered. "Let me come too."

"Certainly." He gestured toward the passenger seat with a courtly wave. "Any number can play."

Once in the car, they headed down the highway as fast as a Ford could go. Gradually, Adela distracted him from his original mission and they ended up at her house eating bacon and scrambled eggs at three in the morning. Adela says Jack went to sleep on the sofa and forgot about killing Mayer until the next time.

It was also during this summer that Jack began to carry a gun. A number of writers have mentioned this as evidence of Jack's growing instability and paranoia. But a good many of Hollywood's rich and famous carried pistols in the same way many of today's celebrities keep bodyguards on the payroll. Burglaries of stars' homes were common, even more so than today when most stars have security systems the CIA would envy. Muggings of big spenders happened at least as often. And Depression-era kidnappings were starting to make nationwide news. Leatrice received a kidnapping threat and as a result, I grew up with iron bars on my bedroom windows.

Jack, however, had other reasons in mind for carrying a gun. He was sure, according to Adela, that he was being followed by men hired by

Louis B. Mayer. Mayer, through Eddie Mannix, had previously employed detectives to gather compromising evidence on an enemy or an errant actor. John Lee Mahin tells the story, for example, of the time Wallace Beery claimed to have severe leg cramps during the shooting of *Treasure Island*. He went ashore from Catalina to seek medical aid and rest. Actually he wanted to go fishing. Mannix had a cameraman follow him home, then to a trout stream, then to a tavern afterward, filming all the way. Beery's fishing excursion cost him a five-thousand-dollar fine. Most surveillances, however, were not so amusing. It would have been entirely characteristic of Mayer to hire detectives to watch Jack, peer through his window, harass him, even break into his house in order to obtain evidence that might aid in voiding his contract.

I told Adela a story that George Oppenheimer told me. He and Jack were at a party together. Jack had arrived late, after everyone else had gone in for dinner. As he sat down, he unstrapped his gun, which was not a small one, and laid it casually on the table. People exchanged startled glances, but they tried to ignore the weapon and went on with their dinner conversation. Nothing unusual happened, and after dinner Jack picked up his gun, said good-bye to his friends, and left. Herman Mankiewicz arrived still later, and George Oppenheimer told him about Jack's bringing a gun to the dinner table. "What are you getting excited about?" Mankiewicz asked. "How much can a gun eat?"

Adela knew about the gun. She'd also heard the Oppenheimer story, plus a couple of different versions of it. She seemed to shrug it off:

> There are one or two things you should understand about Jack. The first thing was that he was fighting a war of nerves with Louis Mayer, but he wasn't entirely a passive victim. Jack landed a few blows of his own. The second thing to know is that Jack fully realized that everything he did would be talked about and promptly reported to the studio. If Mayer did have people following him, Jack wanted Mayer to know he had a gun and was ready to use it, and calmly laying it down on the dinner table at a party was one sure way.

After filming *The Phantom of Paris*, Jack was given another assignment, this time right away. It was called *West of Broadway*. He had high hopes at first that this picture might match the quality of his last, because his friend Paul Bern was producing and another good friend, Gene Markey, was brought in to polish the script. But one look at the story and the assigned cast showed him that this was *Gentleman's Fate* all over again. His co-star, Lois Moran, would be making her last picture and retiring from the screen, her contract not renewed. The director was an embittered Harry Beaumont, who couldn't understand why he was being assigned nothing but lightweight program pictures after winning a 1928–29 Academy Award for *The Broadway Melody*. The rest of the cast was made up of obscure character actors or newcomers to Hollywood, notably Ralph Bellamy, for whom this was his second picture.

As Gene Markey tells it:

Jack had a good friend in Paul Bern. He was intent on getting a good vehicle for Jack, and so was I. But a story came along [*West of Broadway*] and I was given the insurmountable task of trying to make it come alive. It was written by a couple of actors who decided they were screenwriters too. It was a flimsy story. I never believed in it, but I did the best I could. It was not the vehicle Jack should have had, but the studio chief cockroaches thought it would be good to give Jack a change of pace. The damn thing had no pace at all. It was poorly directed, and I must confess that my script was no great shakes. That's what happened to what could have been an opportunity for Jack to have a galloping, romantic picture.

Ralph Bellamy said, "*West of Broadway* was not so much a western as a run-of-the-mill B picture. It was mediocre. Jack was the Easterner who had inherited the ranch, as I remember, and he'd come west to look it over. I was the foreman, which was amusing because I had actually only recently come from the East myself. Jack told me that the studio had put him in this picture hoping he'd refuse to do it, thus breaking his contract. His words were, 'I'll do anything. I'll clean the spittoons if those bastards tell me so, until this contract is up.'" Bellamy says that Jack stayed very much to himself during the shooting, and that he drank a lot. "But he was a professional, and he was right there every day working under very difficult circumstances. We were on location out in the Mojave Desert. Some days the temperature would be a hundred and twenty degrees. Jack gave it his best and he always knew his lines. He had no fear of the microphone, either."

West of Broadway was previewed in Glendale and reviewed in the Hollywood *Herald*: "If it was the purpose of MGM to lead John Gilbert to the guillotine and end the waning popularity of one of the most popular stars the silver screen has ever known, then *West of Broadway* is a great success. Unless this was the purpose, the picture may be described as the most monumental piece of cinematic stupidity on record. To make a man of Gilbert's former standing and favor with screen audiences the world over play a yellow-livered, unchivalrous drunken brute throughout the entire picture and then expect the audience to acclaim him as a hero in the last ninety-five feet, immediately after he has shaken his wife around the room in the manner of a terrier destroying a rat, just because he draws her to his bosom and cries, 'I love you,' is just a little too much for anyone to accept and enjoy."

After the preview, *Variety* announced that sixty thousand dollars' worth of retakes were being made, new scenes added to "sweeten up John Gilbert's part." Later reviews reflect modest improvement in a picture that many of those involved in subsequently omitted from their film biographies. The New York *World-Telegram* said: "Mr. Gilbert is good in the role and does much to overcome the deficiencies of what is laughable to refer to as a plot."

Liberty magazine said: "John Gilbert seems to be on the edge of another comeback. . . . The picture is nowise notable save for showing that this star is his old self again. All he needs now is a real role. His performance is tense, sharply defined. His voice is as good as any on the screen."

·seventeen·

I N OCTOBER 1931, after finishing the retakes of *West of Broadway*, Jack's contract provided for a three-month vacation. He'd planned to spend all of it in Europe, as far from Hollywood as possible, visiting places he'd missed when he was there with Ina Claire. He especially wanted to go back to England, which he loved, and intended to spend a full month there traveling alone and at his own pace.

But by this time he'd entered into an affaire with Lupe Velez, the pretty and wildly impulsive Mexican actress. Lupe announced to Louella Parsons, "Yes, I love John Gilbert and I'm going to follow him to Europe just as soon as I can get my passport. Love," she said, sighing, "was never like this."

Seasickness was never like this either. Lupe was violently ill all the way over. She no sooner recovered than she got sick again, flying in bad weather from Paris to Cherbourg. Jack cut the trip short and they headed homeward in early November. Lupe threw up most of the way home aboard the *Mauretania*. Jack did not pursue the relationship. He sent Lupe back to California, where she "fell in love like never before" with Gary Cooper, who dumped her, and Johnny Weissmuller, who married her.

Jack remained in New York for several weeks and was frequently seen with Ina Claire. Rumors began to circulate that the two were getting back together again. They became thick enough that Ina felt the need to make a formal announcement to the press: "I have no intention of re-marrying Mr. Gilbert. I like him as a friend and hope we will remain friends. But rumors that I am going to remarry him are very embarrassing."

Jack particularly enjoyed this New York stay because *The Phantom of Paris* had opened to quite good reviews while he was there. A great many old friends offered their congratulations and encouragement. But Jack knew that *West of Broadway* would be opening a few weeks later, and he also knew what kind of response it would get. He headed back to Hollywood on the train. There were two more pictures to go on his contract. The studio had now given up hope that Jack would settle with them financially, so they grimly prepared for the end of the charade.

Something seems to have snapped in Jack during the beginning of 1932. It might have been the realization that he was now in the last year of his contract. It would be all over in seven months. It almost didn't matter what his next two pictures were like, or that *The Phantom of Paris* was then playing to favorable reviews, or that the cruel jokes and myths about his speaking voice now seemed to be turning to praise. His audience was gone, it had been too long, his popularity was a memory. He was alone.

At various times he'd spoken with considerable enthusiasm about the new roads that would be open to him after the contract's termination date, July 31, 1932. He'd be financially secure for some years to come, perhaps indefinitely if he invested wisely. He'd be free to write and produce plays and movies that had meaning. He could direct, using all the techniques he'd learned from Tourneur, von Stroheim, Vidor, and even Monta Bell and Clarence Brown. From his own joy and pain he would draw performances from actors truer than anything they thought possible. Perhaps he would act, or perhaps not. To hell with being a movie star. He had yearned for years to do something of more substance than standing in front of a camera speaking another man's words or moving to another man's instructions. He knew so much more. He could do so much more.

But with the coming of the year 1932, he looked out across the months to the time when his new life could begin, when the contract that precluded projects of his own no longer kept him in golden handcuffs, and now he seemed to see only a black hole. His confidence had been eaten away.

And he was ill. His troublesome stomach had developed bleeding ulcers. Any amount of drinking made him sick. A single Scotch-and-soda had the intoxicating effect of five. But still he drank, because the Scotch seemed to help keep away the night. His insomnia had worsened and with it his private fears. Jack could never find the release of sleep in which other men found their balance.

More and more he kept to himself in that house on Tower Road. Friends tried to draw him out, inviting him to lunch and to parties. He would sometimes accept but would seldom appear unless his friends came and got him. Although he claimed to prefer solitude, there were times, usually in the hours before dawn, when he could not bear to be alone. He would call King Vidor or Colleen Moore or Adela and beg them to come over. They usually came. They came largely out of friendship but also out of the fear that Jack might destroy himself if they did not. His gun, though he no longer carried it about, was now kept much too accessible on the table beside his bed.

King Vidor tells of answering a call one night and going to stay with him. Jack finally fell asleep and King got up to visit the bathroom. When he returned to Jack's bedroom, King, framed in a back-lit doorway, saw Jack kneeling on the bed, eyes wide, and the gun pointed squarely at his—King's—chest.

"Jack," he said calmly. "It's only me. Put the damned thing away."

Jack blinked away the haze that caused him to forget that King was in the house. He grimaced an apology and then buried the weapon in a bedroom drawer.

Irving Thalberg was deeply saddened at Jack's condition, worried about him, and bone-tired of his own escalating conflicts with Mayer. Thalberg decided he'd try to give Jack a present.

He called Lenore Coffee into his office and said he'd dusted off an old story that Jack had written four years earlier in hopes of getting Erich von Stroheim to make a picture from it. Nothing had come of the project at the time because the part Jack had written for himself was thought to be too unsympathetic. The story was a black comedy called *Downstairs*, about the goings-on of servants and nobility in an aristocratic Viennese household. Jack's part was that of a cheerfully immoral and lecherous chauffeur. The story's theme was similar to that of the modern classic television series *Upstairs, Downstairs*, and is thought by some to have been the latter's inspiration. Thalberg told Lenore Coffee that now he'd like to assign the picture to Jack if she would work with him to write the necessary dialogue. Lenore agreed with pleasure.

Thalberg seemed determined to do this one right. Erich von Stroheim was out of the question as director—in fact, he was never allowed to complete a sound picture—but Monta Bell could be counted upon to do it justice. He cast the venerable Reginald Owen and Olga Baclanova as the baron and baroness. Paul Lukas was carefully chosen as the butler and Bodil Rosing, a gifted Austrian actress, was to be Sophie the cook. The female lead, that of a young maid named Anna, was given to a delicate blonde newcomer named Virginia Bruce.

When told all of this, Jack was at first disbelieving. Then, as it sank in, he suddenly leaped at Irving Thalberg, hugging the smaller man and picking him up off his feet. His mood soared from its depths and stayed there. He told a reporter, "I am happier than I have been in years," and then enthusiastically described the project. "It's a psychological study, a cross-section view of two strata of life. . . . The part [of Karl, the chauffeur] is a swaggering Don Juan who makes up in audacity what he lacks in conscience. He is an outright villain but nevertheless a fascinating chap. He will be hated for his villainy but he's bound to be interesting."

The plot, in bare bones and without the witty dialogue that makes it a comedy, has Jack arriving at the baron's house on the day the butler, Albert, marries the young maid, Anna. Being a lecher, Karl flirts openly with the maid. Being a cad, he blackmails the baroness upon learning she has a lover and he extorts money from the cook. He eventually seduces Anna while her husband is off with the baron and baroness on a fishing trip. Albert finds out and tries to have him fired. But the baroness can't fire him, because he knows her secret. It comes to a head when Jack tries to get the maid to run off with him on Sophie's money. When she refuses, he tries to take her by force. Albert comes to the aid of his repentant wife and ends up drowning Karl in a wine vat during a violent fight in the wine cellar.

Jack thought the wine-vat drowning was a nice touch and was very pleased with himself for writing it. But upon the picture's release, a few theater managers insisted on a new ending that would leave this engaging rogue alive to work other mischief. In the alternative ending, Karl escapes the wine vat and goes off to a job in another household where the cycle begins again.

Except for the alternative ending, the picture was everything Jack hoped it would be. He got to play an anti-hero, his favorite type of role. Monta Bell, a great admirer of Erich von Stroheim, made a picture that was filled with suggestions of the gifted Viennese director. Von Stroheim's meticulous realism is all there, as well as his attention to detail and his favorite sub-theme of the gentle decadence of the nobility versus the stalwart plodding virtue of the working classes. *Time* magazine raved about the picture's style and sophistication, going so far as to pronounce that "*Downstairs* has brought Gilbert back to the top of the Metro-Goldwyn-Mayer stable of stars."

Modern audiences agree. Kenneth Anger, writing in 1975, said, "Jack's [voice] was in truth not bad. . . . Proof is to be found in the brilliant 1932 comedy *Downstairs*, written by Gilbert himself, in which his delivery is excellent. The harm had already been done, however, and columnists and fan magazines spread the word that Gilbert was finished. His fine performance in *Downstairs* encourages one to lend some credence to the rumor that the sound engineers at MGM, at the order of Louis B. Mayer who at that point wanted to smash Gilbert's career and get rid of him, played havoc with the trebles and deliberately gelded Gilbert's voice."

Some of those fan magazines, by the way, went back into action after the release of *Downstairs*. One said: "*Downstairs* may be said to give what remains of Mr. Gilbert's popularity a push downward. Not because of any glaring deficiency in his performance, but rather because he has written for himself a part that antagonizes and alienates the fan. Why did the studio permit it?"

Whether innocently or not, such reviews missed the point. Throughout Jack's career he had gone out of his way to play varied and unstereotyped roles involving interesting character studies. "That," he said, "is clearly what acting is about."

There's a scene near the end of the picture in which Jack tries to get the naïve, beautiful Virginia Bruce to run away with him. He admits to her that he's been a liar and a cheat and deserving of every terrible thing she thinks about him, but, "Listen, Anna. I never had much of a chance. I never had anyone tell me the right thing to do. I've had to fight my way through life alone. Bad men, bad women. I've never been in love with anyone good like you before. I don't know how to treat you."

Lenore Coffee said, "You often hear about actors living their parts or staying partly immersed in a role after the cameras have stopped. All the good ones did that. Jack was by no means an exception. Neither was Virginia. That girl just opened those big blue eyes, and Jack was ready to fall in. It was inevitable. She was so fresh and young and so astonishingly beautiful. She was not by any means a Hollywood regular. She was innocent. She was nothing from the past. And Jack fell madly in love. They both did."

For a little while, Jack's friends rejoiced when he married Virginia. She seemed to be the one thing that might bring him back from his lonely exile. Lewis Milestone said, "What was so terribly frustrating about Jack was that everything was still there. He was marvelous-looking, he was a splendid actor, with a keen, interesting mind. He was a courteous man, a good friend, but inside was this dark destructive force at work. You couldn't get your hands on it. You couldn't stop it. Then along came Virginia and we all held our breath."

Their engagement was announced in June, during the filming of *Downstairs*, and the wedding was planned for August, when Jack's divorce from Ina Claire became final. Paul Bern rushed to the set with his congratulations when he heard the news. Bern was doubly happy because he too had decided to forsake the bachelor life. Jean Harlow had consented to be his wife. In July, Jack was their best man.

Other things in Jack's life seemed to be going spectacularly well. MGM bought another plum assignment for him, a play by Wilson Collison called *Red Dust*. It was a tough, romantic adventure set in the tropics. The original thought was that Fred Niblo would direct and Garbo might even be given the female lead. But Irving Thalberg decided that Jean Harlow's look and manner were more suited to the role. In place of Niblo, he assigned the French director Jacques Feyder, who had come to Hollywood at the end of the silent era and who had directed *The Kiss*, the last silent film for both Garbo and MGM.

Production was started with only ten pages of script, written by Jack's friend John Lee Mahin. While he was working on it, a chance conversation between Mahin and the producer, Hunt Stromberg, brought Jack's fragile world crashing down again. "I was preparing the script for *Red Dust* ," said Mahin. "Irving Thalberg was going to cast Jean Harlow with Jack Gilbert. She was considered a hot number at the studio and they thought it would be great for his sagging image. I said to Hunt Stromberg, 'You really ought to see a guy I saw on the set, a little kid, eyes like a little boy but he was built like a bull. He was really something.' It was Clark Gable and I suggested that Stromberg go look him up. Stromberg did. He took one look and that was it. He went to Irving Thalberg and said he wanted to take Jack Gilbert out and put Gable in. It was awfully hard but they did it. They took Feyder off the picture too, and gave it to Victor Fleming, and they doubled the budget. Of course it made Gable a star."

Jack was utterly crushed. And Jacques Feyder decided he'd had enough of Hollywood and returned to France, where he continued a distinguished career.

Jack might have fallen apart were it not for Virginia. As she recalled:

> I was working on another picture when Irving Thalberg took Jack out of *Red Dust* and put Clark Gable in. It nearly killed him. Of course Jack had been driven half crazy by the time I married him but I didn't know that. I loved him madly. I was very young, only twenty-one, and he was thirty-three.
>
> Jack sent me a telegram at the studio on August tenth asking me to come to his dressing room at six P.M. for the wedding. I had no more notice than that. I finished work at five-thirty, took off my makeup and changed my clothes, and we were married right on the lot. Irving Thalberg and Norma Shearer were our witnesses.

But before that there was all the business about a marriage contract. My father arranged it, not Jack. Jack agreed to write a new will leaving everything to me and my family. In the contract, I was guaranteed to be a virgin—my father's idea. Jack thought it was hilarious but I think he was also excited about it. I don't think he'd known many virgins in his life. I know this sounds crazy, but my father allowed me to spend one night with Jack before we were married so that he could see for himself that I was a virgin. But he had to promise to return me to my father in the same pristine condition.

All the time I knew Jack, I never saw him so happy as when we were shooting *Downstairs*. He had such high hopes. We were so happy working together. Life was so full and worth living. All he needed was work. But then he lost *Red Dust* and the studio had nothing else for him right away. He owed them one more picture under the old contract but they weren't in any hurry to do it.

Actually, Jack's contract had expired before he and Virginia were married. Technically, he was entitled to full payment of the remaining $250,000 whether he made a movie or not. But there was little point in making an issue out of that or going to court. MGM's lawyers would simply stall, holding up his money no matter what a judge said. Anyway, he had a honeymoon to think about. Jack decided that the third attempt at seeing Europe might be the charm.

"Jack invited my parents along on the honeymoon to Europe," Virginia told me. "We were simple people from North Dakota and it was like coming into a dreamworld. We weren't used to that kind of luxury. Jack just loved Europe. He was so curious about everything, always asking people questions. We saw everything, I promise you. We even went to see a sex show in Paris. But I spent a lot of time in our hotel room trying to cheer him up. Jack would get into these deep depressions and not want to see anyone."

There was good reason for at least one deep and lasting depression. Word reached him that his friend Paul Bern, after only two months of marriage to Jean Harlow, had put a gun to his temple and pulled the trigger. Paul left a note of apology that Louis Mayer tried unsuccessfully to keep from the police. It was a private note that professed his deep love for Jean and his shame over a vague humiliation. It's generally believed that Paul Bern's genitals were underdeveloped. It's also generally and tragically believed that Jean Harlow, a very decent human being, would have cared no less for him because of it.

Jack was profoundly affected by Paul Bern's death. What struck him most deeply was a sense of terrible waste. Paul had had so much talent, so much to give, and his grace had touched the lives of so many, that the reason given for throwing all that away seemed stunningly trivial. The effect, far from turning Jack's thoughts toward self-destruction, made him want all the more desperately to work.

As Virginia Bruce later said:

Work was his god. Jack only wanted one thing in the world and that was to work. I thought at first that he needed a wife, that he needed companionship. He seemed to want me there, on the spot, all the time. I was ready to give up my career. I told that to Irving Thalberg and he agreed to put me on indefinite suspension so I could come back anytime. But I was wrong. What Jack needed all the while was to do what he knew how to do. He had all that energy pent up inside him, and all that anger at what they'd done to him.

When they finally did put him in a movie, it was nothing. Just some B picture. It was no good for him, but he did it. He was determined to live out that damned contract. There was some clause saying he could not be seen drunk in public or otherwise disgrace himself, so he drank at home. Sometimes he'd be awake drinking all night; then in the morning he'd get me to throw him into the swimming pool so he could clear his head. I'm sure the shock must have been bad for him. He had bleeding ulcers. He used to throw up blood in the morning until he fainted.

Jack's doctor was Sam Hirshfield, a kindly man. Hirshfield would come over to the house and inject sodium amytal into Jack's veins so he could sleep; otherwise he'd stay awake for days. Once when we were at Malibu, Jack was terribly sick. One of his veins collapsed and became infected. Hirshfield sent a nurse to look after him. She was a little red-haired girl who promptly fell in love with him. He was not very pretty to look at, he had all kinds of infections, and this girl stood at the foot of the bed with tears streaming down her face. Jack was something, the effect he had on people.

When Jack was feeling himself, he was the most charming, exciting, intelligent man I've ever known. He had a beautiful body and he was a tender and considerate lover. Very patient. I think that's why his love scenes came off so well on the screen. They were real, or at least they rang true. And he'd take his time until the woman in the picture and all the women in the audience were ready. I never understood how that kind of lovemaking could go out of style, because it certainly didn't in real life. What came into style was the treat-'em-rough type of lover like Gable or the cool type like Robert Montgomery. I think it was because they appealed to more men. Men could be like Gable, or think they could. But they knew they couldn't be like Gilbert.

And he was so much more than a lover. Jack had a brilliant, educated mind and he attracted friends who were just as bright as he was. He adored the English, Ronnie Colman and Herbert Marshall, and they loved him. To the end he had friends who adored him. Not the MGM crowd. They left him flat. I suppose they were afraid of Mayer. Except for Cedric Gibbons, who wasn't afraid of anybody.

There was no one like Jack when his spirits were up. But when he was down, he was . . . Oh, you can't describe it. It was like death.

Jack's last picture under the "damned contract" was a negligible piece of work directed by Tod Browning, called *Fast Workers*. It was taken from a play, *Rivets*, by John McDermott, about life with the construction workers on the tall buildings going up in New York. Again, Jack played a villain, Gunner Smith, a temperamental and sometimes sullen lover. "He drinks freely, punches men he does not like, mistreats his women, deceives his friends and shows himself to be an intolerable braggart," said *The New York Times*. "In real life the Gunner would have been pitched from a convenient skyscraper by his fellow workers for one tenth the things he does in the picture."

The cast included Mae Clarke, best known for having a grapefruit shoved in her face by Jimmy Cagney the year before (speaking of a new style of lovemaking), and Robert Armstrong, best known a year later as the white hunter who brought in King Kong. Virginia Cherrill, who played the beautiful blind girl in Chaplin's *City Lights* also had a part. (She was about to marry Cary Grant, the first of five husbands, eventually working her way up to the ninth Earl of Jersey.) Tod Browning, the director, was being punished. This was his only film of the year. He'd made *Freaks* the year before, an expensive, ghastly, and grotesque picture (and underground classic) that had to be drastically cut and later shelved after a San Diego preview in which a woman ran screaming up the aisle.

Fast Workers, according to the New York *Daily Mirror*, was a picture that "makes small use of the celebrated Gilbert charm. . . . Gilbert does the best he can in this unfortunate role."

The New York *Evening Post* said: "That such an indifferent story should have been allotted to Jack Gilbert is a matter to be regretted. . . .

He had always been an excellent performer, although the fact seems to have been largely overlooked in recent years. In his current film he give a capable performance . . . but he is obviously handicapped by the limits of the piece."

The long game was over. Jack could finally pack up his belongings and go home. But MGM had saved one insult for last. When he arrived on his final Saturday morning to pick up his check and his personal effects, workmen were already at work remodeling his dressing room for David Selznick's office. "Please, gentlemen," Jack said, wanting to be left in peace for a few minutes, "the corpse isn't even cold yet."

· eighteen ·

U NDER the studio star system that prevailed from the silent days well into the 1950s, a contracted star was the absolute property of the studio. It is not much of an exaggeration to say that most of these stars sold their souls for fame and wealth. They certainly sold their personae. A look at Article 7 of Jack's contract is instructive. In it, the artist (Jack) gave the producer (MGM) sole and exclusive rights to any artistic activity he might choose to do. He couldn't perform or produce anything or allow his name to be used. He was absolutely locked into MGM for the duration of his contract.

Next came Article 8, the morals clause, which said the star couldn't do anything to offend anybody either.

Leatrice, who was an independent, could do plays or go on vaudeville tours, while Jack could not. He could not exploit his own name by writing a book, appear in a play or radio show, or produce a pet project film. He was even forbidden to use his name to endorse commercial products, and discouraged from talking to the press without benefit of the publicity department, because "the average artist is not well qualified by experience to talk unguidedly for publication."

When a star's contract was about to expire, therefore, he saw that event with a mixture of apprehension and excitement. The money would not be coming in as dependably, but he would serve no master but himself. He would have his pick of projects from all those producers with whom he quietly lunched or who approached him at cocktail parties.

In truth it almost never happened that way. A star without a contract was like the rest of us without a job. One's value becomes vague and ill defined. One becomes something of an untouchable. This was generally true even for an actor who remained good "box office" or who had retained some measure of good will among the studio heads. Many stars found that in order to work again they either had to turn to the stage or go to Europe. But once they did either, even successfully, they were rarely welcomed back. They had violated the system. They were bad examples.

Jack understood the game as well as anyone, and yet he allowed himself to believe that talent and the will to work were the most important ingredients for success. But, except for a series of indifferent plays and talk of one or two British-made films, no offers came. Again a depression set in. Again he withdrew from the company of those who were working. His insomnia and his stomach problems, both of which had abated for a short period after his marriage to Virginia, returned in earnest. He would drink, often with his neighbor John Barrymore, who was at least Jack's equal at self-destruction, and he would get sick. Collen Moore said that Barrymore once tried to introduce Jack to hard drugs. "Jack wasn't that crazy. He said to Barrymore, 'My God, no! I can't even hold my liquor.'" A lifelong aversion to drugs and doctors led Jack one night to order Dr. Hirshfield out of his house while waving that gun at him. Colleen said that some friends had caused Jack to wonder what sort of "feel-goods" Dr. Hirshfield was shooting into his veins. When Hirshfield was vague in his reply, Jack became both horrified and furious. Hirshfield then made the mistake of telling Jack he had just the thing to calm him, and Jack reached for the gun. Although Hirshfield might have been entirely innocent, Colleen points out that there was no shortage of "Dr. Feel-Goods" in Hollywood who amassed small fortunes making house calls to stars in need of mood elevators.

The one bright spot in Jack's idle disintegration that year came in December, when the Gilberts announced that they were expecting a child. He seems to have pulled himself together for a while after that, but not to the point of quitting drinking. But he did appear to be slowly coming to terms with his bitterness at being toppled from his pinnacle.

In April 1933, Jack and Virginia took a cruise to New York by way of the Panama Canal. He was still a big enough name to attract a crowd of reporters at the pier. When he was asked about his future, Jack answered that he had no particular plans. He was looking for a play but had not been excited about any that were offered to him. He added that his own uncertainty was nothing compared to the troubles that were then plaguing Hollywood. Paramount and RKO had gone into receivership that January, as had Fox's West Coast theater subsidiary. MGM and Warners were managing to stay one step ahead of bankruptcy, largely because of the pulling power of their star rosters. "The Depression has finally caught up with them," Jack said to a *Times* reporter. "They never thought it would. As a result, it looks as if the days of the big studios are over and that a chance for individual expression may come out of the general reorganization now being undertaken."

Asked by a *World-Telegram* reporter how he felt about his sharp decline in popularity, Jack answered, "Oh, what the hell. They liked me once. A man is an ass to squawk about life. Especially me." He paused for a moment to fondle a baby squirrel he had picked up in Guatemala. "You know what started all this, my so-called decline, was the terribly unfortunate role in which I broke into talkies. *His Glorious Night.* I played a passionate love scene à la silent-film stuff. You know, all gushing, blahh . . . My God, the people just laughed. I couldn't blame them.

"I said, 'For God's sake, withdraw it and I'll make you another one for nothing.' But they wouldn't and I had to suffer. Well, hell, I don't feel passé. I've got my health and my vigor and I hope my talent. Something is bound to break. If a man has lost his box-office draw, what can you do about it? It's the stage, it's the movies, it's business, it's life. It's silly to get maudlin about it.

"This is a great age," he continued. "No time for hokum and the baloney of spectacles and silly stuff. Social and economic dilemmas created an Ibsen, a Goethe and other great writers. I think that the trend is serious and I'd like to do sober, substantial roles."

The interviewer concluded that Jack was a class act, showing no blame or bitterness toward anyone. Jack's performance was "great theater," the reporter wrote.

But nothing did break for the next three months. A new management team at Fox approached Jack about directing for them, offering him first a consultancy on a Sally Eilers–Norman Foster picture called *Walls of Gold.* However, Jack regarded the consultancy as a disguised "freebie," since it paid no salary and gave him no real responsibility. He declined the offer and continued to sit by the phone.

"I stayed home waiting," he later told the New York *Telegraph,* "hoping I would be offered work somewhere. Had it not been for my wife, who understood, and my friends, I probably would have lost my mind. Then one day, while I was leaving the house, the telephone rang. . . ."

The phone call was from Walter Wanger, then a producer at MGM, of all places. It seemed that Greta Garbo, who had recently returned from an eight-month holiday in Sweden, had started production of her new costume epic, *Queen Christina.* The problem, however, was that they couldn't seem to find anyone capable of playing her love interest.

After rejecting a number of male stars who they feared would be over-whelmed by Garbo, the studio had settled on a brilliant young English actor named Laurence Olivier and they'd brought him over. But Garbo seemed to stiffen every time he or anyone else did a love scene with her. Would Jack, Walter Wanger asked, consider coming down to the set and see if he might help Garbo relax?

Jack happily agreed. He had not laid eyes on Garbo for more than a year, and had not spoken to her except at parties for more than three years. When he got to the set, he was asked if he'd dress in costume and try an informal sort of dress rehearsal. Walter Wanger observed that Garbo seemed delighted to see Jack. She was more relaxed and happy than she'd been in weeks. They rehearsed the scene with the cameras rolling and the microphones switched on. Apparently without quite re-alizing it, Jack had made a screen test. A day later, Walter Wanger told him he had won the role from Laurence Olivier and asked him to come down to the studio at once. Jack answered that it was ridiculous. No possible good would come of it. Louis B. Mayer would never permit it in a million years. "Get down here," Wanger answered. "Mayer's al-ready approved."

Colleen Moore said it was all Garbo's doing:

> She knew Jack was having trouble finding work and that his spir-its were down. And Garbo had a long memory. She knew that Jack had given her equal billing when she was barely established and she remembered all the times he'd helped her career. So she sim-ply marched into Louis B. Mayer's office and said it would be Gilbert or nobody. Maybe she had already seen the tests, I don't know. Mayer went through the roof, of course. They'd just gotten rid of Jack a few months before; they certainly didn't want him back again. Mayer screamed and ranted, and Garbo, as always, said nothing until he was finished. Mayer knew it was useless to argue with her. You can't really argue with someone who's just as happy to go home if she doesn't get her way.

On August 23, 1933, *Queen Christina* began shooting, with Jack in the role of the Spanish ambassador who captivates the queen and pre-cipitates her abdication. During the first week, both Jack and Greta came down with the flu, holding up production for several days. The talk was that Jack had a bad case of nerves and also needed the time to dry out and settle his stomach. That may or may not have been true. However, Garbo had a well-known penchant for being "indisposed" on days when she didn't feel up to giving her best. And, during the filming of *As You Desire Me* the year before, Garbo had timed her illnesses to those of Erich von Stroheim, another giant who'd been humiliated by MGM and was attempting a very nerve-wracking comeback. Given the kindness she'd already shown Jack, it's reasonable to believe that she did the same for him. Given the pressure Jack must have felt, it's reasonable to believe he needed it.

Jack himself said, "I want to tell you that she was magnificent to me while we were working together. She knew that I was nervous, raw, almost sick with excitement and the thrill of the thing. And never once did she fail in consideration of me, in tact, in saying and doing the right thing at the right moment. She was gracious and friendly. She sensed every one of my feelings and was tender toward them.

"It was hard work, of course, making that picture. I was nervous and gun-shy. I felt that only Garbo really wanted me there. I was sick a lot and Garbo was sick. There were delays and retakes and troubles like that. The executives were looking at me with the old-time and too familiar suspicion and hostility. I didn't care. I was working again."

The extent of Jack's nervousness can only be imagined. Whatever the other actors thought of Jack or his ability, they knew he'd been rammed down Louis Mayer's throat and were not about to appear overtly supportive of him to the possible detriment of their own careers. It was also the big chance, the good picture, that Jack had been praying for for so long. Then there was the matter of Garbo herself. It seems unlikely that all the old passions had entirely cooled and the memories faded into an uncomplicated friendship. Garbo developed a relationship with the director, Rouben Mamoulian, during the filming. It seems to have stopped short of being a hot romance, but they were obviously and perhaps painfully close. Jack had to do love scenes with Garbo. It's impossible to believe that would not have awakened old feelings.

Garbo herself may have sensed that happening. After one scene, in which Jack as the Spanish ambassador took the disguised Queen of Sweden into his arms with enthusiastic passion, Garbo took Mamoulian aside and reminded him that Jack was a married man. He also had a new baby—another daughter, named Susan Ann, who had been born earlier that month. Garbo thought, all things considered, that the love scenes between them should be played with less fervor. Mamoulian reported this to Jack, who smiled his understanding and said, "Backward, turn backward, O Time, in your flight."

Several other things weighed heavily on Jack's mind during the filming of *Queen Christina*. One was the contract he had to sign in order to do this picture. He'd signed a standard seven-year MGM contract. It paid him only a tenth of what he'd made for a single film under the old one. It gave MGM the right to use him. It's been written that Jack had signed in haste and read the fine print later—to his horror. This, of course, is nonsense. Harry Edington was still Jack's agent and would have fully understood the contract's terms. He knew that *Queen Christina* would either boost Jack's box-office draw, in which case he could demand more money and more choice assignments, or it would not, in which case the terms of the contract scarcely mattered except that they theoretically prevented Jack from working elsewhere. But MGM would have no reason to hold him.

Another pressure—or, rather, a great sadness—came with the death of Renée Adorée, Jack's co-star in *The Big Parade*, *La Bohème*, *The Cossacks*, and *Redemption*. She was also a former lover who had become a dear and affectionate friend. Renée died of tuberculosis at the age of thirty-five. "It's just devastating," he said, "that a sweet decent girl like Renée should be gone at such an age. God knows there are enough bullies and bastards around to fill the graveyards, but they just seem to go on and on while we lose people like Renée and Paul Bern."

Finally, Jack's marriage to Virginia Bruce seemed to be crumbling at its foundations. They were never strong to begin with. Jack, out of whatever need, had married a fresh, pure, and beautiful young woman. She was innocent of the tawdry side of Hollywood and of life in general. That same innocence, however, soon came to be seen as ignorance. Her naïveté became foolishness. She and Jack had little in common and even less to talk about because of their difference in age and their much vaster difference in experience and acquired education. Moreover, once the filming of *Queen Christina* began, Jack was totally absorbed in it. It was *his* film, *his* opportunity. He had little time for his wife or for his new daughter. When rumors began appearing that all was not well in the Gilbert household, it was suggested, of course, that his reunion with Garbo was to blame. Gilbert is still painfully in love with Garbo, they said. Gilbert wants Garbo back. Gilbert is leaving Virginia Bruce to make room for Garbo. Although there doesn't seem to have been any real substance to these rumors, one can't help thinking that Virginia would have fared poorly in any comparison with Greta. And such a comparison, however involuntary, was probably inevitable.

Queen Christina was finished in mid-December of 1933. Jack was pleased, for all the problems, with the picture and his performance in it. In a moment of reckless euphoria, he telephoned Louis B. Mayer. Jack said, "I was feeling on top of the world and I thought I'd call up just to say thank you for the part, for the chance, for everything. I got him on the phone. I started to say thank you to him. I'd hardly opened my mouth before he opened up on me and let me have it, foul abuse, threats, damnation, and all hell broke loose. I tried to scream into the phone that I was just trying to say thanks. I didn't want any more dough. I tried to tell him so."

If there was ever any doubt, Jack now knew that nothing short of the threatened loss of Garbo's services had got him the part in *Queen Christina*. He also knew that nothing short of a roaring success would get him another MGM role. Two were already being discussed. One was a remake of *The Merry Widow*, to be directed by Ernst Lubitsch, and the other was an original story, *Sacred and Profane Love*, directed by Clarence Brown and co-starring Joan Crawford and Robert Montgomery. These were to be important big-budget releases and they would be Jack's if *Queen Christina* proved his popularity had returned.

It did not. After the film's opening, on the day after Christmas of 1933, *The New York Times* said: "Mr. Gilbert's make-up may be more than slightly extravagant [they gave him the thick eyebrows, mustache, and long oiled hair of a period Spanish don] but there are scenes in which he acts very well. . . . Ian Keith is highly satisfactory as the villain, Magnus [a much jucier part]. It is indeed almost a pity that Mr. Gilbert was not put in the Magnus role and Mr. Keith into that of the Spaniard."

In London, where the picture opened a few weeks later, John Betjeman wrote a bit more effusively in the *Evening Standard*: "I am glad John Gilbert was cast for the part. 'The world's most perfect lover,' as he used to be five years ago when he and Garbo were together in *Flesh and the Devil*, has lost none of his power."

Critics then and ever since have been impressed with one long scene that Jack and Garbo played almost as a silent. They are in a white washed room at an inn, where they'd spent their first night together. As Jack watches, bemused and beguiled, Garbo moves slowly around the room touching, kissing, caressing all the items of furniture as if to burn them into her heart before she leaves her lover and returns to the royal court. Few words are spoken. But it is Gilbert and Garbo at their best, their most moving, their most tenderly erotic.

Many of the movie fans were thrilled by that scene, although disappointed that there wasn't more Gilbert and Garbo in the picture as a whole. The real problem was that there weren't enough fans. Film historians have written about *Queen Christina* as the picture in which John Gilbert made an abortive comeback try in a part that Garbo handed him over the objections of everyone concerned. The truth is that the picture didn't do much for Garbo or anyone else concerned either. Depression audiences had been drifting away from her and from costume epics for some time. Their affections were turning toward Shirley Temple and to big brassy Busby Berkeley musicals. In 1933, Garbo was a shaky fourth on the list of top box-office draws. By 1934, she had fallen to thirteenth place! As for the part being handed to an undeserving John Gilbert, Laurence Olivier told Douglas Fairbanks, Jr., in 1976, "I did the best I could in *Queen Christina*. I wanted the part very badly. Then I went to the studio and saw the tests. Here I am, supposed to be one of the greatest actors in the world, and this fading Jack Gilbert's test was infinitely better than mine. It was perfectly obvious. They didn't have to tell me." It was a generous comment.

Good test or not, good performance or not, it was also perfectly obvious that Gilbert and Garbo had lost their drawing power. Gilbert, it could be assumed, would have substantially less by himself. *The Merry Widow* remake was promptly assigned to Maurice Chevalier, on loan from Paramount. *Sacred and Profane Love* went through several script changes and became *Chained*, with Clark Gable replacing Gilbert. Although MGM did not release Jack from his one-sided contract, the studio clearly had no further use for him.

Louis Mayer, it should be mentioned, was perfectly willing to grit his teeth and accept the miraculous resurrection of John Gilbert if such a miracle happened to be thrown in his lap. But he was not about to help it along. All the MGM advertisements for *Queen Christina* trumpeted GARBO'S TRIUMPHANT RETURN TO THE SCREEN after a year of absence. But there was no mention of Jack except for his name in very small letters at the bottom of the page. *Variety* noticed that "Metro is chastising John Gilbert again. The *Queen Christina* trailers mention all the featured male support but Gilbert."

Jack knew that he was finished at MGM, perhaps in the movie industry as well. His one genuine "comeback" attempt had failed. It did not help to know that Garbo was a failure as well. But in what should have been the depths of despair, something ultimately positive seems to have begun stirring in Jack. With the disappointment, there now came a curious sense of relief, a greater clarity of purpose that often comes to one whose options have been slashed. Anyone who's been fired after living with the fear of that happening knows the feeling. Jack went back to his house and told Virginia that he needed to be alone for a while to sort out his life. He asked her to move out, back with her parents, until he'd chosen a direction for himself. Perhaps they would make it together, find a better life to share, or perhaps not. He needed time.

For Virginia, however, enough was enough. She filed for divorce after a marriage that had effectively lasted only eighteen months. She would no longer exist at Jack's convenience, or tolerate his moods or his drinking. Nor would she try any longer to compete against the exotic Garbo, or the intelligent Ina Claire, or the ghost of Renée Adorée, or even the memory of the struggling early years with Leatrice Joy.

Jack could not blame her. Although he characteristically took full responsibility for the breakup, expressing his profound regret to the press, he did little or nothing to try to keep Virginia.

"I am sorrier," he said, "about the loss of Virginia than I am about anything that has ever happened to me in my life before. It was my own fault, of course. I was sick over the way I was playing my part in *Christina*. I was afraid of giving a bad performance. I was working under terrific pressure. I felt the conditions around me were unfriendly. The whole thing kept twisting in me like a knife. Perhaps I thought that she would understand. I forgot how young she is. I lost sight of the fact that, after all, who am I to suppose that I can go through life being arrogant and expecting people to understand.

"And that this should happen to me just when it did! There was a diabolical timeliness about it. Because for the first time in my life I was becoming conscious of the fact that to put greasepaint on my face is a contributory part of life, but not all of it. . . . But it is over now and I shall not see Virginia again. I don't believe in Hollywood's super-friendly divorces. I love Virginia and I wanted her for my wife or not at all.

"I am probably through with marriage. . . . I would feel ridiculous if I should start to court a girl again. I can't imagine any girl taking me seriously. After a while it does become ridiculous."

A divorce settlement was worked out without difficulty. Jack agreed to give Virginia two insurance policies, forty-two thousand dollars' worth of property, and a hundred and fifty dollars per month for the support of their daughter. He was no longer bound to provide for Virginia or Susan Ann in his will. He would think about that, and change the will when he had reached a decision.

Unwilling to talk further to the press, and still wanting time to himself, Jack left in February 1934, on a solitary voyage to Hawaii. He slipped aboard the S.S. *Monterey*, insisting that his name not appear on the passenger list, and spent most of the trip in his cabin. When the ship docked in Honolulu, he waited until all passengers were ashore and then dashed for a taxi to his hotel. When the press finally learned that Jack was in town and tracked him down at the hotel, he told them that he was traveling for his health and refused to be interviewed.

Upon returning, Jack pressed a suit against MGM either to give him work or to release him from his seven-year contract. MGM hesitated. The jury was still out on *Queen Christina*. They mentioned a compromise but were vague about its terms and timing. Jack knew exactly what they were doing and had no intention of being humiliated save for the slim chance that a ground swell of ticket-buying adulation would arise across the United States and Europe. He insisted that they either assign a picture too good to refuse or release him. When MGM stalled further, he carried the battle to the public. On March 20, 1934, there appeared a message on the back cover of the Hollywood *Reporter*:

Metro-Goldwyn-Mayer

will neither

offer me work

nor

release me from

my contract

Jack Gilbert

The ad brought a wave of public sympathy, and the studio quickly released him. With a measure of pride intact, Jack retired to his beach house and resumed meditating on the direction his life would now take.

Film historians usually dismiss Jack Gilbert's life after the disappointment of *Queen Christina* and the final separation from Virginia Bruce by saying he crawled into a solitary hole and commenced to drink himself to death. The image is of an unshaven, uncommunicative, bleary-eyed, and self-destructive sot. For the film historian, such a write-off becomes a convenient way to close out the "Great Lover who couldn't talk" subject and move on to another.

Colleen Moore, Jack's nearest neighbor, acknowledged that Jack was often depressed, often drank too much, and usually got sick as a result. She said he had come to terms with the end of his popularity as a screen star just as she had. (Colleen's film career ended in 1934.) But he had not yet come to terms with the way it was done, the deliberate destruction that he was sure had been engineered by Louis Mayer and his abandonment by Irving Thalberg, a man he'd thought to be the closest of friends:

I kept hoping, encouraging him to put it all behind him, to make a new success at something else. Like writing. But it wasn't that Jack was holding on to the past. He didn't need to be a star, he needed to be an *actor*. There's a big difference. He wanted to be a director even more. Everyone knew Jack could direct but the offers didn't come, not because of drinking or Louis Mayer but because word had gotten around that his health was so precarious. He'd lost a lot of time during the Garbo movie. When you hire a director, you have to know that he's going to be there every day. But even in bad health he could have been a writer. He was reading plays people were sending him all the time when he should have been writing them. Instead of amusing himself planning the perfect-crime murder of Louis Mayer, he should have been writing a story about it.

A number of literary agents had been sending plays to Jack. Although he never found one he believed in strongly enough to do, he read them all carefully and gave thoughtful written responses that belie the image of a wasted drunk.

Colleen Moore also rejected the notion that Jack was wasting away in an alcoholic fog during that period:

> Sure he was depressed about not being offered any kind of work and about not feeling well so much. But he was never what you'd call suicidal. Suicidal people and alcoholics don't keep themselves looking great and neat like Jack always did. We talked about people we knew who killed themselves. People like Paul Bern and Karl Dane. He could never understand people giving up like that. He was too full of life.

Karl Dane, the giant Dane who played Jack's sidekick in *The Big Parade* and appeared with him in *La Bohème* and *Bardelys the Magnificent*, had also put a gun to his head that year. A thick accent effectively ended his career with the coming of sound. Over the past four years, he'd managed to get only one small role in a serial. Otherwise he made a living as best he could as a mechanic and carpenter. He was running a hot-dog stand when he decided that life wasn't worth the effort.

Colleen Moore warmed to the subject of Jack's still having plenty of life in him:

> Once I had a bunch of very square guests for dinner. I can't remember who they were, but it was terribly important that I make a good impression. The dinner went beautifully and we were sitting around over coffee when my maid appeared and began giving me frantic signals. I excused myself and went to see what was wrong.
>
> She said, in a panic, "Madam, Mr. Gilbert is upstairs. *He's in*

your bed." I had to go see for myself. Sure enough, there he was, under the covers, sitting up and grinning, "Here I am, you lucky woman." I tried to be angry but how could you? Here was that good-looking idiot sitting up in my bed, knowing that all those stuffed shirts were downstairs. Well, you never saw anybody get rid of guests faster than I did. I practically handed them their hats and showed them the door. Then I went back upstairs, but he was gone. He must have climbed down the drainpipe, not thinking I'd come up.

Jack proposed to me about that time. We weren't in love at all but we were awfully good friends. We agreed we didn't need each other's money but we did enjoy each other's company. I turned him down but we kept right on being friends.

One evening, Jed Harris joined us for dinner. He happened to say that he didn't think a woman could be friends with a man once she turned him down. I said, "Oh, yes, she can. What do you say, Jack?" He smacked me gently on the behind and said, "Absolutely."

Once we were sitting by the pool, and I said to him, "Jack, darling, the parade's gone by. Here we are, a couple of old crocks. Tell me, who was the greatest love of your life? Was it Garbo?" He didn't answer me at first. He just looked far, far away. Then he said quietly, "No, the one I loved the best was Leatrice. She was the girl who really broke my heart."

I said, "Why did you two ever break up?" and he shook his head. "It's me. I can't seem to hang on to anything I love."

In June of 1934, Jack told interviewer Gladys Hall, of *Movie Classic*, "I have been on the screen for twenty years and I have managed to squeeze out of it complete unhappiness. Today I can't get a job. I mean exactly that. I-can't-get-a-job. Four short years ago I had a contract calling for $250,000 a picture. Today I can't get a job for $25 a week or for nothing at all. It doesn't make sense but there it is.

"What am I to do? . . . People advise me to go to Europe. What for? I don't want to go to Europe. I don't even want to go to Honolulu. I want to work. I want the simple right of every creature that walks the earth, the right to earn my own living."

As if in response, a small miracle occurred. The phone finally rang with a movie offer. Jack's old friend Lewis Milestone had gone to bat for him with Harry Cohn, president of Columbia Pictures. Milestone had a part in a picture he was planning that he thought would be absolutely perfect for Jack, and he convinced Cohn to give Jack the chance. He telephoned Jack and asked him to come to the studio for a test.

Suddenly Jack was scared to death. A test? What if he couldn't pull if off? What if he got sick again? And the thought of going from Louis B. Mayer to Harry (Get-in-the-fuckin'-bed-or-get-lost) Cohn could not have been comforting. But Milestone would not allow Jack to beg off:

It made me mad to see Jack sitting there going to rot. He had everything right there, all his talent, everything, and no one was usuing it. It wasn't hard to convince Cohn. Cohn had no use for Louis Mayer. He hated the bastard and he really enjoyed the idea of making Jack a big star again just to show him. Cohn did the same thing with Clark Gable. Mayer got mad at Gable for telling a reporter that Mayer paid him not to think, and he punished him by lending him to Columbia. They called Columbia the "bargain basement" but we were turning out some pretty good pictures. Well, Cohn put Gable together with Claudette Colbert in *It Happened One Night* and won all the Academy Awards. Gable went back to MGM a bigger star than ever, and Mayer almost died.

Anyway, Cohn thought he'd do the same thing with Jack. But I couldn't get him to go down for a test. He was really gun-shy. Metro had nearly destroyed him. He had no confidence left at all. Finally I promised I would shoot the test at six o'clock in the morning. Nobody around to see him, just ourselves and a skeleton crew. I didn't think he'd show up, but he did and he made a hell of a good test. Cohn agreed it was fine and signed him for the picture, *The Captain Hates the Sea.* Cohn said to Jack, "If you behave yourself, stay sober, and do your work, you'll be a star again. I'll bet my shirt on you. It's up to you."

Well, Jack dried up almost immediately. He told me he had a good night's sleep for the first time in months. He showed up ahead of time in the morning looking great.

A lot of the action took place on an old boat that was moored at San Pedro Harbor. The story was about a newspaperman who's trying to stop drinking and get a book written. That was Jack. In the beginning he says good-bye to his sweetheart, gets aboard the cruise ship, and sails away. She's going to meet him in New York. It's the usual voyage story, little dramas between passengers. Jack's novel never gets written and he weaves off the boat in New York an unrepentant failure. It was a nice little movie.

But we had a terrible time shooting it. We took the old boat away from the dock and sailed it around the harbor, and around, and around. The weather was bad and the people were sick. Meanwhile, just about every drunk in Hollywood managed to get a job on that picture. There was Walter Connolly, Walter Catlett, Fred Keating, Leon Errol, and Victor McLaglen. They all kidded around and played endless practical jokes. Jack started out with every good intention but it was hopeless. There was more wet stuff flowing inside the boat than out. There was one delay after another. Finally, Harry Cohn wired me: HURRY UP. THE COSTS ARE STAGGERING. I wired him back: SO IS THE CAST. We finally finished the damned thing. Jack did a good job, despite being drunk most of the time. When he wasn't drunk, he was being sick at home. He had bleeding ulcers and sometimes fever and hallucinations—raving out of his mind. When it was over, Jack knew Cohn would never hire him again. He was too much trouble.

Walter Connolly had promised his old friend Ina Claire that he would keep an eye on Jack during the picture. Since Walter was known to take a drink himself, he decided he'd better farm out the responsibility. He asked his good friend Carole Lombard, also under contract to Columbia but not in the picture, to be Jack's guardian angel. Carole tried her best to keep him sober. She hovered about his dressing room and made outrageous passes at him whenever distraction was required. She would pour out drinks and then consume both of them herself. Carole probably kept Jack a good deal more sober than he would have been otherwise, but her task was next to impossible. Jack's role called for him to drink almost constantly. The character he played is the first to arrive in the ship's bar each day and his cabin is almost as fully stocked. No matter how often Lewis Milestone set out bottles filled with colored water, some member of the cast would toss them overboard and replace them with the real stuff. Jack's character was supposed to have a buzz on almost all the time and he did.

Jack's performance, however, was remarkable. He suggests drunkenness only by an understated swaying and a sad smile that occasionally flickers across his face. Of all his talking pictures, *The Captain Hates the Sea* is the closest to today's movies in terms of content and treatment. It is a wry, cynical film, not so much a comedy as an irony. Walter Connolly, as the captain, sets the mood in the beginning by saying, "I detest the sea. . . . I'd like to see any damn-fool women and children beat me into a lifeboat. . . . I'd break them in two with my own hands."

For all the boozing, Milestone found Jack to be the same finely intuitive actor he'd always been. Even his back could be extremely expressive. Milestone gave him one long tender sequence played almost entirely with his back to the camera. Alexander Walker wrote of it in his book *Stardom:* "Gilbert must have savored, and may even have inspired, the irony of the moment in *The Captain Hates the Sea* when the writer unpacks his cabin trunk and finds that his wife has brought him a new suit for the voyage—a rather flashy 'ice cream' suit for tropical wear which reminds him of his palmier days in Beverly Hills. Gilbert eyes it hollowly for a second, then puts it back in the trunk; and with an undertone of contempt for all it represents to him, he quips, 'I know I lived in Hollywood, but after all you got to remember I came from Chicago.' For a man whom the talkies supposedly ruined, he managed to have a caustic last word."

The picture was largely ignored by the press and the public. Critic Otis Furgeson, noting that Columbia seemed to have lost heart very early after having made a boldly different sort of movie, called it the "absolute best neglected picture of two years."

"Gilbert was drinking heavily throughout the shooting," Alexander Walker wrote, "and his very slightly swaying stance in scene after scene conveys the unsettling feeling that he is not just acting drunk, though his voice comes through unslurred and dryly cynical. In place of the old romantic fire he had developed a raffish Errol Flynnish charm. With his slightly fuller face he could almost pass for Flynn's double. The picture ends with his wife collecting him on the quayside when the cruise ship docks again. 'Did you stop drinking?' she asks him. 'No.' Did you start your book?' she asks. 'No,' he answers again. And that was the last heard on the screen from John Gilbert."

·nineteen·

I T WAS after the completion of *The Captain Hates the Sea*, in the latter months of 1934, that Marlene Dietrich first came into Jack's life.

Marlene had arrived in Hollywood four years earlier. She'd been an important actress in her native Germany but was suddenly launched into international stardom by her performance in the German production of *The Blue Angel*. Paramount signed her and immediately began touting Marlene as their answer to the gradually fading Garbo. The director Josef von Sternberg, who had discovered her, promptly began molding Marlene Dietrich into a glamorous and sensual legend through a series of six remarkably exotic and lyrical films.

One hesitates to say too much about Marlene's screen accomplishments because there was, and is, so much more to her as a human being. She'd been in Hollywood only a year or so when word began to get around that, for example, it had been Marlene who paid the overdue rent owed by that studio secretary who lost her job, or the hospital bill run up by the child of the studio electrician. When thanked, Marlene would try to deny any knowledge of it. When caught red-handed, she would stammer in embarrassment. It may be understandable, therefore, that I have been unsuccessful in my efforts to get Marlene to tell me about her year with Jack and all she did for him during that time. I can only offer what I've been able to gather from other sources. I refuse, however, to let Marlene Dietrich off that easily, and offer the following about her even though it is not germane to her relationship with my father and even though it jumps ahead in time.

In 1937, Marlene was in England doing a film. She was approached by Joachim von Ribbentrop, later Hitler's Foreign Minister. At the time, however, he was the German ambassador to England. Von Ribbentrop carried a message and a very generous offer from Hitler himself, asking her to return to Germany. Marlene refused, and her films were promptly banned in her native country. She then became an American citizen. When the war broke out, Marlene put her career considerations aside and began tirelessly entertaining U.S. troops all over the world, participating in bond drives and servicemen's canteens, and making anti-Nazi broadcasts in German. For entertaining under battle conditions "despite risk to her life," she was awarded America's highest civilian award, the Medal of Freedom. For the same reason, the French made Marlene a chevalier of the Legion of Honor.

Getting back to 1934, for one reason or another this magnificent woman decided that something ought to be done about Jack Gilbert. She knew what he'd been, she knew what had happened to him, and she saw that he was now utterly lost and virtually unhirable because of his poor health and his drinking. He was killing himself and she would not have it. Marlene simply took over. By whatever means, she persuaded Jack that the drinking, all of it, must stop at once. So must the self-imposed exile. She made him go to a psychiatrist. She began dragging him out of the house to one Hollywood social event after another, to parties given by her friend Ouida Rathbone, and to all the major movie premieres. They were seen together at restaurants and on the beach at Malibu, at art galleries and concerts. Whatever they went, Marlene stayed close by his side, steering him away from arguments, or getting him to tell funny stories, or helping him through any temptation to accept a drink. After a while there was talk of Jack being asked to do one picture or another, and even a rumor that Irving Thalberg was planning to offer him a new contract. Why not? He seemed his old self again, except unfailingly sober and much calmer.

In October of that year, when I was ten years old, I'd invited Catherine Heerman to come for lunch one day. It was a Saturday and we usually went to the movies. This day we decided to stay home and write letters to our favorite movie stars. I wrote to Katharine Hepburn, Shirley Temple, and Norma Shearer. I asked Miss Shearer for a photograph of her dog Flush in *The Barretts of Wimpole Street* and later received not only that, but a large picture of herself as Elizabeth Barrett Browning.

Catherine's father, Victor Heerman, and mother, Sarah Y. Mason, were then a famous writing team in Hollywood. We both grew up in the picture business and saw famous people all the time, but we were just as awed by stars as anybody else. We were also very selective about whom we asked for pictures. You didn't want just anyone hanging on your wall. We wrote our letters carefully and it took most of the afternoon.

Just before Catherine left, I had an impulsive thought. "I'll write to my father," I said. "I don't have a picture of him. I'm not even sure he has a picture of me. I'll send him one."

Catherine thought it was a fine idea. I began the letter several times before I got it right.

October 24, 1934

> *Dear Daddy,*
>
> *I would like very much to have a picture of you to hang by my bed. I am sending you one of me taken at camp with a fish. I am the one on the right. I miss you.*
>
> *With my love,*
 Tinker
>
> *P.S. The collie dog you gave me, Laddy-Jack, died of distemper.*

Neither Catherine nor I knew his address, so we sent the letter to the Metro-Goldwyn-Mayer studio in Culver City. I then forgot all about it.

The fan pictures soon began arriving in the mail. Most of the stars knew who we were and wrote little notes sending love to our mothers and fathers, and we received full-sized portraits, not the cheap little glossies they usually sent to the fans.

It was several weeks before I heard from my father. The letter probably lay at the studio for a while before anyone bothered to forward it. I came home from school one afternoon and found a huge bouquet of spring flowers on the downstairs hall table. I asked the maid why my mother had ordered the flowers. Were we having a party? She said, "No, they're for you," and she handed me the card.

It read, *For Tinker Bell from her Daddy.*

I was speechless. I had completely forgotten, and for a moment I could hardly catch my breath. Then I noticed a special delivery letter there beside the flowers. I couldn't open it at first. I carried the letter upstairs and locked myself in the bathroom. I had never received a letter from my father before; I didn't know what to expect. Finally, I ripped it open.

> *Darling Tinker,*
>
> *Receiving your letter was the nicest thing that ever happened to me. I had hoped you would write to me someday, just as I hoped that one day you will want to find out what kind of bloke this father of yours is. So when you decide to come around, please do. I assure you we'll have fun.*
>
> *I have been very ill, angel. So ill, in fact, that I cannot write this*

letter myself but I am slowly recovering. If all goes well I leave in about three weeks for New York to do a play. It is an entirely new adventure for me and to be truthful I am scared to death. So have a good wish for me, darling.

I am sorry about Laddy-Jack. If you would like to have another dog I will send you one, or a dozen, but I must say my experience with them has been unfortunate. They were either stolen, or poisoned, or ran away or died. I know we must all die someday but to learn to love a doggie for so short a time and then have disaster fall is too much. However, let me know how you feel about it. Scotties are the aristocrat of dogs.

I was delighted to read the letterhead on your stationery [Leatrice Joy Gilbert]. I had heard stupid rumors about changing your name.

Give my love to your sweet mama, and for yourself if you want it, keep all my heart.

Daddy

I could almost feel the pages burning in my hands. It was a miracle. I had dashed off a foolish fan letter and discovered a father who loved me. His telephone number was scribbled on the corner of the paper and I called him that evening. He was sick but he came to the phone and we talked. He said I could visit him as soon as he was well again.

Being brought up as a Christian Scientist, I did not take his illness at all seriously. It never occurred to me, therefore, to ask what was the matter with him or how grave it might be. All I felt was impatience at having to wait for our first visit.

His health continued to improve but not soon enough for him to go to New York for the play. Eventually, we selected the day for our visit and my mother prepared me for the great event. She ordered a dress for me of white silk organdy, with a pink satin sash and a wreath of pink roses for my hair. I must have looked like Little Bopeep and I felt very uncomfortable. I was not a girl for pink and white dresses. I was a tomboy who wore blue jeans most of the time and climbed trees and played kick-the-can with the neighborhood gang. But Mother had decided I would go full costume and that was that.

Father sent his limousine to collect me and I rode in splendor across the city and up the hillside to the Spanish house on Tower Road. He stood waiting for me at the top of the stairs. He was wearing gray flannel trousers and a white sweater. I remember looking up the long red tile stairway, a cool light coming through the high, leaded panes. I thought he didn't look sick at all.

We had a pretty good time that day after a beginning that was a little stiff and tentative. But soon we were laughing. We looked at our faces together in the mirror to see how alike we were. We pulled each other's long noses, and he comforted me by promising that my face would grow to fit it someday. He told me his mother had a long nose and she was considered very beautiful. For the first hour, I kept tripping over my unfamiliar long dress. He was very understanding about my having to wear it. He finally hitched it up in back under my sash so I could walk around better. I sat on the arm of his big leather chair and we talked. He asked questions about school and my lessons. He particularly wanted me to learn French, and I promised I would. (I'm still valiantly trying to this day.)

I stayed only about an hour and a half the first time, but after that I went up frequently and stayed longer. He showed me all over the house and I could tell that he loved it. There was a secret panel in the alcove off the living room, and a button under one of the bookshelves on the left of it that opened the door to a secret stairway leading to the basement. There used to be a bar down there before Prohibition was repealed. We talked about Prohibition. Mother was strongly in favor of it, but Father explained that it never worked and even did more harm than good "for the same reason that Adam ate that apple back in the Garden of Eden. He probably would never have even noticed the silly thing if he hadn't been told he couldn't have it."

I saw a lot of him during the next months. I never saw him take a drink or even a bottle of liquor in the house. He never seemed sad or depressed either. On the contrary, he seemed very much at peace with himself. He was full of dreams and plans and a sort of astonished awareness of all life had to offer, as if he'd just found out about it. I remember the bemusement on his face when he once said to me, "There really is a whole world out there, Tinker. A big and beautiful world. You can do almost anything. Anything at all." He was saying the words to me, but even at ten I knew he was talking to himself.

I was sent away to camp for the summer of 1935, but we kept exchanging letters. I made him a pair of bookends in arts and crafts that were shaped like movie cameras. I told him about them and about all the fun we were having in the High Sierras where there were still big snow patches we could slide down on our bottoms.

Dearest Tinker,

Receiving a letter from my grown-up daughter is always an exciting event and I look forward to each day's mail. I am a bit worried about you using your backside in lieu of a sled. Be careful, angel. You will have lots of use for your sitter-downer for many years. I am dying to see the bookends and will say "thank you, ma'am," in advance.

Later I asked him to send autographs to my friends, and he replied: "As for the autographs, I have a suggestion to offer. Let's keep our association and correspondence outside the realm of movie fame. What do you say? We have seen very little of each other and have a great deal of affection and understanding to give each other. I would like you to love me for myself rather than for my being a trademark like Grape Nuts or Eskimo Pie. I would like to be your very good friend. You know, a true friend is a rare animal and far more dependable than a sweetheart or even a father. At least that's the way I have found it. But as I said, this is only a suggestion. And if you foolishly persist in being proud of a slightly tarnished movie star and really want me to send the darn autographs, I will do so. I will do anything you want me to do."

He'd also send me riddles. "A man left his country house for the city, leaving his butler to forward some important papers that were due in the mail the morning after he left. But he went off with the mailbox key in his pocket. . . ." The answers would come the following week. He'd send me books to read. One I remember was Ernest Thompson Seton's *Lives of the Hunted*, which turned me against blood sports forever. That was, I know, exactly the effect my father hoped for. I'd written him about our plans to hunt squirrels and jackrabbits. He never said I shouldn't, he just sent the book.

In July of 1935, Jack told Louella Parsons he was embarking on a personal-appearance tour. She wrote: "Jack Gilbert, whose devastating sense of humor and his absolute disregard of the powers of the studio have all but wrecked his career, has completely reformed. . . . He leaves with Hollywood rooting for his success, and if Jack succeeds there is no doubt that he can make the right return to the screen. Certainly a man who was at the top only a brief few years ago is not entirely through. All he needs is the right vehicle."

His first appearance was set for August 9 in Baltimore, where he was to act in a series of sketches with other players. But suddenly the "right vehicle" seemed to appear. Through the influence of Marlene Dietrich, Jack was invited to make a test at Paramount for a role in Marlene's new picture, *Desire*. It was an Ernst Lubitsch picture, to be produced in in color. Gary Cooper was signed as co-star and Jack would play Marlene's suave jewel-thief companion.

The test was successful, Lubitsch was pleased, and Jack got the part. That test still exists. It was Jack's only appearance in Technicolor except for his Romeo and Juliet skit in *The Hollywood Revue of 1929*. In it he looks much older than his thirty-six years, and deadly serious. He may have been lighted and made up that way for his part as the dissolute jewel thief; I remembered him as much younger and more full of life in person. But near the end of the test, someone off-camera asks for a smile and for a moment the years peel off and he lights up the screen. The old radiance was still there.

Once again, however, it seemed as if somebody up there didn't want Jack back in pictures. I've often thought that the somebody, down deep, was Jack himself. In any case, shortly before the filming was to begin, Jack had a mild heart attack while swimming in his pool with Marlene. The production of *Desire* was too far along to be held up and Jack had to be replaced by the veteran leading man John Halliday.

A chance occurrence at about the same time, ultimately a devastating one, led to a cooling of Jack's relationship with Marlene. Marlene was at Jack's house when a battered Packard pullèd up outside. It was Garbo's car. Jack rushed out to talk to her. From where Marlene stood watching, it apparently seemed to her that too much of the old fire still burned. She never knew, or asked, what words passed between them. But she saw a pantomime that she interpreted as desire on Jack's part to take up where he left off years before. Garbo could simply have been inquiring about Jack's health, for all she knew, and Jack could have been urging a reluctant Garbo to come into the house and visit. Whatever Marlene saw or thought she saw, a touch, a kiss, or a look, it's impossible to believe that Jack, to say nothing of Garbo, could or would have done much more than that while standing in his driveway. Anyway, Garbo was about to return to Sweden at about this time for one of her annual vacations. Marlene, nevertheless, assumed the worst but did not ask, and in doing so allowed herself to feel deeply hurt. She stayed away from Jack, who was probably thoroughly confused by her behavior, and began being seen around town with Gary Cooper.

When I visited him just before Thanksgiving in 1935, he seemed in low spirits. People have since told me that he had several small heart attacks after the rift with Marlene, but I could see only that he was sad and a little pale, with no idea why. Still, he went out of his way to make me feel especially welcome. We played Gilbert and Sullivan records and he read aloud from one of his favorite books about animals. Later we went walking up behind the house to watch the sun go down. Walk carefully, he said, because there might be rattlesnakes, and you had to let them know you were coming. From the top of his hill you could see all Los Angeles out to the ocean, and Santa Catalina Island hunched over the bright skyline. As the sun dipped below the horizon and the lights of Los Angeles winked on, he taught me a poem Edna St. Vincent Millay wrote of a contented evening on a hilltop of her own, "Afternoon on a Hill."*

> I will be the gladdest thing under the sun!
> I will touch a hundred flowers and not pick one.
> I will look at cliffs and clouds with quiet eyes,
> Watch the winds bow down the grass and the grass rise.
> And when the lights begin to show up from the town,
> I will mark which must be mine and then start down.

He carried me down on his back. "You fill a great void in my life," he told me.

A few weeks later, at the beginning of December, he had another heart attack. Marlene rushed back to him when she learned of it. Whatever she'd felt about Jack and Garbo didn't seem so important anymore. Marlene once again took over the job of nursing him back to health. Soon he felt well enough to call and invite me for a visit on the day before Christmas.

This time, standing at the foot of the stairs, I looked up and saw a magnificently tall and glittering tree. It was decorated with frosted-glass ornaments and ablaze with real candles in the German tradition. Marlene had done it, but she slipped away before I arrived so that Father and I could have a private Christmas together. There were presents, all of them for me, wrapped in heavy gold paper and silk gauze-like ribbons. They looked almost too beautiful to open but that didn't slow me down a bit. He laughed at what must have looked like a feeding frenzy and advised me to open the presents more slowly to make the pleasure last as long as possible. Like all eleven-year-olds, I had long since rejected that useless adult Christmas-morning philosophy. I plunged right in.

The gifts were wonderful impractical things. There was a pink satin nightgown, with a matching slip and panties, that made me feel like Norma Shearer. And a doll with real hair and a charm bracelet with tiny gold animals. There were books, and a wristwatch, an ivory chess set, and a blue silk dress the color of a summer sky with a lace collar— so much, I can't remember it all.

That afternoon, when it was time to leave, I begged him to ride home with me in the car. He had never done that before but I wanted him to

*From *Collected Poems* (New York: Harper & Row). © 1917, 1945 by Edna St. Vincent Millay.

see my own Christmas tree. He said no, it might embarrass my mother. I insisted it wouldn't. Before he could say no again, I said, "Come on," and took his hand. I led him downstairs to the waiting limousine. He barely had a chance to snatch up his green Alpine hat as I whisked him out the door.

I thought he looked splendid and I was proud to be riding in the car with him. As we approached my house, I reminded him that I expected him to come inside and see the tree. He said, "Absolutely not, young lady."

"Oh, do," I said. "It would make me so happy."

"No, it's no use, Tinker. You're arguing with a Gilbert."

"That's nothing," I said. "So are you."

He laughed and surrendered.

Leatrice was standing on the stairs when we came to the door. She and Jack had not met in several years, and for the longest time they just stood there like stones, looking into each other's faces. Finally, Father smiled and took her hand. Mother had a habit of clutching her necklace when she was nervous, and I saw her free hand creeping up toward her throat. They must have spoken to each other, but all I remember is the looks and the staring, Mother looking straight into his eyes from the first step and Father standing there holding his green hat. After a few moments, he just nodded to her, she nodded back, and he left. I don't think he even noticed my Christmas tree.

Later that night, Leatrice said, he telephoned and asked her to think about coming back to him. She cried that she could not do that. She admitted that her marriage was not a perfectly happy one, but at least her life was settled. She could not bear to tear it up again. He said he was sorry she felt that way but asked that she remember that he loved her.

I was to go to his house again on New Year's Day. He wanted to talk to me about perhaps coming to England with him that following summer. He and Marlene had been offered a movie there that would be finished by the time school got out. He then wanted to take me on a long automobile tour of the Cotswold country and the Midlands. His mother's ancestors came from there. Father said we might even look up some distant cousins.

But on the morning of New Year's Day, he sent me a bouquet of roses with a note:

January 1, 1936

Dearest Tinker,
   Am so sorry that I'm sick and that we must suffer the disappointment of not seeing each other today.

Just as soon as I am strong enough I'll call you and hope you will come up and see me soon.

I love you very much, Tinker.

Daddy

During the night of January 9, Jack had trouble sleeping and a nurse he'd hired gave him an injection. The next morning, he was dead. The nurse called the fire department and they rushed to Tower Road with their resuscitator and tried to pump air into his lungs. Marlene Dietrich's doctor, Leo Masden, arrived and administered adrenaline but it was no use. He was declared dead at 9:05 in the morning. The cause of death was listed as heart failure.

Cedric Gibbons was shaving when he heard the news on the radio. With the soap still drying on his face he got into his car and raced up the hill to Jack's house. He arrived just in time to prevent news photographers from invading Jack's bedroom and taking pictures of his distorted, anguished face. Cedric spoke to both the nurse and the doctor and returned home in a rage. He told his wife that the nurse had given Jack a shot for sleeping the night before, but had not bothered to stay with him to check the drug's effect. She left him alone and Jack choked to death on his own tongue.

"Nobody cared," he said bitterly. "Goddamn them, it didn't make any difference to them. Nobody cared."

·twenty·

I WAS in school when they called me to the principal's office. My mother was there waiting for me and she broke the news as we drove home together. I don't remember feeling grief as such, only a cold numbness. Mother and I spent the day with Mrs. Conrad Nagel and her daughter. The Nagels were newly divorced, and something about losing a father touched young Ruthie Nagel. I remember seeing tears in her eyes, although mine remained steadfastly dry. I realized that my father was dead, I guess, but the loss seemed even greater than that, more like the end of the world.

The funeral date and its location were kept secret. Even so, a squadron of twenty-five policemen were assigned, just in case. No one wanted a repetition of the Valentino circus funeral.

I heard the Episcopal prayers for the dead for the first time in that Beverly Hills mortuary chapel: "I am the Resurrection and the life. . . ." The room was crowded with people, some standing against the walls. Gary Cooper was there, and Marlene, John Barrymore, and Irving Thalberg, who was one of the pallbearers. Also Virginia Bruce, Sam Goldwyn, Monta Bell, Robert Florey, King Vidor, Cedric Gibbons, Myrna Loy, and many others. David Selznick came with his wife, Irene Mayer. Louis Mayer stayed away. Marlene collapsed and fell coming down the aisle. Gary Cooper helped her up, and sat with her as she sobbed through the service.

Mother and I were among the first to leave when it was over. On the way to the car, Irving Thalberg ran after us and spoke to Mother. He said, "You know, Leatrice, Jack was on the verge of a real comeback. He had a contract waiting to be signed, but I honestly don't believe he wanted it anymore." It was then that I saw the odd look in Thalberg's eyes that I didn't understand at the time. Several people told me much later that Thalberg was tormented by his failure to stand up against Mayer for the man who had been his close friend. As for the contract, assuming there was one, I don't believe Jack would have signed it. Certainly not with MGM. Enough was enough.

Irving Thalberg helped us into the car and said good-bye. The following week, he arranged a showing of *The Big Parade* for me in a private projection room at the studio. I had never seen a silent movie before and I was disappointed. It looked old-fashioned and stilted. But I loved seeing my young father. It made him seem still alive. But I missed hearing his voice; I didn't feel any connection with him on the screen.

Eight months later, Irving Thalberg himself was dead, of pneumonia, at the age of thirty-seven.

In England, William Mooring, of British International Pictures, said he was stunned to hear of Jack's death. He'd been negotiating with Jack only a week earlier about the film Jack and Marlene were to make at his Eltree Studio. Mooring said that Jack had lost all interest in trying to make a comeback in Hollywood. He was also determined to stop fighting life and to start enjoying it. "Life hits back too hard," Jack told him.

Garbo was told of Jack's death as she stood in the foyer of a Stockholm theater during the intermission of Schiller's play, *Maria Stuart*. Following advice Jack had given her years ago in the early days of her career, she received the news with great self-control and refused comment, and returned to her seat in the theater. But she left soon after, avoiding the press, and went into seclusion at her home for several days.

Soon after the funeral, Marlene telephoned Leatrice. She had read about Jack's will in the newspapers, the one he'd written on the eve of his marriage to Virginia Bruce. It left her his entire estate except for a few small bequests to his friends and his servants. He left ten thousand dollars to me.

But Marlene said that Jack had written another will and that she'd seen it. The witnesses were his Filipino houseboys. She pointed out that Virginia had relinquished all claims to Jack's estate in their divorce agreement, and suggested that Mother get a lawyer and find the will. Mother tried, but no will was ever found. She says she was told that if she contested the will and lost, I could end up getting nothing. I didn't care about Jack's estate, certainly not then, but Marlene was terribly upset that Jack was being denied his wishes and I was possibly being cheated.

Much more important than the will was my relationship that developed with Marlene herself.

A week or so after the funeral, I received a gorgeous bouquet arranged on a lace doily and tied with pink ribbons. The card, in Marlene's handwriting, said, *I adored your father. Let me adore you.*

For several years, she went out of her way to fill the emptiness he left in my life. She took me to theater openings, informal evenings at her house, and long walks and talks as I'd had with my father. Often we'd end up in her kitchen, with Marlene baking a cake or making cookies for me to take home. She was like a fairy godmother. Presents arrived for no particular reason—a miniature painting of my father, a tiny star ruby pendant on a platinum chain, also a charm bracelet from London and a souvenir cup of the coronation of Edward VIII that I particularly treasured. These last two were special favorites because Father had loved England so. She produced a duplicate of the gold watch Father gave me, a duplicate because I sent the original to the laundry in one of my white middy blouses. Marlene replaced it at once.

I wonder if Marlene Dietrich realized what a difference her presence made to me. Although the full realization of my loss did not come until later, my dreamworld had collapsed. No part of the real world seemed very inviting. Marlene's loving care helped me put off the day when I would have to face the permanance of my loss and bear it. She was a great star then, at the peak of her career. Yet she found time for a plain and sober little girl, with her father's long nose, and for a while turned her into a princess.

Marlene was even more incensed when she learned that Virginia Bruce was putting all Jack's property up for public auction. Virginia was selling *everything*. The auction included Jack's clothes, his tennis racquets, phonograph records, books, all household furnishings, even his toothbrush and the sheets he died on. This last was too much for Marlene. She sent an agent, who bought up all the bed linens before the auction began. Her instructions were to pay any price at all.

I went to the auction with my governess. Marlene had to be in England, but she had her agent attend with an additional list of things she didn't want to fall into the wrong hands.

I bought a makeup box that I thought was his, but it turned out to be his mother's. It was a battered old thing with worn-out powder puffs and ancient tubes of greasepaint. I also bought a cameo bracelet he wore in *Cameo Kirby*, and a few books. Clarence Brown bought a leaf from the Gutenberg Bible, the prize of Jack's collection, for only a hundred and fifty dollars. The members of an angling club made a collective bid on Jack's huge collection of fishing tackle. In all, there were a thousand items listed in the auction catalogue.

Marlene's agent bought up virtually all the bedroom furniture, rugs, wall hangings, and draperies. But there was spirited competetive bidding on Jack's bed itself, which was more than eight feet wide. A Pittsburgh bedspring maker and a Detroit mattress manufacturer and a couple of hotels were among those bidding against her. The auctioneer held up the bidding to let the agent cable Marlene in London asking how high he could go. But Marlene could not be reached in time, and anyway the prices were getting ridiculous. The agent let it go to the management of the Summit Hotel outside Uniontown, Pennsylvania. They announced after paying $1,250 for the bed that it was to be installed in the John Gilbert Honeymoon Room with other bric-a-brac from the auction. A daily drawing would be held and the room rented to a lucky couple for twenty-four hours. Marlene was appalled, but Leatrice said Jack would have laughed himself sick.

Jack's body was cremated and the ashes were buried at Forest Lawn Memorial Park in a section called Whispering Pines. I visited his grave fairly often when I was growing up, but then I moved East and thirty years went by before I saw it again.

In 1973, I returned to Los Angeles. I was thinking about this book, talking to people and collecting stories. The day I chose to go to Forest Lawn was a rare one for Southern California. The air was clean and bright, the way I remembered it as a child, and memories came flooding back. I began to shake; my hands trembled on the steering wheel. I knew I was touching strong emotions, even after all these years. I was suddenly cold—and when I stopped to buy some red carnations I was choking back tears.

The grave is on a steep hill, very hard to find, and I walked up and down several times before I saw it, a bronze plaque set in the grass, engraved in his own handwriting, *John Gilbert*. I put down the flowers, sat on a bench, and waited for whatever was going to happen. It was a little like a sea wave rising; I didn't know where it would take me.

Suddenly, a loud cheerful voice said, "Hello there!" A gravedigger was passing by on a yellow bulldozer. "Are you any kin of Mr. Gilbert?" Without waiting for an answer he dismounted and sat down beside me. "It's funny, I've been here at Forest Lawn since 1945, and I never saw any family come to visit him. You'd think there'd be someone, a big star like that."

He was right out of *Hamlet*, a comic gravedigger, for God's sake! I explained that I was Jack's daughter and that I lived in the East.

"Is that so?" He talked and talked. I couldn't get rid of him. By the time he finally climbed back on his machine and rolled away down the hill, whatever had been rising in my heart was stilled. I sat for a while under the pine trees, thinking of the man who had been my father. There were so many sides to him, so many paradoxes.

"He could have been a brilliant director."

"He was on the threshold of a wonderful new career."

"A drunk, a hermit."

"No better friend."

"Unstable, self-destructive."

"God, how I loved that man!"

I'd heard people say all of those things over the years. As they sifted through my mind I remembered something else that David Selznick told Mother on the set of *Gone With the Wind* the year after father died. "You and I know, Leatrice, we buried the man who should have played Rhett Butler."

I certainly hadn't met anyone like him in the years that followed. I knew I never would. There would always be a void in my life, lingering unfinished business, until I discovered what kind of man John Gilbert really was. He had touched so many lives, some, like mine, far too briefly, and he managed to leave such vivid memories that almost fifty years could not erase them.

The light was gone from the sky and the air had a chill to it when I started down the hill. I hated to leave him there alone; even the red carnations couldn't warm the place. But I knew that when I returned some day, I would know him a lot better and perhaps find a few people along the way who cared as much as I did.

But there's more to the story. After years of neglect and near oblivion, Jack's name began to surface again. It began in England with Kevin Brownlow, in *The Parade's Gone By*, and film critic Alexander Walker, in his book *Stardom*, taking a second look at Jack's career and finding a mystery there. Then, some of Jack's movies began to appear on public television in the States. In 1979, Kevin Brownlow and David Gill produced a series for Thames Television, *Hollywood: The Pioneers*, with Jack's story a highly dramatic feature. Garson Kanin wrote *Moviola*, which later appeared on television. People began to call me, or write, from universities and film libraries asking about my father. I was invited to speak at Boston University, then London.

I had thought by writing the story of his life as I discovered it that I could rekindle interest and appreciation of his career. But even before this book was written, people were beginning to discover him on their own. Jack had a growing following made up of those who remembered seeing his films long ago, as well as new film students suddenly aware of his glamour.

In November of 1982, I went to London as the guest of Thames Television. They were presenting *Flesh and the Devil* at the Dominion Theater, on Tottenham Court Road. For the first time I could remember, I saw his name in lights, over the marquee of a glittering movie palace, in one of the greatest cities of the world. People were jostling in line for tickets, kids with punk haircuts and leather jackets nudging older women with white hair and little fur capes. Bessie Love was there and Charlie Chaplin's family.

I stood with Kevin Brownlow and David Gill, who had engineered this event, watching the crowd. Suddenly, without warning, the tears I had been holding back for so many years came coursing down my cheeks. All the tears I couldn't shed at his funeral, or even at his grave-side at Forest Lawn, or in the many movies of his I'd seen, came embarrassingly, like a river, and I found myself sobbing like a child on David Gill's obliging shoulder.

It wasn't from a sense of sadness, or loss of a father I loved, but because I knew then that Jack would always be alive. As long as there are movies, as long as people want to know how it all began—John Gilbert lives.

FILMOGRAPHY

Matrimony. Ince–Triangle, November 28, 1915.
Director: Scott Sidney
Cast: Louise Glaum, Julia Dean, Howard Hickman, Gilbert—extra

The Aryan. Ince-Triangle, April 29, 1916.
Director: William S. Hart, with Clifford Smith
Cast: William S. Hart, Bessie Love, Louise Glaum, Gilbert—extra

Aloha Oe. Ince–Triangle, December 12, 1915.
Director: Richard Stanton
Cast: Willard Mack, Enid Markey, Margaret Thompson, Frank Borzage, J. Frank Burke, J. Barney Sherry, Gilbert—extra

The Corner *(The Corner in Wheat).* Ince-Triangle, January 1916.
Director: Walter Edwards
Cast: Willard Mack, Clara Williams, George Fawcett, Gilbert—extra

Civilization. Ince-Triangle, July 1916.
Director: Raymond B. West
Cast: Herschel Mayall, Howard Hickman, J. Frank Burke, Lola May, Ethel Ullman, Gilbert—extra

The Last Act. Ince—Triangle, February 27, 1916.
Director: Walter Edwards
Cast: William S. Hart, Bessie Barriscale, Clara Williams, Robert McKim, Gilbert—extra

Hell's Hinges. Ince–Triangle, February 26, 1916.
Director: William S. Hart and Charles Swickard   *Scenario:* C. Gardner Sullivan
Cast: William S. Hart, Clara Williams, Jack Standing, Alfred Hollingsworth, Robert McKim, Louise Glaum, J. Frank Burke, Robert Kortman, Gilbert in unbilled bit part.

Bullets and Brown Eyes. Produced by K. B. for Ince–Triangle, March 12, 1916
Director: Scott Sidney
Cast: William Desmond, Bessie Barriscale, Jean Hersholt, Jack Gilbert

The Apostle of Vengeance. Ince–Triangle, June 25, 1916.

Director: William S. Hart and Cliff Smith   *Scenario:* Monte Katterjohn
Cast: William S. Hart, Nona Thomas, Joseph J. Dowling, Fanny Midgely, Jack Gilbert

The Phantom *(Phantom Faraday).* Ince–Triangle, July 2, 1916.
Director: Charles Giblyn
Cast: Frank Keenan, Enid Markey, Jack Gilbert

The Eye of [the] Night. Ince–Triangle, July 16, 1916.
Director: Walter Edwards
Cast: William H. Thompson, Margery Wilson, Jack Gilbert

Shell 43! Ince–Triangle, August 13, 1916.
Director: Reginald Barker   *Scenario:* C. Gardner Sullivan
Cast: H. B. Warner, Enid Markey, Jack Gilbert, George Fisher, Margaret Thompson, Louise Brownell

The Sin Ye Do. Ince–Triangle, December 17, 1916.
Director: Walter Edwards
Cast: Frank Keenan, Margery Wilson, Jack Gilbert

The Weaker Sex. Ince–Triangle, January 7, 1917.
Director: Raymond West
Cast: Dorothy Dalton, Charles Ray, Louise Glaum, Jack Gilbert

Princess of the Dark. Ince–Triangle, February 18, 1917.
Director: Charles Miller
Cast: Enid Bennett, Jack Gilbert (first lead), Alfred Vosburg, Walt Whitman, J. Frank Burke

The Dark Road *(The Price).* Ince–Triangle, April 1, 1917.
Director: Charles Miller   *Art Director:* Robert Brunton
Cast: Dorothy Dalton, Robert KcKim, Jack Gilbert

Happiness (Seeking Happiness) *(The Soapsuds Trust).* Ince–Triangle, May 13, 1917.
Director: Reginald Barker   *Photography:* Robert Newland   *Art Director:* Robert Brunton   *Scenario:* C. Gardner Sullivan
Cast: Enid Bennett, Andrew Arbuckle, Charles Dunn, Thelma Salter, Jack Gilbert, Gertrude Claire, Adele Belgrade, Leo Willis

The Millionaire Vagrant. Ince–Triangle, May 27, 1917.
Director: Victor Schertzinger
Cast: Charles Ray, Sylvia Breamer, Jack Gilbert

Hater of Men. Ince–Triangle, June 24, 1917.
Director: Charles Miller   *Scenario:* C. Gardner Sullivan
Cast: Bessie Barriscale, Charles K. French, Jack Gilbert

The Mother Instinct *(Every Mother).* Ince–Triangle, July 15, 1917.
Directors: Roy William Neil and Lambert Hillyer

Cast: Margery Wilson, Enid Bennett, Rowland V. Lee, Todd Burns, Jack Gilbert

Golden Rule Kate. Ince–Triangle, August 12, 1917.
Director: Reginald Barker
Cast: Louise Glaum, Gertrude Claire, William Conklin, Mildred Harris, Jack Gilbert

The Devil Dodger. Ince–Triangle, October 13, 1917
Director: Cliff Smith
Cast: Belle Bennett, Roy Stewart, Josie Sedgwick, Jack Gilbert

Doing Her Bit. Triangle, September 1917 (possibly not released).
Director: Unknown
Cast: Ruth Stonehouse, Carl Ullman, Jack Gilbert

Up or Down. Triangle, November 10, 1917.
Director: Lynn F. Reynolds
Cast: George Hernandez, Fritzi Ridgeway, Jack Gilbert

One Dollar Bid. Paralta, January 1918.
Director: Ernest Warde
Cast: Louise Glaum, Jack Gilbert, Leatrice Joy

Nancy Comes Home. Triangle, March 24, 1918
Director: Jack Dillon
Cast: George Pierce, Myrtle Lind, Jack Gilbert

Shackled. Paralta-Hodkinson, June 1918.
Director: Wallace Worsley
Cast: Louise Glaum, Lawson Butt, Charles West, Roberta Wilson, Jack Gilbert

Wedlock. Paralta–Hodkinson, August 3, 1918
Director: Wallace Worsley
Cast: Louise Glaum, Jack Gilbert

More Trouble. Pathé, July 14, 1918.
Director: Ernest Warde
Cast: Frank Keenan, Jack Gilbert, Joseph Dowling

The Mask of Riches *(The Mask).* Triangle, September 8, 1918.
Director: Thomas Heffron,
Cast: Claire Anderson, Jack Gilbert

Three X Gordon. Paralta–Hodkinson, November 30, 1918.
Director: Ernest C. Warde
Cast: J. Warren Kerrigan, Lois Wilson, Jack Gilbert, Leatrice Joy

Sons of Men. Paralta-Hodkinson, circa November 1918.
Director: Unknown

Cast: J. Warren Kerrigan, Jack Gilbert

The Dawn of Understanding. Vitagraph, November 23, 1918.
Directors: David Smith and Charles R. Seeling
Cast: Bessie Love, Jack Gilbert

The Busher. Paramount–Ince, May 1919.
Director: Jerome Storm
Cast: Charles Ray, Colleen Moore, Jack Gilbert

The Man Beneath. Haworth for Robertson-Cole, July 5, 1919.
Director: William Worthington   *Scenario:* Edmund Mitchell
Cast: Sessue Hayakawa, Helen Jerome Eddy, Pauline Curley, Fanny Midgley, Jack Gilbert, Fontaine LaRue, Wedgewood Nowell

The White Heather. Tourneur–Hiller and Wilk, June 29, 1919.
Director: Maurice Tourneur
Cast: Mabel Ballin, Ralph Graves, Jack Gilbert, Ben Alexander, Spottiswoode Aitken, Gibson Gowland, E. H. Herbert

The Red Viper. Tyrad Pictures, September 6, 1919.
Director: Jacques Tyrol
Cast: Ruth Stonehouse, Gareth Hughes, Irma Harrison, Jack Gilbert

Widow by Proxy. Famous Players–Lasky, September 28, 1919.
Director: Walter Edwards
Cast: Marguerite Clark, Brownie Vernon, Nigel Barrie, Gertrude Claire, Jack Gilbert

The Heart o' the Hills. First National, November 17, 1919.
Director: Sidney Franklin   *Photography:* Charles Rosher
Cast: Mary Pickford, Harold Goodwin, Allan Sears, Fred Huntley, Claire McDowell, Sam De Grasse, W. H. Barinbridge, Jack Gilbert, Betty Bouton, Henry Herbert, Fred Warren

Should a Woman Tell? Metro, December 28, 1919.
Director: John E. Ince   *Scenario:* Finis Fox
Cast: Alice Lake, Jack Mulhall, Lydia Knott, Richard Headrick, Jack Gilbert

The White Circle. Famous Players–Lasky, August 15, 1920.
Director: Maurice Tourneur   *Scenario:* Jack Gilbert and Jules Furthman, based on "The Pavilion on the Links," by Robert Louis Stevenson
Cast: John Gilbert, Janice Wilson, Jack McDonald, Spottiswoode Aitken, Wesley Barry, Harry Northrup

The Great Redeemer. Metro, September 1920.
Director: Clarence Brown, supervised by Maurice Tourneur   *Scenario:* Jack Gilbert and Jules Furthman
Cast: House Peters, Marjorie Daw, Joseph E. Singleton, Jack McDonald

Deep Waters. Famous Players–Lasky, October 10, 1920.

Director: Maurice Tourneur   *Scenario*: Jack Gilbert   *Photography*: Alfred Ortlieb

Cast: Jack Gilbert, Barbara Bedford, Florence Deshon, Jack McDonald, Henry F. Woodward, George Nichols

The Bait. Paramount–Artcraft; Hope Hampton Productions, Distributed by Paramount Pictures, January 2, 1921.

Director: Maurice Tourneur   *Scenario*: Jack Gilbert   *Photography*: Alfred Ortlieb

Cast: Hope Hampton, Harry Woodward, Jack McDonald, James Gordon, Rae Ebberly, Joe Singleton, Poupee Andriot, Dan Crimmins, Jr.

The Servant in the House. H. O. Davis, (for F.B.O.) Distributed by Federated Exchange of America, Walgreene Film Corporation, ca. February 26, 1921. (Made in 1919 by Film Booking Office, copyrighted March 1, 1920.)

Director: Jack Conway   *Scenario*: Lanier Bartlett   *Photography*: Elgin Lessley

Cast: Jean Hersholt, Jack Curtis, Edward Peil, Harvey Clark, Clarence Horton, Zenaide Williams, Claire Anderson, Jack Gilbert, Mrs. George Hernandez

Love's Penalty. Hope Hampton Productions. Distributed by Associated First National, June 1921.

Director: Jack Gilbert   *Scenario*: Jack Gilbert   *Photography*: Alfred Ortlieb   *Technical Director*: Henry Menessier   *Title Editor*: Katherine Hilliker

Cast: Hope Hampton, Irma Harrison, Mrs. Phillip Landau, Percy Marmont, Jack O'Brien, Virginia Valli, Douglas Redmond, Charles Lane, Mrs. L. Faure

Shame. Fox, July 31, 1921.

Director: Emmett J. Flynn   *Scenario*: Emmett J. Flynn, Bernard McConville   *Photography*: Lucien Andriot

Cast: John Gilbert, Mickey Moore, Frankie Lee, George Siegmann, William V. Mong, George Nichols, Anna May Wong, Rosemary Theby, Doris Pawn, "Red" Kirby

Ladies Must Live. Mayflower Photoplay Corporation, October 30, 1921. Distributed by Paramount.

Director: George Loane Tucker   *Scenario*: George Loane Tucker, based on *Ladies Must Live*, by Alice Duer Miller

Cast: Robert Ellis, Mahlon Hamilton, Betty Compson, Leatrice Joy, Hardee Kirkland, Gibson Gowland, John Gilbert, Cleo Madison, Snitz Edwards, Lucille Hutton, Lule Warrenton, William V. Mong, Jack McDonald, Maria Manon, Arnold Gregg

Gleam o' Dawn. Fox, January 8, 1922

Director: Jack Dillon   *Scenario*: Jules G. Furthman   *Photography*: Don Short

Cast: John Gilbert, Barbara Bedford, James Farley, John Gough, Wilson Hummel, Edwin Booth Tilton

Arabian Love. Fox, April 9, 1922.

Director: Jerome Storm *Story-Scenario:* Jules Furthman *Photography:* Joe August

Cast: John Gilbert, Barbara Bedford, Barbara La Marr, Herschel Mayall, Robert Kortman, William H. Orlamund

The Yellow Stain. Fox, May 21, 1922.

Director: Jack Dillon *Story-Scenario:* Jules Furthman *Photography:* Don Short

Cast: John Gilbert, Claire Anderson, John P. Lockley, Mark Fenton, Herschel Mayall, Robert Daly, Mace Robinson, James Hemphill, May Alexander

Honor First *(Honor Bright).* Fox, August 27, 1922.

Director: Jerome Storm *Scenario:* Joseph Franklin Poland *Photography:* Joseph August

Cast: John Gilbert, René Adorée, Hardee Kirkland, Shannon Day, Wilson Hummel

Monte Cristo. Fox, September 3, 1922.

Director: Emmett J. Flynn *Scenario:* Bernard McConville *Photography:* Lucien Andriot

Cast: John Gilbert, Estelle Taylor, Robert McKim, William V. Mong, Virginia Brown Faire, George Siegmann, Spottiswoode Aitken, Ralph Cloninger, Albert Prisco, Renée Adorée

Calvert's Valley. Fox, October 8, 1922

Director: Jack Dillon *Scenario:* Jules Furthman *Photography:* Don Short

Cast: John Gilbert, Sylvia Breamer, Philo McCullough, Herschel Mayall, Lule Warrenton

The Love Gambler. Fox, November 12, 1922.

Director: Joseph Franz *Scenario:* Jules Furthman *Photography:* Joe August

Cast: John Gilbert, Carmel Myers, Bruce Gordon, Cap Anderson, William Lawrence, James Gordon, Mrs. Cohen, Barbara Tennant, Edward Cecil, Doreen Turner

A California Romance. Fox, December 24, 1922.

Director: Jerome Storm *Scenario:* Charles E. Banks *Story:* Jules G. Furthman *Photography:* Joseph August

Cast: John Gilbert, Estelle Taylor, George Siegmann, Jack McDonald, Charles Anderson

While Paris Sleeps *(The Glory of Love).* Hodkinson, January 23, 1923. (Made at Paramount in 1920.)

Director: Maurice Tourneur *Photography:* Renee Guissart

Cast: Lon Chaney, Mildred Manning, John Gilbert, Hardee Kirkland, J. Farrell McDonald, Jack F. McDonald

Truxton King. Fox, February 18, 1923.

Director: Jerome Storm   *Scenario:* Paul Schofield   *Photography:* Joseph August

Cast: John Gilbert, Ruth Clifford, Frank Leigh, Mickey Moore, Otis Harlan, Henry Miller, Jr., Richard Wayne, Willis Marks, Winifred Bryson, Mark Fenton

The Madness of Youth. Fox, April 8, 1923.

Director: Jerome Storm   *Scenario:* Joseph Franklin Poland   *Photography:* Joseph August

Cast: John Gilbert, Billie Dove, Daniel Hatswell, George K. Arthur, Wilton Taylor, Ruth Boyd, Luke Lucas, Julanne Johnston

St. Elmo. Fox, September 30, 1923.

Director: Jerome Storm   *Scenario:* Jules G. Furthman   *Photography:* Joe August

Cast: John Gilbert, Barbara La Marr, Bessie Love, Warner Baxter, Nigel de Brulier, Lydia Knott

The Exiles. Fox, October 14, 1923.

Director: Edmund Mortimer   *Scenario:* Fred Jackson

Cast: John Gilbert, Betty Bouton, John Webb Dillon, Margaret Fielding, Fred Warren

Cameo Kirby. Fox, October 21, 1923.

Director: John Ford   *Scenario:* Robert N. Lee   *Photography:* George Schneiderman

Cast: John Gilbert, Gertrude Olmstead, Alan Hale, Eric Mayne, William E. Lawrence, Richard Tucker, Phillips Smalley, Jack McDonald, Jean Arthur, Eugenie Forde

Just Off Broadway. Fox, January 30, 1924.

Director: Edmund Mortimer   *Scenario:* Frederic Hatton, Fanny Hatton   *Photography:* G. O. Post

Cast: John Gilbert, Marion Nixon, Trilby Clark, Pierre Gendron, Ben Hendricks, Jr.

The Wolf Man. Fox, February 17, 1924.

Director: Edmund Mortimer   *Scenario:* Frederic Hatton, Fanny Hatton   *Photography:* Don Short, Michael Farley

Cast: John Gilbert, Norma Shearer, Alma Francis, George Barraud, Eugene Pallette, Edgar Norton, Thomas R. Mills, Max Montisole, Charles Wellesley, Richard Blaydon, D. R. O. Hatswell, Mary Warren, Ebba Mona

The Lone Chance. Fox, May 18, 1924.

Director: Howard Mitchell   *Scenario:* Charles Kenyon, from a story by Frederick I. Jackson   *Photography:* Bert Baldridge

Cast: John Gilbert, Evelyn Brent, John Miljan, Edwin Booth Tilton, Harry Todd, Frank Beal.

His Hour. MGM, September 29, 1924.

Director: King Vidor *Scenario:* Elinor Glyn *Titles:* King Vidor, Maude Fulton *Photography:* John Mescall *Art Director:* Cedric Gibbons *Assistant Director:* David Howard *Gowns:* Sophie Wachner (Production supervised by Elinor Glyn.)

Cast: Aileen Pringle, John Gilbert, Emily Fitzroy, Lawerence Grant, Dale Fuller, Mario Carillo, Jacqueline Gadsdon, George Waggoner

Married Flirts. MGM, October 27, 1924.

Director: Robert G. Vignola *Scenario:* Julia Crawford Ivers *Titles:* Frederic Hatton, Fanny Hatton *Photography:* Oliver Marsh *Settings:* Charles L. Cadwallader *Film Editor:* Frank E. Hull

Cast: Pauline Frederick, Conrad Nagel, Mae Busch, Huntly Gordon, Paul Nicholson, Patterson Dial, Alice Hollister *Cameo Appearances by:* John Gilbert, Hobart Henley, Robert Z. Leonard, May McAvoy, Mae Murray, Aileen Pringle, Norma Shearer

He Who Gets Slapped. MGM, December 22, 1924.

Director: Victor Seastrom *Adaptation:* Carey Wilson, Victor Seastrom *Photography:* Milton Moore *Sets:* Cedric Gibbons *Film Editor:* Hugh Wynn *Costumes:* Sophie Wachner

Cast: Lon Chaney, Norma Shearer, John Gilbert, Tully Marshall, Marc MacDermott, Ford Sterling, Harvey Clarke, Paulette Duval, Ruth King, Clyde Cook, Brandon Hurst, George Davis

The Snob. MGM, November 10, 1924.

Director: Monta Bell *Photography:* Andre Barlatier *Sets:* Cedric Gibbons *Film Editor:* Ralph Lawson *Costumes:* Sophie Wachner

Cast: John Gilbert, Norma Shearer, Conrad Nagel, Phyllis Haver, Hedda Hopper, Margaret Seddon, Aileen Manning, Hazel Kennedy, Gordon Sackville, Roy Laidlaw, Nellie Bly Baker

The Wife of the Centaur. MGM, December 1, 1924.

Director: King Vidor *Adaptation:* Douglas Z. Doty *Photography:* John Arnold *Art Director:* Cedric Gibbons *Film Editor:* Hugh Wynn *Assistant Director:* David Howard *Costumes:* Sophie Wachner

Cast: Eleanor Boardman, John Gilbert, Aileen Pringle, Kate Lester, William Haines, Kate Price, Jacqueline Gadsdon, Bruce Covington, Philo McCullough, Lincoln Stedman, William Orlamund

The Merry Widow. MGM, August 26, 1925.

Director: Erich von Stroheim *Adaptation-Scenario:* Erich von Stroheim, Benjamin Glazer *Titles:* Marian Ainslee *Photography:* Oliver T. Marsh, Ben Reynolds, William Daniels *Sets:* Cedric Gibbons, Richard Day *Film Editor:* Frank E. Hull, *Musical Score:* William Axt, David Mendoza *Assistant Directors:* Eddy Sowders, Louis Germonprez *Costumes:* Richard Day, Erich von Stroheim

Cast: Mae Murray, John Gilbert, Roy D'Arcy, Josephine Crowell, George

Fawcett, Tully Marshall, Albert Conti, Sidney Bracy, Don Ryan, Hughie Mack, Ida Moore, Lucille van Lent, Charles Margelis, Harvey Karels, Edna Tichenor, Gertrude Bennett, Zalla Zarana, Jacqueline Gadsdon, Estelle Clark, D'Arcy Corrigan.

The Big Parade. MGM, November 5, 1925.
Director: King Vidor *Scenario:* Harry Behn *Titles:* Joseph Farnham *Story:* Laurence Stallings *Photography:* John Arnold *Art Directors:* Cedric Gibbons, James Basevi *Film Editor:* Hugh Wynn *Musical Score:* William Axt, David Mendoza *Wardrobe:* Ethel P. Chaffin
Cast: John Gilbert, René Adorée, Hobart Bosworth, Claire McDowell, Robert Ober, Tom O'Brien, Karl Dane, Rosita Marstini

La Bohème. MGM, February 24, 1926.
Director: King Vidor *Continuity:* Ray Doyle, Harry Behn *Titles:* William Conselman, Ruth Cummings *Story:* Fred De Gresac *Photography:* Henrick Sartov *Sets:* Cedric Gibbons, Arnold Gillespie *Film Editor:* Hugh Wynn *Musical Score:* William Axt *Costumes:* Erte
Cast: Lillian Gish, John Gilbert, Renée Adorée, George Hassell, Roy D'Arcy, Edward Everett Horton, Karl Dane, Frank Currier, Mathilde Comont, Gino Corradel, Gene Pouyet, David Mir, Catherine Vidor, Valentina Zimina, Blanche Payson

Bardelys the Magnificent. MGM, September 30, 1926 (Los Angeles premiere; released November 21, 1926).
Director: King Vidor *Adaptation:* Dorothy Farnum *Photography:* William Daniels *Sets:* Cedric Gibbons, James Basevi, Richard Day *Wardrobe:* Andre-Ani, Lucia Coulter
Cast: John Gilbert, Eleanor Boardman, Roy D'Arcy, Lionel Belmore, Emily Fitzroy, George K. Arthur, Arthur Lubin, Theodore von Eltz, Karl Dane, Edward Connelly, Fred Malatesta, John T. Murray, Joseph Marba, Daniel G. Tomlinson, Emile Chautard, Max Barwin

Flesh and the Devil. MGM?, December 25, 1926.
Director: Clarence Brown *Screenplay:* Benjamin F. Glazer *Titles:* Marian Ainslee *Photography:* William Daniels *Sets:* Cedric Gibbons, Frederic Hope *Film Editor:* Lloyd Nosler *Assistant Director:* Charles Dorian *Wardrobe:* Andre-Ani
Cast: John Gilbert, Greta Garbo, Lars Hanson, Barbara Kent, William Orlamund, George Fawcett, Eugenie Basserer, Marc McDermott, Marcelle Corday, Polly Moran (unbilled bit)

The Show, MGM, January 22, 1927.
Director: Tod Browning *Screenplay:* Waldemar Young *Titles:* Joe Farnham *Photography:* John Arnold *Sets:* Cedric Gibbons, Richard Day *Film Editor:* Errol Taggart *Wardrobe:* Lucia Coulter
Cast: John Gilbert, Renée Adorée, Lionel Barrymore, Edward Connelly, Gertrude Short, Andy MacLennan

Twelve Miles Out. MGM, July 9, 1927.
Director: Jack Conway *Screenplay:* A. P. Younger *Titles:* Joe Farnham *Photography:* Ira Morgan *Sets:* Cedric Gibbons, Eugene Hornbostel *Film Editor:* Basil Wrangell *Wardrobe:* Rene Hubert
Cast: John Gilbert, Ernest Torrence, Joan Crawford, Eileen Percy, Paulette Duval, Dorothy Sebastian, Gwen Lee, Edward Earle, Bert Roach, Tom O'Brien

Man, Woman and Sin. MGM, November 19, 1927.
Director: Monta Bell *Scenario:* Alice D. G. Miller *Story:* Monta Bell *Titles:* John Colton *Photography:* Percy Hilburn *Sets:* Cedric Gibbons, Merrill Pye *Film Editor:* Blanche Sewell *Wardrobe:* Gilbert Clark
Cast: John Gilbert, Jeanne Eagels, Gladys Brockwell, Marc MacDermott, Phillip Anderson, Hayden Stevenson, Charles K. French, Aileen Manning

Love. MGM, November 29, 1927 (New York premiere; released January 2, 1928).
Director: Edmund Goulding *Producer:* Edmund Goulding *Continuity:* Frances Marion *Titles:* Marian Ainslee, Ruth Cummings *Adaptation:* Lorna Moon *Photography:* William Daniels *Set Design:* Alexander Toluboff *Film Editor:* Hugh Wynn *Musical Score:* Ernst Luz *Song:* "That Melody of Love," by Howard Dietz, Walter Donaldson *Wardrobe:* Gilbert Clark
Cast: John Gilbert, Greta Garbo, George Fawcett, Emily Fitzroy, Brandon Hurst, Philippe DeLacey

The Cossacks. MGM, June 23, 1928.
Director: George Hill *Adaptation-Continuity:* Frances Marion *Titles:* John Colton *Photography:* Percy Hilburn *Sets:* Cedric Gibbons, Alexander Toluboff *Film Editor:* Blanche Sewell *Wardrobe:* David Cox *Technical Advisor:* Theodore Lodi
Cast: John Gilbert, Renée Adorée, Earnest Torrence, Nils Asther, Paul Hurst, Dale Fuller, Mary Alden, Josephine Borio, Yorke Sherwood, Joseph Mari

Four Walls. MGM, August 11, 1928.
Director: William Nigh *Continuity:* Alice D. G. Miller *Titles:* Joe Farnham *Photography:* James Howe *Sets:* Cedric Gibbons *Film Editor:* Harry Reynolds *Wardrobe:* David Cox
Cast: John Gilbert, Joan Crawford, Vera Gordon, Carmel Myers, Robert S. O'Connor, Louis Natheaux, Jack Byron

Show People. MGM, October 20, 1928.
Director: King Vidor *Continuity:* Wanda Tuchock *Titles:* Ralph Spence *Treatment:* Agnes Christine Johnston, Laurence Stallings *Photography:* John Arnold *Sets:* Cedric Gibbons *Film Editor:* Hugh Wynn *Song:* "Crossroads," by William Axt and David Mendoza *Wardrobe:* Henrietta Frazer (Sound effects and synchronized musical score by Movietone.)

Cast: Marion Davies, William Haines, Dell Henderson, Paul Ralli, Tenen
Holtz, Harry Gribbon, Sidney Bracy, Polly Moran, Albert Conti
Cameo Appearances by: Renée Adorée, George K. Arthur, Charles Chaplin,
Karl Dane, Douglas Fairbanks, John Gilbert, Elinor Glyn, William S.
Hart, Leatrice Joy, Rod La Rocque, Mae Murray, Louella Parsons,
Aileen Pringle, Dorothy Sebastian, Norma Talmadge, Estelle Taylor,
Claire Windsor

The Masks of the Devil. MGM, November 17, 1928.
Director: Victor Seastrom *Continuity:* Frances Marion *Titles:* Marian
Ainslee, Ruth Cummings *Adaptation:* Svend Gade *Photography:*
Oliver Marsh *Sets:* Cedric Gibbons *Film Editor:* Conrad A. Nervig
Song: "Live and Love," by William Axt and David Mendoza *Assistant
Director:* Harold S. Bucquet *Gowns:* Adrian (Sound effects and syn-
chronized musical score. Also silent version.)
Cast: John Gilbert, Alma Rubens, Theodore Roberts, Frank Reicher, Eva von
Berne, Ralph Forbes, Ethel Wales, Polly Ann Young

A Woman of Affairs. MGM, December 15, 1928.
Director: Clarence Brown *Continuity:* Bess Meredyth *Titles:* Marian
Ainslee, Ruth Cummings *Photography:* William Daniels *Art Director:*
Cedric Gibbons *Film Editor:* Hugh Wynn *Song:* "Love's First Kiss,"
by William Axt and David Mendoza *Assistant Director:* Charles Dor-
ian *Gowns:* Adrian (Sound effects and synchronized musical score.
Also silent version.)
Cast: Greta Garbo, John Gilbert, Lewis Stone, John Mack Brown, Douglas
Fairbanks, Jr., Hobart Bosworth, Dorothy Sebastian

Desert Nights. MGM, March 9, 1929.
Director: William Nigh *Scenario:* Lenore Coffee, Willis Goldbeck *Titles:*
Marian Ainslee, Ruth Cummings *Adaptation:* Endre Bohem *Story:*
John Thomas Neville, Dale Van Every *Photography:* James Howe *Art
Director:* Cedric Gibbons *Film Editor:* Harry Reynolds *Wardrobe:*
Henrietta Frazer (Sound effects and synchronized musical score. Also
silent version.)
Cast: John Gilbert, Ernest Torrence, Mary Nolan

A Man's Man. MGM, May 25, 1929.
Director: James Cruze *Scenario:* Forrest Halsey *Titles:* Joe Farnham *Photography:* Merritt B. Gerstad *Art Director:* Cedric Gibbons *Film Editor:* George Hively *Song:* "My Heart Is Bluer Than Your Eyes, Cherie,"
by Al Bryan and Monte Wilhitt *Wardrobe:* David Cox (Sound effects
and synchronized musical score. Also silent version.)
Cast: William Haines, Josephine Dunn, Sam Hardy, Mae Busch, Gloria
Davenport *Cameo Appearances by:* Greta Garbo, John Gilbert

The Hollywood Revue of 1929. MGM, June 20, 1929.
Producer: Harry Rapf *Director:* Charles Reisner *Dialogue:* Al Boasberg,

Robert E. Hopkins *Skit:* Joe Farnham *Photography:* John Arnold, Irving Ries, Maximilian Fabian, John M. Nickolaus *Art Directors:* Cedric Gibbons, Richard Day *Film Editing:* William S. Gray, Cameron K. Wood *Score Arrangers:* Arthur Lange, Ernest Klapholtz, Ray Heindorf *Dance Ensembles:* Sammy Lee, George Cunningham *Recording Engineer:* Douglas Shearer *Sound Assistants:* Russel Franks, William Clark, Wesley Miller, A. T. Taylor *Assistant Directors:* Jack Cummings, Sandy Roth, Al Shenberg *Production Manager:* Joe Cohn *Costumes:* David Cox, Henrietta Frazer, Joe Rapf *Electrician:* Louis Kolb
Cast: Conrad Nagel, Jack Benny, John Gilbert, Norma Shearer, Joan Crawford, Bessie Love, Lionel Barrymore, Cliff Edwards, Stan Laurel, Oliver Hardy, Anita Page, Nils Asther, The Brox Sisters, Natacha Natova and Company, Marion Davies, William Haines, Buster Keaton, Marie Dressler, Charles King, Polly Moran, Gus Edwards, Karl Dane, George K. Arthur, Ann Dvorak, Gwen Lee, the Albertina Rasch Ballet, The Rounders, the Biltmore Quartet

His Glorious Night. MGM, September 28, 1929.
Director: Lionel Barrymore *Screenplay-Dialogue:* Willard Mack *Photography:* Percy Hilburn *Art Director:* Cedric Gibbons *Film Editor:* William Le Vanway *Musical Score:* Lionel Barrymore *Conducted by:* William Axt *Sound:* Douglas Shearer *Wardrobe:* David Cox (Also silent version; French and German versions directed by Jacques Feyder, with photography by William Daniels, and a different cast.)
Cast: John Gilbert, Catherine Dale Owen, Nance O'Neil, Gustav von Seyffertitz, Hedda Hopper, Doris Hill, Tyrell Davis, Gerald Barry, Madeleine Seymour, Richard Carle, Eva Dennison, Youcca Troubetzkoy, Peter Hawthorne

Redemption. MGM, April 5, 1930.
Director: Fred Niblo *Screenplay:* Dorothy Farnum *Dialogue:* Edwin Justus Mayer *Titles:* Ruth Cummings *Photography:* Percy Hilburn *Art Director:* Cedric Gibbons *Film Editor:* Margaret Booth *Recording Engineer:* Douglas Shearer *Gowns:* Adrian
Cast: John Gilbert, Renée Adorée, Conrad Nagel, Eleanor Boardman, Claire McDowell, Nigel de Brulier, Tully Marshall, Mack Swain, Sidney Bracy, Dick Alexander, Erville Alderson* (Also silent version.)

Way for a Sailor. MGM, November 6, 1930.
Director: Sam Wood *Scenario-Dialogue:* Laurence Stallings, W. L. River *Additional Dialogue:* Charles MacArthur, Al Boasberg *Photography:* Percy Hilburn *Art Director:* Cedric Gibbons *Film Editor:* Frank Sullivan *Recording Engineers:* Robert Shirley, Douglas Shearer *Wardrobe:* Vivian Beer

* Charles Quartermaine has occasionally been credited with Tully Marshall's role, Agostino Borgato with Erville Alderson's.

Cast: John Gilbert, Wallace Beery, Jim Tully, Leila Hyams, Polly Moran, Doris Lloyd

Gentleman's Fate. MGM, June 1931.
Director: Mervyn LeRoy   *Story:* Ursula Parrott   *Dialogue:* Leonard Paskins
   Photography: Merritt B. Gerstad   *Film Editor:* William S. Gray
Cast: John Gilbert, Louis Wolheim, Leila Hyams, Anita Page, Marie Prevost,
   John Miljan, George Cooper, Ferike Boros, Ralph Ince, Frank Reicher,
   Paul Forcasi, Tenen Holtz

The Phantom of Paris*(Cheri-Bibi)*. MGM, November 1931.
Director: John S. Robertson   *Continuity:* Bess Meredyth, based on the novel
   by Gaston LeRoux.   *Dialogue:* Edwin Justus Mayer, John Meehan
   Photography: Oliver T. Marsh   *Film Editor:* Jack Ogilvie
Cast: John Gilbert, Leila Hyams, Lewis Stone, Jean Hersholt, C. Aubrey
   Smith, Natalie Moorhead, Ian Keith, Alfred Hickman

West of Broadway. MGM, November 1931 (New York premiere: January
   1932).
Director: Harry Beaumont   *Story:* Ralph Graves, Bess Meredyth   *Adaptation-
   Dialogue:* Gene Markey   *Photography:* Merritt B. Gerstad   *Film Editor:*
   George Hively
Cast: John Gilbert, El Brendel, Lois Moran, Madge Evans, Ralph Bellamy,
   Frank Conroy, Gwen Lee, Hedda Hopper, Willie Fung, Ruth Renick

Downstairs. MGM, August 1932.
Director: Monta Bell   *Screenplay:* Lenore Coffee, Melville Baker   *Story:* John
   Gilbert   *Photography:* Harold Rossen   *Film Editor:* Conrad A. Nervig
Cast: John Gilbert, Paul Lukas, Virginia Bruce, Hedda Hopper, Reginald
   Owen, Olga Baclanova, Bodil Rosing, Otto Hoffman, Lucien Littlefield,
   Marion Lessing, Karen Morley (unbilled)

Fast Workers. MGM, March 1933.
Director: Tod Browning   *Screenplay:* Karl Brown, Ralph Wheelwright, Lau-
   rence Stallings (Adapted from *Rivets*, by John McDermott)   *Photography:*
   Peverell Marley   *Art Director:* Cedric Gibbons   *Film Editor:* Ben Lewis
Cast: John Gilbert, Robert Armstrong, Mae Clarke, Muriel Kirkland, Vince
   Barnett, Virginia Cherrill, Muriel Evans, Sterling Holloway, Gay Usher,
   Warner Richmond, Robert Burns

Queen Christina. MGM, December 1933.
Director: Rouben Mamoulian   *Producer:* Walter Wanger   *Screenplay:* Salka
   Viertel, H. M. Harwood   *Story:* Salka Viertel, Margaret F. Levine   *Di-
   alogue:* S. N. Behrman   *Photography:* William Daniels   *Film Editor:*
   Blanche Sewell   *Musical Score:* Herbert Stothart
Cast: Greta Garbo, John Gilbert, Ian Keith, Lewis Stone, C. Aubrey Smith,
   Elizabeth Young, Reginald Owen, Georges Renevent, David Torrence,
   Gustav von Seyffertitz, Ferdinand Muncier, Cora Sue Collins

The Captain Hates the Sea. Columbia, November 1934.

Director: Lewis Milestone *Continuity:* Arnold Belgrade *Screenplay:* Wallace Smith (From the novel by Wallace Smith.) *Photography:* Joseph August *Film Editor:* Gene Milford

Cast: Victor McLaglen, Wynne Gibson, Alison Skipworth, John Gilbert, Helen Vinson, Fred Keating, Leon Errol, Walter Connolly, Tala Birell, Walter Catlett, John Wray, Claude Gillingwater, Emily Fitzroy, Geneva Mitchell, Donald Meek, Luis Alberni, Akim Tamiroff, Arthur Treacher, Inez Courtney, The Three Stooges

MISCELLANEOUS FILMS

A talkie trailer of MGM stars, presented in London at the Empire Theater, c. February 1929. John Gilbert, Norma Shearer, Ernest Torrence, George K. Arthur, Marion Davies. Reference in *Photoplay*, Vol. 35, no. 3 (Feb., 1929), p. 132, in Herbert Howe, "Just a Hollywood Day."

We Tune in on Hollywood. MGM, July 1931.

For German release. Paul Morgan (German comedian) makes a tour around the MGM studios. In cameo roles and skits: Buster Keaton, John Gilbert, Ramon Novarro, Heinrich George and Nora Gregor (two German film stars in Hollywood at the time), and Adolphe Menjou. Reference in *New York Times*, July 26, 1931. "News of the Berlin Screens," by Curt L. Heymann (correspondent in Berlin doing film criticism).

Pirate Party on Catalina Isle. MGM, released early in 1936.

Technicolor two-reel featurette, with Errol Flynn, Lili Damita, Marion Davies, Cary Grant, Virginia Bruce, Chester Morris, Lee Tracy, John Gilbert. Reference in George Morris, *Errol Flynn* (New York: Pyramid Publications, 1975), p. 26.

BIBLIOGRAPHY

Allen, Frederick Lewis. *Only Yesterday*. New York: Harper & Brothers, 1964.

Ardmore, Jane. *The Self-Enchanted*. New York: McGraw-Hill, 1959.

Astor, Mary. *A Life on Film*. New York: Delacorte Press, 1967.

Bainbridge, John. *Garbo*. New York: Holt, Rinehart, and Winston, 1971.

Berkman, Edward O. *The Lady and the Law: The Remarkable Story of Fanny Holtzman*. Boston: Little, Brown, 1976.

Brownlow, Kevin. *Hollywood: The Pioneers*. New York: Knopf, 1980.

———. *The Parade's Gone By*. New York: Knopf, 1968.

———. *The War, the West, and the Wilderness*. New York: Knopf, 1979.

Corliss, Richard. *Greta Garbo*. New York: Pyramid, 1974.

Crawford, Joan, with Jane Ardmore. *A Portrait of Joan*. Garden City: Doubleday, 1962.

Courtney, Marguerite. *Laurette*. New York: Rinehart, 1955.

Crowther, Bosley. *Hollywood Rajah*. New York: Dell, 1960.

———. *The Lion's Share*. New York: E.E. Dutton, 1957.

Curtiss, Thomas Quinn. *Von Stroheim*. New York: Farrar, Straus & Giroux, 1971.

Davis, Henry R. "A John Gilbert Index." *Films in Review*, October 1962.

De Mille, Cecil B. *Autobiography*. Englewood Cliffs: Prentice-Hall, 1959.

Eames, John Douglas. *The M-G-M Story*. New York: Crown, 1975.

Gilbert, John. "Jack Gilbert Writes His Own Story." *Photoplay*, June-September, 1928.

Glyn, Anthony. *Elinor Glyn: A Biography*. Garden City: Doubleday, 1955.

Griffith, Richard. *The Movie Stars*. Garden City: Doubleday, 1970.

———, and Arthur Mayer. *The Movies*. New York: Bonanza, 1957.

Head, June. *Star Gazing*. London: Peter Davies, 1931.

Hecht, Ben. *A Child of the Century*. New York: Simon and Schuster, 1954.

Higham, Charles. *Hollywood Cameramen*. Bloomington/London: Indian University Press, 1970.

Hopper, Hedda. *From Under My Hat*. Garden City: Doubleday, 1952.

Lahue, Kalton C. *Dreams for Sale: The Rise and Fall of the Triangle Film Corporation*. Cranbury: A. S. Barnes, 1971.

Lauritzen, Einar, and Lundquist, Gunnar. *American Film Index, 1908–1915*. Stockholm: Film Index, 1976.

———. *American Film Index, 1916–1920*. Stockholm: Film Index, 1984.

Marion, Frances. *Off With Their Heads*. New York: MacMillan, 1972.

Marx, Samuel. *Mayer and Thalberg*. New York: Random House, 1975.

Moore, Colleen. *Silent Star*. Garden City: Doubleday, 1968.

Negri, Pola. *Memoirs of a Star*. Garden City: Doubleday, 1970.

Oppenheimer, George. *A View from the Sixties*. New York: McKay, 1966.

Pensel, Hans. *Seastrom and Stiller in Hollywood*. New York: Vantage Press, 1969.

Pratt, George C. *Spellbound in Darkness*. Greenwich: New York Graphic Society, 1973.

Quirk, Lawrence J. "John Gilbert." *Films in Review*, March 1956.

Ragan, David. *Who's Who in Hollywood*. New Rochelle: Arlington House, 1977.

Robinson, David. *Hollywood in the Twenties*. London/New York: Zwemmer/Barnes, 1968.

Rosenberg, Bernard, and Harry Silverstein. *The Real Tinsel*. New York: MacMillan, 1970.

Stewart, Donald Ogden. *By a Stroke of Luck!* London: Paddington Press, Ltd., 1975.

Thomas, Bob. *Thalberg: Life and Legend*. New York: Bantam, 1970.

Vidor, King. *A Tree is a Tree*. New York: Harcourt, Brace & Company, 1952

Walker, Alexander. *The Shattered Silents*. New York: Morrow, 1979.

——. *Stardom*. New York: Stein & Day, 1970.

Weinberg, Herman. *Stroheim: A Pictorial Record of His Films*. New York: Dover, 1975.

Wilson, Robert, ed. *The Film Criticism of Otis Ferguson*. Philadelphia: Temple University Press, 1971.

Zierold, Norman. *Garbo*. New York: Stein & Day, 1969.

The American Film Institute List of Feature Films, 1921-1930. 2 volumes. New York: R.R. Bowker, 1971.

Periodicals

Cinema Art
Exhibitor's Herald
Film Daily
Los Angeles Times
Motion Picture Story
Motion Picture Classic
The Nation
The New York Times
The New Yorker
Photoplay
Picture Play
Theatre
Time
Vanity Fair
Variety

INDEX